SOME PROBLEMS IN
ROMAN HISTORY

Ten Essays

bearing on the administrative and legislative work of Julius Caesar

by

E. G. HARDY, M.A., D.Litt.

Principal of Jesus College, Oxford

THE LAWBOOK EXCHANGE, LTD.

Clark, New Jersey

2007

ISBN-13: 978-1-58477-753-3
ISBN-10: 1-58477-753-2

Second printing 2008

The quality of this reprint is equivalent to the quality of the original work.

THE LAWBOOK EXCHANGE, LTD.
33 Terminal Avenue
Clark, New Jersey 07066-1321

Please see our website for a selection of our other publications and fine facsimile reprints of classic works of legal history:
www.lawbookexchange.com

Library of Congress Cataloging-in-Publication Data

Hardy, Ernest George, 1852-1925.
Some problems in Roman history : ten essays bearing on the administrative and legislative work of Julius Caesar / E. G. Hardy.
p. cm.
Originally published: Oxford : The Clarendon press, 1924.
Includes bibliographical references.
ISBN-13: 978-1-58477-753-3 (cloth : alk. paper)
ISBN-10: 1-58477-753-2 (cloth : alk. paper)
1. Caesar, Julius. 2. Rome--History--Republic, 265-30 B.C. 3. Roman law. I. Title.
DG262.H3 2007
340.5'4--dc22 2006034315

Printed in the United States of America on acid-free paper

SOME PROBLEMS IN

ROMAN HISTORY

Ten Essays

bearing on the administrative and legislative

work of Julius Caesar

by

E. G. HARDY, M.A., D.Litt.
Principal of Jesus College, Oxford

OXFORD
AT THE CLARENDON PRESS
1924

TO MY WIFE

ANNE HARDY

WITHOUT WHOSE ENCOURAGEMENT AND STIMULUS

THIS BOOK WOULD NEVER HAVE APPEARED

PREFACE

CONTRARY to the anticipations to which I gave expression in the Preface to the *Monumentum Ancyranum*, I have found it possible to collect and republish a selection of the articles contributed by me to various periodicals during recent years. I am greatly indebted to the kindness and courtesy of the Delegates of the Clarendon Press, which have enabled me to do this, as well as to the Editors of the *Journal of Roman Studies*, the *Journal of Philology*, and the *Classical Review* for allowing me to reprint my articles.

I have entitled my volume 'Some Problems in Roman History', and the title indicates the somewhat heterogeneous character of its contents. The various articles were suggested to me in all sorts of accidental ways, and I can claim little continuity or unity of purpose amongst most of them. They do, however, all of them, even that on *Iudicia Populi* (which was intended to lead up to the cases of Rabirius and Cicero), have a direct bearing on points, either legal or political, in the career of Julius Caesar. His position in 'Cicero's year', 63, would have admitted of more connected treatment, and I should have liked to have supplemented the papers on the Rullan proposal and the trial of Rabirius with one on the Catilinarian affair. But this would have unduly overloaded the volume, and I am therefore publishing the last-mentioned article as a separate monograph. All the essays are literally restudies, perhaps in some cases reinterpretations of the original authorities. Some views put forward are, as far as I know, new, and these I submit to the judgement and criticism of my fellow labourers in the field of Roman history.

That the treatment of so vexed a subject as the *lex Iulia Municipalis* would involve controversial matter was inevitable, and, unless I was to withdraw my original article, to the conclusions of which I adhere, I was bound to reply to Professor Reid's courteous and temperate criticisms of it.

I am indebted to my friend, Mr. Seymour, for putting the articles in order for the press, and to Mr. Faire for his assistance in correcting the proofs.

JESUS COLLEGE, OXFORD
25 *January*, 1924.

CONTENTS

I

SOME NOTABLE JUDICIA POPULI ON CAPITAL CHARGES

THOUGH I have described my paper as 'some notable *judicia populi*', I must make the somewhat paradoxical explanation that more than half the cases dealt with never reached the stage of being *judicia populi* at all. Still, but for suicide or voluntary exile, or the dropping of the preliminary trial, they would all of them have had to come before the people, and I hope that this will justify my title.

I may state at the outset that it has not been my aim in the following pages to which I prefix this preliminary explanation, to propound any new theory of my own on the procedure illustrated by these trials, and still less to criticize the two distinguished English scholars whose books will always hold a foremost place in the European literature on earlier Roman law. My object has been rather, by the genetic method of recording the details of the most notable trials, always from the original authorities, in a strictly chronological order, to illustrate the general principles of procedure, the systematic treatment of which is given by Mr. Strachan-Davidson and Dr. Greenidge.[1] The advantage of this method is that, presented in this orderly procession, the cases supplement one another more obviously, gaps in this case being filled by details in that, and mark the cumulative character of the evidence more forcibly than when they are merely referred to in footnotes or in pieces, as they must be in a more systematic treatment.

All that I claim as anything that can be called a contribution of my own is to have shown that there are practically no abnormal cases, and that, whether we have a highly complicated case like

[1] Greenidge: *Legal Procedure in Cicero's Time.* Strachan-Davidson: *Problems of the Roman Criminal Law.*

that of Rabirius, or a comparatively simple but badly reported one like that of Metellus, they all rigidly conform to the general type.

In referring by name to the two scholars I have mentioned I have almost of necessity adopted the Tacitean maxim, 'si qui diversa prodiderint'. With two views of Dr. Greenidge I have been compelled to disagree. I cannot follow him in thinking that *provocatio* ever became unnecessary or fell out of use; nor can I admit that after the time of the Gracchi the plebs tended to regain some of its ancient criminal jurisdiction. On the former point I follow Mr. Strachan-Davidson, and on the latter, though I do not remember that he has expressed an opinion, I hope that I am not in disagreement. With Mr. Strachan-Davidson himself I have ventured to disagree on certain points connected with the cases of Rabirius and Cicero. I have done so in the former case in order to assert the consistency of the procedure involved; in the latter I have done my best to vindicate the consistency of Caesar's attitude.

1. We must commence with the trial of Horatius[1] which, though not historical, may be regarded with Mommsen and Strachan-Davidson as archetypal in some of its essential features. Horatius, the survivor in the fight against the Curiatii, had slain his sister and thereby excited horror in the minds of patres and plebs. He was accordingly seized and hurried to the king's tribunal. The king, in order to avoid the personal conduct of the trial and the execution of the punishment, announces: 'Duumviros qui Horatio perduellionem judicent secundum legem facio.' The *lex* was no doubt, as Mr. Strachan-Davidson explains, the formula or instruction given by the king to his delegates. It was to the effect: 'Duumviri perduellionem judicent. Si a duumviris provocarit, provocatione certato: si vincent, caput obnubito: infelici arbori reste suspendito: verberato, vel intra pomerium, vel extra pomerium.' On these instructions the duumviri, whatever their view of the moral guilt of the accused, had clearly no alternative but to condemn, and accordingly one of them proceeded to pass sentence: 'P. Horati, tibi perduellionem judico. I, lictor, conliga manus.' On the approach of the lictor, Horatius, in accordance

[1] Livy, i, 26.

with the formula, and with the additional encouragement of the king, utters the word 'provoco'. Then 'de provocatione certatum ad populum est'. The appointment of the duumviri and the instructions given to them had been in the presence of the *concilium populi*, and possibly the *judicium* of the duumviri was also publicly conducted. The people, moved by the appeals of the accused's father and by the unfaltering behaviour of Horatius himself, acquitted him, their decision being brought about, as the historian declares, 'admiratione magis virtutis quam jure causae'.

Now while some points of the procedure embodied in this story are undoubtedly archetypal and abiding, others hardly less important are not. In the first place it was always henceforth the case that the highest magistrates with imperium, consuls and praetors, could themselves exercise criminal jurisdiction in capital cases if they chose, but that, like king Tullus, they abstained from doing so. On the other hand the reason for this abstention was different from that stated by Livy. The king stood aside because he disliked to undertake a lamentable and invidious *judicium*, or to be responsible for an atrocious sentence of death. The consuls and praetors abstained as a consequence of the Valerian laws, because it was not consonant with their dignity to pass a sentence which might be quashed by the popular assembly.

In the second place capital trials are always actually held by subordinate officials or magistrates without the imperium, as in this case by the *duumviri perduellionis*; but the subordinate position of the judge or prosecutor is in this connexion the only archetypal point. There is no certain evidence, though there is one doubtful rumour to be alluded to below, that *duumviri perduellionis* were ever appointed again till the admittedly artificial and antiquarian case of Rabirius. We cannot, I think, say that they fell into desuetude, for there is no evidence of any custom being established, and it is futile therefore to agree or to disagree with Mommsen as to whether these shadowy officials were or were not elected by the people. All through the republic, as the cases described below will show, capital charges were in the hands of regular magistrates, quaestors, aediles, and especially tribunes of the plebs.

A third archetypal point was that capital trials conducted by a magistrate always ended with a sentence which, apart from *provocatio*, either conceded or required by law, would be final. The details of historical trials differ much from those described in this case. For the *lex* or formula given to the duumviri by the king is substituted a recognized procedure, whether based on customary or on statute law, and this procedure comes to involve not a single hearing, but a triple *anquisitio*, the sentence only being pronounced at the end of the third stage. Again, while the formula given to the duumviri clearly necessitated condemnation and precluded acquittal, it was open to the tribunes and quaestors either to acquit or to pronounce a sentence less than capital.

I follow Mommsen and Mr. Strachan-Davidson in regarding as a fourth archetypal point, the appeal from the sentence of the judge or magistrate to the people. It is true that in this case the right of appeal is a voluntary concession made by the king, and that after it was established by law the actual appeal is rarely mentioned in the recorded cases. This, however, is one of the questions to be discussed later, and I will only insist here that in the Horatian case the *concilium populi* is beyond all doubt a court of second instance, and that, wherever in subsequent cases there is or is to be a *judicium populi* after a sentence pronounced by a magistrate, the same conclusion must follow.

Lastly, the case of Horatius is clearly archetypal in establishing the point that, though there was always involved in a *judicium populi* a *certatio* between the magistrate, or, as he now becomes, the accuser, and the condemned person, the *provocatio* was in its essence not so much an appeal for a revised judgement on the part of the people as an appeal for mercy or pardon. In certain cases, no doubt, though I am not sure that we have one on record, the people might reverse the magistrate's sentence on the ground that it was unjust, but in principle its acquittal, as in this case, was an act of sovereign pardon. It would perhaps have been more logical if the two cases had been in some way distinguished, but at least the paradox of our own procedure was kept out of sight, in which a condemned person may receive the royal pardon for a crime which there is good reason to believe he never committed.

Before we come to our next instance of a capital trial the republic had taken the place of the kingship, and the change had been marked by the all important lex Valeria of 509 B.C., the first law passed in the comitia centuriata. Cicero [1] states the law thus: 'ne quis magistratus civem Romanum adversus provocationem necaret neve verberaret.' The appeal to the people in capital cases was no longer a voluntary concession but a legal necessity.

2. In 477 B.C. an agrarian law was proposed by two tribunes and, as usual, resisted by the patricians. In retaliation, the two tribunes brought a capital charge against T. Menenius on the ground of his having been responsible for a recent military disaster: 'T. Menenio diem dicunt.' Great efforts were made by the patricians, and the reputation of the accused's father was appealed to, with the result that 'in multa temperarunt tribuni cum capitis anquisissent'. Menenius was accordingly fined 2,000 asses and the case ended. At the beginning of the next year the ex-consul Sp. Servilius was similarly brought to trial (*die dicta*) by two other tribunes. He followed a bolder course 'non tribunos modo, sed plebem oratione feroci refutando exprobrandoque Menenii damnationem', with the result that 'periculum discussit'.[2]

From the meagre and untechnical account of Livy it is difficult to be sure of the real procedure. It is clear, however, that the tribunes had begun to bring capital charges. It is practically certain that they conducted an *anquisitio* before the public. It is possible that this was followed in the case of the ex-consul by an appeal to the people, though it would, I suppose, be open to contend that the tribunes were not yet magistrates and therefore not bound by the lex Valeria. Menenius had no need to appeal, because his fine was below the maximum allowed. Whether the triple *anquisitio* was as yet developed we have no means of deciding from this case. A more important question is how we are to explain the phrase: 'non tribunos modo, sed plebem refutando.' Mommsen and Greenidge believe that prior to the Twelve Tables, the *concilium plebis* may have claimed and exercised the power of life and death over citizens.[3] It is possible, therefore, that the case of Servilius went before the plebs on appeal from the tribune's sentence and that he was acquitted. The word *plebs*, however, is often used by Livy for the public

[1] *de Repub.* ii, 31, 54, cf. Livy, ii, 8.
[2] Livy, ii, 52. [3] *Staatsrecht*, iii, p. 387.

assembly present at a *contio*,[1] and on the whole I should prefer to explain it so here and to suppose that, in the face of public feeling and the failure in the case of Menenius, the tribunes desisted from the prosecution.

At any rate all claims to capital jurisdiction on the part of the plebs were authoritatively set aside by the Twelve Tables in 451 B.C. We have the evidence of Cicero[2] that of the 'leges praeclarissimae de xii tabulis translatae' one of them 'de capite civis rogari nisi maximo comitiatu vetat'.[3] That this law was observed till at any rate the time of Gaius Gracchus is, I think, admitted by all authorities. That the procedure contemplated in such cases by this code was dependent on *provocatio* is also proved by Cicero,[4] who declares, with some inexactness which need not here be dwelt upon, 'ab omni judicio poenaque provocari licere indicant xii tabulae'.

A few years later, as a means of guarding against the practical abrogation of the lex Valeria by a régime like that of the decemviri, one of the leges Valeriae Horatiae enacted 'ne quis ullum magistratum sine provocatione crearet; qui creasset, eum jus fasque esset occidi: neve ea caedes capitalis noxae haberetur'.[5] It is in the light of this legislation that we have to consider the instances of capital charges which immediately follow.

3. In 446 B.C., immediately after the decemviral legislation, the tribune Virginius accused the hated Appius Claudius, 'diem Appio Virginius dixit'. Appius came down to the forum with a retinue of young patricians and was arraigned by the tribune. Though Appius expected nothing, either from the tribunician *auxilium* or from the *judicium populi*, he nevertheless appealed to the other tribune and also uttered the word *provoco*, the 'vox una vindex libertatis'. Then 'inter contionis murmur' he made the usual speech of self and family glorification. Virginius replied, and then, though the plebs was almost overawed by this sign of its own freedom, Appius was thrown into the carcer, and

[1] Livy, iii, 57; vi, 20; xliii, 16.
[2] *de Legibus*, iii, 19, 44.
[3] Cf. also iii, 4, 11.
[4] *de Repub.* ii, 31, 54.
[5] Livy, iii, 55. In all probability not only the creation of a magistrate exempt from appeal, but the death penalty inflicted by any magistrate without appeal, would be covered by this sanction. In this case Mommsen's explanation of 'improbe factum' in Livy, x, 9, 6, given by Mr. Strachan-Davidson, vol. i, p. 144, would be confirmed.

'tribunus ei diem prodixit'. So far all this is plain. There seems to have been a single *anquisitio* in the presence of a *contio*, and the public present at it is called the *plebs*. We have here expressed, what usually has to be assumed, the utterance of the word *provoco*, though this was probably after and not before the speeches referred to, and to ensure the presence of the defendant on the *dies prodicta*, that is, the day for the *judicium populi*, he is arrested, a step which no tribune was found to veto. In the interval his relatives tried to move the pity of the people by appearing in mourning in the forum, but as this failed, 'priusquam prodicta dies adesset, Appius sibi mortem conscivit'.

Where, I wonder, is there any justification in this account for Dr. Greenidge's contention that it proves the tribunes to have brought before the tribes cases of *perduellio* having no connexion with plebeian interests, immediately subsequent to the decemviral legislation (p. 328)?

As the *judicium populi* was not held, its constitution is not specified, but as Livy records that, apparently while Appius was actually in prison, the Twelve Tables were engraved and set up in public, we may conclude with absolute certainty that the court of appeal would have been the comitia centuriata.[1]

4. We have, in Livy, vi, 20, what is unquestionably a very important account of a capital trial falling in the year 384 B.C. which must have been as memorable as that of Horatius itself. Marcus Manlius, the saviour of the Capitol, had had a renowned military career, but at home he had been turbulent and seditious. Things had come to an open breach with the patricians and he was suspected of aiming at the position of king. For once the patricians and tribunes were at one, and Manlius was summoned by the latter to appear and stand his trial, 'diem Manlio dicunt'. When the day came, the charges made were, according to Livy's authorities, riotous meetings, seditious language, and ostentatious gifts to individuals; charges in fact 'pertinentia proprie ad regni crimen'. Livy himself seems to think that there must have been more direct evidence than this, 'cum damnandi mora plebi non in caussa, sed in loco, fuerit'. This will be explained by what follows. Manlius produced as witnesses 400 persons who had

[1] Livy, iii, 56–8.

benefited by his liberality, showed his civic and mural crowns, recounted his exploits and, turning to the Capitol, concluded with an impassioned prayer to the gods. Without stopping to tell us the result of the *anquisitio* in the forum, Livy at once proceeds 'in campo Martio cum centuriatim populus citaretur, et reus, ad capitolium manus tendens ab hominibus ad deos preces avertisset', the tribunes saw that the voting must be out of sight of the Capitol, and so *die prodicta* assembled the *concilium populi* outside the porta Nomentana: 'ibi crimen valuit et obstinatis animis triste judicium invisumque etiam judicibus factum.' The sentence was executed, and Manlius was hurled from the Tarpeian rock.

We get in this account very clearly the distinction between the hearing in the forum on the *dies dicta* and the summons of the comitia centuriata to the Campus. There is nothing, however, to show whether or not the triple *anquisitio* was yet developed. The result of the first hearing seems to have been that the plebs, that is, the public in the *contio*, though not without hesitation owing to the associations of the spot, approved of the tribunes' sentence. This is how I interpret the inexact phrase of Livy quoted above. Taking Livy's account as it stands we should have to suppose that, when the comitia met in the Campus after the necessary twenty-four days, the tribunes, who clearly presided, prorogued them to a later date. This would be inconsistent with the rule laid down by Cicero,[1] that in case of the comitia not being held on the day fixed, or being interrupted, the whole proceedings fell to the ground. Perhaps Mommsen is right in regarding this rule as no more than custom, but more probably Livy has here confused what happened. The tribunes must have foreseen, from what took place in the forum, what would happen in the Campus, and therefore, in fixing the day for the comitia centuriata to meet (*prodicta die*), they at once named another spot. In this way we get rid of the tiresome repetition of Manlius and the gods, and give *prodicta die* its usual technical sense. That this was a case of *provocatio* it was impossible to doubt. Even Dr. Greenidge does not put what he believes to have been the growing disuse of *provocatio* till after the third Valerian law; but if Livy's silence about *provocatio* is admittedly in this case no argument against its having taken place, the

[1] *de Domo*, 17, 45.

argument *a silentio* as applied to later cases will have equally to be discounted.

One point remains. After recounting the condemnation by the people, Livy states that, according to some authorities, the condemnation took place 'per duumviros, qui de perduellione anquirerent, creatos'. He rejects this version and we cannot traverse his judgement; but it is curious that he should regard this course as an alternative to condemnation by the people, whereas it could clearly only be an alternative to the *anquisitio* of the tribunes. With regard to the kind of execution we can hardly believe that Livy is correct or that a death sentence passed by the comitia centuriata would not have led to execution by the axe.

In 300 B.C. the third lex Valeria was passed,[1] 'eodem anno Marcus Valerius consul de provocatione legem tulit, diligentius sanctam. Tertia ea post reges exactos lata est, semper a familia eadem.' I will not stop here to discuss Livy's somewhat obscure distinction between earlier and later sanctions, only suggesting as possible that while the second law by a rough-and-ready method declared the magistrate who disregarded it a public murderer, liable to be killed by any one, the present law probably, followed in this respect by the lex Porcia, provided for a formal process of *perduellio* against him. Very possibly too it was from this time that the dictator within the city was made subject to *provocatio*.

5. We now come to a series of interesting and important capital trials no one of which by itself enables us to follow the matter through all its stages, but which by their joint and cumulative evidence serve to settle most doubtful points. In 212 B.C. much chicanery on the part of publicani was revealed in the matter of provisioning the armies across the sea. The senate for political reasons would take no step, but two tribunes, both named Carvilius, instituted proceedings against Postumius, the most notorious offender, and sentenced him to a fine of 200,000 asses;[2] 'ducentum millium aeris multam M. Postumio dixerunt.' That this sentence was the result of a triple *anquisitio* Livy does not state, but as in the very next year we shall see that this was the

[1] Livy, x, 9. [2] Livy, xxv, 3 and 4.

course adopted in a case exactly similar to this in its first stages, we may safely assume it here. So far the case was not a capital one; but the fine was over the maximum allowed to a magistrate, and therefore there was an appeal to the *comitia tributa*. Livy does not say this in so many words, but his language is capable of no other interpretation: 'cui certandae[1] cum dies advenisset, conciliumque tam frequens plebis adesset, &c.' At the meeting of the people Postumius, having failed to secure the *intercessio* of a friendly tribune, caused so much riot and disorder that on the advice of the consuls it was dissolved. Then, after a decree of censure passed by the senate, 'tribuni plebis, omissa multae certatione, rei capitalis diem Postumio dixerunt'. Postumius, though he had been compelled to give bail, did not appear on the day. Therefore 'Tribuni plebem rogaverunt, plebesque ita scivit; si M. Postumius ante kalendas Maias non prodisset, citatusque eo die non respondisset, neque excusatus esset, videri eum in exsilio esse: bonaque ejus venire, ipsi aqua et igni placere interdici'.

In this case therefore there was no *anquisitio*, no sentence by the tribunes and no *judicium populi*, for the simple reason that Postumius did what every accused person could do if he had not been arrested, he went into voluntary exile. This step was not usually taken till the completion of the *anquisitio*, though Cicero was more precipitate than Postumius, and did not wait even for the *diei dictio*. Postumius clearly scented the possibility of arrest and decided not to take the risk. But at whatever stage prior at least to the actual meeting of the centuries the step was taken, the result seems always to have been a decree not of the centuries but of the plebs. This decree, however, was declaratory, not judicial, for there was no longer any need of a sentence, and the plebs merely registered the fact that the accused had gone into exile as a means of escaping punishment: that it was a case of *justum exsilium* and that he was in the position of a person outlawed on whom the ban of *aquae et igni interdictio* had been passed.

[1] The word *certare* in connexion with provocatio is found both in the case of Horatius and in the *locus classicus* from Cicero to be cited below. Whether the tribunes 'multam dixerunt' at the end of their *anquisitio* and 'multam inrogaverunt' in the comitia, as Dr. Greenidge and others hold, has been made more than doubtful by Mr. Strachan-Davidson, vol. I, pp. 175 ff.

6. In the very next year[1] we are told that 'Gaius Sempronius Blaesus die dicta Cn. Fulvium, ob exercitum in Apulia amissum in contionibus vexabat'.

The charge was not at first a capital one, and on the first two days of the *anquisitio* only a pecuniary penalty was contemplated 'Bis est accusatus, pecuniaque anquisitum'. But on the third day the evidence was such 'ut capite anquirendum contio subclamaret'. Accordingly 'cum tribunus bis pecunia anquisisset, tertio capitis se anquirere diceret'. An objection was made to this but was overruled, and Sempronius gave his judgement 'perduellionis se judicare Cn. Fulvio, dixit'. At the same time, as the condemned man either appealed or was assumed to have appealed to the people, the tribune requested permission from the praetor to preside at the comitia centuriata on a certain day 'diemque comitiis a praetore urbis petit'. Fulvius had some hopes of securing a famous brother's presence at the *judicium populi*, but when that failed, 'exulatum Tarquinios abiit'. The final step was 'id ei justum exsilium esse scivit plebs'.

We should be happy if Livy had always been as explicit in his accounts of capital cases. It is clear that the triple *anquisitio* is now fully developed, as laid down in Cicero's *locus classicus* 'nam cum tam moderata judicia populi sint a majoribus constituta, ut . . . ne inprodicta die[2] quis accusetur, ut ter ante magistratus accuset intermissa die quam multam inroget aut judicet, quarta sit accusatio trinum nundinum prodicta die, quo die judicium sit futurum, &c.'[3]

A second point clearly established by this case as well as by the words of Cicero, is that the third *anquisitio* held in the presence of a *contio* ended with a sentence pronounced by the magistrate. But if this was so, then the *judicium populi* was necessarily and always a court of second instance. Dr. Greenidge overlooked this point when he wrote the following: 'circumstances combined to render the act of *provocatio* almost unnecessary. Customary law dictated that the magistrate should not pronounce a sentence which he knew must lead to the appeal,

[1] Livy, xxvi, 2 and 3.

[2] The constant use of *prodicta dies* by Livy shows that *ne inprodicta die* is explained by the words which follow. Why Mr. Strachan-Davidson should take it differently I do not understand.

[3] *de Domo*, 17, 45.

and consequently, when he held that the crime deserved such a sentence, he made no provisional pronouncement of his own but went directly to the people' (p. 311). It seems to me that all the evidence we have and indeed the very nature of *anquisitio* is against this view. I demur to the statement of Dr. Greenidge (p. 345) that the procedure of a *judicium populi* consisted of two stages, the *anquisitio* and the proceedings before the comitia. On the contrary these were two separate trials. In all matters not calling for *provocatio,* the *quaestio* of the magistrate, dependent as it was on his *coercitio,* was the only trial necessary. In capital cases after the lex Valeria, no doubt with the view of making possible the satisfactory working of the appeal, the *quaestio* was developed, perhaps gradually, into the more public and more formal *anquisitio.* This was held three times, each time in the presence of a *contio,* and formed, like the original *quaestio,* its forerunner, a separate trial ending with a sentence passed by the magistrate. It was only when this sentence was appealed against that a *judicium populi* took place at all, and, even then, if the condemned man, after appealing, went into exile, no *judicium populi* was necessary. The *anquisitio,* that is, the formal and regulated magisterial *judicium,* is not a stage of, but preparatory to the *judicium populi,* and was developed as the only means by which *provocatio* could become really effective. This in my opinion is how the words of Cicero are to be understood 'omnibus magistratibus . . . judicia dantur . . . ut esset populi potestas ad quam provocaretur'.[1] If this view of the *anquisitio* as a magisterial *judicium* is correct, Dr. Greenidge's ingenious distinction (p. 345) between the magistrate who, recognizing his limitations, went direct to the people, and the magistrate who, not recognizing them, gave rise to *provocatio,* falls to the ground. The system of *anquisitio,* the 'ne inprodicta die' rule, made it impossible for him to go direct to the people. The only way in which he could do so was in a case like that of Postumius, or perhaps that of Cicero, where, owing to the premature withdrawal of the delinquent, no magisterial *judicium* had taken place. And in such cases he went to the people, not assembled as a judicial body to get a capital sentence passed, but to the *concilium plebis* to register an administrative decree

[1] *de Leg.* iii, 12, 27.

of outlawry. Dr. Greenidge's whole treatment of this subject is vitiated by his confusion of these two aspects. While admitting in one passage (p. 318) that the act of outlawry pronounced against Cicero by the plebs never claimed to be a judicial sentence, he nevertheless on page 329 speaks of the plebs as having passed on Postumius,[1] 'a sentence of aquae et igni interdictio'.

A third point brought out clearly by this case, and surely brought out typically, is that not only was the *judicium populi* to have been a court of second instance, or in other words a court of appeal, but that it was to have been before an assembly over which the praetor and not a tribune would in the ordinary course preside; and this assembly must have been, in accordance with the Twelve Tables, the comitia centuriata. As there can be no matter of doubt about this in the present case, and as, notwithstanding, the decree of outlawry came from the plebs, it will be as well to lay it down once for all, with a view to future cases, that this latter fact offers no presumption, whether in Cicero's case or in any other, that the *judicium populi* would not have been held by the centuries.

7. The next case, that of Scipio Africanus in 187 B.C., need not detain us so long. He was suspected of having defrauded the aerarium of booty taken in war, and two tribunes 'diem dixerunt'. There was much difference of feeling about the merits of his case 'donec dies dicendae causae venit'. On the first day of the *anquisitio* Scipio was escorted to the forum by a huge crowd and was ordered to plead his cause 'sine ulla criminum mentione'. He delivered a dignified speech recording his own achievements. Then the tribunes 'suspicionibus magis quam argumentis pecuniae captae reum accusarunt'. The hearing went on till night when 'prodicta dies est'. On the second day the tribunes took their seats on the rostra and Scipio, on being summoned again, appeared with his retinue and after another magnificent oration left the forum and, attended by the whole *contio*, proceeded to visit the Capitol and the other temples, the

[1] It is difficult to see how the case of Postumius justifies Greenidge's assertion on page 328 that the tribune still hears cases of *perduellio* before his own peculiar assembly. That charge was not heard anywhere, and if it had been, the case of Fulvius proves conclusively that it would have been before the centuries.

tribunes being left alone on the rostra. Perhaps to allow time for popular feeling to cool down, there was a longer interval before the day fixed for the third *anquisitio*: 'die longiore prodicta'. But Scipio disdained to plead his cause any more, and before the day arrived he had retired to Liternum. 'Ubi dies venit, citarique absens est coeptus,' his brother pleaded illness as an excuse, which the tribunes, who had now apparently summoned the *concilium plebis*, refused to accept, putting down his absence to the same arrogance through which on the second day he had left the 'judicium et tribunos plebis et contionem'. Some of the other tribunes, however, interposed, and proposed that the excuse should be accepted 'diemque a collegis prodici'. Another tribune, Tiberius Gracchus, went still further and declared that he would place his veto on any more proceedings against Scipio. This practically ended the matter. The accusers declared that they must reconsider their action and the *concilium plebis* was dissolved.

I cannot agree with Mommsen[1] that the three days of the *anquisitio* were all held, and that 'die longiore prodicta' refers to the meeting of the comitia. A careful reading of the whole passage[2] will show that there had been only two days in the forum before Scipio went into exile, and that on the last day there was a meeting, not of the comitia centuriata at all, but of the *concilium plebis*. Why then was the plebs called together when Scipio failed to make his third appearance? I think that the two former cases, and especially that of Postumius, give the answer. It was to pass the formal declaration that the defendant was an exile and an outlaw. When Gracchus came forward, a known enemy of Scipio, the action which he took was a surprise, for all were expecting 'tristiorem sententiam', which can only have been the usual bill of outlawry as passed against Postumius and Fulvius. If we take this view, the case falls into line with the others in every respect.

8. About twenty years later, in 169 B.C., we have another very interesting case. The censors C. Claudius Marcellus and Tib. Sempronius Gracchus had not only made themselves unpopular by depriving many equites of the *equus publicus*, but had issued

[1] *Staatsrecht*, iii, p. 356. [2] Livy, xxxviii, 50–2.

an edict refusing to allow any *publicani* who held or had contracted for the *vectigalia* under the previous censors to be bidders at their own *locatio*. The *publicani* in question, after appealing in vain to the senate, secured the aid of Rutilius, a tribune whose *intercessio* in another matter the censors had ignored. Rutilius accordingly promulgated a *plebiscitum* to the effect that all contracts accepted from the present censors were invalid and that from the new *locatio* no bidder should be excluded. At the *contio* following on this *promulgatio* the censors spoke against it, and when Claudius was interrupted by clamour he took steps to maintain order. Thereupon Rutilius left the *contio*, consecrated the property of Gracchus for the previous neglect of the *intercessio*, summoned Claudius to appear on a certain day (*diem dixit*) for having broken up the *contio*, and finally 'utrique censori perduellionem se judicare pronuntiavit, diemque comitiis a praetore urbano petiit'.

Livy's account here is evidently very condensed, and the various steps in the procedure are omitted, but may be supplied with some exactness from the other cases. Rutilius seems to have begun by dealing with the two censors in different ways, taking action against Gracchus under the sanction of the *leges sacratae*, while Claudius was treated as a political offender in the ordinary way. It is clear, however, that on second thoughts Gracchus was included under the same charge as his colleague, and no doubt had to appear on the same day. The capital sentence evidently immediately preceded the request for a day from the praetor, and we cannot possibly believe with Mr. Strachan-Davidson (vol. i, p. 134) that 'it took place at the commencement of the proceedings'. Livy has simply passed over in this case the three days of *anquisitio* and has hurried on to the result at the end of the third day. On this occasion, however, the censors, who of course had appealed, did not go into exile but stood their ground to await the decision of the centuries. The *comitiis perduellionis dies* arrived and the case of Claudius was taken first. He was less popular than his colleague, and, though both censors seem to have been confident of acquittal, it was by no means certain that he would escape. They did not, however, really risk their lives, for the practice of allowing those accused of a capital charge to save themselves by voluntary exile was by this time fully established. We have already had several instances of exile so incurred before the beginning of the comitial *judicium*, but even after this had begun it was still open to the accused to withdraw as long as the vote of a single century was wanting to a majority for condemnation.[1] If indeed all the tribunes were agreed, the accused might, like Appius Claudius, be arrested, and if condemned might actually suffer the death penalty, but this was a rare and improbable case. In the present instance Rutilius was evidently acting alone and the censors were therefore quite safe from arrest; nevertheless, when the trial came on, Claudius was nearly condemned. The voting actually reached the point when only eight centuries were required for condemnation. What saved Claudius was not 'jus causae' but the popularity of Gracchus: he solemnly declared to the people (*plebs* is the word used), who had made it clear that he was himself in no danger, that 'si collega damnatus esset non expectato de se judicio, comitem exsilii ejus futurum'. The result was the acquittal of Claudius and the withdrawal of the charge made against Gracchus.[2]

9. It would be interesting if we could add to these earlier cases the details of the accusation of T. Quinctius Rocus by the quaestor Manius Sergius. It probably belonged to this earlier period, but all that we know of it is derived from a few extracts made by Varro from a document which he calls 'commentarium vetus anquisitionis Mani Sergii quaestoris, qui capitis accusavit T. Quinctium Rocum'.[3] But while we do not know the exact nature of the charge or how the case ended, we have some interesting light thrown on some of the procedure implied in the preceding trials. I venture, in spite of Mr. Strachan-Davidson's treatment of the *commentarium*, to go into it again, because I find myself compelled to give a different interpretation at least to certain points of it. No doubt the document as a whole contained instructions to the quaestor for the conduct of the case *ab initio*; but the two extracts quoted by Varro only concern certain steps to be taken at the end of the last day of *anquisitio*,

[1] The μία φυλή in Polybius, 6, 14, is an obvious slip. [2] Livy, xliii, 16.
[3] See Bruns, appendix, p. 59, and Strachan-Davidson, i, 156 ff.

and at the beginning of the day on which the centuries were to meet. It will be convenient to cite the passages in full and then to translate them, in order to express what I believe to be their meaning. The first passage runs: 'Auspicio operam des et in templo auspices. Dum aut ad praetorum aut ad consulem mittas auspicium petitum, comitiatum praeco populum vocet ad te, et cum de muris vocet praeco, id imperare oportet. Cornicinem ad privati januam et in arcem mittas, ubi canat. Collegam roges, ut comitia edicat de rostris, et argentarii tabernas occludant. Patres censeant exquaeras et adesse jubeas; magistratus censeant exquaeras, consules praetores tribunosque plebis collegasque tuos in templo adesse jubeas omnes; ad comitias contionem advoces.' We have to suppose that the *judicium* before the quaestor is over and Rocus condemned. At this point the quaestor is thus instructed: 'Take care to remember the auspices and you will have to take them in the "templum". Provided that you send to secure the auspices either to the praetor or the consul, the herald may summon the people to the comitia under your presidency, and when the herald makes this summons from the walls, he should give orders to that effect. You should send a horn-blower to sound his horn at the door of the accused and at the arx. You should ask your colleague to make formal edict for the comitia to meet, from the rostra, and to notify the bankers to close their shops on that day. You should ask the senators for their approval and invite their attendance, likewise the magistrates. You should invite all of them to attend in the "templum". You should then summon in advance the *contio* for the comitia.'

This translation brings out the fact that the quaestor is being here instructed what to do when he has condemned the accused on the last day of the *anquisitio*. He is of course not to take the auspices on that day, but he is reminded that he will have to take them, and he is told to get leave at once from the higher magistrates to take them on the day fixed for the meeting of the comitia, still twenty-four days distant. He is in fact merely told in more technical terms to 'ask a day from the praetor', which had to be done immediately after the appeal. The actual date of the comitia is to be announced by the *praeco* from the walls, and more formally by the other quaestor from the rostra. The *cornicen* is sent to the house of Rocus, who had presumably gone home as soon as the sentence was given. Finally, when the messages to the senators and magistrates are dispatched, in the explanation of which I follow Mr. Strachan-Davidson, he is to issue his own summons for the *contio* in the Campus twenty-four days later, which, on the magistrate's bidding, will arrange itself as the comitia centuriata. I have adopted Mommsen's conjecture 'ad comitias' instead of the manuscript reading 'ac cum mittas'.

The second citation is expressly said by Varro to be at the end of the *commentarium*, though this point has generally been overlooked. It runs as follows: 'Item quod attingat qui de censoribus classicum ad comitia centuriata redemptum habent, uti curent eo die quo die comitia erunt, in arce classicus canat circumque muros et ante privati hujusce T. Quincti Roci scelerosi ostium canat, et ut in campo cum primo luci adsiet.'

The initial *item* shows that the fragment is a part of other instructions for the proceedings of the final day.

'Further as regards the persons who have engaged a trumpeter from the censors for the comitia centuriata, they must see that the said trumpeter shall blow his trumpet at the arx and round the walls and before the door of the said wicked individual Titus Quinctius Rocus on the day when the comitia shall be held, and that the accused shall be present in the Campus at the dawn of day.'

It is clear that no arrest of accused was contemplated. That this instruction refers to a different occasion from the former is surely proved by the fact that the summons to Rocus is given now, not by a *cornicen* but by a *classicus* in the service of the censors. The point is also made clear by Varro's comment: 'inter id cum circum muros mittitur et cum contio advocatur tempus interesse apparet ex his quae interea fieri scriptum est': that is, an interval has elapsed, namely twenty-four days, prior to the sending of the *classicus* round the walls, from the previous summons of the *contio*. The further instructions to the quaestor, as to the course to be pursued when the centuries have met, are unfortunately not preserved.

The capital trials which we have considered have given us almost every possible variety. In one case, that of Menenius, the prosecution was abortive. In two, those of Horatius and the censors, the *judicium populi* was actually held and ended in acquittal. In one, that of Manlius, it ended in condemnation and execution. In one, that of Appius Claudius, the accused anticipated the *judicium populi* by suicide. In three, those of Postumius, Fulvius, and Scipio, the *judicium* was anticipated by voluntary exile. This, however, was in one case after the third *anquisitio*, in another after the second, while Postumius did not even wait for the first. It is clear that all the cases were, or would have been, tried before the centuries. The actual sentence of the magistrate is only definitely stated in three trials, but it is implied wherever the *anquisitio* reaches its final stage, and wherever it is implied the *judicium populi* becomes of necessity a court of second instance.

It is true that only in two cases is the act of *provocatio* mentioned; but on the other hand we should remember that there are only three others in which we could possibly have expected it, those of Manlius, Fulvius, and the censors; and as Fulvius made no practical use of the right, we may reduce them to two. We have had nothing so far to indicate either that *provocatio* was becoming unnecessary and growing out of use, or that the enactment of the Twelve Tables with regard to capital cases going before the *maximus comitiatus* was becoming 'the doctrine of mere constitutional purists'. At the same time, from a number of instances sufficient to establish it as the normal practice, we have seen that, when an accused or condemned person had evaded by voluntary exile the *judicium* either of the magistrate or of the people, it was the assembly of the plebs which registered, as an accomplished fact, the ban of *aquae et igni interdictio.*

While the foregoing cases have all depended upon the leges Valeriae, which by establishing the right of appeal necessitated both the *judicium populi* and the public *anquisitio*, the cases now to be considered must have depended on the leges Porciae, probably belonging to the first half of the second century B.C., or on subsequent enactments like that of Gaius Gracchus or that of Clodius. Whatever may have been the effect of the Porcian legislation in extending the right of *provocatio* outside Rome or Italy, it probably made no essential difference in the procedure of *judicia populi.* Livy (x, 9) makes the lex Porcia merely sharpen the sanction of the third Valerian law; 'gravi poena, si quis verberasset necassetve civem Romanum sanxit'. Cicero [1] confirms this 'neque vero leges Porciae . . . quicquam praeter sanctionem attulerunt novi'. I agree with Dr. Greenidge, though his interpretation seems hardly consistent with his view of *provocatio* having long since become unnecessary, that these laws did not make death by the axe or by scourging in themselves illegal 'but merely submitted the threat of such punishment to appeal' (p. 321). But obviously the more rigidly *provocatio* was enforced, with its interval of twenty-four days between the sentence of the magistrate and its confirmation by the people, the more certainty there was that a person condemned by a magistrate might if he chose withdraw before his final trial. This is surely all that Caesar could have meant when he said [2] that the lex Porcia as well as other laws, namely the Valerian, 'condemnatis civibus non animam eripi sed exsilium permitti jubent'. Assuming therefore that the Porcian laws were essentially laws enforcing *provocatio*, and remembering that the importance of *provocatio* as a real and valuable privilege is implied both by the franchise proposal of Fulvius Flaccus in 125 B.C. and by the lex Acilia of 122 B.C., we may proceed with our instances of capital trials before the people with tolerable certainty that their ultimate basis was still what Livy calls the 'unicum praesidium libertatis'.

10. In 123 B.C. Publius Popilius Laenas, one of the consuls of 132 B.C. was prosecuted for *perduellio* by Gaius Gracchus. Such a prosecution was almost certainly called forth owing to the severe sanction of the lex Porcia, which had been violated by Popilius. He had in fact, after the death of Tiberius Gracchus, put citizens to death without a *judicium populi* [3]; but it is doubtful whether the lex Porcia alone would have applied to his case, because he had been empowered by the senate to hold a special *quaestio* on the adherents of Gracchus 'cum senatus . . . Laenati . . . mandasset ut in eos qui cum Graccho consenserant more majorum animadverteret'.[4]

In such cases, customary law, perhaps because the magistrate was acting administratively and not judicially, allowed *provocatio* to be ignored. To prevent this evasion of the Porcian law in

[1] *de Repub.* 2, 31, 54. [2] Sall. *Cat.* 51. [3] Plut. *Tib. Gracc.* 20.
[4] Val. Max. 4, 22: cf. the *crudeles quaestiones* of Velleius, 2, 7.

future, Gaius Gracchus passed his law 'ne de capite civis Romani injussu vestro judicaretur',[1] while in order to punish Popilius he made the law retrospective. From this time there could be no capital *judicium* except either a *judicium populi* or a special *quaestio* established by the people, not by the senate, or a *quaestio perpetua*. It was under this retrospective law that Gracchus prosecuted Popilius, and perhaps his colleague Rutilius as well. It was an *actio perduellionis*, as Cicero implies that his own case would have been if he had not run away.[2] What happened in regard to the trial, it is hard to gather from the isolated references to it which are all we have. It seems clear that Popilius never actually appeared before a *judicium populi*.[3] Cicero says that he escaped 'vim caedemque' and that he was afterwards 'restitutus'. These expressions, as well as the statement of Diodorus (xxxv, 26) that he was conducted from the city μετὰ δακρύων ὑπὸ τῶν ὄχλων, imply voluntary exile. On the other hand, the statement of Cicero in the same speech (15, 37) that on behalf of Popilius, his young sons 'propinquorumque multitudo populum Romanum est deprecata', and of Velleius (2, 7) that he fell a victim to ill feeling stirred up 'judiciorum publicorum merito' imply that he was present at least at some of the stages of the *anquisitio*. Dr. Greenidge believes that Gaius Gracchus, in passing the law referred to, 'widened the power of the people and the magistrates by giving to the plebs, as well as to the populus, capital jurisdiction in this particular case': that 'he contemplated the cognizance of the plebs' and that therefore 'the clause of the Twelve Tables which claimed capital causes for the centuries was abrogated as far as this particular jurisdiction was concerned' (pp. 324, 325). The case of Cicero to which the same hypothesis is made to apply, will be considered later. In the case of Popilius I cannot think that Dr. Greenidge adduces any arguments which justify his view. It is true that Cicero[4] speaks of Popilius and Metellus as driven away 'tribuniciis rogationibus', but that surely only means that the ultimate cause of exile was in the one case the law 'ne de capite, &c.' and in the other the clause in the agrarian law requiring the oath. The other passage on which Dr. Greenidge depends, is to me conclusive

[1] Cic. *pro Rab.* 4, 22. [2] *pro Mil.* 14, 36. [3] Cic. *post Red. in Sen.* 15, 38.
[4] *post Red. in Sen.* 15, 38, and *de Domo*, 32, 87.

that the case of Popilius was on all fours with the earlier trials and especially with that of Fulvius. In the *de Domo*, 31, 82, Cicero asks 'ubi enim tulerat ut mihi aquae et igni interdiceretur quod Gaius Gracchus de Popilio . . . tulit?' I interpret this to mean not that a sentence was pronounced on Popilius by the plebs as a *judicium populi*, but that when he had withdrawn into exile, the *concilium plebis* did what we have seen it do in the case of Fulvius, register its declaration that Popilius was by his own act an exile and an outlaw.

11. Of far greater constitutional importance was the prosecution in 120 B.C. of Lucius Opimius and his trial and acquittal by the people. Whatever may have been the case with the adherents of Tiberius Gracchus, there can be no doubt that those of Gaius Gracchus and Fulvius Flaccus had put themselves in armed and riotous opposition to the state authorities. The senate was precluded by the law of Gracchus himself from setting up a summary *judicium* to deal with these seditious citizens, but it established a new precedent by passing the so-called *senatus consultum ultimum*. This was in itself merely a decree, as Plutarch puts it,[1] σώζειν τὴν πόλιν ὅπως δύναιτο. The official formula we get from Cicero[2] 'decrevit quondam senatus ut L. Opimius consul videret ne quid respublica detrimenti caperet'. I believe with Mommsen and Mr. Strachan-Davidson[3] that this did no more than point out to the consul 'that a state of civil war has begun, that there are enemies about, and that he is advised to deal with them accordingly'. What it practically came to was that it was left to the discretion of the consul how much of the old unlimited imperium he must use to save the state. Opimius acted on the decree without scruple. All the authorities agree that not only were Gracchus and Fulvius killed, but a large number (Plutarch says 3,000) of their followers were either slaughtered in the street fighting or taken to the carcer and executed.[4]

Now in doing this Opimius certainly did not contravene the law of Gracchus, which only made illegal a special *judicium* not set up by the people, but he undoubtedly acted in violation of the Porcian and Valerian laws by putting citizens to death not only

[1] *Gaius Gracc.* 17. [2] *in Cat.* 1, 2, 4. [3] i, 245.
[4] Plut. *G. Gracc.* 16 and 17; App. 1, 26; Sall. *Jug.* 31; Liv. *Epit.* 61; the point about the carcer comes from Sallust and Livy.

without *provocatio* but without a *judicium* of any kind. On the face of it therefore he was liable to prosecution for *perduellio.* This was the view taken by the tribune Q. Decius. Livy's account of the trial would have been invaluable. The epitomator merely says 'Lucius Opimius accusatus apud populum a Q. Decio tribuno plebis quod indemnatos cives in carcerem congessisset absolutus est'. We must assume that the usual *anquisitio* took place, that *perduellio* was pronounced against the accused by Decius, and that Opimius, feeling confident of influential support, stood his ground and was tried before the centuries. Dr. Greenidge seems a little inclined to apply his theory of capital jurisdiction by the plebs to this trial as well as to that of Popilius. But the words 'apud populum' are against this view and so is the very fact of acquittal, which might not have been so certain if the plebs had had the decision. We gather from Cicero[1] that, either at the *anquisitio* or at the *judicium populi*, C. Carbo, one of the consuls, spoke in favour of Opimius. Opimius admitted the facts alleged, admitted even that he had acted 'contra leges', that is, the Porcian, not the Sempronian, but pleaded that he had done it in a time of war for the sake of saving the state at a time when the people had been called to arms by the decree of the senate. Decius on the other hand maintained 'ne sceleratissimum quidem civem sine judicio jure ullo necare potuisti'.[2] It was a momentous trial because, if Opimius had been condemned, a deathblow would have been struck at the new senatorial method of dealing with seditious citizens without awaiting for the cumbrous process of a *judicium populi*. The acquittal on the other hand established and gave some kind of legal sanction to the new precedent. The interpretation given to the *senatus consultum ultimum* by the result of this trial was clearly the interpretation put upon it by Caesar in the famous passage where he admits its applicability in the case of Gracchus and Saturninus: 'Quotienscumque sit decretum, darent operam magistratus, ne quid respublica detrimenti caperet, qua voce et quo senatus consulto populus Romanus ad arma sit vocatus, factum in perniciosis legibus, in vi tribunicia, in secessione populi, templis locisque editioribus occupatis; atque haec superioris aetatis exempla expiata Saturnini atque Gracchorum casibus

[1] *de Oratore*, 2, 25, 106.
[2] Cic. *Part. Orat.* 30, 104; cf. *de Orat.* ii, 30, 132.

docet.'[1] To him the essence of the decree clearly was that by it the Roman people were called to arms and that it therefore legitimized acts of war under the direction of the consul. I shall argue below that his action and attitude in 63 B.C. was perfectly consistent with this view. Cicero argues that the execution of the five Catilinarians could similarly be justified as an act of war. Caesar at any rate did not take this view, and I believe that he was perfectly right.

12. The next trial to be dealt with is that of Quintus Metellus Numidicus in 100 B.C. The case presents several features both of interest and of ambiguity. The agrarian law of Saturninus contained a clause which required all senators to take oath to its observance within five days of its being passed, on pain of being expelled from the order and paying a fine of twenty talents.[2] Metellus alone refused to swear to a law passed by violent means[3] and accordingly Saturninus 'Metello Numidico eo quod in eam non juraverat diem dixit'.[4] It is perfectly clear from all accounts that Metellus did not await the *judicium populi*, but retired into voluntary exile at Rhodes. Cicero is indeed fond of comparing his own action with that of Metellus in this respect, although the latter went away through motives of dignified patriotism, while Cicero simply took fright and lost his head. It appears to me certain, however, that Metellus stayed through the *anquisitio*. In the first place Livy states that he was defended 'a bonis civibus'. In the second place it appears from Appian, as I interpret the passage quoted below, that he did not leave until after the day was fixed by Saturninus for the *judicium populi*, and that could only have been on the third day of *anquisitio*. In the third place, how are we to account for the capital charge made against Metellus when the clause in the agrarian law only specified a fine? I believe that the answer is found in the case of Fulvius. Metellus must have been accused at the first, perhaps also at the second *anquisitio* with a view to the exaction of the pecuniary penalty, and for this eventually the capital charge was substituted in the

[1] *Bell. Civ.* 1, 7. The plural *Gracchorum* need not be pressed so as to imply that the *senatus consultum ultimum* was passed in the case of Tiberius. All the evidence implies that it was not.

[2] App. 1, 29. [3] Cicero, *pro Sestio*, 47, 101. [4] Livy, *Epit.* 69.

last stages of the tribunician trial. That he was to have been tried before the comitia centuriata we can hardly doubt; indeed even Dr. Greenidge admits this,[1] though he does so through accepting the obvious mistake of Appian, that the charge was brought jointly by Glaucia and Saturninus (p. 351).

Our fullest account of this trial comes from Appian (i, 31), and if we correct one gross but palpable error, the case falls into perfect consistency with that of Fulvius. In order to establish my point, I must quote the passage *in extenso*. After relating (what may or may not be true) that Saturninus sent his *viator* to drag Metellus from the curia and that, when this was resisted, he declared to the people that they would never have their land till Metellus was got rid of, Appian proceeds: *ψήφισμά τε φυγῆς ἐπέγραφον αὐτῷ, καὶ τοὺς ὑπάτους ἐπικηρῦξαι προσετίθεσαν, μηδένα Μετέλλῳ κοινωνεῖν πυρὸς ἢ ὕδατος ἢ στέγης. ἔς τε τὴν δοκιμασίαν τοῦδε τοῦ ψηφίσματος ἡμέραν προὔγραφον.* Metellus, to avoid civil strife, withdrew. On this, *τὸ ψήφισμα ὁ Ἀπουλήιος ἐκύρου, καὶ τὰ ἐν τῷ ψηφίσματι Μάριος ἐπεκήρυττεν.*

Appian's mistake is his description of the first step, attributed by him to Saturninus and Glaucia but really taken by Saturninus alone. The *ψήφισμα φυγῆς*, that is, the registration or declaration of outlawry, of course came at the end of the whole affair, as we have seen it do in so many previous cases, and for this there was no need for any previous announcement such as that implied in Appian's words: *ἐς τὴν δοκιμασίαν τοῦδε τοῦ ψηφίσματος ἡμέραν προὔγραφον.* Appian is clearly describing what took place after the last stage of the *anquisitio*, and what he meant was that 'Saturninus perduellionem Metello judicavit'. If we accept this correction, all falls into perfect order. Saturninus, having pronounced sentence, asked the praetor for a day and fixed the date for the decision of the centuries to be given, *ἐς τὴν δοκιμασίαν τοῦ ψηφίσματος.* Metellus, however, withdrew, and then, on the proposal of Saturninus, the plebs took the course described in the case of Fulvius and 'justum ei exsilium esse scivit', this being the *ψήφισμα φυγῆς.* This is perfectly consistent, too, with what

[1] Cicero, in a passage quoted above, says that both Popilius and Metellus were driven out *tribuniciis rogationibus.* Dr. Greenidge argues from this that Popilius was, or was to have been, tried by the plebs, and yet he admits here that Metellus was not. The words of Cicero would at any rate indicate that the procedure was the same in both cases.

Cicero states,[1] 'ubi enim tuleras ut mihi aqua et igni interdiceretur, quod . . . Saturninus de Metello tulit?'

The direction to the consuls to publish the decree is more doubtful. It is impossible to accept Mr. Strachan-Davidson's suggestion (ii, p. 63) that such a magisterial proclamation was the normal proceeding, being in fact a warning to the *interdictus* of his danger, and only unnecessary when the latter 'went away briskly'. It is clear that Metellus had already gone away, as also had Postumius, Fulvius, and Cicero, before the *interdictio* was 'fulminated', or, as I should prefer to say, registered and notified. I should rather agree with Dr. Greenidge that it was an unusual proceeding, though there could not have been, as he suggests, a 'consular bill'. Appian and Cicero both state distinctly that the bill of outlawry was passed by Saturninus; the latter writer even accentuates the point in his *de Domo* (33, 87) by the antithesis 'rogationibus tribuniciis, non . . . comitiis centuriatis'. Besides, Appian is quite clear that the consuls were not to pass a bill, but only to proclaim τὰ ἐν τῷ ψηφίσματι. If Appian is right, it must have been, I imagine, an exceptional step, to be explained by the nature of the coalition between Marius and the popular leaders.

Before passing to the two last cases which the title of this article forbids me to shirk, I will deal very briefly with three minor cases, the first two because Dr. Greenidge believed that they give support to his view as to the capital jurisdiction of the plebs.

13. In 104 B.C. Marcus Silanus was accused by the tribune Gnaeus Domitius because five years previously 'adversum Cimbros rem male gesserat'. The matter came before the people and Silanus 'plenissime absolutus est, nam duae solae tribus damnaverunt'.[2] If this was a capital charge at all, the penalty must have been modified in the course of the *anquisitio* to a pecuniary one, as we have seen it in the case of Menenius, so that the appeal came before the tribes, or more probably this military offence from the first was threatened only with a fine, as that of Fulvius had been in its first stages.

14. The next case I give in Dr. Greenidge's own words: 'In

[1] *de Domo*, 31, 82. [2] Ascon. *in Corn.* p. 80.

98 B.C. P. Furius, who had opposed the recall of Metellus, was ... accused by C. Appuleius Decianus before the people. Decianus was tribune and the place of trial was the forum ; the case, therefore, must have come before the plebs.' This, however, does not follow, because Valerius Maximus, who tells the story (viii, 1, 2, *init.*) when he says ' pro rostris ' may be referring to the *anquisitio* and not to the *judicium populi*, as he certainly is later in the same chapter, when he speaks of Galba being accused ' pro rostris ', but immediately adds that the *contio* was afterwards conciliated. Dr. Greenidge goes on : ' The accused was acquitted by the tribes, but torn in pieces by the mob ; ' and refers to Dio Cass. *Frag.* 105. A reference to Dio shows that he says nothing about the tribes and only states that Furius was killed ἐν τῇ ἐκκλησιᾳ.

15. The last case, before the establishment of the *quaestiones perpetuae* by Sulla made *judicia populi* comparatively rare, was that of Merula and Lutatius Catulus in 87 B.C. Although the prosecution, clearly a capital one, was in the midst of the Marian massacres, the usual triple *anquisitio* would seem from Appian (i, 74) to have taken place, although he does not understand it and says that they ought to have been convicted four times: τετράκις δὲ ἐχρῆν κηρυττομένους ἐν ὡρισμένοις ὡρῶν διαστήμασιν ἁλῶναι. The only irregularity was that the accused, though not arrested, were shadowed, φυλασσόμενοι ἀφανῶς, and so, being unable to go into exile, they committed suicide in the interval between the *anquisitio* and the *judicium populi.*

16. It has been possible so far, by adhering strictly to the authorities and deducing from precedents more or less firmly established, to explain with some consistency the procedure of all the trials hitherto considered. Will the same method fail us when we come to that crux of cases, the trial of Rabirius in 63 B.C.? We cannot doubt that the whole affair was set on foot by Caesar's agency. It was a critical year for the popular party, and Caesar had failed, through want of judgement, in his agrarian scheme earlier in the year. It must have been obvious that the rumoured plots which were in the air might before the end of the year lead to a revolution, and quite possibly there was some irresponsible talk in senatorial or equestrian circles about repeating, in such an

eventuality, the repressive measures of the famous year 100 B.C. This may have suggested to Caesar the otherwise somewhat far-fetched idea of taking a test case from that very year and thereby raising a popular cry by the reassertion of the 'unicum libertatis auxilium', and perhaps also of guarding against possible eventualities.

I cannot believe that Caesar intended to raise the question of the validity of the *senatus consultum ultimum*, though no doubt Cicero intended to create that impression.[1] The impression must have been a false one, for Caesar was not a man to change his principles, and he deliberately, towards the end of his career, not only recognized the validity of the senate's action in the sense established by the trial and acquittal of Opimius, but specifically admitted its justification on the occasion of the Appuleian riots.[2] But though the matter had been lost sight of amid the reactionary excitement of the time, Saturninus, it would seem, had not met his death, as Gracchus had, in the course of actual civil war, or even in obedience to direct orders from Marius the consul. Florus (ii, 4), who is evidently following Livy, but more fully than the epitomator, says that Saturninus and others shut up in the Capitol, after a message expressing penitence, were received into the curia with some guarantee of safety, and that it was the mob and not the armed bands of Marius which put him to death. With this version Appian agrees. According to him, Saturninus and Glaucia gave themselves up and were guarded by Marius in the curia, with a view to legal action in the future, ὡς ἐννομώτερον ἐργασόμενος, and it was the mob which broke in and massacred the prisoners. This may not have been the true or the only account, but it was clearly the one which it suited Caesar's purpose to adopt. It certainly put a very different complexion from that conveyed by Cicero's whole speech on the case. The civil war, it seems, was over. Saturninus was no longer an overt *perduellis*. The immediate safety of the state did not require his summary death, and that death was not the act of the consul acting on the senate's decree. Whether, by his previous conduct, Saturninus had laid himself open to a charge of *perduellio* was another question which might have been decided as Marius had intended, ἐννομώτερον. That this was Caesar's point and not

[1] *pro Rab.* 1, 1, &c. [2] See pp. 23 and 24.

an attack upon the 'summum auxilium majestatis atque imperii' is shown by Cicero himself, who refers to the persistent contention of Labienus that 'fides Saturnino data est'.[1] He attempts to answer the argument, first, by suggesting that Rabirius was not bound by a guarantee given by Marius, although his whole case depends on the assumption that Rabirius was acting under the orders of the consul, and, secondly, by the strange assertion that Marius had no right to give the guarantee without a decree of the senate.

It happened that Rabirius, the person who by some accounts had actually killed Saturninus, was still alive, and Caesar conceived the perhaps not altogether happy idea of calling him to account, after thirty-seven years, for this political murder by having him prosecuted for *perduellio*; but if the design showed doubtful judgement, the procedure adopted was still more open to criticism. Caesar, probably for the sake of creating a deeper impression on the public mind, determined to revive the obsolete procedure which tradition assigned to the trial of Horatius. I have already expressed the belief that the *duumviri perduellionis* had never been called into existence since that occasion. At any rate, as far as I can see, the procedure was now to be exactly the same in every respect, even including the grim punishment specified in the *horrendum carmen*. But in one respect there was bound to be a difference; there was no king to create the duumviri and therefore the initiative must come from the now sovereign people. The tribune Labienus was Caesar's agent in the matter, and I agree with Dr. Greenidge that the only inference to be drawn from the confused account of Dio Cassius (37, 27) is that Labienus passed a tribunician law establishing the duumviral court, arranging the method of appointment and embodying the ancient formula with all its grotesque barbarity handed down from the legendary trial. The duumviri were apparently to be appointed by lot out of persons selected by the praetor.[2] It was doubtless pure bad luck that Caesar, who for every reason must have preferred to keep in the background, was one of the two on whom the lot fell. There was no reason for delay, and I assume that, as soon as the law was passed and the duumviri appointed, the trial before them took place.

[1] *pro Rab.* 10, 28.

[2] Cf. 'sorte ductus' in Suet. *Caes.* 12.

It was clearly very brief, as indeed it was bound to be if the Horatian precedent was followed. I called attention to the point that the formula given to the duumviri by the king precluded any verdict save one of condemnation. So it must have been in the present case. Cicero[1] distinctly says that condemnation was compulsory and that the trial was conducted 'indicta causa'. Suetonius (loc. cit.) says that Caesar condemned so hastily as to prejudice the cause of the prosecution with the *judicium populi* 'ac sorte judex in reum ductus tam cupide condemnavit, ut ad populum provocanti nihil aeque ac judicis acerbitas profuerit'. The duumviral trial was to be a mere form preparatory to and rendering possible the decision of the people in the comitia centuriata, bringing home to the people the vital issues at stake by the gruesome preparations which accompanied the condemnation. We need not suppose that in any case the execution would have been carried out. The demonstration was all that Caesar wanted. Whether after the duumviral condemnation the *trinundinum* necessary in republican trials would have intervened before the popular *judicium* is, I think, very doubtful, but the point cannot be settled.

In any case, Cicero was ready. Caesar, not for the first time in this year, had made a tactical mistake in insisting on the exact reproduction of obsolete forms. The whole thing was contrary to the spirit of the age. The duumviral procedure with its compulsory condemnation[2] could at best only suit cases where the facts were undisputed, and in this case there was apparently strong evidence forthcoming that Rabirius had not himself killed Saturninus at all. It was scandalous violation of what, at least by the *mos majorum* if not by statute law, had come to be the recognized method of dealing with *perduellio*, namely, by tribunician prosecution. It was an attempt to revive punishments which were essentially *inusitata*[3] as well as barbarous, and which were a 'vestigium crudelitatis regiae' unknown in the free republic since the expulsion of the kings.[4] In an ordinary *anquisitio*, held in the publicity of a *contio*, no magistrate would venture to condemn without some visible signs of approval from the assembled people,

[1] *pro Rab.* 4, 12.
[2] Cf. the phrase 'indicta causa condemnari coegit', *pro Rab.* 4, 12.
[3] *pro Rab.* 4, 13. [4] ibid. 3, 10.

and therefore it might well be argued that the condemnation by the duumviri without a hearing, without such approval from the public, and in mechanical obedience to a formula imposed, was *injussu populi*, and this in spite of the fact that the court itself was established by means of a law.[1]

By urging these considerations and by interposing in some way the authority of the senate, Cicero succeeded in getting the verdict of the duumviri, and indeed the whole proceedings so far instituted for *perduellio* on the lines of the Horatian legend, formally quashed. He afterwards declares[2] 'ego in Rabirio perduellionis reo . . . interpositam senatus auctoritatem sustinui contra invidiam atque defendi'. More explicitly still he speaks of the 'perduellionis judicium . . . a me sublatum'[3] and quite as emphatically and to the same effect declares 'quam ob rem fateor atque etiam, Labiene, profiteor . . . te ex illa crudeli, importuna, non tribunicia actione sed regia, meo consilio, virtute, auctoritate esse depulsum'.[4] By what exact means Cicero and the senate intervened is not clear, but I do not see how the conclusion is to be avoided that in some way the whole duumviral proceedings were brought to an abrupt end.

Caesar's original plan therefore was defeated, though he had probably never seriously intended to carry out the gruesome farce to its bitter end, but only to make a solemn and awe-inspiring demonstration. But at the same time Rabirius was not to have got off with a mere fright. I am happy for a moment to be able to follow Mr. Strachan-Davidson (p. 198). 'Meanwhile,

[1] Cf. *pro Rab.* 4, 12. 'C. Gracchus legem tulit ne de capite civium Romanorum injussu vestro judicaretur, hic popularis a duumviris injussu vestro non judicari de cive Romano sed indicta causa civem Romanum capitis condemnari coegit.' Mr. Strachan-Davidson (i, 196) finds the words 'injussu vestro' inconsistent with the view that the duumviral court was established by a tribunician law. I am inclined to think that the phrase like *indicta causa* qualifies not *coegit* but *condemnari.* If so, the words are of course not used in the same sense as in the first clause, and a false antithesis is suggested between the action of Labienus and the action required by the Sempronian law, but the *suggestio falsi* produced by the repetition of the phrase is by no means inconsistent with Cicero's oratorical methods. It is abundantly clear that it was Labienus who in some way got the duumviri appointed, and there was no means by which a tribune could do this except by a tribunician law. In fact the gravamen against Labienus was not that he had established a *judicium injussu populi*, but that he had misled the people into establishing one based on a shadowy and barbarous precedent out of harmony with the free republic and suited only to the age of the kings.

[2] *in Pison.* 2, 4. [3] *pro Rab.* 3, 9. [4] ibid. 5, 17.

parallel to the proceedings for *perduellio*, another attack was opened. The tribune Labienus had piled up a long and miscellaneous list of charges against Rabirius; official abuses, secret assassination, disgraceful offences against morals are heaped together as counts in his *multae irrogatio*. For these misdemeanours he announced the infliction of a fine. . . .'

The scene therefore changes to the forum, where this prosecution had of course to go through the usual three stages of *anquisitio* and would then, as a pecuniary and not a capital case, have gone on appeal to the *comitia tributa*. Clear traces of this *anquisitio* presided over by Labienus are found in the words 'nunquam profecto istam imaginem . . . in rostra atque in contionem attulisses'.[1]

We have already seen in the case of Fulvius and perhaps of Metellus that a pecuniary charge might in the course of the *anquisitio* develop into a capital one for *perduellio*. This is what I believe happened in the present case. When the duumviral *perduellionis judicium* was quashed by the action of Cicero and the senate, Labienus received instructions to turn the final stages of his *anquisitio* into an ordinary tribunician prosecution for *perduellio*. The *publica judicia* therefore, that is, the hearings in the forum before Labienus, began with the charges piled up in the *multae irrogatio*[2]; but though Cicero naturally refers to these in his speech, and couples the *multatio bonorum* with the *ignominia judiciorum publicorum* as part of the calamity which Rabirius had to pass through, it was the murder of Saturninus as an act of *perduellio* which was the charge in the final hearing. The pecuniary penalty was therefore dropped, and what now awaited Rabirius if condemned was *miserum exsilium*, or, if he did not seek this *perfugium supplicii* in time, even death.[3]

There is of course nothing in this theory of how the case developed which is inconsistent with the maxim laid down by Cicero 'ne poena capitis cum pecunia conjungatur',[4] since, as in

[1] *pro Rab.* 9, 25. [2] ibid. 3, 8.

[3] The whole passage in *pro Rab.* 5, 16 evidently refers to the tribunician trial, which, however objectionable, was at least in accordance with the forms of the free republic. 'Misera est ignominia judiciorum publicorum, misera multatio bonorum, miserum exsilium; sed tamen in omni calamitate retinetur aliquod vestigium libertatis. Mors denique si proponitur, in libertate moriamur, carnifex vero et obductio capitis et nomen ipsum crucis absit.'

[4] *de Domo*, 17, 45.

the case of Fulvius, we must suppose the capital charge to have been substituted for and not added to the pecuniary penalty.

From this point the whole case becomes normal. Labienus must have pronounced the usual sentence of *perduellio* at the final *anquisitio*, and the *judicium populi* before the centuries was the result of *provocatio*, not from the duumviri whose whole *judicium* had been quashed, but from the sentence of Labienus. The tribune therefore would of course have received permission to preside in the comitia centuriata, and this explains how it is that Cicero in his extant speech so often addresses himself to Labienus. That Cicero's speech was delivered at the final stage before the comitia centuriata seems to me certain. Apart from the improbability that he would make his great effort at any but the final stage, there are several passages which can only be explained on this assumption:

(1) (*pro Rab.* 2, 5) 'precorque . . . ut hodiernum diem et ad hujus salutem conservandam et ad rem publicam constituendam inluxisse patiantur.' There seems no way of evading the obvious inference from this passage.

(2) There are two passages (ibid. 2, 5 and 12, 35) in which Cicero distinctly speaks of the *suffragia* which his hearers are called upon to give, words which would be wholly inapplicable if addressed to a *contio* which did not vote.

(3) In 3, 8, he speaks of 'non modo homines sed prope regiones' as having assembled for the defence of Rabirius, an obvious allusion to the country voters who might flock in to attend the comitia centuriata, but would certainly not be present at a mere *contio*.

I need not repeat the familiar story told by Dio Cassius[1] of how the praetor, probably not without the connivance of Caesar, pulled down the flag on the Janiculum and so broke up the assembly. Considering the course which the whole case had taken, Caesar might well have felt equally embarrassed at an acquittal or a condemnation, and possibly after Cicero's speech there may have been significant signs that the former was the more probable issue. We can hardly imagine that his somewhat ill-judged demonstration had to any serious extent served its purpose. If it had, we

[1] Dio Cass. 37, 28,

might perhaps have been deprived of the last case with which this article will deal.

On the case of Rabirius I have studied Mr. Strachan-Davidson's interesting if not convincing chapter, and I am struck, as all must be, with the lucidity and candour with which he treats views not adopted by himself. His own theory of the case seems to me to break down in the following points. First, his explanation of 'perduellionis judicium a me sublatum' seems very unconvincing. According to it, neither the trial by nor the sentence of the duumviri was quashed at all, for at the stage when Cicero spoke, the proceedings before them are supposed not yet to have taken place: all that Cicero did was, by either preventing the arrest of Rabirius or setting him free if already arrested, to make it possible for the accused through voluntary exile to escape the barbarous punishment provided by the *carmen horrendum.* The words surely imply more than this, and there is no indication whatever that the arrest of Rabirius was either effected or contemplated. Secondly, Mr. Strachan-Davidson does not consider that the sentence of the duumviri, when it came, was quashed by Cicero, and on his view it was the only sentence on a capital charge: it follows, therefore, that the appeal to the centuries was an appeal from the duumviri. Clearly, however, Labienus, and not one of the duumviri, was presiding on the occasion when Cicero made his speech, and so it is found necessary to assign the speech to the occasion of 'a commonplace accusation for a fine' before a *contio.* I have already adduced passages from the speech wholly inconsistent with this view. Thirdly, how can it be the case that the accusations on the capital charge before the duumviri and on the pecuniary charge before Labienus 'were parallel and simultaneous' (p. 189) if at the time when Cicero made his speech in the last stage of the latter accusation, 'the great trial before the duumvirs was still in the future' (p. 200)? Fourthly, the 'hodiernum diem' passage referred to above, which as Mr. Strachan-Davidson admits, gives him some anxiety, surely receives a wholly insufficient and improbable explanation on p. 202. An acquittal on a mere pecuniary charge would have been a very slight *praejudicium* in favour of an acquittal on the capital charge of *perduellio* which had still to go through both its preliminary and its final stage.

Dr. Greenidge's account of the trial is vitiated by the impossible supposition (p. 357) that the sentence of the duumviri would have to be followed by the triple *anquisitio* in the forum. The two proceedings were of course alternative to one another. The mistake is a corollary of his view, which I have already criticized, that the *anquisitio* was not a separate trial but only the first stage of the *judicium populi.*

If I am right in the view taken above of Caesar's position in regard to the prosecution of Rabirius, he had so far made no protest against the validity of the *senatus consultum ultimum* as acted upon by Opimius, that is, as urging administrative action against men who by overt act were enemies of the state. Saturninus had (or at least Caesar adopted the view that he had) been killed in the first place after a guarantee of safety had been given him, and in the second place by a man not acting under the orders of the consul, but constituting himself a 'tumultuarius miles'. It was all very well for Nasica to have done this in 132 B.C.,[1] but I apprehend that the *senatus consultum ultimum* had at least the good effect of abolishing the independent 'tumultuarius miles' in future.

17. It remains to consider whether in Cicero's case either Caesar or Clodius, who no doubt acted on Caesar's instructions and initiative, assailed the principle implied in the acquittal of Opimius. In 58 B.C. Clodius promulgated and passed a tribunician law to the effect that 'qui civem Romanum indemnatum interemisset, ei aqua et igni interdiceretur'.[2] It was universally recognized that this law was occasioned by Cicero's execution in the carcer, as a consequence of the *senatus consultum ultimum*, of the five Catilinarians in 63 B.C. Why was this law called for? It was not a re-enactment or a re-enforcement of the lex Sempronia, unless indeed Cicero's consultation of the senate was interpreted as a *judicium*, and though I believe that Cicero sailed dangerously near the wind in the course he took, the wording of the Clodian law is against this view.

If, however, Cicero is to be taken seriously, as Mr. Strachan-Davidson seems to take him (p. 244), when he argues that 'Caesar

[1] See Strachan-Davidson, i, p. 241, note 1.
[2] Vell. 2, 45; cf. Livy, *Epit.* 103.

has not hesitated to pronounce on these men in spite of the law of Gracchus', the question of a *judicium* would seem to have been raised, for the law of Gracchus was concerned with that point alone. It was, on the other hand, a distinct re-enactment of the lex Porcia. Just as the lex Sempronia had been intended to stop one kind of evasion of that law, so the Clodian law was declaratory of the fact that there had been a violation of the Porcian law which must be dealt with as the sanction of that law directed. It was not, therefore, retrospective in any sense which Caesar could have criticized, as Dio Cassius (38, 17), obviously through some misunderstanding, says that he did. What was the violation alleged to have been perpetrated by Cicero? Mr. Strachan-Davidson (p. 240) asks the question what was the distinction between the action of Popilius which was forbidden by the Sempronian law, and that of Cicero which was not. That, however, is not the relevant question. The relevant question is, what was the distinction between the action of Opimius which his acquittal established as legal, and the action of Cicero which the Clodian law implied to be illegal. Mr. Strachan-Davidson's answer, adopted from Cicero, to his own question, is that Cicero's action 'was not a judicial execution of citizens, but an act of war against enemies'. This is an admirable description of the distinction between Popilius and Opimius, but it unfortunately ignores, as it was Cicero's whole object to ignore, the really relevant question.

Cicero, though he had run away very precipitately on the first announcement of Clodius' law, afterwards convinced himself that he might have stood his ground and established the point that he had not executed Roman citizens at all, but public enemies, that in fact the precedent of Opimius would have saved him. We may with confidence accept, as Mr. Strachan-Davidson does, the doctrine of Mommsen that the *perduellis* 'by the very act, passes out of the citizen ranks into the category of public enemies'. But who is the *perduellis?* Mommsen expressly makes his statement with regard to the more heinous species of *perduellio*, and there is a very vital distinction between the *perduellis* by overt act of war or actual sedition, and the *perduellis* by construction and on suspicion.

It does not follow that because the former could be dealt with summarily by virtue of the *senatus consultum ultimum* without trial, the latter could be treated in the same way. To argue that it does, would indeed be, in Mommsen's words, 'a party doctrine, contravening law'. It seems to me, I confess, that to defend Cicero's application of the *senatus consultum ultimum* as Mr. Strachan-Davidson does, by representing it as a 'deduction from the legal doctrine of *perduellio*', is to ignore the distinction between the *perduellis* by overt act and the *perduellis* by construction, and that, if logically followed out, it would represent as superfluous and unnecessary all the *judicia* for *perduellio* which we have been considering.

We are now in a position to answer the question as to how Cicero had violated the lex Porcia in a way that Opimius had not, and why therefore the Clodian law was called for. He had exercised the right of martial law against men who were possibly *perduelles*, but *perduelles* by construction only, and not yet by overt act. Cicero had convinced himself from information received, whether trustworthy or untrustworthy, that the five men were engaged in a plot which was to end in incendiarism, assassination, and revolution. He had even got evidence in their own handwriting of some treasonable correspondence with a Gallic tribe. He very likely had damning evidence of their guilt, but they had not actually carried any of these designs into effect. If they had, Cicero's action would have been covered by the precedent of Opimius and Marius and others, but there was no precedent for acting as he did towards men whose guilt was presumptive only.

Still even so, if he could have shown that the only way of saving the state, of preventing these designs from being carried out, was the execution of these five men, there might have been a justification,[1] though it would have established a new and dangerous precedent, and Caesar, as we shall see, pointed out to him what steps he might have taken. Mr. Strachan-Davidson adopts Cato's argument that the executions were necessary in view of the armed force in Etruria under Catiline and Manlius, and declares that they actually had the effect of dissipating that

[1] As a matter of fact, Cicero had already been publicly thanked by the senate on the previous day for having saved the state, and in view of the revulsion of popular feeling after his speech to the people ('mutata mente Catilinae consilia execrari, Ciceronem ad caelum tollere': Sall. *Cat.* 48), it is clear that all practical danger was over.

force; but it is obvious that Cicero never regarded the rising in Etruria as really dangerous. If he had done so, he would never have been so anxious for Catiline to join it, or have given the conspirators in the city the fullest opportunity of doing the same thing.

That Cicero himself had some hesitation on these points seems clear from the fact that he took the unnecessary step of laying the matter before the senate. There was of course no reason why he should not do this. Every magistrate in his position could take advice when and how and where he chose. His action did not in itself turn the senate into a judicial body, but at the same time by formally asking for the opinions of the senators in turn, by putting the question formally to the vote, and by making it understood, as he undoubtedly did, that he would feel himself bound to act on the decision of the majority, he virtually admitted that his administrative action required, shall we say, a semi-judicial sanction, and thereby, I repeat, came dangerously near to a violation of the Sempronian law. He goes so far as to assert (*in Pison.* 7, 14) that he has only obeyed the senate, 'qui senatui parui', and even declares: 'nam relatio illa salutaris et diligens fuerat consulis, animadversio quidem et judicium senatus.' If he had been as explicit at the time, there would have been no doubt as to whether the senate was being used as a criminal court.

The most interesting point in the senatorial discussion is the attitude of Caesar. As his *sententia* reported by Sallust is partly at least confirmed by Cicero,[1] we may accept it and perhaps also the general purport of the speech. He could not have regarded the meeting of the senate as a *judicium*, for in that case he must have pointed out the glaring violation of the lex Sempronia. We have no right, therefore, to speak of his pronouncing on the men, for if his speech ended with a pronouncement or sentence upon the prisoners, there is no escape from the conclusion that the senate was acting as a *judicium*. Cicero might choose to speak of it as such, because in that case, if the lex Sempronia was violated, Caesar would share with himself the responsibility of violating it.[2] Caesar must have assumed that the consul, before taking administrative action, was merely asking for the advice of individual senators. When his turn came he had no alternative but

[1] *in Cat.* 4, 5, 10. [2] Cf. *in Cat.* 4, 6, 11.

to give a *sententia* of some kind, though in view of current rumours and suspicions he must have felt his position a difficult one.

The pertinent part of his advice seems to me to come to this: 'I advise the consul not to impair the dignity of the state by an act of vengeance or panic. I advise him not to disregard precedent. New precedents are dangerous both to their author and to the state, and they seldom remain where they start. I advise him to remember that the Porcian laws are still in existence, and that by their operation there is an interval during which even the *perduellis* condemned by a magistrate may go into exile. Assuming the truth of what the consul has told us, I have no doubt that the men deserve death and worse, but I do not advise him to inflict it. As he insists on my advice it is this: if he is sure that he can prove the men to be *perduelles*, I suggest that as a precaution he should either instruct a quaestor to confiscate their property, or get a tribune to consecrate it, and that by his own coercive power he should hand over the men themselves to be kept in prison in responsible Italian towns, while to ensure their retention we may pass a resolution forbidding any magistrate to intervene on their behalf.' Sallust's version of the *sententia* is 'ita censeo: publicandas eorum pecunias, ipsos in vinculis habendos per municipia quae maxume opibus valent: neu quis de eis postea ad senatum referat, neve cum populo agat'. This is not a judicial pronouncement and implies no sentence to be passed by the senate: it is merely a suggestion of administrative action which, if accepted, it would be for the consul alone to take. The right of confiscating property did not belong to the senate any more than the right of passing a death sentence. Confiscation was either the result of judicial proceedings or was an administrative act taken under certain circumstances by the magistrate on his own initiative or sometimes on the exhortation of the senate.[1] It suits Cicero's immediate purpose to say[2] 'ut nihil de capite civis aut de bonis sine judicio senatus aut populi . . . detrahi possit', but he knows perfectly well that Opimius had done both,[3] and we have already seen a tribune consecrate the property of a

[1] This is all that is implied by Val. Max. vi, 3, 3, cited below, where it is a pity that Dr. Greenidge translates 'the senate *ordered* the confiscation of his goods', p. 515.

[2] *de Domo*, 13, 33.

[3] Plut. *G. Gracchus*, 17.

censor whom he is about to try for *perduellio*. In the present case, though the men were not overt *perduelles*, the same suspicious circumstances which warranted their arrest might warrant the precautionary confiscation. Whether the *publicatio* or *consecratio* became finally effective would depend on the dénouement of the case. The point was perhaps not a very practical one, for the men were probably already bankrupt, and Cicero's allusion to the 'corporis egestas' and 'mendicitas' which would result from it, sounds hollow and unreal. The internment of the prisoners in Italian towns was certainly within the administrative power of the consul, and would serve the double purpose of removing their dangerous presence from Rome and of making possible proceedings against them for *perduellio* when calmer counsels prevailed. According to Appian, Caesar's proposal was that the prisoners should be reserved for future trial, and I believe that this is really not inconsistent with Sallust. Obviously, wealthy towns were to be selected as least likely to sympathize with the revolutionary cry for *novae tabulae*. I see no indication that Caesar was suggesting perpetual imprisonment. Cicero's 'aeternis tenebris vinculisque mandare'[1] can be nothing but his own rhetorical amplification: it is certainly not suggested in the version of Sallust. While virtually agreeing with Mr. Strachan-Davidson's objection to Mommsen's view of Caesar's *sententia* (p. 165), I cannot but think that the lifelong imprisonment, which he accepts, is a delusion which my explanation gets rid of. The perpetuity of the imprisonment could only depend on the magistrates proving amenable to the exhortation of the senate not to intervene. I agree with Dr. Greenidge (p. 515) that this is how the passage of Val. Max. vi, 3, 3, should be explained: 'publicatis enim bonis ejus, ipsum aeternis vinculis puniendum censuit.'

The tone of Caesar's speech is extraordinarily guarded throughout, but his actual *sententia* was far from being either a piece of bluff or an impudent proposal. It was on the contrary a practical piece of advice which would have met the case exactly, and which, if followed, would have saved Cicero from the mistake which he actually made. If Caesar's attitude, both in the case of Rabirius and in that of the Catilinarians, is what I take it to

[1] *in Cat.* 4, 5, 10.

have been, it was in every respect consistent with the memorable passage of the *Bellum Civile.* Where open enemies of the state are dealt with by an act of war, he is ready to stand aside; but where an individual, acting without consular leading, takes the law into his own hands, or where a consul treats suspected conspirators as if they were already overt enemies, he protests.[1]

Before the Clodian law was actually passed, but probably not before Caesar had supplemented the guarded menace of his speech in the senate by an open condemnation of Cicero's action in a *contio*,[2] Cicero withdrew from Rome and soon from Italy. What followed is, *mutatis mutandis*, a mere repetition of what we have seen taking place in the cases of Postumius, Fulvius, Popilius, and Metellus. The difference between Cicero's case and theirs only strengthened the position of Clodius and made his course more clear. The above-mentioned, with the exception of Postumius, had all awaited their trial before the magistrate, and even Postumius had waited for the formal notice of prosecution (*diei dictio*). Cicero, on the other hand, by his own admission, lost his head and threw up his case at once. What Clodius had to consider and to act upon was not the motive of Cicero's action, but the self-evident fact that he had taken it. His second *plebiscitum* was, with perhaps one trifling exception, in strict accordance with all the precedents. It was the usual declaratory affirmation by the *concilium plebis* that the withdrawal was accepted and recognized and registered as equivalent to *justum exsilium*, and that Cicero by his own act was an outlaw and interdicted from fire and water. The series of sanctions introduced by Clodius into his bill, obviously futile, but suggested by the recall of Popilius and Metellus, need not detain us. It was,

[1] I cannot but think that Sallust's famous summary (*Cat.* 29) of the powers called into existence by the senate's decree was from the popular point of view carelessly and injudiciously framed, and that Caesar, if it had been submitted to him, would have revised it The words 'maxima per senatum potestas magistratibus permittitur' are inexact and misleading. The 'coercere omnibus modis socios atque cives' must be limited to citizens and others acting like public enemies. The 'summum judicium habere' can only mean that punitive power of summary execution which can be described as *judicium* merely in a non-technical and non-legal sense. I am inclined to doubt Dr. Greenidge's view that the *senatus consultum ultimum* allowed the magistrate a 'summary trial' at which he could use a *consilium*. The passage from *de Amicitia*, 11, 37, does not prove it, for Popilius was not acting on the *senatus consultum ultimum* but was presiding over an extraordinary *judicium*.

[2] Dio Cass. 38, 17.

of course, not a judicial sentence, and if Cicero, which I doubt, ever tried to argue that it was (the passage in *pro Sest.* 30, 65, on which Dr. Greenidge relies, does not prove it), he was disingenuous. It was indeed to guard, quite unnecessarily, against this possible interpretation that Clodius seems to have deviated from the usual formula by using the phrase 'ut interdictum sit'[1] instead of 'ut interdiceretur'. As a matter of fact the meaning of the latter and usual formula is clearly expressed by Livy where he gives it in full in the case of Postumius (see above, pp. 9, 10). The deviation from tralatician usage, though perfectly logical, was unnecessary, and gave Cicero, who was always a word-splitter, an opportunity of futile protest, and that is all that need be said on the point. I do not agree with Dr. Greenidge (p. 363) that any protasis like that employed in the case of Postumius was necessary. He was declared to be interdicted if he did not appear on a certain day, but Postumius had waited long enough to be summoned and then had failed to appear on the first day of *anquisitio*, but he was given the chance of appearing on the second. Cicero had taken the course of despair by not waiting to be summoned at all, and this had cleared the way for Clodius to take the final step. It is unnecessary, after what has preceded, to comment further on this last case of a threatened *judicium populi*. All the arguments and criticisms and complaints with which Cicero occupied his period of exile might have been urged with equal force and equal futility by Popilius and Metellus, but they would not have increased our respect for either of them.

It is perhaps superfluous to ask what form a *judicium populi* would have taken in a case where the initial steps calling for one were not started, but I can see no reason whatever for Dr. Greenidge's suggestion that it would have been a trial before the plebs. I can only remember one passage where Cicero seems to look so far ahead as the possible final scene before the people, and in that he declares that if Clodius had summoned him, 'fecissem ut ei statim tertius a praetore dies diceretur',[2] which seems to imply that when the praetor was asked for a day, he would have waived the interval of a *trinundinum* and demanded an immediate trial before the centuries, as perhaps the censors had done in 169 B.C.[3]

[1] *de Domo*, 18, 47. [2] *de Harus. Resp.* 4, 7. [3] Livy, xliii, 16.

II

THE TRANSPADANE QUESTION AND THE ALIEN ACT OF 65 OR 64 B.C.

IN the course of my essay on the Lex Iulia Municipalis (*v.* below, No. ix), I had occasion to criticize the interpretation given by Mr. J. M. Nap to an important passage of Dio Cassius (xxxvii, 9) in connexion with a dispute between the censors of 65 on the subject of the Transpadani, and a subsequent Alien Act passed by a tribune named Papius. Not having his own article, which is written in Dutch,[1] accessible, I had gathered his views from the paper of a not unfriendly critic in a French review, and I only dealt with them incidentally as bearing upon the date assigned by him to the so-called lex Iulia Municipalis. Since then, Mr. Nap has pointed out to me that, at least in one particular, I had misapprehended his meaning; he has also very kindly sent me a copy of his article, and has developed and elucidated his views in several letters. I have in consequence carefully re-studied the statements of Dio and I propose to examine somewhat more in detail Nap's interpretation and hypotheses, and at the same time to set forth by their side my own reconstruction of the situation, as far as the Transpadani and the Alien Act are concerned.

It will be convenient at the outset to cite in full the passage to be examined. After describing the portents and rumours of conspiracy which marked the year 65, Dio (loc. cit.) goes on:

Ταῦτά τε ἐν ἐκείνῳ τῷ ἔτει συνέβη. Καὶ οἱ τιμηταὶ περὶ τῶν ὑπὲρ τὸν Ἐριδανὸν οἰκοῦντων διενεχθέντες (τῷ μὲν γὰρ ἐς τὴν πολιτείαν αὐτοὺς ἐσάγειν ἐδόκει τῷ δὲ οὔ) οὐδὲν οὐδὲ τῶν ἄλλων ἔπραξαν, ἀλλὰ καὶ τὴν ἀρχὴν ἀπεῖπον. Καὶ διὰ τοῦτο καὶ οἱ διάδοχοι ἀυτῶν ἐν τῷ ὑστέρῳ ἔτει οὐδὲν ἐποίησαν, ἐμποδισάντων

[1] *Dateering en Rechtskarakter der z.-g. lex Iulia Municipalis.* Verhandelingen der koninklijke Akademie van Wetenschappen te Amsterdam Deel xi, no. iv.

σφᾶς τῶν δημάρχων πρὸς τὸν τῆς βουλῆς κατάλογον δέει τοῦ μὴ τῆς γερουσίας αὐτοὺς ἐκπεσεῖν. Κἀν τούτῳ πάντες οἱ ἐν τῇ Ῥώμῃ διατρίβοντες πλὴν τῶν τὴν νῦν Ἰταλίαν οἰκούντων ἐξέπεσον Γαίου τινὸς Παπίου δημάρχου γνώμῃ, ἐπειδὴ ἐπεπόλαζον καὶ οὐκ ἐδόκουν ἐπιτήδειοί σφισιν εἶναι συνοικεῖν.

I. THE POLITICAL AND JURISTIC POSITION OF THE TRANSPADANI

Nap's first point is that the term 'Transpadani' in this, as in other passages of our authorities, is used loosely to cover all the inhabitants of Gallia Cisalpina; that the Transpadani and the Cispadani were in precisely the same legal and juristic position; and that the questions at issue in 65 B.C. properly concerned the Cisalpini as a whole, and not the Transpadani alone. While specifying no other passage in which this confusion may be detected, he rests his contention on two grounds. (1) He argues that the so-called lex Rubria, instead of belonging to the Caesarian period, was the 'lex provinciae' of Cisalpine Gaul, being the original 'lex data' framed by Sulla, when he established the province. But, as the law treats all communities north and south of the Po on the same juristic principles, there could have been no difference of status between different parts of the province.[1]

I have dealt in detail with Nap's arguments as to the nature and date of this law below (No. vii). They rest largely on the internal and doubtful evidence of legal procedure, but partly on what seem to me unsupported and improbable hypotheses. I will only remark here (*a*) that from the contents of the extant chapters, as well as from the titles of magistrates compared with those on the Table of Heraclea, the uniformity of status throughout the province would seem to find its best explanation in the possession by all the communities of the Roman civitas; while at the very least they must all, when the law was passed, have been 'fundi' of Roman law. Neither, however, of these two conditions can be assumed earlier than 49 B.C. (*b*) The remaining fragments are very different from what we should expect to find in the 'lex data' of a newly constituted province. As a matter of fact, an examination of the condition of Cisalpine

[1] Het iudicium legitimum in de Romeinsche wetgeving. Overgedrukt uit *Themis*, 1912, pp. 18–31.

Gaul in Sulla's day makes the uniformity of status, unwisely insisted on by Nap as implied by the law, one of the strongest arguments against his hypothesis as to its date. (2) This becomes more apparent when we come to Nap's second reason for believing in an identity of legal position between Transpadani and Cispadani. He relies upon a statement made by Mommsen,[1] taken, I must observe, out of its context, to the effect that very probably the lex Pompeia conferred the 'ius Latii' collectively on all the 'civitates foederatae' of Gallia Cisalpina. But, Mommsen goes on to observe, since north of the Po a considerable number of 'civitates foederatae' were affected by the measure, while south of the river Ravenna perhaps stood alone, the operation of the law has been erroneously limited to the Transpadane region. The difference, however, between the two parts of the province was really political rather than juristic.

I quite accept Mommsen's assumption that the lex Pompeia treated alike all 'civitates foederatae' within the area of Cisalpine Gaul, and I believe that it also treated alike, probably on lines already laid down by the lex Iulia of the previous year, all Latin colonies within the same area, in other words that it made them all Roman communities. But, if this is granted, the juristic identity between the Transpadane and Cispadane regions, on which Nap insists, will merely mean that certain categories of towns were treated in the same way in both. On the other hand, the political difference, which after all was the important factor, stands out in sharp relief. In the Cispadane region there were (*a*) such already existing Roman colonies as Mutina and Parma; (*b*) the Latin colonies of Placentia, Bononia, and Ariminum (see below) now made Roman; and (*c*) a considerable number of fora, which Mommsen (loc. cit.) must be right in regarding as settlements of Roman citizens, though not strictly urban communities. It follows that, with the possible exception of Ravenna, the Cispadani after 89 B.C. were practically all Roman citizens. It was of course in reference to these Roman communities south of the Po that Cicero wrote in 65 B.C.: 'videtur in suffragiis multum posse Gallia.'[2] On the other hand, in the much larger area north of the Po, with the exception of two colonies, Dertona and Eporedia, already in Mommsen's opinion Roman, and two others, Cremona

[1] *Jurist. Schriften*, i, 183. [2] *ad Att.* i, 1, 2.

and Aquileia, made Roman by the lex Pompeia, the Transpadane communities were towns possessing only the 'ius Latii'. Under such conditions, where are we to find the identity of legal status throughout the province for which Nap contends? Is it not manifest that the political and legal questions still requiring solution after 89 B.C. would be, as all our authorities represent them, Transpadane and not Cisalpine questions?

II. THE LEX POMPEIA AS THE LEX PROVINCIAE OF GALLIA CISALPINA

If we accept Mommsen's hypothesis that the operation of the lex Pompeia was not confined to the Transpadane country, but affected also what we know as the Cispadane portion of the province, I think we are bound to explain how it came to do so. On Mommsen's view, usually accepted, the province was not in existence till Sulla created it in 82 or 81 B.C. When it was created, it was of course necessary that some definite dividing line, whether the Aesis or the Rubicon, should be fixed as the boundary between Italy and the province. But why, on this view, should this or any dividing line have been selected in 89 B.C. to distinguish the spheres within which the lex Iulia and the lex Pompeia should operate? It is true that the population immediately south of the Po had originally been largely or mainly Celtic, and even that the country as far down as Ariminum was known as 'ager Gallicus'. But though this racial distinction was long recognized, and marked by a line running from the Arnus on the west to the Aesis on the east, and in spite of a difficult passage of Livy, in which Ariminum is spoken of as a 'provincia' allotted to a praetor late in the third century B. C. (Liv. xxi, 44), it is certain that there was no administrative distinction between Italy and the 'ager Gallicus', and that, in fact, the whole peninsula up to the Alps was regarded as Italy.[1] The whole country, like the rest of Italy, was under the general direction of the consuls; colonies, both Roman and Latin, were founded in it in considerable numbers, and most of its other towns became members of the Italian confederacy. No doubt the Transpadane region was still thoroughly Celtic, and conditions north of the river were in many

[1] See Liv. xxxix, 54, and Polyb. ii, 14.

ways essentially different from those in the south. But between those in the Cispadane part of the 'ager Gallicus' and those in Etruria and Umbria there was practically no difference at all.

Now these being the conditions in 90 and 89 B.C., it is intelligible that the government would think it well to treat north Italy in a different way from the rest of the peninsula, and therefore not to apply to it the operation of the lex Iulia, which would have meant the elevation of all its towns to the status of Roman 'municipia'. Hence the advisability of a separate law, the lex Pompeia; but unless some drastic change of administration was contemplated, the obvious dividing line between the operation of the two laws was the Po, marking a concrete difference of conditions, and not the old Arnus-Aesis line, marking a nearly obsolete racial distinction. This, however, according to Mommsen, was not the course adopted, for the lex Pompeia changed the status of all 'civitates foederatae' within the area of the old 'ager Gallicus'. The position is not made easier by Mommsen's inference from the words of Aulus Gellius (3, 4, 3), 'universo Latio lege Iulia civitas data est', that Aquileia, Cremona, Placentia, and Bononia received the civitas from the latter law, so that both laws operated in the Transpadane and Cispadane regions, though affecting different classes of towns.

I believe that we may escape from these difficulties and gain a more reasonable view of the policy adopted after the Social war if we discard the hypothesis that Cisalpine Gaul was made a province by Sulla, and place its creation in 90–89 B.C.. It is notorious that no ancient writer assigns its establishment to Sulla. The only passage where his name is coupled with the province is a fragment of Licinianus (ed. Teubn., p. 32) referring to a date some years before the dictatorship: 'data erat et Sullae provincia Gallia Cisalpina.' I do not pretend to explain the statement, but it seems almost to imply the existence of the province some years earlier than Mommsen's hypothesis assumes. At any rate, whatever the statement means, we may safely reject the inference drawn from it by Nap, who believes that the province was 'given' to Sulla, while dictator, for the purpose of receiving a 'lex data', and heroically calls in the lex Rubria, to fill the part. But while that law is conspicuously inappropriate to the known conditions of the country at the time, what we know of the details of the lex Pompeia corresponds exactly with what we should expect to find in a 'lex provinciae', settling the political and juristic relations within a newly created province.

The enfranchisement of Italy meant the disappearance of the Italian confederacy, and if, for perhaps sufficient reasons, the government declined to include in the new arrangement the purely Celtic and non-Romanized region in the north, some other substitute for a military confederacy, now out of date, would have to be provided. In view of the constant danger from Alpine tribes, a danger recognized by the settlement of military colonists at Comum by Pompeius,[1] the immediate conversion of the country into an armed province was an obvious course. The emergency arose at once, when the league ceased to exist, and would surely have been met at once, and not have been left for Sulla to deal with after an interval of eight or nine years.

Whoever were the statesmen responsible for the settlement after the Social war, it was admirably adapted to the situation, and I believe that the establishment of a Cisalpine province was an essential part of it. But the lex Iulia admitted of no delay, and while the claims of the 'civitates foederatae' would have to be considered separately, it was essential to give the civitas at once *en bloc* to all Latin colonies, it being impossible to make a distinction between those in Italy and those which were henceforth to be provincial towns; hence the 'universo Latio' of Gellius. But when in the following year effect was given to the scheme of creating a Cisalpine province by the lex Pompeia, this grant of citizenship to the Latin colonies was naturally confirmed, or rather taken over by the provincial law. In this way we escape the difficulty involved in Mommsen's view that within the same area one law dealt with the Latin colonies, another with the 'civitates foederatae'. That the lex Pompeia conferred the 'ius Latii' on the Transpadane towns we know very precisely from Asconius,[2] and this fixing of graduated status is exactly what a 'lex provinciae' would effect. Equally appropriate to such a law was the arrangement, testified to by Pliny,[3] of 'attributing' native tribes to the urban communities, an arrangement which also implies another characteristic of a provincial law, viz. the delimitation of municipal and colonial territories. Moreover, it is

[1] Strabo, p. 213. [2] *in Pison.* 3. [3] *H. N.* iii, 10, 138.

now possible to understand what Mommsen's dating of the province leaves unexplained, why the operation of the law extended south of the Po. For whenever a province of Cisalpine Gaul came into existence, it was bound by its very name to include all that the 'ager Gallicus' had once included. It is true that the southern portion would remain, as far as political status was concerned, 'Italia verius quam provincia'; but this was perhaps no disadvantage, as furnishing a useful administrative background to the new province, as well as a type to be gradually attained by the rest. If the considerations which I have put forward have weight, it follows almost of necessity that the original boundary of the province was the old Arnus-Aesis line. Later on, as we know from Strabo[1] and the incidents of Caesar's time, it was the Varus on the west and the Rubicon on the east. We may accept Mommsen's hypothesis that it was Sulla who made the change, and that his claim to extend the 'pomerium'[2] was based on the consequent extension of Italian soil. I would note, however, that Mommsen vitiates his own hypothesis by making this extension coincide with the creation of the province, which was in itself a limitation and not an extension of Italy.

III. THE TRANSPADANI AS LATINS WITH THE 'LATER LATINITAS'

Suetonius speaks of the Transpadane towns as 'coloniae Latinae', and we learn from Asconius[3] how this term is to be understood. 'Pompeius enim non novis colonis eas (Transpadanas) colonias constituit, sed veteribus incolis manentibus ius dedit Latii, ut possent habere ius quod ceterae Latinae coloniae, ut petendo magistratus civitatem Romanam adipiscerentur.' The Transpadani therefore possessed the 'later Latinitas', the distinguishing mark of which is noted by Asconius; but 'the other colonies' possessing it are not specified. Nap agrees with Beloch[4] that they were the 'duodecim Latinae coloniae quae Q. Fabio et Q. Fulvio consulibus (209 B.C.) abnuissent milites dare';[5] but these colonies were: Circeii (393), Suessa and Cora (?) Ardea (412),

[1] v, i, 11, p. 217 ad fin.: *ὅριον δὲ τῆς χώρας ταύτης, ἣν ἐντὸς Κελτικὴν, καλοῦμεν πρὸς τὴν λοιπὴν Ἰταλίαν τό τε Ἀπέννεινον ὄρος τὸ ὑπὲρ τῆς Τυρρηνίας ἀπεδέδεικτο καὶ ὁ Αἶσις ποταμός, ὕστερον δὲ ὁ Ῥουβίκων.*

[2] Tac. *Ann.* xii, 23, and Sen. *de brev. vit.* 13. [3] *in Pison.* 3.

[4] *Der Ital. Bund*, p. 157. [5] Liv. 27, 9; 29, 15.

Sutrium (383), Nepete (383), Setia (382), Cales (334), Interamna (312), Alba (303), Narnia (299), Carseoli (298),[1] and therefore all of more or less early foundation. But (1) we should expect to find the 'later Latinitas' in the latest Latin foundations; and (2) I fully agree with Mr. Strachan-Davidson[2] that, if the magistrates of these Latin colonies, who play a prominent part in the affair of 209, had had the right alluded to by Asconius, Livy must have mentioned it. As a matter of fact twelve Latin colonies were founded later than any of the foregoing towards the end of the third and the beginning of the second century B. C. Ariminum (268) being the earliest, and Aquileia (181) the latest; and of these no fewer than four, Ariminum, Placentia, Bononia, and Aquileia, were within the limits of the 'ager Gallicus'. It seems to me beyond a doubt that Mommsen is right in identifying these with the 'duodecim coloniae' alluded to by Cicero in *pro Caecin.* 35, 102, and explicitly associated by him with Ariminum and that it is in these later foundations that the 'later Latinitas' resided.[3]

Nap, however, refuses to accept this view, contending that the existence of two separate groups, known as the 'duodecim coloniae', is incredible, while he gives his own interpretation to the passage in *pro Caecin.* In reply to the objection that Caecina, as a citizen of Volaterrae, a town disenfranchised by Sulla, could not claim an inheritance by Roman law, Cicero says: 'Sulla ipse ita tulit de civitate ut non sustulerit horum nexa et hereditates. Iubet enim eodem iure esse quo fuerint Ariminenses; quos quis ignorat duodecim coloniarum fuisse, et a civibus Romanis hereditates capere potuisse?' It is not disputed that Ariminum is cited as having been a Latin colony possessing the 'ius commercii'; but Nap argues that the 'duodecim coloniae' are those spoken of by Livy, and that Ariminum is cited, not as one of them (which of course it was not) but as having been put in their juristic position. But (*a*) Ariminum is clearly taken as the type of a class, and therefore far more likely to be the first and most conspicuous instance of a new class than a mere annexe to a well-known and long-established group. (*b*) The phrase 'duodecim coloniarum

[1] I take the dates at which these colonies were founded from Marquardt, *Röm. Staatsverwalt.* i, pp. 49–50 (1881).

[2] *Problems of Rom. Crim. Law*, i, p. 151.

[3] Mommsen, *Rom. Hist.* Engl. trans. (1872), i, 433, note.

fuisse' has no meaning unless Ariminum was actually included under 'the twelve', and as it was certainly not one of Livy's list, it must have belonged to another group. Nor is there any point in Nap's repudiation of two separate groups of 'twelve colonies', for there is not the smallest necessity to assume the existence of more than one. A referencc to Livy's narrative and a glance at the list of twenty-eight Latin colonies founded before Ariminum will show that Livy's 'duodecim coloniae Latinae' is a distributive and not a collective expression and that they were merely the colonies, happening to be twelve, which took the common action in 209, but were in no other way marked out from the other fifteen.

We may therefore assume that the Latin colonies taken by Pompeius as his model were the Ariminum-Aquileia group, possessing the later 'ius Latii'.

IV. THE MILITARY SERVICE OF THE TRANSPADANI

Up to the Social war and as long as the Italian confederacy existed we know that the Latin communities and the 'civitates foederatae' had to furnish soldiers 'ex formula togatorum', i.e. in accordance with a military register, drawn up in each and sent to Rome.[1] It was indeed in connexion with this requisition of soldiers that the trouble arose in 209 with Livy's twelve Latin colonies. But after the Social war the Italian confederacy ceased to exist, while by the operation of the lex Iulia and lex Pompeia there were no more 'civitates foederatae', and the only Latin towns were the new Transpadane colonies, which were without the military substratum hitherto essential in colonies. It is therefore a question whether, and in what form, the burden of military service was imposed upon the Transpadani in the following period. Nap appears to hold that the conferment of Latin rights, and inscription on the 'formula togatorum' involved one another; that Pompeius accordingly inscribed the Transpadane colonies on the 'formula', but that, when the country became a province, a difficulty arose, the position of the Transpadani, or as he prefers it, of the Cisalpini, became the subject of dispute,

[1] Cf. *lex agrar.* 21: 'sociumve nominisve Latini quibus in terra Italia ex formula togatorum milites inperare solent'.

and a settlement by means of legislation was in the air. For this view I can see no evidence whatever, though it is no doubt true that inscription on the 'formula' was properly intended for Italy for the simple reason that the confederacy was a purely Italian confederacy. (1) In the first place, the words of the lex agraria, where alone 'formula togatorum' is mentioned, show that it was no more associated with Latin communities than with the other 'socii' or 'civitates foederatae'. It was in fact an essential detail of the Italian confederacy, and inscription on the 'formula' was in no sense a political privilege, but a military burden. (2) In the second place, the difficulty involved in the supposed inscription of the Transpadani on the 'formula' by Pompeius would not have arisen from the creation of the province, but from the fact that the military confederacy, which alone had given meaning to the 'formula togatorum', had ceased to exist. So far from admitting that conferment of 'Latinitas' and inscription on the 'formula' were equivalent to one another, I am inclined to affirm that they belonged to two entirely different military and political systems.

As long as Rome was the head of a military league, the *raison d'être* both of 'civitates foederatae' and of Latin colonies was to discharge their league obligations, while enjoying a guaranteed internal autonomy. When, as an example, 6,000 colonists were sent to Placentia to act as a 'propugnaculum imperii', exchanging their Roman status for the rights of Latins, it would have been a misuse of terms to describe the proceeding as the conferment of the 'ius Latii' upon Placentia, just as the conclusion of a 'foedus' with some Italian town did not imply the conferment on that town of any special honour or privilege. In both cases, however, inscription on the 'formula togatorum' would be a compulsory concomitant of the step. On the other hand, when the Italian League was replaced by an enfranchised Italy, Latin communities and 'civitates foederatae' alike, if they survived at all, could find no place except in the provinces. This was what happened, but the meaning both of 'Latinitas' and of 'federate' status was changed. It is from this time that it becomes correct to say that they were conferred, and conferred as a reward, or a mark of distinction or political privilege. With regard to the 'ius Latii', this comes out clearly in the action of Pompeius, as described by Asconius. The Transpadani, without receiving military colonists or undertaking military obligations, were promoted to a higher grade of juristic and political status, intended probably to be preparatory to complete absorption in the citizen body. It was precisely the course adopted afterwards by Caesar in Narbonensis and elsewhere, and which reached its climax when Vespasian conferred the 'ius Latii' on all non-privileged towns in Spain.

I hope I have shown that the 'formula togatorum' was out of date and out of place when Pompeius constituted, as I believe he did, the province of Cisalpine Gaul. But the inhabitants, and not least those of the non-Roman Transpadane portion, were excellent material for soldiers, and they must have been somehow utilized. As a matter of fact, a passage in Caesar's commentary on the civil war (iii, 87) proves that they were. In 48 B.C. Labienus speaks of Caesar's forces in Epirus as largely made up from recent levies in Gallia citerior, and specifies 'plerique ex Transpadanis coloniis'. The implication certainly is that these men were legionaries, and this creates a difficulty, for it is certain that Latins were not eligible for the legions, and, now that there were no 'cohortes sociorum' in the old sense, would serve among the 'auxilia'.[1] How the Latin citizens in the numerous Latin towns under the Principate were made subject to military service I confess I do not know, and the two fragmentary charters of Salpensa and Malaca throw no light on the subject. But with regard to the question in Gallia Cisalpina, we must remember that the practice of reinforcing the Roman army from the provinces was still in its infancy, and though there was no difficulty in getting legionaries from the numerous colonies in the south, the arrangements for recruiting Transpadani were probably vague and largely dependent on the discretion of the proconsul. Still, I would suggest three considerations which may help to explain the statement of Labienus: (*a*) the number of Roman citizens in the Transpadane colonies had been yearly increasing between 89 and 48 by the continuous enfranchisement of magistrates and their families, so that there would in this way have been a considerable body of persons in each Latin town available for legionary service; (*b*) more than a year before the date of

[1] Cf. the phrase 'Transpadani alarii' in Cic. *ad Fam.* ii, 17, 7.

Labienus' speech the lex Roscia had been passed, enfranchising all the Transpadane colonies, so that in all levies held in the last nine months of 49 Transpadani could have been enlisted in the legions; (*c*) it is highly probable that Caesar, with or without legal authorization, may have anticipated the practice, very common in the period of the civil wars, of recruiting 'peregrini', but giving them the 'civitas' on enlistment. It is possible even that Pompey caused the same thing to be done by his legates in Spain, since a comparison of *Bell. Civ.* i, 85, 6, with ii, 20, 4, shows that a 'legio vernacula' (the name given to legions containing such soldiers) under Varro had been recently raised in the Further province.

V. THE TRANSPADANE QUESTION IN 65

It appears therefore that the Transpadane towns after the creation of the province were not only treated differently from the towns of Italy, which, either at once or gradually, were enfranchised by the operation of the lex Iulia, but found themselves in an inferior political status to that of practically all the Cispadane communities, and even of a few colonies north of the Po. Of their inhabitants some were Roman citizens, and the number of these was slowly increasing with every year, but the majority were politically and juristically Latins, possessing indeed the 'ius commercii', but probably without the 'ius conubii', and certainly lacking the 'ius suffragii' and the 'ius honorum'. In these circumstances there was bound to be a Transpadane question. The Latin colonies were certain sooner or later to put forward a claim to full citizen rights, and some section of politicians in Rome was sure from interested or disinterested motives to support their claim. This was precisely the situation in 67, as revealed by Suetonius (*Iul.* 8). The Latin colonies were then 'de civitate Romana agitantes', and clearly received some sort of encouragement from Caesar. One would have thought the phrase of Suetonius sufficiently explicit, but Nap, with what I can only call a perverse ingenuity, represents the agitation as due to difficulties experienced by these Latins in exercising the old Latin right of voting, when in Rome, in one of the tribes. He believes that this grievance must have been rectified before 65, because in that year Cicero writes: 'videtur in suffragiis multum posse Gallia'.[1] It seems hardly necessary to point out that the two passages are wholly out of relation to one another, for Cicero is referring to the Roman communities of the province which he thought of canvassing.

Next we come to Dio's statement about the year 65, showing that the agitation of 67 was now affecting party struggles in Rome. We know from Plutarch that Crassus and Lutatius Catulus were censors in 65, and Dio, without giving names, says that the censors were hopelessly at variance on the question of admitting the Transpadani εἰς τὴν πολιτείαν. So bitter was the dispute that they resigned office without completing any of their censorial duties, the 'lectio senatus', the census, or the business of state contracts. The difficulty is to explain the *locus standi* of the censors in deciding this question of Transpadane enfranchisement, which Crassus, as we should expect from his close association at this time with Caesar, favoured, and Catulus in the interest of the optimates opposed.

It is obviously not a sufficient explanation to say that the inclusion or non-inclusion of the Transpadani in the register of the Roman census was the point at issue, for the census lists could only include Roman citizens, and the Transpadani were not yet brought εἰς τὴν πολιτείαν. Mommsen sought to evade the difficulty by representing Crassus as trying by the enrolment of the Transpadani on the burgess register to give effect to the 'standpoint of the popular party' that they were already legally entitled to the franchise, and needed no further act of legislation.[2] In this case Dio must have misunderstood his authorities, for his words εἰς τὴν πολιτείαν ἐσάγειν imply that they were still excluded from the civitas. Still how could the Transpadani be legally entitled to the franchise unless some law had granted it? There is no trace however, of any such law, whereas Mommsen himself accepts the evidence of Asconius as to the Latin rights conferred by the lex Pompeia. But surely Mommsen's case is

[1] *ad Att.* i, 1, 2.

[2] *Rom. Hist.* Engl. trans., iv, p. 158. One would have hoped that this ill-considered view would have been modified in later works, but it is reasserted in a comparatively late article: 'es nahmen die Caesarianer an, dass die Transpadaner das Bürgerrecht bereits besassen'. (*Juristische Schriften*, i, p. 181.)

effectually put out of court by the fact that in 49 Caesar, in spite of this standpoint of the popular party, thought it necessary to confer the franchise on the Transpadani by an act of legislation.[1]

We must therefore find some other clue to the situation in which the censors of 65 figure so prominently. Mr. Nap supplies us with a new one. Considering his repeated insistence that the point at issue was the inclusion or non-inclusion of the Cisalpini as a whole, and not of Transpadani alone, and that the latter were in the same legal position as the Cispadani, I hardly wonder at M. Besnier's inference that in Nap's opinion the Transpadani were already Roman citizens. At any rate, the inference is not correct, for Nap admits them to have been still Latins with the rights of the 'duodecim coloniae', as he understands that term. But there was nevertheless a party in Rome in 65 which advocated their inscription on the Roman census list. This inscription, he argues, would not have implied that the Cisalpini were Roman citizens; on the contrary if Crassus had had his way, they would have been enrolled, not on the ground that they were Roman citizens, but on the ground that they were men capable of serving in the Roman legions as if they were Roman citizens. The last six words give the case away, for they imply, what it is surely unnecessary in these days to establish, that the privilege or burden of legionary service belonged exclusively to Roman citizens. It is enough to take Nap's own instance. He declares that the senate ordered the recalcitrant Latin colonies in 209 to be included in the Roman census. A reference to Livy (29, 15) shows that on the contrary each colony was ordered to take its own census in accordance with a 'formula', i. e. scheme of tabulated schedules, supplied by the Roman censors. The whole affair

[1] Dio (xli, 36) places the grant in 49; *καὶ τοῖς Γαλάταις τοῖς ἐντὸς τῶν Ἄλπεων ὑπὲρ τὸν Ἠριδανὸν οἰκοῦσι, τὴν πολιτείαν, ἅτε καὶ ἄρξας αὐτῶν, ἀπέδωκεν.* Strabo (210) states the same fact without a date, but implies a long interval between it and the enfranchisement of Italy: *ὀψὲ δέ ποτε, ἀφ' οὗ μετέδοσαν Ῥωμαῖοι τοῖς Ἰταλιώταις τὴν ἰσοπολιτείαν, ἔδοξε καὶ τοῖς ἐντὸς Ἄλπεων Γαλάταις . . . τὴν αὐτὴν ἀπονεῖμαι τιμήν, προσαγορεῦσαι δὲ καὶ Ἰταλιώτας πάντας καὶ Ῥωμαίους.* The law, as we know from the Atestine Fragment, was passed by L. Roscius, praetor in 49, on 11th March. I notice that Nap, applying his own canons of internal probability, regards the lex Roscia as granting to Caesar full powers to make and unmake laws, and as annexing Gallia Cisalpina to Italy. The latter point seems a misunderstanding of Strabo's statement, which records, not very clearly, two separate events. Italy was extended to the Alps, as we know from Dio (xlviii, 12) in 41. As to Nap's other assertion we may await his evidence for it.

indeed related to the 'formula togatorum', which had nothing to do with the legions, and nothing to do with the Roman census or the Roman censors, though the latter might supply the 'formula' (in the sense given above) to be used. This confusion about legionary service vitiates Nap's explanation, while it is open to the same objection as Mommsen's, that, as long as they were non-citizens, the Transpadani could not possibly be enrolled in the census either for military or political objects. I may add that Nap's explanation of the dispute as one merely concerned with the military service of the Transpadani, not only ignores Dio's εἰς τὴν πολιτείαν ἐσάγειν, but makes the whole situation unintelligible, for it represents Crassus as wishing to impose a military burden on Caesar's protégés, not to confer a political privilege.[1]

I am convinced that the only satisfactory way of explaining the attitude of the censors in 65, without riding rough-shod over Dio, and in accordance with the known situation, is to assume Caesar's intention of marking the year by the enfranchisement of the Transpadani. He had given encouragement to their claims in 67; he had, according to an historian cited by Suetonius,[2] intrigued with them at the beginning of this very year; and their enfranchisement might greatly further his own plans and those of Crassus in the immediate future. For we may take it as highly probable that they had already determined to make the consular and tribunician elections in 64 a trial of strength. If Cicero hoped much from the votes of Cispadane Gaul,[3] how much more important would be the more numerous Transpadane towns if they could be enfranchised in time?

Caesar certainly had some following in the tribunician college, for he tried 'per partem tribunorum' to get a command in Egypt, and I believe that a law to enfranchise the Transpadani was to have been part of the year's programme. This is not a mere conjecture in the air, but the only means of explaining the irreconcilable opposition of the censors on the question of the Transpadane citizenship. For the censors had no *locus standi* in the matter till the time came for the enrolment of the new citizens in the burgess lists, and this could only be when an

[1] This is clear from the supposed inclusion in the Roman census of the Latin colonies in 209, which was the result of disobedience.

[2] *Iul.* 11. [3] *ad Att.* i, 1, 2.

enfranchising law had qualified them for such enrolment. As the law was not passed, the practical question never came before the censors, who indeed could not have touched even their preliminary function of a 'lectio senatus', since we find it attempted by the censors of the following year (cf. also οὐδὲν τῶν ἄλλων ἔπραξαν). But the censors on entering office knew what might come, and they represented irreconcilable views. Crassus might have declared that, unless opposition to the measure was withdrawn, he would block every censorial act; or Catulus might have threatened to make the law inoperative, at any rate for the moment, by refusing his co-operation in the enrolment in tribes and centuries. Under such circumstances their resignation was inevitable, and owing to that, and the energetic action of the optimates this year, the law was not proposed.

VI. THE CENSORS OF 64

I again have to join issue with Mr. Nap. He declares that if, after the fiasco of 65, censors were again created in 64, it must have been because the cause of dispute had been in the interval settled definitely one way or the other. To have created fresh censors merely to be driven to the same deadlock was, he argues, inconsistent with Roman statesmanship. It is true, he admits, that Dio's words καὶ διὰ τοῦτο imply that the fresh censors were wrecked on the same rock as their predecessors, viz. the Transpadane question, but for the reasons given he must be mistaken.

In what way then was this Transpadane, or, as Nap will have it, Cisalpine question settled after the resignation of the censors in 65 and before the creation of the next pair in 64? He finds the settlement in a lex Papia, which is preserved on the Table of Heraclea in lines 143 to 159. This law, by providing that in future a Roman census should be accompanied by a census in all 'municipia', 'coloniae', and 'praefecturae' within Italy, implicitly excluded from the Roman census the Cisalpini or Transpadani because they were not within but outside Italy, and therefore cleared away all difficulties on this score from the path of the new censors. Now Nap does not pretend that there is any reason for connecting this law with Papius or the year 65 except that it meets the situation. But does it? The 'municipia', 'coloniae', and 'praefecturae' within Italy were all fully enfranchised towns, and the law explicitly orders a census of the Roman citizens in those towns. It is true that this excludes the Transpadani, but it only excludes them in the sense that it has nothing to do with the Transpadane question; it only excludes them as it excludes the towns of Sicily or of Africa. The words 'in Italia' have no doubt a limiting force, for they rule out all 'municipia', 'coloniae', and 'praefecturae' of Roman citizens outside Italy, which in the year 65 would have meant the Cispadane colonies and the four colonies north of the Po. But this would clearly not have helped the censors of 64, whose difficulty, on Nap's own showing, was the enrolment of men who, though not Roman citizens, might, if enrolled, be capable of serving in the legions. As a matter of fact, no law was required to exclude non-citizens; they were excluded by the very nature of the census; while on the other hand, if an enfranchising law was once passed, nothing could legally prevent their enrolment, though the temporary obstruction of particular censors might delay it. The supposed lex Papia therefore did not settle the question between the censors, for it was as completely out of relation to it as Nap himself makes the other two leges Papiae which he declares to have been passed on the same day.[1]

Nor do I see the force of the argument that new censors would

[1] The three leges Papiae are (1) the Alien Act, mentioned by Dio, of which we have the conclusion in lines 1 to 19 of the Table of Heraclea, and of which Nap's interpretation will be discussed below; (2) a law dealing with aedilician duties, also on the Table; (3) the law about the census. Nap's reference of this last law to the dispute between the censors is open to a further objection, which I need not here insist on, in that he includes in it the regulations as to municipal senates, obviously irrelevant to what he makes the essential aim of the law.

On Nap's view of matters military and political the third lex Papia would seem to have had little effect. Its object was to exclude the Transpadani from the census, and this involved non-eligibility for service in the legions. Notwithstanding this, he infers from *Bell. Civ.* iii, 87 (quoted above) that Transpadani did serve in Caesar's legions. They could do this, he thinks, because Latins were not 'peregrini' but 'municipes'. But, if as 'municipes' they could join the legions without being on the census, why did their advocates in 65 take so much trouble to get them on the census? If we discard facts and evidence for theories and conjectures, we must expect disconcerting contradictions of this kind. On Latins as 'municipes' see below.

not have been created till the dispute between the former ones had been settled by legislation. For it did not follow that the next censors would also hold opposite views on the matter, and each party might well hope to secure two censors favourable to itself. It was desirable, too, to complete the 'lectio senatus' and if possible the whole census, while state contracts would be requiring renewal. Even if another deadlock ensued, it would merely mean the *status quo*. At any rate, fresh censors entered office, and it seems to me impossible to doubt that they both belonged to the popular party. That they belonged to the same party is indicated by the fact that both equally were opposed by the tribunes, and that both resigned through the same apprehension of trouble to themselves; that they belonged to the popular party is shown by the Alien Act, unintelligible, unless some relief for the Transpadani was anticipated by the optimates. On this assumption, we can, I think, understand all that followed, the attack by tribunes, left by Nap without a motive, and the Alien Act, irrelevant on Nap's view to its context. There was still the possibility of an enfranchising law, and, if this could be rushed through, the popular leaders might even, with two friendly censors, get the new citizens enrolled in time for the elections in July. To meet this danger, the optimates took two steps, perhaps almost simultaneous. In the first place, they put up certain tribunes to block by their 'intercessio' the first censorial act, the 'lectio senatus'. If this was persisted in, there was no alternative but resignation, and the censors, fearing that resistance would be visited by an impeachment for 'perduellio', or, as Dio less correctly puts it, by loss of senatorial rank, followed the example of their predecessors and laid down office. Nap, objecting to the καὶ διὰ τοῦτο of Dio, argues that they could not have resigned both on account of the tribunes' veto and of the Transpadane difficulty. I hope I have shown that the two causes were intimately connected. But at the same time, as a precaution and a manifesto, one of the tribunes, C. Papius, was instructed to pass an Alien Act, expelling from Rome any expectant beneficiaries of an enfranchising law who might happen to be in the city.

VII. THE ALIEN ACT OF PAPIUS

Before dealing with the precise scope of this Alien Act, it is necessary to discuss Nap's representation of it. In the first place, as he insists that all his leges Papiae were passed on one and the same day, and as the whole *raison d'être* of his third law requires it to have been passed in 65 before the censors of 64 entered office, he is compelled to place the Alien Act in the interval between the two pairs of censors. If there were the slightest evidence for the third lex Papia, or for its object being what Nap assumes, there might be some reason for ignoring the order of events as implied by Dio, but an examination of the census clause on the Table of Heraclea has shown that there is none. But Dio, after describing the failure of the censors in 64, goes on: *καὶ ἐν τούτῳ οἱ ἐν τῇ Ῥώμῃ διατρίβοντες κτλ* and the introductory words can only mean 'while this was going on', i.e. in 64. But on Nap's view of the Alien Act, it really does not matter whether it was passed in 65 or 64, or for that matter in 66 or 63, for it has no relation to the Transpadane question, and there seems no reason why Papius should have passed it on the same day as his law excluding them from the census, or why Dio should have mentioned it in such close connexion with the two censorial failures. It is agreed that Dio's phrase *οἱ ἐν τῇ Ῥώμῃ διατρίβοντες* means the 'peregrini in Rome at the time', but Nap roundly declares that the Transpadani were not and could not have been expelled by the Act, because as Latins they were not 'peregrini' but 'municipes', and as 'municipes' they had the legal right of residence in Rome. The last point needs evidence, but it is enough to say that this supposed right of residence did not prevent Latins being expelled under the two earlier Alien Acts of 126 and 95. The latter is described by Cicero (see below) as a law 'de sociis et Latinis redigendis', while the former provoked the revolt of Fregellae. But 'municipes', as a class intermediate between 'peregrini' and full citizens, had long since passed out of existence; and a 'municeps' was simply the citizen of a 'municipium'. If the 'municipium' was one of Roman citizens, as all in Italy now were, he was a Roman; if it was one with Latin rights, like Salpensa or Malaca, he was a Latin. Nor can it be maintained that Latins were not 'peregrini'. Latin colonies were after all simply the most favoured class of 'civitates foederatae'.[1] They were not usually called by this name, because their position was not due to a separate 'foedus', with Rome, but was a survival from the common 'foedus', which had once bound together the members of the Latin League, the nucleus out of which the Italian confederacy had grown. But I should be content to let the point be determined in a simpler and more direct way. Latins, as we have seen, were affected by the two earlier Alien Acts, and yet the general object of both measures is given by Cicero as the expulsion of 'peregrini'. 'Male etiam qui peregrinos urbibus uti prohibent eosque exterminant, ut Pennus apud patres nostros. . . . Nam esse pro cive qui civis non sit rectum est non licere; quam legem tulerunt . . . consules Crassus et Scaevola; usu vero urbis prohibere peregrinos sane inhumanum est.'[2]

But if the 'peregrini' expelled were not Transpadani, who were they? Nap's answer is that they were the foreigners of non-Italian extraction, especially the heterogeneous Greeks and Orientals who were residents or visitors in Rome, and who thronged or disturbed the 'contiones'.[3] I can find only one point in favour of this view, and that is the reason suggested by Dio for the expulsion, namely, that they were persons regarded as too numerous and *οὐκ ἐπιτήδειοι συνοικεῖν*. This, however, is outweighed by other considerations, and merely suggests to my mind that Dio, while correctly giving from his authorities the scope and date of the measure, did not appreciate its exact relation to its context in his own narrative, and allowed himself a somewhat foolish conjecture. It is more important to determine the nature of the class exempted from the operation of the law, *πλὴν τῶν τὴν νῦν Ἰταλίαν οἰκούντων*. Nap takes this to mean 'except those who were natives of Italy and Cisalpine

[1] That the Latin colonies fell under the class of 'civitates foederatae' in its widest sense is indicated by Cicero's phrase 'Latinis, id est, foederatis' in *pro Balb.* 24, 54.

[2] *de Offic.* iii, 11, 47.

[3] *pro Flac.* 28, 66.

Gaul', i. e. of Italy in Dio's own time. But why should Dio have brought in τὴν νῦν Ἰταλίαν in this sense? The exempted class were of course 'peregrini', and in Italy proper there were no native-born 'peregrini' after the Social war.[1] The only 'peregrini', who in the wide sense were not of extra-Italian origin, were those in Cisalpine Gaul, and Dio could never thus have paraphrased his authorities' description of these. I believe that he did not paraphrase it at all, but that τὴν νῦν Ἰταλίαν is his rendering of their actual words.

But Nap is more interested in a more problematical class of exempted persons, of whom Dio gives no hint. He believes that within the ranks of Greek and Oriental foreigners a certain number could obtain exemption by making a declaration before a magistrate (professio) to the effect that they were teachers, or physicians, or professors of some liberal art. As a proof that there were exemptions, Nap cites *de leg. agrar.* i, 4, 13, where a Glaucippus 'illa lege qua peregrini Roma eiciuntur excipitur'. As an indication that physicians had to make a 'professio', he adduces a passage of Suetonius (*Iul.* 42) where Caesar presented with the citizenship 'medicinam Romae professos et liberalium artium doctores'. Finally, as confirmation of his hypothesis that these persons, if they claimed exemption, had to make a 'professio', the first nineteen lines of the Table of Heraclea are declared to be the conclusion of, or a corollary to, the Papian Alien Act.

With regard to Glaucippus, Cicero's argument implies rather that he was a solitary exception than one of a class of exempted persons, and I think I can find room for him among Dio's exceptions. As to the 'professi medicinam', they are of course not 'physicians who had registered', but 'men who practised medicine'. Nor is there the smallest reason to identify the 'professi' of the Table of Heraclea with these supposed teachers, physicians, and artists, who, according to Nap, were seeking exemption from the Alien Act. On the other hand, there are two fatal reasons against it. Nap's applicants would *ex hypothesi* be 'peregrini'; the 'professi' of the Table were demonstrably

[1] It would be perhaps cruel to press the point that on Nap's view neither were there any native-born 'peregrini' in the Cisalpine province, if the Transpadani were, as he contends, not 'peregrini'.

Roman citizens. For (1) there is a strict prohibition against allowing them to benefit by the 'frumentationes', a prohibition only intelligible in connexion with Roman citizens, since Greek and Oriental 'peregrini' had, as even Nap must admit, no claim whatever to receive corn. (2) It appears that women and minors (whom we should hardly expect to find among Nap's applicants) might make the required declaration through legal 'tutores', a point which absolutely rules out Nap's hypothesis that these women and youths came under the category of extra-Italian 'peregrini'.

But of course the possibility of an Alien Act such as Nap assumes does not necessarily stand or fall with this unhappy interpretation of the opening lines of the Table. It falls nevertheless from the total absence of evidence in its favour. Such an heroic measure as the expulsion of the foreign population of Rome was unique and unparalleled, and if actually carried, must inevitably have left some traces behind. Nap can point to none; he does not even attempt to show that the 'contiones' were less disorderly in the succeeding years, and he as utterly fails to explain why Papius should have practically tacked on this sweeping expulsion of foreigners to a law on the census of the Transpadani, as why he should have included in what was to all intents and purposes a 'lex satura' a parochial measure on repairing roadways and limiting traffic. I return to my own conception of the situation at the opening of 64. There were two censors favourable to the popular policy, and if a law enfranchising the Transpadani could be hurried through, there might be a chance of enrolling them in the tribes and centuries in time to use their votes at the elections in July. But the optimates paralysed the censors and made their resignation inevitable by causing their first act, the 'lectio senatus', to be blocked by tribunician 'intercessio'. Under the circumstances the idea of an enfranchising law, which could no longer affect immediate issues, was given up, and has left no trace, except as explaining the quarrel between the censors of 65, and throwing light upon the second move of the optimates, the Alien Act of Papius. There is indeed an extraordinary, and surely not accidental, parallel between the circumstances of 65–64 and those of 126 and 95. In the first year there was known to be impending, with a view to ease the agrarian situation, the proposal of Fulvius Flaccus, actually made next year, to grant the 'civitas' to the Italians, i. e. to the Latin and federate towns. In 95 there was violent agitation among the Italians, and many of them 'summa cupiditate Romanae civitatis' illegally anticipated the exercise of full civic rights.[1] In 65, as a sequel to local agitation for the franchise among the Latin colonies, we find violent dissensions in Rome, reflected in the attitude of the censors, as to whether it was expedient τοὺς ὑπὲρ τὸν 'Ηριδανὸν οἰκοῦντας εἰς τὴν πολιτείαν ἐσάγειν. On these respective antecedents what followed? In the first case a tribune, Iunius Pennus, passed an Alien Act, by which 'peregrini', no doubt limited by some excepting clause to those expecting enfranchisement, were expelled from Rome.[2] In the second case the lex Licinia-Mucia was passed—a more complicated measure, for it had to deal with actual usurpation of citizen rights, but in part an Alien Act, expelling 'socii et Latini' from Rome.[3] In precisely the same way, if we believe Dio and Cicero,[4] an Alien Act was passed on the occasion we are considering, expelling 'peregrini' from Rome. Can we avoid the conclusion that the expelled 'peregrini' were in this case too some of those about whose admission to the 'civitas' parties were divided?

But does Dio's description and specification of the persons expelled tally with this view? They were οἱ ἐν τῇ 'Ρώμῃ διατρίβοντες πλὴν τῶν τὴν νῦν 'Ιταλίαν οἰκούντων. The words τὴν νῦν 'Ιταλίαν are the only difficulty, and I have already argued against the supposition that Dio uses them from his own point of view. It is far more likely that the excepting clause is taken straight from the authority, and is the historian's rendering of what he found. I take the exempting clause to be: 'with the exception of any "peregrini" now in Rome, who have a domicile in Italy, as now determined.' Considering that the

[1] Ascon. *in Cornel.* 67. [2] *de Off.* iii, 11, 47.

[3] It is this double character of the law which explains Cicero's mixture of praise and blame. As dealing with usurped rights he approves it; as an Alien Act he condemns it. He says in *pro Sest.* 13, 30, 'nihil acerbius socii et Latini ferre soliti sunt quam se, id quod perraro accidit ex urbe exire a consulibus iuberi.' The reference, according to Schol.-Bob., is to the law of 95, by which it was enacted: 'ut redire socii et Latini in suas civitates iuberentur.'

[4] *de leg. Agr.* i, 4, 13.

boundary of Italy had been altered not more than sixteen or seventeen years earlier, this careful precision is what we should expect in a law of the kind; it would, e.g., safeguard the position of 'peregrini' domiciled in Ariminum. But this interpretation of the clause represents as the exempted persons exactly the class which, on Nap's view, was expelled. For the only 'peregrini' domiciled in Italy at this time were foreigners of non-Italian origin, and all of these, whether domiciled in Rome itself, or visiting Rome from other domiciles, were unaffected by the Papian law. On the other hand, any 'peregrini' domiciled outside Italy, and therefore any Transpadani from the Latin colonies in the Cisalpine, who happened to be in Rome, would have to leave.

Of course, such an Alien Act could not by itself prevent the passing of an enfranchising law. The Act of Pennus did not prevent the proposal next year of Fulvius Flaccus, though it may have done something towards its defeat. Similarly, the lex Licinia-Mucia did not hinder Livius Drusus from taking up the cause of the Italians, and perhaps did more to intensify than to dissipate the agitation. Still, the lex Papia, especially coming after the action of the tribunes, might have considerable moral effect, would serve as an optimatist manifesto, and if, as is probable, a good many Transpadani had been attracted to Rome, it might put a practical stop to much intrigue and agitation.

It remains to notice two individual sojourners in Rome, whose treatment under the lex Papia differed as much as that of the chief butler and of the chief baker. Cicero[1] speaks of a Glaucippus whose exemption from the Alien Act was as marked as Pompey's exemption from the requirement to hand in 'manubiae'. Nap regards him as one of a class of registered exempts, whereby the point of comparison with Pompey is lost. I take him to be a foreigner domiciled in some Transpadane town, whose presence in Rome therefore brought him under the Papian Act, but who, not coming under its intention, had received special exemption. On the other hand, in the year 51 a citizen of Novum Comum found himself in Rome just at the time when

[1] *de leg. Agr.* i, 4, 13.

the government had legally or illegally declared the town to be a Latin and not a Roman colony. Marcellus, on some pretext not specified by the historians, seized this man and had him publicly scourged, as a practical demonstration that he was not a Roman citizen. I suggest that the consul may have used as a pretext for his action the Alien Act of Papius, which, however ephemeral its immediate object, may nevertheless have remained on the statute book, a trap for unwary Transpadani.

III

THE AGRARIAN PROPOSAL OF RULLUS IN 63 B.C.

CICERO'S speeches 'against Rullus' would seem not only to have given its quietus to the Lex agraria brought forward under the name of that man of straw, but to have decided also the verdict of history on the nature, object, and statecraft of that still-born scheme. It is not my intention in this paper to make any attempt to controvert this practically unanimous verdict of modern historians. I say 'of modern historians', because somewhat strangely the extraordinary and revolutionary project which was to cost the Roman people its *pax*, its *libertas*, and its *otium*, has attracted practically no notice from ancient writers. Cicero, looking at the scheme as a whole and at the indirect, not to say underhand, method of its proposal, was justified from all points of view in opposing it. Its acceptance by the people, the political situation being what it was, could, it might well be argued, hardly have failed to impair the financial stability of the State, might even have precipitated civil war, and in any case might have stirred up too many animosities both in Italy and in the provinces to give any reasonable chance of success to the ostensibly agrarian portion of the measure.

But it does not follow either that all the arguments employed to secure a verdict on the measure are fair or satisfactory representations of the facts, or that all the sections of this complicated law deserve equal condemnation, or are to be described as *vinolentorum somnia* or *optata furiosorum*.

It has seemed to me on re-reading Cicero's speeches, and comparing them with the deductions drawn from them by the authorities to whom we mainly look for guidance, that it may be worth while to review once more this notorious proposal, to draw fresh attention to some ambiguities and not a few disingenuous misrepresentations on the part of Cicero, to disentangle, if possible, a little more thoroughly than our historians have taken the trouble to do, the numerous schemes comprised under the law, and to inquire whether after all there are no traces in it of *consilia siccorum* or even of *cogitata sapientium*.

It is, however, obviously only worth while to make this attempt on the assumption, made equally by Cicero and by later historians, that the bill really emanated from more important personages than Rullus. If it had really been the conception of a tribune without antecedents, and so insignificant that his name never re-emerges in a period offering so many chances to able adventurers, the episode would deserve no place in history, and would require no mention except as having afforded Cicero an occasion for a somewhat easy oratorical triumph. It was indeed, as it seems to me, the fatal mistake made by Caesar at this point that he put this easy victory within Cicero's reach by entrusting his measure to a man of straw, and then, as far as we can see, simply leaving it to take its chance. No doubt he might well have hesitated to have come forward in open opposition to Pompey, but at the same time, if he really desired, as it seems agreed by all that he did, to obtain through this law some position of vantage against that general, and if he laid any stress, as I shall argue that he did, upon the scheme of Italian colonization, he, as a matter of fact, wrecked both objects, not so much by the extreme character of some of the proposals, as by providing the bill with no adequate or responsible support.

Cicero undoubtedly regarded the law as seriously meant by its authors, and as the outcome of a deliberate and dangerous design to overawe, if not to destroy, the republican government, but he is able to represent it as an impudent challenge to Pompey by Rullus, as a shameless bid for self-aggrandizement and self-enrichment at the expense of the State by Rullus. It is Rullus who will manipulate the election of commissioners by the seventeen tribes; who will be the leading spirit among them; who will decide the future fate of Egypt; who will sell the very ground under Pompey's camp; who will use his powers of land purchase in Italy in the interests of his father-in-law and himself, and who in the end will appropriate goodly portions of the rich *ager Campanus*. This mode of attack was perfectly safe—we may measure the insignificance of Rullus by the outrageous lengths to which Cicero ventured —and must have been very effective with the people. While even in the Senate he affected to ignore the other commissioners; *tu Rulle—missos enim facio ceteros*. But more than once Cicero allows himself to drop this thin disguise, and to allude, though in cautious language, to those whom he well knew to be the real authors of the law. 'For what security', he asks the Senate, 'do you suppose will be left you in the republic, or in the maintenance of your liberty and dignity, when Rullus and those whom you fear far more than you fear Rullus have got possession of Capua and the cities round Capua?'[1] Again, still more unmistakably: 'and the men who aim at all this are wont again and again to complain that every land and sea has been handed over to Gn. Pompeius' (ii, 17, 46). We may add such expressions as 'neque ipse (Rullus) neque illi horum consiliorum auctores' (ii, 8, 20) and 'tibi nos, Rulle, et istis tuis harum omnium rerum machinatoribus totam Italiam inermem tradituros existimasti' (i, 5, 16).

We may take it, therefore, that Cicero, while openly directing his attack against the impudent and self-seeking designs of Rullus, was well aware that he was really dealing with the formidable and carefully devised scheme of serious politicians. But if we admit this, it surely follows that many if not most of Cicero's most effective arguments are irrelevant to the real scheme, the scheme as conceived by Caesar himself. That Cicero should have taken the opportunity, unguardedly put into his hands by Caesar, and avoided almost all discussion of the bill on its merits, is only natural. He was professedly speaking as the champion of Pompey's interests (see especially ii, 18, 49 ff.), and it may even be doubted whether he had detected any policy in the proposal at all except the obvious intention to neutralize or undermine Pompey's commanding position.

When we turn to modern historians, what seems surprising

[1] *De leg. Agr.* i, 7, 22.

to me is that while scouting the idea that Rullus was more than a man of straw, and advowedly attributing the whole scheme to Caesar, or to Caesar and Crassus, they seem nevertheless content to accept the description of the law as assigned by Cicero to Rullus. Mommsen accepts the view that a purely personal position was aimed at *legis agrariae simulatione.* Mr. Strachan-Davidson seems to admit that the main lines on which Caesar was about to work were foreshadowed in the law, but as far as its agrarian character is concerned, he merely suggests that the democratic leaders 'would have ample means at their disposal to provide for their more hungry partisans' (*Cicero*, p. 104). Mr. Heitland sees no serious purpose in the law beyond the aim of the moment. 'As a practical means of relieving poverty or ridding Rome of a surplus population, the bill was a sham. Caesar of course knew this, but he wanted a cry to serve his real purposes' (vol. iii, p. 87). Mr. Ferrero simply assigns to the law the double end of destroying Cicero's popularity and of raising again the great question of Egypt (vol. i, p. 259).

I confess that I am not entirely satisfied with any of these accounts of the matter. They do not go much beyond Cicero's declaration that from the first chapter to the last he can find nothing in the law except the establishment of a *decemvirale regnum.* They do not take into account what Cicero, when he made his speeches, had no means of doing, the later programme and policy of Caesar. Was the position of Pompey so all-absorbing that there was no room for social legislation or financial readjustment? Or was Caesar only a serious politician after 59? In that year he passed two genuine agrarian laws. May it not be possible to find their antecedents in his abortive scheme of 63? At any rate, I propose to make an attempt to get at the meaning of those provisions of the law which can be extracted from the three speeches of Cicero, unfortunately our sole evidence. How imperfect our knowledge of the law, as a whole, must be, is shown by the fact that while Cicero's criticisms relate to not more than about ten of its clauses, the provision about the 'Sullan lands' was Chapter 40, and this certainly came before the chapters dealing with the colonial scheme. It is sometimes said that the law was clumsily drawn up, with clauses vaguely and ambiguously worded, and containing 'loose general expressions capable of still wider application'. This may have been the case, but I suspect that the vagueness and ambiguity which hangs over the law is due to Cicero's method of presenting it to his audiences. His *praeco* stood beside him with a copy of the law in his hands, but Cicero rarely quotes from it, and when he does, it is usually only the first few words, the purport of the clause, as he wished his hearers to understand it, being merely a paraphrase of his own. We have therefore to trust to a hostile critic, and though we may sometimes suspect, we must take the contents of the law as Cicero gives it. It is, however, possible in certain cases to check or explain statements made in the speech to the people by corresponding passages in that to the Senate. Sometimes, too, we can distinguish between Cicero's interpretations of a clause and its actual wording, while in one or two instances this interpretation can be shown to be unwarranted by his own statements elsewhere.

Whatever its real object, the law was entitled a *lex agraria* and its proposer was an otherwise unknown P. Servilius Rullus with whom several of his colleagues were associated. An agrarian law was always taken to imply the settlement by the State of Roman citizens on public or at least on publicly provided land, and Cicero as a *consul popularis* is careful to declare that such laws may be worthy of all praise, like those of the two Gracchi, *clarissimos ingeniosissimos amantissimosque plebei Romanae viros* (ii, 5, 10). The proposal of Rullus was that an extensive scheme of colonization should be carried out by the State in Italy. So far it hardly went beyond the proposals of Livius Drusus in 122 B.C. and his son in 91 B.C., and neither of these had been considered revolutionary, though they had ended in nothing. But at these dates there had been considerable quantities of public land in Italy, which, though perhaps not without some friction, might be resumed for the purpose. In 63 B.C., however, with the exception of the *ager Campanus* and the *ager Stellas*, which had been untouched by previous agrarian laws, there was practically no public land in Italy which had not in one way or another been disposed of. All that was left was to be used for the purposes of the scheme, but the bulk of the land required for it was to be obtained by purchase on a large and systematic scale. To provide for this, and perhaps to make the scheme a permanent and continuous one, an extraordinary fund of money was to be established, partly by the immediate alienation and realization of certain categories of *ager publicus* in the provinces, partly, as I shall argue, by such a readjustment of the financial system as would keep it supplied for the future, or at least for the next few years, with a regular income. The creation of this fund by the various methods prescribed in the law, together with its management and disposal in the necessary purchase of land, and finally in the foundation or enlargement of the contemplated colonies, were to be in the hands of a board of ten commissioners, elected by the seventeen tribes, and invested with extraordinary judicial and administrative powers for five years. Cicero declares, whether correctly or not, that no land was to be purchased until all the sales were completed and the money realized (Ante omnia veneunt, ante pecuniae coguntur . . . quam gleba una ematur, ii, 27, 71), and though quite possibly the *ager Campanus* might have been parcelled out at once, it will be better to take that part of the law first which contained the scheme for raising the required fund. It was mainly through these clauses that the democratic leaders hoped to obtain a position in the provinces which would put them on even terms with Pompey, or, as Cicero preferred to put it, that the *decemviri* would become kings over all the provinces, the free peoples, the client kingdoms, and in short over the whole world (ii, 6, 15).

(1) What Cicero calls the *primum genus venditionis* is given in his own words, not those of the law. *Ut liceat ea omnia vendere de quibus vendendis senatus consulta facta sunt M. Tullio et Gn. Cornelio coss. postve ea* (ii, 14, 35). The provision need not detain us long. The offer for sale from time to time *propter angustias aerarii* of public sites in the city, and other state assets like the willow plantations at Minturnae, was one of the most unsatisfactory and undignified contrivances of Roman finance, and quite possibly, as Cicero declares, the responsible magistrates had sometimes shrunk from acting on these senatorial decrees. But at any rate the promoters of the law were

taking no unprecedented course, and in raising an extraordinary fund for a special object it was natural enough to adopt this among other methods, especially as the Senate had already marked out these particular properties for sale. Cicero complains that they are not specified, and suggests that this is either due to a sense of the shameful character of such sales, or points to a sinister intention on the part of Rullus to sell under senatorial sanction whatever he chose. The latter insinuation is perfectly gratuitous, while if the Senate was not ashamed of its decrees there was no reason for Rullus to be ashamed of his clause.

(2) The next provision is perhaps the crux of the law. However, we begin hopefully with some actual words of the clause, and Mr. Strachan-Davidson (p. 101) remarks that we could hardly believe the extraordinary nature of the project 'if the very words of this clause had not been preserved to us by Cicero'. Unfortunately the only words of the clause preserved to us are these: *qui agri quae loca aedificia aliudve quid.* At this point Cicero abandons quotation for paraphrase and sums up the provision thus: *quicquid igitur sit extra Italiam quod publicum populi Romani factum sit L. Sulla Q. Pompeio consulibus* (88 B.C.) *aut postea, id decemviros jubet vendere* (ii, 15, 38). Now it is to the designs discovered by him to be lurking under this chapter that Cicero allows himself to apply the expressions already cited, *somnia vinolentorum*, &c. What are those designs? In the first place, towns like Ephesus, Smyrna, Miletus, and Mytilene, with all their territories, and in fact the whole province of Asia, might be brought under the terms of the clause, since having been lost in the second Mithridatic war they had been recovered after 88 B.C. The whole of Asia might therefore be sold. Again, the kingdom of Bithynia had been inherited by the Roman people within the period specified. It too was saleable. More monstrous still, Alexandria and the whole of Egypt was alleged to have been bequeathed to Rome by the will of King Alexander in 81 B.C., *ergo ex sua lege vendet Alexandream, vendet Aegyptum* (ii, 16, 43). But what according to Cicero was even more scandalous than this wide power of selling Roman property was the unlimited judicial authority belonging to the *decemviri.* It was not only for Rullus and his colleagues to decide the legal question whether Egypt was or was not the rightful inheritance of the

Roman people, but they might make a tour of the whole empire, adjudicating on the claims of the Roman people to this or that territory, and either appropriating and selling it, or exacting heavy blackmail for their forbearance.

For my part I profess myself unable to accept this interpretation of the clause. No doubt it was vaguely worded, though it is hardly doubtful that the *aliud quid*, where Cicero finds it convenient to stop, received some explanation or limitation in what followed. It is perfectly clear that neither Asia nor Bithynia nor Egypt was mentioned by name. But Bithynia and Egypt, and Cicero might have added Cyprus, would come under the terms of the clause, and he was undoubtedly right in recognizing that the open attempt made in 65 B.C. by the democratic leaders to get a standing in Egypt was being replaced by this less direct and more subtle method. That Egypt, with its position, its wealth, and its resources, was to be the real set-off against Pompey is admitted by all, and need not be further insisted upon. After his failure of two years before, Caesar naturally omitted all mention of Egypt, and left his clause vague. Cicero partly sees this, but cannot resist the insinuation that the vagueness was meant to cover all sorts of other possibilities. We cannot be sure that some action would not have been taken in Cyprus and Bithynia, but the suggestion that the whole of Asia would have been brought under the clause on the ground of its release from Mithridates is preposterous, and was of course intended to blind the equestrian order. Macedonia and Achaia might equally have been included. Cicero inadvertently proves his own suggestion to be dishonest. In introducing the next provision he in both his speeches emphasizes the fact that he is passing from a clause which impaired the dignity of the empire, and caused unrest and alarm in all its parts, to one which weakened its resources, attacked the *aerarium*, and laid hands on the *vectigalia*. *Cum se sociorum cum exterarum nationum, cum regum sanguine implerint* (the exaggeration is ridiculous, and only in Egypt was a foreign nation or king threatened), *incidant nervos populi Romani, adhibeant manus vectigalibus vestris, inrumpant in aerarium* (ii, 17, 47, and i, 1, 2). The suggestion, therefore, that Asia, the richest of the provinces, was to be handed over to the *decemviri* and 'sold' was evidently unfounded and dishonest.

With regard to Bithynia, we shall find that the royal domain lands in that province were to be sold under the next clause, but if, as Cicero implies, the whole *regnum Bithyniae* was liable to be sold under this one, the royal domains would have been included. In all probability, therefore, in spite of its general terms, the provision was intended to apply to Egypt alone, and Cicero must have known this, but the vague wording gave him an opportunity for alarming suggestions of which he made skilful use.

With regard to the judicial powers of the *decemviri*, by which they were to decide the question as to the will of Alexander, and to terrorize and pillage the whole empire, we can only describe Cicero's argument as audacious sophistry, which was only not libellous because the *decemviri* were not yet in existence. In the first place, the question whether Egypt did or did not belong to the Roman people was diplomatic and not legal, and the Senate, as Cicero himself admits (ii, 16, 41), had already taken action on the assumption that the will was genuine. The *decemviri* would simply proceed on the same assumption. In the second place, we can hardly doubt that the judicial powers of the commissioners were specified in the law, though Cicero keeps this out of sight, and in any case his picture of the unscrupulous uses to which it would be put is a reflection of his insinuation that the *decemviri* would be composed of Rullus and his like, whereas he knew perfectly well that however *improbi* politically, they would number men of position and responsibility. To brand this still unelected body with infamy may have been effective at the moment, but we may surely dismiss it as not worthy of serious consideration.

The question arises, what are we to understand by the statement that the *decemviri* were empowered 'to sell' such properties of the Roman people as Egypt, or, if we like to add it, Bithynia? That much movable property would be actually sold and realized is probable, but it is ridiculous to talk of selling a province or a kingdom, or any considerable part of either, in the ordinary sense. Besides, it is by the carrying out of the next clause as distinct from the present one that *praesens pecunia certa numerata* is looked for. I have no doubt myself that *vendere* is here used not in the sense of *alienare* (where Cicero uses this word, it is always in connexion with the next clause) but in the sense in which the censors are said sometimes *vendere*, sometimes *locare*, the usufruct of either *vectigalia* or lands. The system, whatever it might be, in force in the older provinces for getting the *vectigalia* from *ager publicus* was not interfered with, but in the case of these new acquisitions, certainly Egypt, and possibly Bithynia and Cyprus, the *decemviri* were to make the necessary arrangements, selling the usufruct of the land, and possibly selling or farming out the *vectigalia* from it, but not actually alienating any immovable property of the Roman people. For the next five years at any rate all that accrued from these arrangements would be at the disposal of the commissioners for purposes of the agrarian scheme. It was of course an audacious interference with the ordinary financial system, and it foreshadowed the anti-senatorial and personal policy of the first triumvirate, but reduced to its true proportions it was something more than the mere dream of madmen or drunkards.

Mr. Heitland says (vol. iii, p. 85), 'the extent of the power of sale under this head may be gathered . . . by observing that the recent annexations of Pompey were included also.' This was most certainly not the case. If it had been, we may be sure that Cicero would not have been absolutely silent on the point. Pompey's annexations were indeed affected by the law, but, as we shall see, under two other clauses, not under this. As a matter of fact, Pompey was still engaged in framing the various *leges datae* for the new provinces and their divisions, and until this was completed, they were not technically the property of the Roman people, though the royal domains of Mithridates might be claimed, as appears from the next clause, as part of the public *patrimonium* immediately on his deposition. Cicero's fancy picture of the ground under Pompey's camp being sold by Rullus belongs to the clause with which we have next to deal, while we shall see in a still later clause that the appropriation of the *vectigalia* from the new provinces was to date from the end of 63 B.C. Indeed the whole of that clause would have been redundant if Pompey's annexations had been included under the present one.

(3) If the terms of the preceding clause were vague and general, the same complaint can certainly not be made against the next (i, 1, 2 to 2, 6; and ii, 18, 47 to 21, 56). The present

clause, unlike the former, is a direct attack upon the *aerarium.* Its object is to secure *praesens pecunia certa numerata*—in other words, a fund of ready money, available for the immediate purchase of Italian land. It not only permitted but ordered the actual sale and alienation of certain specified portions of *ager publicus.* Nothing that was not so specified was to be touched under this clause. Cicero is very explicit on this point in both speeches. *Imperat ut decemviri vestra vectigalia vendant nominatim* he says in the second speech, and proceeds to give the list exhaustively. Again, in the first speech: *perscribit in sua lege vectigalia quae decemviri vendant, hoc est, proscribit auctionem publicorum bonorum,* and again he gives the list, but not so completely. I call attention to the limited sense in which the phrase *auctio publicorum bonorum* is used, because Mr. Heitland (p. 85) makes Cicero speak of 'a sale of the Roman people's effects', which is misleading, for it was a sale of quite a small portion of them. It was, however, in this case to be actual sale of lands and not merely of their usufruct. It makes no difference under this clause whether the sale is said to be of lands or of *vectigalia,* since the latter was involved in the sale of *agri vectigales* (ii, 24, 64). That it was actual sale appears from the phrase *venire nostras res proprias et in perpetuum a nobis abalienari* (ii, 21, 55), and the phrase *vectigalia abalienare* wherever it occurs refers to this clause and to this clause only.

What, then, were these properties of the Roman people that were to be immediately realized? In Italy there was the *silva Scantia,* some woodland probably leased by the censors, but unlike the *ager Campanus,* not suitable for assignation. Besides this, all the remaining *possessiones,* nothing being omitted, were to be sold. This need not detain us, since, as we shall see later, there was practically nothing left under this category. We pass to Sicily. *Nihil est in hac provincia quod aut in oppidis aut in agris majores nostri proprium nobis reliquerint quin id venire jubeat* (ii, 18, 48). It was, however, certainly not the whole of Sicily which was to be sold. In the first speech he puts it this way; *persequitur in tabulis censoriis totam Siciliam.* I infer from this that it was only that part of Sicilian land *a censoribus locatus* which came under this clause. It is clear that some of the land in Sicily came under another clause, that by which *pergrande vectigal* was to be imposed on public lands, because the *ager Recentoricus* is made an exception to that clause. *Excipit in vectigali imponendo agrum Recentoricum Siciliensem* (i, 4, 10). It would be irrelevant here to enter into the intricate question of land tenure in Sicily. My point is that it was not the whole of Sicily, as Cicero's words to the people would imply, which was to be sold, but only a part and perhaps the smaller part of it. Farther afield we find put up for sale the territories of certain communities in Cilicia, captured in war by Servilius Vatia, such as the Attalenses, the Phaselites, the Olympei, and others. To these are to be added the royal domain lands in Bithynia, and also those in Macedonia, both of which properties, like the saleable lands in Sicily, *a censoribus locati sunt et certissimum vectigal adferunt.* Belonging to the same category were the domain lands of the Attalids in the Chersonese, and those of King Apion in Cyrene, while all that remained of the Corinthian territory was to be disposed of. In the west there were certain lands near Nova Carthago, acquired by the two Scipios, and 'ancient Carthage'. This expression must have meant more than the mere site of the destroyed city, since exception is made of certain land on the coast, originally assigned to the use of Massinissa's children and then occupied by Hiempsal, on the ground that this occupation had been sanctioned by a treaty. How much, however, of the former territory of Carthage was included we cannot say. Cicero's insinuation (ii, 22, 58) that this exception was *quaestuosa* seems gratuitous, since the same exception was made from the sale of African land in 111 B.C. (*Lex Agr.* v, 81). The last category of land to be sold under this clause, though probably not the most valuable, was what most excited Cicero's indignation. It consisted of the royal domain lands of Mithridates in Paphlagonia, Pontus, and Cappadocia. It can hardly have been more than bluff which induced Caesar to insert these lands, or possibly their insertion might be useful in further negotiations with Pompey. Cicero complains that it was irregular to interfere with these lands, while the arrangements for the new provinces were still *sub judice*, and the *leges datae* not yet issued. I suggest that this objection would have been fatal to bringing these provinces under the preceding clause, but that Mithridates once deposed, his domains passed *ipso facto* to the Roman people.

At any rate the picture of Rullus summoning Pompey by letter, and conducting his auction midway between the two camps, is too silly and far-fetched to have imposed even upon a Roman mob.

We must remember that there was at least one precedent for the sale of provincial land, for some of the African and some of the Corinthian land had been sold in 111 B.C. On that occasion too some of the land had been sold by the commissioners on the spot, another arrangement which Cicero complains of, contrasting it with the censor's *locatio*, which had always to be in Rome. Local sales were of course the obvious way of guarding against the glutted market which otherwise would have been inevitable. The clause, though far less sweeping than is generally represented, was no doubt a serious interference with the financial authority of the Senate; it was laying hands on the *vectigalia* and it meant the loss to the treasury of not unimportant revenue. Saturninus, in a law not defeated on its merits, had apparently contemplated the appropriation of these same lands for the settlement of the Marian veterans, since it can hardly be a mere coincidence that the provinces mentioned in connexion with his scheme were Africa, Sicily, Macedonia, and Achaia. Caesar's later schemes of transmarine colonization, too, meant the withdrawal from revenue of what would otherwise have been *agri vectigales*. If Italian colonization was desirable, and later events showed that it might be made a success, then some sacrifice of revenue for the purchase of land was justifiable, and it was a policy deliberately adopted afterwards both by Caesar himself and by Augustus.

(4) The next provision is more vague, though the vagueness is almost certainly due to Cicero and not to the law. Cicero, however, begins with the actual words of the clause, of which unfortunately he only gives us the first four: *omnes agros extra Italiam* (ii, 21, 56). His own paraphrase is best given to the Senate (i, 4, 10); *jubet enim eosdem decemviros omnibus agris publicis pergrande vectigal imponere*. This, like the preceding clause, has no time limitation, *infinito ex tempore*. As the *decemviri* were to have unlimited judicial power, Cicero represents this as enabling them to visit any province, any free community, or any client kingdom, and either to levy this impost on whatever land they

chose to declare public, or to exact blackmail for themselves for all land which they exempted. This imputation of an intended *nundinatio juris et fortunarum* against men not yet elected is surely more dishonouring to Cicero himself than to any one else. But what does the clause mean? Mr. Heitland says (p. 85): 'it was of course clear that all the vast territories potentially affected by the bill could not in practice be actually sold. To meet this difficulty, power was given to lay a rent or tax on whatever was not disposed of by sale.' This explanation is wholly inadmissible. If vast territories were potentially saleable, which I have argued was not the case, it could only be under the first clause, and between that and the present one there was no possible connexion, since the former was subject to the consulship of Sulla and Pompey as time limitation, and the latter is *infinito ex tempore.* It is clear that the lands on which this *vectigal* was to be imposed stood outside the categories included under the first two clauses. We cannot doubt that the law itself was more explicit than Cicero, both as to the lands affected and the nature of the tax. The term *pergrande* can only be Cicero's description of a specified rate or rates. It is impossible to decide whether the *vectigal* was a lump sum to be paid at once, or an annual impost levied presumably for the next five years, or how far in a province like Asia it would have complicated the ordinary censorial *locatio.* It was at any rate an extraordinary tax to meet an extraordinary need. In Sicily the *ager Recentoricus* was exempted from this *vectigal,* and it appears that this land was in the hands of *possessores* holding by custom, not contract. On the other hand, the land to be sold in Sicily was, as we have seen, *in tabulis censoriis.* Whether this distinction gives us a clue which might be applied to the other provinces is a suggestion which I am not prepared to press.

(5) The next provision by which the land purchase fund was to be increased is at least clear and specific enough. It is partly retrospective, partly prospective. It requires that *aurum argentum ex praeda ex manubiis ex coronario ad quoscunque pervenit neque relatum est in publicum neque in monumento consumptum* (ii, 22, 59) should be accounted for and paid by the generals or their heirs to the *decemviri.* Apart from the difficulties always involved in retrospective enactments, and assuming, what of

course Cicero ignores, that the *decemviri* were to be a responsible financial commission, and not the mere gang of Rullus, there seems little that is unreasonable in this. The money certainly belonged to the State, and only the slack senatorial government was responsible for its misappropriation. Cicero implies that the provision was aimed at Faustus Sulla, the heir of the dictator. Perhaps it was, but probably no one felt more uncomfortable than Lucullus, to whose case Cicero is not anxious to call attention. For the future, or at any rate for the next five years, all generals immediately on leaving their provinces were to account for money falling under these heads to the *decemviri*. To this Pompey for obvious reasons was made an exception. Whether the money was necessary for this particular fund or not, the clause would have put a check on what was probably systematic peculation.

(6) The last provision in this division of the law, though in no way interfering with Pompey's free hand in organizing and framing *leges datae* for his new annexations, would undoubtedly have the immediate effect of offending his dignity. The provision was *ut si qua pecunia post nos consules ex novis vectigalibus recipiatur ea decemviri utantur*. This of course pointed to Pompey's annexations, the *vectigalia* from which *se frui putat oportere* (ii, 23, 62). The same thing is expressed a little differently in the first speech; *quasi vero non intelligamus haec eos vectigalia quae Gn. Pompeius adiunxerit vendere cogitare*. We can gather, I think, from these passages the meaning of the clause. In spite of the word *vendere* in the last quotation, it certainly does not mean that the land in these provinces was to be sold or the *vectigalia* alienated. The money is to come *ex novis vectigalibus*, i. e. from their produce, not from their sale. The *vendere* in the first speech is clearly equivalent to the *frui* or *uti* in the second, and *frui vectigalibus* and *abalienare vectigalia* are sharply contrasted with one another in ii, 13, 33; *vectigalibus non fruendis sed alienandis*. The *decemviri* were therefore to have the usufruct of the new *vectigalia*, and this usufruct they then were empowered to sell, no doubt to *publicani*, just as the censors sold to *publicani* the *vectigalia* of Asia. Mr. Ferrero, I think, speaks of the interests of the equestrian order being jeopardized by the bill. This is not what we should expect from Caesar at such a crisis, and if they lost the royal domains in Bithynia and Macedonia,

they would be more than compensated by these new *vectigalia*. As to the policy of risking offence to Pompey, we may believe that Caesar was far-sighted enough to see that the time must shortly come when Pompey would require some provision for his soldiers. To meet this contingency was probably part of the agrarian scheme, and the legal control of these revenues would facilitate negotiations and rearrangements with Pompey when the time came.

Such was the scheme with its six distinct means of raising the extraordinary agrarian fund required. The only provision affecting every province was that empowering the imposition of a *vectigal*. The actual sale of land was to be carried out in nine provinces out of fourteen, but in almost every case the amount of land affected was very small compared with the whole province. Mr. Strachan-Davidson writes (p. 100): 'Rullus' commissioners were empowered to sell the whole of the property of the Roman people beyond the seas.' Mr. Heitland declares (p. 85): 'the sale was to include . . . all State property abroad (with one or two trifling exceptions), in particular all the acquisitions made in the first consulship of Sulla or since. The extent of the power of sale under this head may be gauged . . . by observing that the recent annexations of Pompey were included also.' The detailed examination of the clauses given above will, I hope, show that such statements have next to no justification, and are utterly misleading. They indeed go far beyond anything which Cicero himself ventures to say.

Still, making every allowance for Cicero's highly coloured and often unfair interpretations of these provisions, we must admit that even their partial carrying out would have created, if not a *decemvirale regnum*, at least a position for Caesar and his adherents more inconsistent with a republic even than Pompey's own. Cicero declares that the ten kings would be practically the nominees of Rullus. Election was to be by seventeen tribes selected by lot, because it was easy to manipulate the lot so as to secure nine tribes ready to vote to order. It is just as likely that Caesar had recourse to this plan as a means of guarding against the flagrant bribery of the aristocrats. It was useless to buy votes when no one knew before the day which tribes would be called upon. Equally unconvincing is the criticism on

Rullus for proposing that the extraordinary powers of the *decemviri* should be confirmed by a *lex curiata.* Cicero knew well enough that there were good constitutional arguments in favour of such a law, and we may be very sure that if Rullus had ignored them they would have been adroitly used against him.

All the clauses of the law so far considered are preliminary to its more properly agrarian provisions. Modern historians have hardly thought these worthy of examination. Cicero took a more serious view of them, though in passing to their consideration he at first professes to find merely *alios immensos et intolerabiles quaestus* concealed under the popular title of an agrarian law (ii, 24, 63). The law provided that out of the immense sums of money in the hands of the *decemviri* they should purchase land in Italy on which a part of the too numerous *plebs urbana* was to be settled in colonies. *Plebem urbanam nimium in republica posse exhauriendam esse.* One would have imagined that Cicero would not have been sorry to see some of what he elsewhere calls the *misera et ieiuna plebecula*, the blood-suckers of the *aerarium*, safely disposed of, especially as he speaks in laudatory terms of the Gracchan scheme. But he can find no precedent for an agrarian law which made use of lands acquired by purchase. *Non esse hanc nobis a maioribus relictam consuetudinem ut emantur agri a privatis quo plebes publice deducatur. Omnibus legibus agris publicis privatos esse deductos* (ii, 25, 65). But with the exception of the Campanian land, to the use of which Cicero is even more opposed than to the purchase scheme, there was no *ager publicus* in Italy left. All that had been in the hands of individual possessors had in one way or another become private property after 111 B.C., and that portion which the law of that year had allowed Italian communities to retain on terms of usufruct, and which is last heard of in the tribuneship of Livius Drusus (App. 1, 35), had certainly been disposed of in the course of Sulla's agrarian arrangements. If, therefore, colonization on a large scale was contemplated, it could only be by a system of purchase, and Cicero's objection on the ground that there was no precedent was simply to ignore the altered agrarian conditions of the time. As a matter of fact, the principle of purchase was from this time accepted in all agrarian arrangements which were not, like those of the second triumvirate, based on robbery and confiscation. It was adopted by Caesar's agrarian law of 59 B.C.; it was again enunciated by the dictator in the settlement of his soldiers after the civil war, and it was the boast of Augustus that all the Italian land on which he settled his veterans was bought and paid for. But it was in the Rullan proposal that this piece of Caesarian policy was first embodied. Cicero, however, is not only opposed to the principle of purchase, but finds in it all sorts of occasions for jobbery and chicanery on the part of the *decemviri.* But all his arguments depend on the assumption that the *decemviri* will be self-seeking rascals, and will therefore behave as such. In answer to Cicero's inquiry as to what particular lands are going to be bought, Rullus reasonably replied that, as there was to be no purchase *ab invito,* it was impossible to say beforehand what lands would come into the market. Only land capable of cultivation would be bought. 'Capable of cultivation' Cicero chooses to interpret as 'not yet cultivated', and the *ne ab invito* provision he takes as an indication that Rullus and his friends have their eyes on certain landowners who will be far from unwilling to part with undesirable land on terms advantageous to themselves but disadvantageous to the State. Two categories of land, he declares, will come into the market, land which is barren and not worth keeping, and land of which the title is not sound, or its original acquisition not creditable. His most effective appeal to the *optimi cives,* who in his letters are the greedy leeches of the treasury, is that they will be giving up their games, their holidays, their corn doles, the money value of their votes, merely to be planted in some barren or pestilential corner of Italy (ii, 27, 71).

Thus the whole scheme is condemned *a priori.* No justification is offered for the outrageous insinuations against the honesty of the commission. They all depend on one fact and one hypothesis, the fact only being relevant if the hypothesis is accepted. The fact is that Valgus, the father-in-law of Rullus, had acquired considerable land in the Sullan times, and was supposed to be anxious to part with it. The hypothesis is that Rullus would be not only one of the *decemviri,* but the leading spirit among them. On the strength of this Cicero is not ashamed to declare that the law has been concocted *non a vestrorum commodorum patrono sed a Valgi genero.*

But was it after all necessary to buy the land owned by Valgus or by any of the other *Sullani homines?* It might very well be the contention of the Marian party and of a Marian tribune that a tenable claim could be made by the State to all the so-called *Sullani agri.* The question indeed as to the legal position of the lands which had changed hands in the course of the Sullan proscriptions, and as to the legal title of their new occupants, was the most difficult agrarian problem of the time, and urgently called for some authoritative solution. It must be remembered that all Sulla's agrarian measures depended for their ultimate validity upon the Lex Valeria, which ratified in advance all his acts. It was this which authorized the confiscation of the lands of many Italian towns, as well as the proscription of individual estates. It was this law again which authorized the sale by auction of much of this public land, and the assignation of other portions of it to his old soldiers. The result of these measures was naturally profound and lasting discontent among many sections of the community, and the *Sullani homines,* whether soldier colonists or purchasers, were objects of hatred to all connected with the dispossessed. Nor was this all. The Lex Valeria was, as even Cicero declared, and as the whole Marian party would certainly agree, a *lex iniquissima et legis dissimillima.* It had been passed without *promulgatio,* and proposed by an *interrex,* whose constitutional function was not to pass laws but to conduct elections. It might therefore be argued that the titles to all these lands were unsound, that the land was still *ager publicus,* and that in the eyes of the law all these *Sullani homines* were no more than *possessores,* liable to be ejected by a new agrarian law. There were other *Sullani homines* whose title was still more unsound. Much of the land made public had remained unsold and unassigned, and had, no doubt with the connivance of Sulla, been simply appropriated by his satellites. These men, therefore, were legally mere *possessores* of public land, although they had for the last twenty years regarded themselves as owners. 'Sunt enim multi agri lege Cornelia publicati nec cuiquam adsignati neque venditi qui a paucis hominibus impudentissime possidentur' (iii, 3, 12). Now it was extremely desirable that the question as to these *Sullani agri* should receive final settlement. Such a settlement was contained in the law of Rullus. Caesar was statesman enough to perceive the only possible solution. Though irresponsible tribunes might talk of a restoration of the Marian exiles, he recognized that it was outside the range of practical politics, and could only lead to economic confusion throughout Italy, to interfere now after twenty years with these *Sullani homines* either with a view of restoration to the original owners, or of saving the State some expense by using the lands for distribution. And in this general settlement it was obviously wise to include the worse titles along with the better. Accordingly—and for once Cicero gives us a complete sentence of the law—clause XL provided: 'qui post Marium et Carbonem consules agri, aedificia, lacus, stagna, loca, possessiones publice data adsignata, vendita, concessa, possessa sunt, ea omnia eo iure sint ut quae optimo iure privata sunt' (iii, 2, 7).

This moderate and on the whole equitable provision puts Cicero in some difficulty, but gives him the opportunity of imputing political inconsistency and corrupt motives to the authors of the bill. He does not venture openly to express the opinion that the *Sullani homines* ought to have been dispossessed, and he would certainly have opposed such a suggestion if Rullus had made it,[1] but he twits the *Marianus tribunus plebis* with political inconsistency intended solely to benefit his father-in-law, and he allows himself to suggest to the *optimi cives* that the *Sullani agri* would have been a useful perquisite for themselves.

It would hardly perhaps be worth while to examine Cicero's criticisms of this clause, unworthy as they are of a serious statesman, were it not that they throw so much light on his methods of political controversy. *Ne ei quidem qui agros publicos possident decedent de possessione, . . . Conversa ratio. Antea, cum erat a tribuno plebis mentio legis agrariae facta, continuo qui agros publicos aut qui possessiones invidiosas tenebant extimescebant; haec lex eos homines fortunis locupletat, invidia liberat* (ii, 26, 68). Previous agrarian laws had been unfavourable to the interests of possessors, this one is not. Therefore, argues Cicero, with

[1] Rullus seems to have represented Cicero as taking up this position: *me gratificantem. . .Sullanarum adsignationum possessoribus agrariae legi et commodis vestris obsistere.* This is certainly not his attitude in the second speech, but Rullus may have referred to some utterances of Cicero while he was still ignorant of the contents of the bill, and suspected an attack on the *Sullani homines*.

an enthusiasm for earlier agrarian laws which he does not always show, and without any regard to the different conditions of the possessors now protected, this is a bad law, and must be due to corrupt motives, though the only trace of these which he can find is the possible case of the unfortunate Valgus. It is on the strength of this that he says: 'you are selling your *vectigalia*, won by the blood and sweat of your ancestors, merely to enrich the Sullan possessors' (ii, 26, 69). In criticizing the wording of the clause, he first suggests that the consulship of Marius and Carbo was taken as the *terminus post quem* in order to disguise the fact that the *Sullani agri* were referred to. But the next year was that of Sulla's dictatorship, and *post Sullae dictaturam* would have cut out the very lands intended by the clause. He then tries to persuade the people—he would hardly have attempted such buffoonery in the Senate—that if these lands were to be *optimo iure privata* they would forthwith be freed from any hypothecations or rates or servitudes to which they were liable.

Before taking leave of this clause, it is necessary to mention one other kind of land the title to which was ambiguous, but would seem to have been safeguarded by it. That the lands in question are not mentioned by Cicero in the course of his speeches is from his later utterances on the subject somewhat surprising. In the year 45 B.C. he wrote to Valerius Orca, one of Caesar's land commissioners, begging him not to interfere with the lands of Volaterrae in Etruria. In a letter written to Atticus at the time of the agrarian proposal of Flavius (*ad Att.* i, 19, 4) it appears that Sulla had confiscated the territory both of Volaterrae and Arretium, but had not made use of them for purposes of distribution. 'Volaterranos et Arretinos quorum agrum Sulla publicaverat neque diviserat in sua possessione retinebam.' The lands were therefore, as confiscated by Sulla's act, *agri publici*, and, as still being allowed to remain with the towns, they were legally *possessiones*, liable at any time to be claimed by the State. A comparison of the phrases *publicaverat neque diviserat* and *publicati nec cuiquam adsignati neque venditi* shows that the legal position of these two territories was exactly that of the *Sullani agri* whose titles were least secure. But it is perfectly clear that Caesar intended by this law to restore full ownership to the towns and so to put an end to a state of uncertainty and suspense. Their case was beyond all doubt covered by cap. XL of the law, and the people of Volaterrae only differed from the *Sullani homines* in being the possessors of land which they had themselves formerly owned, a point which made a difference in equity but not in law.

In view of these conclusions, from which I can see no escape, what are we to make of Cicero's explicit assertion to Valerius Orca in 45 B.C. that he had defended the lands of Volaterrae against the law of Rullus? 'Summo studio populi Romani a me in consulatu meo defensi sunt. Cum enim tribuni plebis legem iniquissimam de eorum agris promulgavissent, facile senatui populoque Romano persuasi, ut eos cives, quibus fortuna pepercissit, salvos esse vellent. Hanc meam actionem C. Caesar primo suo consulato lege agraria comprobavit' (*ad Fam.* xiii, 4). Is Cicero forgetful or disingenuous? or does he confuse the Rullan with the Flavian proposal? Not only is there no word of reference to these lands by name in the extant speeches, but, as we have seen, they are safeguarded by the clause quoted by him. If Cicero really disapproved of this clause, as he wishes the people to believe, the people of Volaterrae might well pray to be saved from their friends, for it was the *lex iniquissima* which defended them, and Cicero who would have prolonged their ambiguous position. Cicero at the date of this letter was living on the memory of his own good deeds, real or imaginary, and as the details of the Rullan law were long since forgotten, was quite safe in making this statement to Orca. What is more striking is that he should have had the effrontery to represent Caesar's action in 69 B.C. as based upon his own. What I think we may safely conclude is that in 59 B.C. Caesar carried into effect, along with other provisions of his own former scheme, this wise acceptance of 'faits accomplis' involved in the confirmation of all ambiguous titles, individual and corporate.

The avowed object of the wholesale purchase of Italian land contemplated in the law was the foundation of colonies. *Scriptum est enim, 'Quae in municipia quasque in colonias decemviri velint, deducant colonos quos velint et eis agros adsignent quibus in locis velint'* (i, 6, 17). Now in all probability Caesar's scheme included colonies of the Gracchan type for the *plebs urbana*, and also colonies of the newer military type for old soldiers. Cicero, however, though plainly aware that colonies of the former kind were contemplated (especially in the passage where he urges his hearers not to give up the pleasures of Rome for life in the country), bases all his arguments against the colonial scheme on the supposition that the colonies will be *praesidia* garrisoned by soldiers and men prepared for violence, sedition, and bloodshed. He gives a false note at once to the discussion by taking colonies in the bygone sense of *propugnacula imperii*, and asking Rullus what suitable strategical sites he had selected (ii, 27, 73). He even suggests that the sites chosen will be those from which pressure might most easily be brought to bear on Rome. The aim of the authors of the law is in his eyes *totam Italiam suis praesidiis obsidere et occupare*; and *vestram libertatem suis praesidiis et coloniis interclusam tenere*. If we add to these expressions a passage in the peroration to the second speech concluding with the words: *ut omnem rempublicam vestris militibus vestris urbibus vestris praesidiis cingeretis*, it will be evident that Cicero saw in the law a scheme for the foundation of military colonies. On what wording of the law he based this belief we do not know, but I cannot believe that he was mistaken. The two points on which he went astray were, first his assumption that these colonies must be instruments of revolution rather than a necessary and useful provision, under present conditions of service, for old soldiers; and secondly his incredulity as to colonies for the *plebs urbana*. It is certain that the carrying out of both kinds of colonies was among the serious and salutary measures of Caesar's dictatorship. In spite of some obscurity, there is reason to believe that his agrarian laws of 59 B.C. were intended both for Pompey's soldiers and for poor citizens who were fathers of three children. Why then, when we find both kinds of colony figuring in this law, admittedly Caesar's and admittedly prepared with care and trouble, should we all blindly follow Cicero, a blind leader indeed where political situations are concerned, and believe that this first agrarian scheme of 63 B.C. meant nothing, or, if anything, revolution? Even politically, apart from other aims which certainly actuated him later, Caesar had much to hope from carrying these schemes. To have the land and the machinery ready for a considerable number of military colonies would give him immense advantages and something very tangible to offer Pompey in the critical negotiations with that powerful general which were bound before long to take place. While to get rid of some of the too powerful *plebs urbana*, devoted as it was to Pompey, would be equally to his advantage.

If I am right in my view that Caesar was serious in his double scheme of colonization, I think we may assume that one part of it was more immediate, and the other more remote. Remembering that the land to be purchased could not be available till after money had been raised in the provinces, and that the veterans, whom Caesar probably had in mind, would not be ready till after Pompey's return, we may perhaps connect these facts and assume that the military colonies would have come later, and would have been mainly on the purchased land. We are of course at a great disadvantage in not having the clauses of the law but only the vague and often misleading diatribes of Cicero, but, as usual we may get something from his own admissions and from a careful reading between the lines. Thus when he complains (ii, 27, 74) that the localities to which colonists are to be sent are not specified, nor the kind of colonists, nor the number for each foundation, he is clearly speaking of the future, not the immediate scheme. How could the localities be specified when the lands were not bought, and the *ne ab invito* proviso made it quite uncertain what would be bought? As to the kind of colonists, if my suggestion about Caesar's motive for making future provision for Pompey's soldiers is correct, he would hardly show his hand by specifying them at present, and I imagine that the *quos velint* was intentionally vague so as to give him a free hand when the time came. The fact too that the number of colonists is not given proves by itself that the colonies were not immediately contemplated, for it was a characteristic of Roman colonies that they were always for a fixed number. On the other hand, there can be no manner of doubt that immediate colonization was contemplated by the law. In this case the locality is specified, the number of colonists fixed, and even certain details of constitution, such as the number of decurions, augurs, and priests determined (ii, 28, 76, and 35, 96). What colonists then were ready for immediate settlement, and what land was available for them?

If Cicero was right in attributing to Rullus or Caesar the

sentiment, *plebem urbanam nimium in republica posse*, this distrust of the people can only be explained by the present popularity of Pompey, and therefore it was politically desirable *sentinam urbis exhaurire* at once before the victorious general's return. As for land, there was still one region of *ager publicus*, which both the Gracchi and Sulla had left untouched, the *ager Campanus* and the adjoining *campus Stellas*. It was proposed by the law that these lands should now be applied to purposes of colonization, five thousand colonists to be sent at once to Capua, there to be settled on the rich territory forfeited after the second Punic war, and others apparently to some of the neighbouring Campanian towns. *Et enim ager Campanus hac lege dividetur . . . et Capuam colonia deducetur* (ii, 28, 76); *nunc omnes urbes quae circum Capuam sunt a colonis . . . occupabuntur* (i, 7, 20).

But though the considerations put forward above would seem to connect the purchased land with future military colonies, and the *ager Campanus* with immediate citizen colonies, Cicero argues against the latter scheme on a different assumption. He is obsessed by the idea, perhaps suggested by Sulla's φρούρια κατὰ τῆς 'Ιταλίας, that 'all Italy' was to be kept down with garrisons and soldiers of the *decemviri*. In accordance with this idea Capua and the other cities are to be colonized by the satellites and *praesidia* of the *decemviri*, by men who are *ad vim prompti, ad seditionem parati . . . armati in cives et expediti in caedem*. We are not here concerned with the historical misrepresentation which ascribes the punishment of Capua to the same motives as that of Corinth and Carthage, or with the futile attempt to stir up obsolete animosities by talking about the *Campana arrogantia* and the danger of an *altera Roma*. It is perfectly clear that in Cicero's eyes the real danger was not in the colonization of Capua or Cumae or Atella, but in the supposed character of the colonists who were to be sent there. I suspect that these ferocious satellites of the *decemviri* existed only in Cicero's imagination. That by the wording of the law itself these lands were intended for the *plebs urbana* is inadvertently admitted by Cicero when he speaks of the *ager Campanus* as *qui vobis ostenditur, aliis comparatur* (ii, 31, 85), while it appears that the colonists were to be taken tribe by tribe, though not in an order which Cicero approved. There is no more solid ground that I can discover for his insinuations as to the desperate character of the Campanian colonists than there was in the equally reckless imputations of corruption and abuse of power in the provinces. Nor is Cicero even honest in his alarm at these new *praesidia* which the distribution of the *ager Campanus* will bring into existence. It appears that, after all, the real motive of these not yet elected *decemviri* is the basest personal greed. They want the rich *ager Campanus* themselves, and these desperate colonists are only to be put in to keep their places warm until, in spite of the clause forbidding sale, they can contrive to buy up the five thousand plots of ten *iugera*. *Nam agrum quidem Campanum quem vobis ostentant ipsi concupiverunt; deducent suos quorum nomine ipsi teneant et fruantur. Coement praeterea*, &c.' (ii, 28, 78). I think we may leave Cicero's two theories as to the destination of the *ager Campanus* to cancel one another. At any rate they cannot both be true, and I can see no reason for believing that either is so. I believe, therefore, that the colonization of the *ager Campanus* was intended by Caesar as a real agrarian reform, and primarily for the benefit of the city proletariate, though not without the hope of political advantage to himself. As a matter of fact, the scheme was actually carried out in 59 B.C. and whether the colonists then were civilians or Pompeian veterans, the political danger of Capua developing into an *altera Roma* was proved wholly chimerical.

Whether the distribution of these Campanian lands, leaving, as it did, to the Roman people *gleba nulla de paternis atque avitis possessionibus*, was justifiable from a financial point of view is perhaps more difficult to decide. They comprised some of the most fertile land in Italy, and were in the hands of tenants, described by Cicero as *aratores* and *milites*, who paid a substantial rack-rent to the State. The Gracchi certainly, and Sulla possibly, had spared them from financial considerations. Cicero states the financial objections very strongly, laying great stress on the certain and unvarying revenue derived from this source. It was all very well to point to the *transmarina vectigalia*, but Asia had paid no *vectigalia* in the Mithridatic war; Spain had produced nothing while Sertorius held out, and Sicily in the slave wars had not had enough corn for itself. *At ex hoc vectigali numquam malus nuntius auditus est*. No doubt it was not one of the best features of Roman finance at this period that it depended more and more exclusively on the provinces, and that the *domestica vectigalia* were one by one relinquished till Cicero can say after 59 B.C. *portoriis sublatis, agro Campano diviso, quid vectigal superest domesticum praeter vicesimam?* It must be admitted too that this loss of the Campanian *vectigalia* might be all the more serious at the present moment, because in the same bill there was involved a good deal of temporary interference with some of the provincial revenues. Still we can hardly help suspecting that Cicero overstates his case. Though rented high the lands were limited in extent and the total receipts must have compared unfavourably, as far as figures went, with other and more precarious sources of revenue. If Cicero's sonorous phrases, *caput vestrae pecuniae, pacis ornamentum, subsidium belli, fundamentum vectigalium, horreum legionum, solacium annonae*, were ever true, it was well over a century earlier, when legions were few, income and expenditure small, and when the crowded city was not yet dependent on foreign corn. At the present time they were ridiculous exaggerations. After all, the real question is—and we cannot answer it—whether the results of the scheme were likely to be worth the money sunk in it. Caesar seems to have thought that they were; for, much to Cicero's disgust, the same scheme formed the substance of his second agrarian law in 59 B.C., and was then carried out. In spite of Cicero's prognostications, there is no evidence that it in any way crippled the financial stability of the State.

With regard to the character and object of the law as a whole, after an examination of all that can be gathered concerning it from a comparison of Cicero's statements with one another, with the probabilities of the case and with known facts, and from a consideration of Caesar's immediate political requirements and his subsequent policy, I am drawn to conclusions very different from those contained in the imaginative peroration to the second speech and in other equally exaggerated passages. The *decemviri* were not to be the reckless and irresponsible gang of Rullus. There is no season to suppose that their judicial powers would have enabled them to declare public or private at will any territories within the empire. They would not be a common danger to all foreign kings, though they might depose the usurper in Egypt, and might come into collision with the King of Cappadocia, in whose country lay some of the domains of Mithridates. They would not have all the free peoples at their mercy, though in imposing a *vectigal* on public lands they might have to readjust the boundaries of free town territories. They were not to 'alienate the *vectigalia*' of the Roman people, though they were empowered to sell certain specified *agri vectigales* in a limited number of provinces. They would not have the supreme control of the *aerarium*, though they would no doubt have the temporary administration of a large and extraordinary fund. In applying this to the purchase of Italian land, there is no indication and little likelihood that they would either use the opportunity to relieve the *Sullani homines* from insecure possessions or would buy undesirable lands at exorbitant prices from their friends or from one another. Lastly, there seems no justification for the suspicion that the *ager Campanus* was either to be the territory of a new and rival capital, held by armed and violent satellites of the *decemviri*, or that it was to find its way into the possession of the leaders themselves.

For all these assertions or insinuations the evidence, if such a term can be used, utterly breaks down. On the other hand, the law, as I understand it, shows unmistakable signs all through of that audacity, disregard of constitutional precedent, contempt of outworn prejudices, of that clear recognition of the end desired and that unscrupulous but dexterous adaptation of means, which characterized Caesar at all stages of his career. So far from containing the mere dreams of madmen, the measure was a singularly cool and adroit piece of statecraft, providing the popular leaders with not one but several 'points d'appui' against the threatened predominance of Pompey, and at the same time containing schemes for the improvement of agrarian conditions in Italy which were in complete harmony with the domestic policy of the popular party.

There can be no doubt that, if the law had been passed, Caesar and Crassus would have been in a very strong position when the time came for Pompey's relations both with the popular party and with the republic to be readjusted. By that time Egypt and its resources would have been practically in their hands, and in all probability a military force have been found necessary in order to complete the annexation. They would also presumably have been in possession already of a very large amount of money. No attempt would of course have been made to interfere with Pompey's settlement of the East, nor is it probable that he, however indignant at the action taken by his political rivals, would have been diverted from this work. Meanwhile in Italy the initiatory steps would probably have been taken to carry out the agrarian scheme by the colonization of Capua and perhaps by the sending of colonists to other Campanian towns. Whether this would have created much enthusiasm in Rome is doubtful, but it might to some extent have dissipated the strength of the *plebs urbana*, and that, as long as Pompey was its idol, would be something gained. With regard to the purchase scheme, though no lands would have been actually bought for some time to come, the prospect of a market and favourable prices would probably have appealed, not as Cicero pretended to believe, to the *Sullani homines*, but to some of those landowners who, having got into debt through excessive speculation supervening on a boom of prosperity, as Mr. Ferrero puts it, saw no way of escape except by sale or *novae tabulae*. Of course a conceivable result of the challenge to Pompey involved in this law would have been civil war, as soon as Pompey's hands were free. But Caesar probably knew Pompey well enough to foresee other more likely contingencies, though if a struggle could not be avoided, the money in the hands of the *decemviri* could easily be diverted from agrarian to military ends. But what was far more likely to happen was negotiation and a coalition. It was to put himself and his followers in a position to conduct these negotiations on at least equal terms that Caesar caused the various provisions of this law to be so adroitly framed. On facing the situation outside his immediate sphere of command, Pompey would have found these provisions more or less in operation. He would almost certainly have seen Egypt on its way to becoming a military base; he would probably have found that the *decemviri* had used their opportunities of securing influence in Macedonia and Achaia. Of course no attempt would have been made to touch the Mithridatic domain lands, but he would have found the men who had decreed their sale, and who had been empowered to dispose of the *vectigalia* from his own annexations, in a very commanding position in

Rome and Italy. Short of entering upon a civil war, how was he to deal with the situation so produced? How was he either to accept arrangements so compromising to his dignity or to counteract them? At such a point Caesar could with great effect have made use of that clause in the law empowering the *decemviri* to settle on the lands still to be purchased in Italy 'any persons they might choose'. To get his veterans safely provided for in this way without having himself to face the task of carrying through an agrarian law would be a strong, if not an irresistible inducement to Pompey to acquiesce in the appropriation of his new *vectigalia*, and the more so, as the arrangement would carry with it of necessity the confirmation of his *acta* during the recent years.

Caesar's aim, therefore, in putting forward this law, involving too many and too distant combinations for Cicero to understand its full meaning, was not wantonly or through mere jealousy to attack Pompey's position, or to rob him of the fruits of his successes, but to compel him by indirect pressure to fall into line once more with the leaders of the popular party. Perhaps some of the powers and actions assigned and allowed to the *decemviri* may seem to have gone beyond this aim, and, as Cicero contended, beyond the necessities of the agrarian scheme, but at any rate they constituted a reserve of force, which it might or might not be necessary to make use of.

The proposal miscarried ignominiously. We can hardly avoid the conclusion that Caesar had calculated to better effect on the results of the law if passed, than on the chances and methods of passing it. Agrarian schemes always needed delicate handling and persuasive authors, and yet this one, unprecedented in several points, involving serious financial innovations and certain to be displeasing to Pompey, he allowed to be put forward by a man of straw, who inspired no confidence and spoke with no authority. It was a course which gave Cicero his greatest oratorical triumph. Whether a somewhat similar mistake later in the year gave him also his greatest political success, is a question which it is not pertinent here to ask or to answer.

As a matter of fact, in spite of the failure of this elaborately contrived scheme, various circumstances, on which Caesar could not possibly have counted beforehand, brought about practically the same situation as that for which the law had been designed to pave the way. Pompey was induced to join in the famous coalition of 59 B.C., and the main inducement was the prospect opened out to him of providing for his soldiers by means of Caesar's agrarian schemes. To secure this end, he was ready enough, as Caesar had foreseen, to fall in with the plan of using the new *vectigalia* for the purpose. The question has often been raised whether Caesar's agrarian laws of 59 B.C. were intended for Pompey's veterans or for poor citizens generally. Later writers declare that fathers of three children were to be preferred. Cicero, when he says that if there was only room for five thousand on the *ager Campanus*, *reliqua omnis multitudo* would be alienated, implies citizen colonies. On the other hand, when we remember the avowed object of the abortive law of Flavius, and Pompey's anxiety to make good his promises to his soldiers, we cannot doubt that they were at least included. Probably the laws were mere repetitions of the Rullan proposals, with this difference, that then the provision for soldiers was more remote, provision for the *plebs urbana* more immediate, while in 59 B.C. the order was reversed. Whether Caesar's first agrarian law, which decreed the purchase of land in Italy for purposes of colonization, was carried out is uncertain. It was soon supplemented by the second law for the distribution of the *ager Campanus*, and on this the activity of the commissioners seems to have been mainly concentrated. In 58 B.C. Pompey is said to have stated in a *contio* that agrarian laws had had to be postponed through the emptiness of the treasury (Dio Cass. 38, 5), and Caesar, trusting to Pompey's *vectigalia*, which would hardly be available at once, had provided no fund of *praesens pecunia*, as he had intended to do by the Rullan law. The full realization of Caesar's agrarian schemes, foreshadowed in 63 B.C. and imperfectly carried out in 59 B.C., was reserved for the dictatorship.

IV

POLITICAL AND LEGAL ASPECTS OF THE TRIAL OF RABIRIUS

CICERO'S speech on behalf of Rabirius must have been delivered within a very few months of his triumphant defeat of the Rullan proposal in January 63 B.C. He alludes in his peroration to the repudiated scheme 'for parcelling out the world in general and the ager Campanus in particular', while he contrasts in almost identical terms the entire absence of danger from abroad with the prevalence of domestic and intestine plots emanating from traitors and revolutionaries (cf. 12, 33 with *de leg. agr.* i, 9, 26). The early months indeed of this year were highly critical, both for the popular party with Caesar and Crassus at its head and for the constitutional or senatorial party and Cicero, who was doing his best to sustain the not easy part of 'consul popularis'. In view of the overwhelming position of Pompey in the East and his impending return, it was essential for Caesar and Crassus both to secure for themselves some locus standi in the empire, and to hold together their followers by the allurement of some kind of popular programme. That Caesar was already looked to by the populares as their real head seems clear, but he was still in an early stage of his cursus honorum, and therefore needed the official and magisterial assistance of others. For the year sixty-three he had, it appears probable, originally counted not only on a college of tribunes mainly devoted to himself, but also on two consuls in the persons of Antonius and Catiline ready to carry through any programme he might dictate. These plans were partly disconcerted by the consular elections in the summer of 64, and instead of having his selected candidates to work with, he found himself confronted by Cicero, who, in whatever sense a 'consul popularis', was known to be at once Pompeian and senatorial in his sympathies. Caesar therefore had to do the best he could with the instruments at his command.

I have already in the preceding Essay (No. III) discussed the policy of the Rullan proposal. I regarded it as an audacious piece of Caesarian legislation, intended as a real and popular agrarian scheme by which colonies, at once for poor citizens and in the future for old soldiers, were to be provided, but at the same time securing for Caesar and his allies a commanding position in many provinces and in Egypt, and by audacious financial innovations establishing a huge fund, primarily for agrarian purposes, but available, if occasion arose, for ulterior ends. But owing to his failure to secure influential magisterial agents, Caesar had entrusted the carrying of this weighty measure to one of his tribunes, a man of no reputation, and whose name commanded no confidence. This, as it turned out, was a grave tactical mistake, and caused the ignominious defeat of the scheme, for it gave Cicero a safe opportunity for two of his most telling accomplishments, unscrupulous misrepresentation and outrageous insinuation, used with perfect impunity against a nonentity like Rullus.

Meanwhile, Caesar still needed a rallying cry to unite the populares against the senatorial government which the new consul was known to favour, and with which it was not impossible that Pompey on his return might ally himself.

The domestic situation in Rome was probably very complicated in this critical year. It can hardly be doubted that, though there was as yet no 'Catilinarian conspiracy', there was a good deal of vague and restless expectation among a certain class in the capital of impending revolutionary changes. This may have been produced or encouraged by incautious and unauthorized expressions let fall by Catiline in his candidature for the consulship about the need for 'novae tabulae' and other drastic measures against the selfish rich. Sallust has no doubt antedated the existence of definite plot, but in the early months of 63 there were indications of coming trouble, clearly alluded to by Cicero in the words 'a turbulentis hominibus atque novarum rerum cupidis ab intestinis malis a domesticis consiliis cavendum est' (*pro Rab.* 12, 33) and as certainly not unknown to Caesar. Whether the candidature of Catiline was still favoured by the latter is uncertain, but Caesar must have realized the probability of serious disturbances in the event of another disappointment. He must have foreseen, too, that to meet them the senate would pass the senatus consultum ultimum, and that Cicero, consul popularis as he might be, would be at least as prepared to carry it into effect as Marius had been to act against Saturninus and his followers in 100 B.C. Cicero indeed made no secret of what he would do. 'Facerem idem quod C. Marius fecit, ad senatum referrem, vos ad rem publicam defendendam cohortarer, armatus ipse vobiscum armato obsisterem' (*pro Rab.* 12, 34).

But to Caesar the possibility of any return on the part of the senate to the methods employed in the tribuneship of Saturninus must have been disquieting. For whatever views he may have held on the constitutional legality of the senatus consultum ultimum, he would be in any case averse to its employment at the present time as likely to increase that influence and prestige of the senate which it was the 'popular' policy to depress. Should disturbances take place later in the year, and should they be suppressed, as those of Saturninus had been, by the senate and consul, the result would be a serious set-back, if not a fatal disaster, to the popular party.

It was in the midst of these embarrassments, caused alike by his recent defeat and the prospect of complications to come, that Caesar hit upon the idea which developed into the much discussed trial of Rabirius for *perduellio*.

Suetonius and Dio Cassius shall give their somewhat meagre statements of what took place. '(Caesar) subornavit etiam qui Caio Rabirio perduellionis diem diceret, quo praecipuo adiutore aliquot ante annos Luci Saturnini tribunatum senatus coercuerat. (*Caes.* 12.) *Τίτος δὲ δὴ Λαβιῆνος Γάιον Ῥαβίριον ἐπὶ τῷ τοῦ Σατουρνίνου φόνῳ γραψάμενος πλεῖστόν σφισι τάραχον παρέσχεν. ὅ τε γὰρ Σατουρνῖνος πρὸ ἓξ που καὶ τριάκοντα ἐτῶν ἐτεθνήκει· καὶ τὰ κατὰ τὸν πόλεμον τὸν πρὸς αὐτὸν οἱ ὕπατοι τότε παρὰ τῆς βουλῆς προσετετάχατο.* (xxxvii. 26.) That the initiative was due to Caesar is carefully kept out of sight throughout Cicero's speech, but is definitely asserted by Suetonius, and is hardly less clearly brought out by the words of Dio, *καὶ ἐπειδὴ τοῦτο διά τε τὸν Καίσαρα καὶ δι' ἄλλους τινάς ἐνίκησε.* It appears from these passages and from statements of Cicero that Rabirius, now an elderly senator of some property and standing, had thirty-seven years before, when a young man and an *eques*, not only joined in suppressing Saturninus, as Suetonius states, but was said actually to have killed him with his own hand. Cicero, like Dio, states this explicitly: 'arguis occisum esse a C. Rabirio L. Saturninum.' (*pro Rab.* 6, 18.) Whatever explanation of his act may be forthcoming, there can be no doubt that it was Caesar's plan of meeting his difficulties to have Rabirius brought to trial for this political murder committed thirty-seven years before. That his object was a political one, and Rabirius a mere man of straw, is of course obvious. It was, I imagine, a double object; to raise a popular cry by vindicting the 'unicum libertatis praesidium', set at naught by the slaughter of Saturninus without trial and without appeal, and at the same time, not indeed to assail the validity of the senatus consultum ultimum itself, but so to expose certain illegalities which had been covered by its supposed sanction, as to discredit a procedure capable of such abuses.

It has usually been held by modern historians that Caesar on this occasion was challenging the legal or constitutional basis of the senatus consultum ultimum, and that it was the standpoint of the popular party all through this period to contest the validity of the senate's action in passing the decree. There seems to me to be no reason whatever either for attributing this attitude to the party, or for finding in Caesar's indictment of Rabirius a covert attack on the legality of the 'last decree'. It is true that Opimius had been brought to trial for killing Roman citizens on the strength of the senate's decree, and Decius, perhaps representing the popular party, had declared that nothing could justify the slaying of a citizen without trial and appeal. But the people had accepted the arguments of Opimius and his advocates, and by their acquittal had legally sanctioned his action, and with it the validity of the senatorial decree. There is every indication that the popular leaders down to the end of the Republic loyally accepted this decision, though regarding this new senatorial prerogative with some suspicion, and insisting that what the people had ratified as the legal sequel to a senatus consultum ultimum was action in strict conformity to that of Opimius. If, therefore, there was a state of war in the city, and riotous citizens with arms in their hands threatened the safety of the state, the senate was justified in passing its decree, bidding the consuls see 'ne quid respublica detrimenti caperet'. The consuls were then justified in 'calling the people to arms', putting themselves at its head, and carrying into effect the state of war. It followed that all riotous citizens who were killed by members of this armed force acting under the consuls' order, lost their lives as overt enemies of the state—*perduelles*—so that neither the Sempronian law requiring trial by the people, nor the Porcian law requiring appeal, was applicable to the case.

In this sense the validity of the senatus consultum ultimum is emphatically asserted by Sallust, who notoriously wrote from the standpoint of the popular party. 'Itaque, quod plerumque in atroci negotio solet, senatus decrevit darent operam consules ne quid respublica detrimenti caperet. Ea potestas per senatum more Romano magistratibus maxima permittitur, exercitum parare, bellum gerere, coercere omnibus modis socios atque cives (i.e. of course those acting as enemies), domi militiaeque imperium atque iudicium summum habere; aliter sine populi iussu nullius earum rerum consuli ius est'. (Sall. *Cat.* 29.)

Still more decisive are two carefully worded pronouncements of Caesar himself. 'Decurritur ad illud extremum atque ultimum senatus consultum quo nisi paene in ipso urbis incendio atque in desperatione omnium salutis et in summa sceleratorum audacia nunquam ante descensum est; dent operam consules praetores tribuni plebis quique pro consulibus sint ad urbem, ne quid respublica detrimenti capiat.' (*Bell. civ.* i, 5.) Again and still more explicitly: 'Quotienscunque sit decretum darent operam magistratus ne quid respublica detrimenti caperet, qua voce et quo senatus consulto populus Romanus ad arma sit vocatus, factum in perniciosis legibus, in vi tribunicia, in secessione populi, templis locisque editioribus occupatis; atque haec superioris aetatis exempla expiata Saturnini atque Gracchorum casibus docet.' (*Bell. civ.* i, 7.) These deliberate utterances were made not more than fourteen or fifteen years after 63; there is no reason whatever to think that Caesar had changed his views, and, if he had not, these passages prove that he did not question either the validity of the senatus consultum ultimum, or the legality of the acts which followed it, provided that there was violence, civil war, and danger to the State, and that any acts of war to avert these dangers were directed by the responsible magistrates. Caesar's words are exactly applicable to the action of Opimius in 121 and of Marius in 100, the justification of which indeed in both cases is expressly admitted.

It seems to me, therefore, quite impossible to maintain that Caesar's political object in instituting this trial was to attack the validity of the senatus consultum ultimum as a means of dealing with revolutionary emergencies. This is, however, undoubtedly the impression which Cicero's speech conveys and was intended to convey to the Roman people. He sounds this note at the very outset. His task is primarily that of a consul, only secondarily that of an advocate, for the real object of the impeachment is not to endanger the life of Rabirius, but 'ut illud summum auxilium maiestatis atque imperi quod nobis a maioribus est traditum de republica tolleretur, ut nihil posthac auctoritas senatus, nihil consulare imperium, nihil consensio bonorum contra pestem ac perniciem civitatis valeret'. (*pro Rab.* 1, 2.) Again: 'agitur enim nihil aliud in hac causa, Quirites, nisi ut sit nullum posthac in republica publicum consilium, nulla bonorum consensio contra improborum furorem et audaciam, nullum extremis reipublicae temporibus perfugium ac praesidium salutis'. (ib. 2, 4.) To the same effect in his peroration: 'Hisce autem malis magnum vobis praesidium maiores vestri reliquerunt, vocem illam consulis "qui rempublicam salvam esse vellent". Huic voci favete, Quirites, neque vestro iudicio abstuleritis mihi . . . neque eripueritis reipublicae spem libertatis, spem salutis, spem dignitatis.' (ib. 12, 33.)

That this view of Caesar's motive should have come to be accepted by historians like Dio Cassius is the natural result of the publication and preservation of Cicero's speech. So we find Dio declaring that as a result of the impeachment *ἡ γερουσία ἄκυρος . . . τῶν ψηφισμάτων ἐγίγνετο*, and that it was highly indignant *ὅτι τὸ πρόσχημα τῆς πολιτείας διεβάλλετο*. I have tried to show in connexion with the agrarian proposal earlier in the year how dangerous it is to accept Cicero's evaluation of political motives and political situations without the most careful criticism. In the present case, I believe that we may find an intelligible motive for Caesar's action without having to attribute to him any change of attitude on the subject of the senatus consultum ultimum.

The charge against Rabirius was that he had killed Saturninus. The fact was denied, and it was even asserted that a slave had long since been rewarded for having done the deed. The point, even if true, is not conclusive, for Saturninus was killed by missiles from above, and Rabirius and the slave may both have hit their mark, though only one claimed the reward. A story retailed by the author of *de vir. illustr.* represents Rabirius as carrying the head of Saturninus about (*de vir. ill.* 73), but after thirty-seven years there was much room for doubt. Cicero is very little concerned with the question of fact. He denies it, but wishes that it were true (*pro Rab.* 6, 18), and in any case all would obviously depend on the exact circumstances of the act. These were differently reported by later writers. The epitomator of Livy (lxix), Velleius (ii, 12), and Dio Cassius (loc. cit.) all speak as if Saturninus was killed in what was virtually open war between him and an armed force commanded by Marius the consul. We shall see too that Cicero's whole case rested on this assumption. This, however, was not the only version of the final act of the drama, but as to the earlier stages there is no dispute. Saturninus and Glaucia with their followers were behaving like public enemies. They had not only murdered Memmius, a candidate for the consulship, but had seized the Capitol with an armed force (*pro Rab.* 6, 20). On this 'fit senatus consultum ut C. Marius L. Valerius consules adhiberent tribunos pl. et praetores, quos eis videretur, operamque darent ut imperium populi Romani maiestasque conservaretur . . . qui rempublicam salvam esse vellent arma capere et se sequi iubent. . . . Arma populo Romano Mario consule distribuente dantur' (ib. 7, 20). Cicero slightly paraphrases the formula to emphasize his point that the consuls were commissioned to save the State, but otherwise his account must be accepted as correct. Among those so armed and led by Marius, including senators and *equites* and indeed all loyal citizens, Rabirius was admittedly one. 'Confiteor interficiendi Saturnini causa C. Rabirium arma cepisse' (ib. 6, 19). More than that, if he had accomplished his object, 'id pulcherrimum facinus esse arbitrarer.' We may at once admit that, on the precedent of Opimius and according to Caesar's own pronouncement, if the

Capitol had been stormed, as it was in A.D. 69, and if in the fighting Rabirius had met and killed Saturninus, Cicero's argument would be final: 'si arma iure sumpta concedis, interfectum iure concedas necesse est.' But the Capitol was not stormed, and Saturninus did not meet his death there at all. Most accounts agree that he was killed in the senate house. Perhaps he escaped there when the water-pipes of the Capitol were cut, and was there attacked and killed by the consul's armed bands. If so, Cicero's argument would still apply. But there was another version as to how Saturninus found himself in the senate house, and how he met his death there. According to Florus, what happened after the seizure of the Capitol was this: 'Sed cum abruptis fistulis obsideretur, senatuique per legatos paenitentiae fidem faceret, ab arce degressus cum ducibus factionis receptus in curiam est. Ibi eum facta inruptione populus fustibus saxisque coopertum in ipsa quoque morte laceravit' (Flor. ii, 4). Appian gives further details. καὶ αὐτοὺς τῆς βουλῆς ἀναιρεθῆναι ψηφισαμένης, ὁ Μάριος ἀχθόμενος ὅμως ὥπλιζέ τινας σὺν ὄκνῳ· καὶ βραδύνοντος ἕτεροι τὸ ὕδωρ ἐπιρρέον ἐς τὸ ἱερὸν διέτεμον. καὶ Σαυφήιος μὲν ἐμπρῆσαι τὸν νεών, ὑπὸ δίψης ἀπολύμενος, ἠξίου, Γλαυκίας δὲ καὶ Ἀπουλήιος ἐλπίσαντες αὐτοῖς ἐπικουρήσειν Μάριον παρέδωκαν ἑαυτούς, οἵδε, πρῶτοι καὶ ἐπ' ἐκείνοις ὁ Σαυφήιος. Μάριος δ', αὐτίκα πάντων αὐτοὺς ἀναιρεῖν κελευόντων, ἐς τὸ βουλευτήριον συνέκλεισεν ὡς ἐννομώτερον ἐργασόμενος. οἳ δὲ πρόφασιν τοῦτ' εἶναι νομίσαντες, τὸν κέραμον ἐξέλυον τοῦ βουλευτηρίου καὶ τοὺς ἀμφὶ τὸν Ἀπουλήιον ἔβαλλον ἕως ἀπέκτειναν, ταμίαν τε καὶ δήμαρχον καὶ στρατηγόν (*Bell. civ.* i, 32).

From these passages it would appear that Saturninus made terms of surrender with Marius, who conducted him under a safe-escort to the *curia*, and guarded him there, intending, according to Appian, to proceed against him in legal form. It was thus while he was an unarmed prisoner in the senate house that the people, and among them Rabirius if he really killed Saturninus, put an end to him with stones and tiles. But if this was the true version, or the version which, true or false, Caesar chose to adopt, the affair bore an entirely different complexion from that put upon it by Cicero, and there is no longer any justification for regarding Caesar's impeachment of Rabirius as a veiled attack on the legality of the senatus consultum ultimum.

In the first place, Saturninus on surrendering and being made prisoner had ceased to be an open *perduellis* in arms against the State, whose safety demanded his instant death. This was recognized by Marius, who set guards to keep the prisoners safe for subsequent trial. In the second place, Rabirius was on this showing not acting under the consul's order at all. On the contrary, he acted against them, eluding the consul's guards, and killing those whom the consul wished to preserve. Such a murder was not authorized by the consul, and was therefore not authorized by the senatus consultum which alone gave him his mandate. It was, in fact, a political assassination committed by an irresponsible individual in defiance of the wishes, orders, and precautions of the consul.

It may be argued that this version, being found only in these late writers, deserves no serious attention. I notice, however, that scholars who are most emphatic in styling Appian a third-rate compiler are ready enough to support their own theories by the most casual expressions found in this contemptible source. But in the present case we have the inadvertent evidence of Cicero himself, not of course for the truth of the story, but for its existence at the time, and its adoption by the prosecution. It is one of our obvious disadvantages that, while we have the main speech for the defence, we have no statement of the case for the prosecution. It is perfectly obvious that the point whether a guarantee of safety was or was not given to Saturninus by the consul was crucial to the case, and must have had a prominent place in the speeches of Labienus. It has no such prominent place in Cicero's defence because it was an awkward point, and because an elaborate *ignoratio elenchi* was the best means of meeting it. But it could not be wholly passed over, and therefore after the sonorous but irrelevant question, 'if Rabirius deserves the cross and the executioner, what does the consul deserve under whose orders he acted?' he makes his sole reference to the point. 'Ac si fides Saturnino data est, quod abs te saepissime dicitur, non eam C. Rabirius sed C. Marius dedit, idemque violavit, si in fide non stetit. Quae fides, Labiene, qui potuit sine senatus consulto dari?' (*pro Rab.* 10, 28). It appears therefore from the words 'quod abs te saepissime dicitur' that this point about the guarantee, only intelligible on the version of Appian and Florus, was persistently urged by Labienus. Cicero has two replies to it, both as illogical as they were audacious. (1) A guarantee given by Marius did not bind Rabirius. (2) Marius had no right to give the guarantee without a special decree of the senate. But if Rabirius was not bound by the consul's decision, what becomes of Cicero's reiterated argument that Rabirius should have been safe from attack just because, like all good men, he had joined the consuls, had received his arms from the hands of Marius, had not refused 'voci atque imperio consulum oboedire', had been among those 'qui consulari imperio paruerunt', and had acted on the conviction that 'virtus et honestas et pudor cum consulibus esse cogebat'? It seems there was a fourth alternative besides the three laid down by Cicero of doing nothing, or joining Saturninus, or following the consuls. There was the course of irresponsible lynching, and that, according to Labienus and Caesar, was the course which Rabirius took. Again, if Marius had no right to give the guarantee without a senatorial decree, Cicero commits himself to the hopeless paradox that the senatus consultum ultimum, while it authorized the consul to kill armed enemies, did not authorize him to abstain from killing men who were no longer armed enemies. No wonder that the orator hastened from the point to a disquisition on the immortality of great men (ib. 10, 29). It is to be hoped that Labienus had made his points with sufficient clearness to expose beforehand the irrelevant sophisms with which Cicero met the alleged facts. 'If you admit that Rabirius had the right to take up arms, you must admit that he had the right to kill Saturninus' (ib. 6, 19). 'If Rabirius has committed a capital crime in taking up arms against Saturninus, what is to be said of all those noble patriots who did the same, and could not be, as he might have been, excused on the score of youth?' (ib. 9, 26). 'If a cross is to be set up in the Campus for Rabirius because he took up arms, what punishment can be devised for the consul who called him to arms?' (ib. 10, 29). 'There is not a loyal citizen in Rome to-day, who is not in the name of Rabirius the subject of a capital charge' (ib. 11, 31). These arguments are in Cicero's best style, but they dishonestly ignore the fact that, according to the prosecution, Rabirius had not been one of the loyal citizens obeying the consul, but one of the irresponsible crowd which had defied his orders.

It was the circulation of this story about Rabirius, whether true or false, which, after the defeat of the Rullan scheme, suggested to Caesar his next move. Here was a case of political murder (the victim having been not only a Roman citizen but a tribune of the plebs) which had remained unnoticed and unpunished for thirty-seven years, during which the reputed murderer had acquired wealth and position. The murder was not exactly a violation of the lex Porcia, for it had not been punishment inflicted by a magistrate; but, on the other hand, it had not been sanctioned by the senatus consultum ultimum, for the victim was a prisoner at the time of his death, being guarded by the consul with a view to future trial. It therefore made no difference that the murdered tribune had been an armed enemy of the State, for he had been disarmed and rendered harmless, and could have been dealt with according to due forms of law. Both the nature of the crime and the long impunity of the criminal demanded from the popular party some extraordinary vindication of the law. Besides, the possibility of such a crime as that of Rabirius suggested grave reflections. It was not the direct result of the extreme senatorial decree, that indeed would have been its sole justification, but it nevertheless could hardly have happened unless that decree had been passed. Without assailing the validity of the method adopted in critical emergencies by the senate, it was essential to the interests of the popular party that two things should be made quite clear. (1) On the sole legally established precedent only armed and active enemies could be killed by the consul and his band. This had not been contravened in 100, but it would have been if Marius after imprisoning Saturninus had executed him, and it might be contravened in future. (2) If the legitimate 'consensio bonorum' degenerated into irresponsible lynching, the government must be held responsible at least to the extent of being bound to see that such incidental effects of their own decree did not go unpunished. Otherwise, under the vague aegis of the last decree all sorts of illegal and riotous acts might creep in. This is how in my opinion the political object of this famous trial may be expressed. It was calculated to rally the popular party round the 'unicum libertatis praesidium'; it threw some slur on the senatorial government which had allowed thirty-seven years' impunity to a lawless and inexcusable murder, and it sounded a significant note of warning, clearly not lost upon Cicero, against careless application of martial law by senate or consuls, or failure to punish regrettable or illegal incidents.

It must be admitted that this idea of rallying his party by a political impeachment, though not without signs of Caesar's characteristic adroitness and resource, was a little far-fetched and *en faute de mieux*. But the legal methods by which the impeachment was to be carried through were still more open to criticism. There was perhaps something, in the exceptional circumstances of the case, to be said for resorting to an impeachment for *perduellio* rather than to an ordinary accusation in the *quaestio de vi* or *de sicariis*. (The distinction is marked by Dio cap. 27: οὐ γὰρ ἁπλῶς, ἀλλὰ τὸ δὴ λεγόμενον περδουελλίωνος ὁ Ῥαβίριος ἐκρίθη.) It is true that such a procedure was something of a survival, but it was still legal and subject to fixed and well-known regulations. But it was not the historical process of *perduellio* which Caesar determined to adopt. He wished to make a more striking and impressive appeal to the popular imagination. It was with this view that the fantastic idea shaped itself of reviving for the occasion the barbarous and obsolete procedure ascribed by tradition to the famous trial of Horatius under the kings. The king had appointed *duumviri perduellionis* to pass sentence in his stead in the words, 'iudico tibi perduellionem'. From this there was an appeal to the people, before whom a *certatio* followed between the condemned and the *duumviri*. If the latter won, the formula prescribed: 'caput obnubito; infelici arbori reste suspendito'. I have argued elsewhere that there is no evidence and as little probability that the *duumviri* or the *carnifex* or the *arbor infelix* ever figured again in trials for *perduellio*. The barbarous and realistic exhibition had given place under the Republic to a tribunician prosecution in three stages, followed in case of condemnation by an appeal to the comitia centuriata after twenty-four days' interval. If this normal course had been adopted, there would have been no room for senatorial opposition, and no need for action by the people. The tribune would simply have fixed a day (diem dicere) for Rabirius to appear before his tribunal. Suetonius supposes that Labienus did this, but the other authorities prove that he is wrong (loc. cit. 'qui C. Rabirio perduellionis diem diceret'). But for the Horatian procedure there was no constitutional machinery in existence, and nothing could be done without legislation.

The agent employed by Caesar, who no doubt as in the agrarian proposal remained in the background, was T. Labienus, one of the tribunes. He was possibly selected because an uncle of his had lost his life with Saturninus in the *curia*. On the promulgation of the scheme there was much consternation and confusion, *σπουδαὶ ταραχώδεις καὶ φιλονεικίαι*. The popular and anti-senatorial motive was apparent: *οἱ δήμαρχοι τήν τε ἰσχὺν καὶ τὴν ἀξίωσιν τῆς βουλῆς καταλῦσαι παντελῶς ἐσπούδαζον καὶ ἐξουσίαν ἑαυτοῖς τοῦ πάνθ' ὅσα βούλοιντο ποιεῖν προπαρεσκεύαζον* (Dio Cass. xxxvii, 26). It was almost certainly represented from the first as a thinly veiled attack upon the senatus consultum ultimum, so that *πᾶς ὁ κόσμος τῆς πολιτείας ἐταράττετο*. We are told by Dio Cassius, in a passage far from clear (cap. 27), that there were two great contests, first *περὶ τοῦ δικαστηρίου*, i.e. whether it should be established or not, and, when that point was won by Caesar and his friends, secondly *περὶ τῆς κρίσεως*.

The first struggle centred round the law which was necessary to bring the duumviral procedure into existence. In the Horatian trial all had rested on the fiat of the king; it now had to emanate from the sovereign people. Accordingly Labienus must have promulgated a bill, providing for the appointment of *duumviri perduellionis*, prescribing the form of sentence to be pronounced, and specifying the gruesome punishment in rigid accordance with the 'horrendum carmen' handed down from the barbarous legend of kingly days. Cicero's allusions to the action of Labienus seem to leave no room for doubt on this point. 'Quam ob rem uter nostrum, Labiene, popularis est, tune qui civibus Romanis in contione ipsa carnificem ... adhibere putas oportere, qui in campo Martio comitiis centuriatis auspicato in loco crucem ad civium supplicium defigi . . . iubes etc.' (*pro Rab.* 4, 11). 'Tu, homo lenis ac popularis, libentissime commemoras: CAPUT OBNUBITO; ARBORI INFELICI SUSPENDITO; quae verba, Quirites, iam pridem . . . luce libertatis oppressa sunt' (ib. 4, 13). So, contrasting the method of C. Gracchus in impeaching Popilius with that of Labienus: 'Sed moreretur prius acerbissima morte miliens C. Gracchus quam in eius contione carnifex consisteret' (ib. 4, 15).

'Si C. Rabirio quod iit ad arma crucem T. Labienus in campo Martio defigendam putavit etc.' (ib. 10, 28). I could quote other passages, but these are surely enough to prove that the trial was to be in every detail a replica of the Horatian. That this extraordinary court was brought into existence by Labienus is clear both from passages already quoted and from such an expression as the following: 'accusatio perniciosa, iudicium acerbum, res tota a tribuno pl. suscepta contra rempublicam' (ib. 12, 35). As tribune, he could only have done it by legislation, and it was during the *contiones* between the promulgation and passing of the law that the violent contests περὶ τοῦ δικαστηρίου took place. I understand that the carnifex and crux said by Cicero to have been brought into his *contio* by Labienus did not appear there in flesh and blood or wood and iron, but only figured in his speeches as having a place in his law. Whether after the sentence of the *duumviri* a cross was actually set up in the campus Martius is another matter which I may notice below.

Among the contents of the law must have been the appointment of, and mandate given to, the *duumviri perduellionis.* Their title is not mentioned by Suetonius nor by Dio, though the latter speaks of the two Caesars as judges. Cicero, however, in a passage soon to be quoted, distinctly does so (ib. 3, 12). Dio speaks of them as μὴ πρὸς τοῦ δήμου, κατὰ τὰ πάτρια, ἀλλὰ πρός αὐτοῦ τοῦ στρατηγοῦ, οὐκ ἐξὸν, αἱρεθέντες. Suetonius speaks of Caesar as 'iudex in reum sorte ductus'. It has been inferred from this, and I have nothing better to suggest, that the praetor urbanus selected a certain number from categories not to be specified, and that from these two were appointed by lot. (One suggestion is that the lot simply decided which of the *duumviri* should pass sentence, but the words 'iudex in reum' are against this.) Whether the lot which fell upon C. and L. Caesar was tampered with must remain uncertain, but I prefer to think that Caesar would have chosen to remain in the background, and that his selection was pure bad luck. Dio's statement that the proper mode of appointment was popular election has no value whatever. There is absolutely no evidence that *duumviri perduellionis* had ever been called into existence under the Republic, and everything points to their being employed now as mere constituents of the legendary model.

As to their mandate, I have no doubt whatever. They were not to try the case, but to pass the gruesome and awe-inspiring sentence. This was clearly all that the archetypal *duumviri* had had to do in the case of Horatius. It also explains, what Suetonius did not understand, the apparent haste of Caesar's condemnation. But what Cicero says of Labienus places the matter beyond a doubt: 'hic popularis a IIviris iniussu vestro non iudicari de cive Romano sed indicta causa civem Romanum capitis condemnari coegit' (ib. 4, 12). The phrases—non iudicari sed condemnari—indicta causa—coegit—are surely as conclusive as words can make anything. As a matter of fact, the duumviral *iudicium* was merely intended as a means to render possible the solemn decision of the comitia centuriata. There must have been a special clause in the law providing for *provocatio*, for otherwise an extraordinary court set up by the people would place in abeyance the operation of the *leges Valeriae*.

This then was the struggle περὶ τοῦ δικαστηρίου, τῶν μὲν ὅπως μὴ συναχθῇ, τῶν δὲ ἵνα καθιζήσῃ δικαιούντων, which was concluded in favour of the tribune διά τε τὸν Καίσαρα καὶ δι' ἄλλους τινάς (Dio Cass. xxxvii, 27). The *duumviri*, having been constituted, would naturally lose no time in performing their allotted task. Suetonius says that Caesar 'tam cupide condemnavit ut ad populum provocanti nihil aeque ac iudicis acerbitas profuerit'. Cicero emphatically declares that the condemnation was compulsory and 'indicta causa'. The sentence was in the formula: 'iudico tibi, C. Rabiri, perduellionem'. What this meant had been foreshadowed in the wording of the law, taken, as Cicero proves, from the 'horrendum carmen' of the archetypal trial. It seems to me not improbable that, when the sentence was pronounced, Labienus may have caused the *crux* or *arbor infelix* to be actually erected on the campus Martius in preparation for the final hearing before the people. Whatever might be the outcome of that hearing, this would have the effect, presumably aimed at by Caesar, of impressing the popular imagination by these relics of obsolete barbarity. No doubt the words 'crucem in campo Martio defigendam putavit' may signify no more than an intention, but I am inclined to refer them to a perpetrated outrage.

It is at this point, as I believe, that we reach the second struggle in the case, marked by Dio's words περί τε τῆς κρίσεως αὖθις συνέβησαν. Dio does not himself explain the nature of this struggle, and seems to imply that the dispute concerned the mode in which the *duumviri* had been appointed, but more light is thrown upon it by Cicero. It had seemed a happy idea to disinter an obsolete procedure with its impressive but inhuman punishments, whereby to safeguard the primary rights of Roman citizens. But it proved to be an error of judgement. Such methods were contrary to the spirit of the free Republic; they were a violation, if not of statute law, at least of long-established *mos maiorum*. If a crime was so heinous as to fall under the head of 'perduellio', a recognized legal procedure had grown up, in which no extraordinary officials were required, and in which a capital sentence, never likely to be carried out, was decently veiled in the formula of 'aquae et igni interdictio'. It might well be represented as a strange and dubious policy for a 'popular' tribune acting for a 'popular' party, to derive his legal precedents from the cruel and hated age of kingly rule.

It was just the situation which gave Cicero the chance of posing for a moment as a 'consul popularis'. The actual course which he took, though several times alluded to and gloried in, is never clearly stated in his extant speech. In some way and in some sense he cancelled or quashed the 'perduellionis iudicium', and his action was bitterly complained of by Labienus. 'Nam de perduellionis iudicio, quod a me sublatum esse criminari soles, . . . utinam, Quirites, ego id aut primus aut solus ex hac republica sustulissem. . . . Quid enim optari potest quod ego mallem quam me in consulatu meo carnificem de foro, crucem de campo sustulisse?' (*pro Rab.* 3, 10). He explains that his agency was secondary to that of the *mos maiorum*, which since the expulsion of the kings had tolerated 'nullum in libero populo vestigium crudelitatis regiae', and to that of previous statesmen, who had substituted equitable laws for barbarous penalties. In another passage he is more ready to take the credit to himself: 'quam ob rem fateor atque etiam, Labiene, profiteor et prae me fero te ex illa crudeli, importuna, non tribunicia actione sed regia meo consilio, virtute, auctoritate esse depulsum' (ib. 5, 17).

These statements can only mean that the whole machinery, based upon this antiquated precedent, which Caesar and Labienus had contrived, was somehow rendered null and void by Cicero's intervention. This intervention is connected by some scholars with Dio's first struggle περὶ τοῦ δικαστηρίου and Cicero is thought simply to have pruned away from the bill of Labienus all traces of the 'carmen horrendum', and to have substituted for the grisly death on the 'arbor infelix' the ordinary capital sentence of 'aquae et igni interdictio'. It seems to me impossible to accept this view. Such a change in the law would have at the outset so completely baulked Caesar's object, if that object was what I have suggested, that he would have caused the bill to be withdrawn. There was nothing impressive or awe-inspiring in the appointment of *duumviri* or in listening to the ordinary sentence which would be now all that they could pass. And yet nothing but this would have been left, if Cicero had brought about the supposed excision. It would have been simpler and even more impressive to fall back on the usual tribunician impeachment. The *duumviri* were only important as having figured in the ancient trial, and if the kernel of that trial was extracted, it was futile to keep the shell. But, as we know, from both Suetonius and Dio, the law was proceeded with, the *duumviri* were appointed and passed their sentence.

I argue therefore from the probabilities of the case, as well as from the phrase itself, 'perduellionis iudicium sublatum', that Cicero's intervention followed rather than preceded the duumviral trial and sentence, and that both were rendered by it invalid, null and void, legally extinct.

Now the grounds on which Cicero based his intervention, his official intervention as consul, may be gathered from his own words, and the method by which it was brought about is also, I think, to be inferred from statements made by himself. The methods of the duumviral trial were 'non solum tenebris vetustatis verum etiam luce libertatis oppressa' (4, 14). They had 'nullam partem aequitatis aut iuris' (ib.). They were 'non ex memoria vestra ac patrum vestrorum, sed ex annalium monumentis atque ex regum commentariis conquisita' (5, 15). They were things of which 'mentio ipsa indigna cive Romano et homine libero est' (5, 16). Lastly, they prove neglect of 'omnia exempla maiorum, omnes leges, omnem auctoritatem senatus, omnes religiones atque auspiciorum publica iura' (5, 17). Making therefore every allowance for rhetorical expressions, we can hardly doubt that the law on which *perduellionis iudicium* had depended was contrary to the whole spirit of Roman legislation, and in a sense of the Roman religion. If so, it was Cicero's 'consulare officium' to protect the Republic against such an outrage. There was only one way of doing this, and that was through the intervention of the senate. We know from several undisputed examples that when laws were passed 'per vim' or 'contra auspicia', or in any way which constituted them 'vitiosae', the senate, whether its action was *de facto* or *de iure*, was in the habit of passing a decree, 'populum Romanum ea lege non teneri.' This had been done in the case of the Apuleian laws in 100, and of the Livian laws in 91 B.C., on which occasions, in Cicero's words, these laws were cancelled and became null and void 'uno versiculo senatus'. I have argued elsewhere that the same course was taken by the consul Marcellus in 51 B.C. with regard to the lex Vatinia, by which Caesar had established a colony at Comum. This power was obviously a useful adjunct of senatorial government, and was, I suspect, when the circumstances were favourable, not unfrequently employed. That the cancelling of the duumviral trial—perduellionis iudicium sublatum—was due to the senate's action on Cicero's initiative is, I think, made in the highest degree probable by what Cicero says a year or two later in his speech against Piso: 'ego in Rabirio perduellionis reo interpositam senatus auctoritatem sustinui contra invidiam atque defendi' (*in Pison.* 2, 4).

I may notice a possible objection to the view that Labienus established the duumviral court by a law, derived from the words 'iniussu vestro' in the passage 4, 12 quoted above. Cicero is contrasting Labienus with C. Gracchus. The latter had prohibited any capital *iudicium*, which was not created by law (iniussu vestro). Labienus is responsible for the compulsory condemnation of a Roman citizen, without a trial and 'iniussu vestro'. How 'iniussu vestro', if a law was passed? The phrase is only a difficulty if it qualifies 'coegit'. It seems to me from its position after 'a duumviris' to qualify 'condemnari'. A tribune in his *contio* would never condemn without some sign of approval from the assembled people, but the *duumviri* had condemned mechanically with no such approval, 'iniussu vestro'. I am not sure that another explanation might not serve, though I prefer the foregoing. After the law had been cancelled Cicero might speak as if there had never been proper legal authorization, and 'iniussu vestro' might be 'by a law which was no law'.

I assume therefore that everything accomplished by the law of Labienus was undone; the procedure was illegal and the sentence invalid. Rabirius had no doubt appealed, as Suetonius and Dio knew, but the appeal would lapse like everything else, and the trial before the comitia centuriata described by Dio was not on an appeal from the *duumviri*. For the moment, indeed, Cicero and the senate had caused the defeat of Caesar's whole elaborate plan. How it would have ended otherwise, it is perhaps idle to speculate, but it is difficult to believe that the barbarous spectacle on the *Campus* would ever have been witnessed.

But at any rate this was not destined to be the conclusion of the incident. It is perfectly clear from what Cicero says about certain imputations made by Labienus against Rabirius, several of which were contained 'in eadem multae inrogatione' (3, 8), that Rabirius was, or had been, on his trial on charges for which a fine, probably a heavy one, was the threatened penalty. The phrase 'multae inrogatio' was far too technical to be used in any but its strict and literal sense. Such charges, like capital charges, would be heard three times by the prosecuting tribune before a *contio*, and after the third hearing, if he condemned—multam inrogavit—and if the fine exceeded a certain amount, appeal was allowed to the comitia tributa. Probably at the commencement of the affair, and while the 'perduellionis iudicium' was being contrived, Labienus summoned Rabirius to appear before him in the forum on a specified day—diem dixit. The tribune may have owed Rabirius a grudge on account of the death of his uncle, who had perished with Saturninus. But his accusation on these minor charges was as likely as not part of Caesar's plan, since they might increase the accused's unpopularity, and so render more certain his final condemnation on the capital charge. It is impossible from Cicero's vague statements to specify the counts comprised under this 'multae inrogatio'. I doubt if they were as numerous as is sometimes contended. Cicero is complaining that the half-hour allowed him by Labienus is too long for an advocate to answer the minor charges, but too short for a consul to deal with the main point. He then mentions as unworthy of any answer a number of imputations on Rabirius which Labienus had clearly made in the course of his accusation (2, 7 to 3, 9). But most of these were merely old charges, raked up to create a prejudice against the accused, not counts in the present indictment. On one charge Rabirius had actually been tried and acquitted; on another a relative of Rabirius had been acquitted, and Rabirius himself not accused at all. Nor could the murder of his nephew have possibly been part of a mere fine-process. Cicero is not interested in repelling any of these charges, because, as we shall see, they had practically dropped out of the case before he made his speech. As for the charge 'de civibus Romanis contra legem Porciam verberatis aut necatis', it could not possibly, as a capital offence, have been visited by a fine, and was probably mere rumour, brought up by Labienus to reinforce his capital charge. As far as I can see, only two counts in the 'multae inrogatio' remain: a violation of the lex Fabia de plagiariis, and a charge of scandalous immorality. That the latter was the foremost count may be inferred from the words 'quod est in eadem multae inrogatione praescriptum'. (I follow Prof. A. C. Clark in reading *praescriptum* rather than *perscriptum*.)

But it was open to a tribune in the course of his three hearings in the forum to convert, if he thought the evidence required it, what had begun as a fine-process into a capital impeachment. Among the earlier cases the one most in point is that of Fulvius, in which, according to Livy, 'cum tribunus bis pecuniae anquisisset, tertio capitis anquirere diceret.' (Liv. xxvi, 3.) If we assume that this is what took place in the present case, it seems to me that we can assign a consistent and intelligible place to the 'multae inrogatio' within the whole process, and that it thus becomes possible to regard the proceeding, when once the interlude of the duumviral farce was excised by senatorial decree as invalid, as in complete accord with established precedent.

Labienus therefore had either already issued the summons for, or had actually begun an accusation against, Rabirius in the form of a fine-process in the forum at the time when by the action of Cicero and the senate the 'perduellionis iudicium' on the model of the Horatian archetype was quashed out of existence. The defeat was mortifying, but it was not fatal, for Labienus at once received instructions to convert his prosecution into a normal tribunician impeachment for *perduellio*, and on these new lines the case proceeded, as with better counsels it might have begun. Whether the change was made at the first or second or even at the third 'anquisitio' there is nothing to show, but I imagine that it may have been marked by the introduction into the tribune's *contio* of the portrait of Saturninus, a fact alluded to by Cicero in the words: 'nunquam profecto istam imaginem . . . in rostra atque in contionem attulisses.'[1] There was nothing of course which could be constitutionally objected to in the course that was now being taken, for the capital penalty was not being illegally added to the pecuniary, but substituted for it. It might well, however, be described as a hardship and calamity for Rabirius after all these years to go through the ignominy of trials in the forum—publica iudicia—and to be threatened first with financial ruin and then with a capital sentence. That is how I interpret the following passage: 'misera est ignominia iudiciorum publicorum, misera multatio bonorum, miserum exilium; sed tamen in omni calamitate retinetur aliquod vestigium libertatis' (5, 16). Even if the sentence must be a death sentence, at least there will be now no *crux* and no *carnifex*.

There are two inferences which in my opinion it is impossible not to draw from Cicero's speech. The first has been already sufficiently enunciated, viz. that all danger of execution on the cross was a thing of the past. The second inference is not less clear, that at the time when the speech was delivered Rabirius was still the defendant in a capital trial, still theoretically, if not practically, in danger of his life. I do not press the title of the speech, *Pro Rabirio perduellionis reo*, for that may have been affixed later, but there is internal evidence which cannot be got over. At the very outset Cicero thinks it necessary to explain his own position, 'in hac defensione capitis, famae, fortunarumque

[1] 9, 25. Where the crux and carnifex are spoken of as present in the contio, I understand the expression figuratively, and refer it to the contio in which the law to set up the duumviral court was promulgated. But it is clear that the portrait was actually produced before the people, and I have no doubt that it was during the trial. Cicero's references are all so vague that it is difficult to nail them down.

omnium C. Rabiri' (1, 1). Again, it is 'vita C. Rabiri' as well as 'salus reipublicae' which is at stake (2, 5). After showing how many good men now dead had obeyed the call of the consul in 100, 'quot ex his qui vivunt' he asks 'eodem crimine in summum periculum capitis arcessas?' (9, 26). Similarly, all loyal citizens 'abs te capitis C. Rabiri nomine citantur' (11, 31). These passages, of which the implication is unmistakable, are by no means weakened in the peroration, which has been strangely adduced by some scholars as an argument against the capital nature of the case. 'Neque a vobis iam bene vivendi sed honeste moriendi facultatem petit, neque tam ut domo sua fruatur, quam ne patrio sepulcro privetur laborat .... Nihil aliud iam vos orat atque obsecrat nisi uti ... eum ... in patria mori patiamini' (13, 37). But this is the 'miserum exilium' of 5, 16 over again, and that *exilium*, which Cicero declares was never by Roman law a punishment, but always 'supplicii perfugium', would be the result of a capital sentence. There were circumstances of course in which a heavy fine might drive a man into exile, but this was not the punishment of which exile was the recognized 'perfugium', and, taken with the passages previously cited, Cicero's concluding words help to establish the point that Rabirius was 'perduellionis reus' when Cicero's speech was delivered.

The case therefore in the later stages of the trial in the forum before Labienus resolved itself into an impeachment of Rabirius for the political murder of Saturninus. We must assume that witnesses were produced on both sides as to the question of fact, for, though Cicero himself makes little of it, it appears that Hortensius, who probably defended Rabirius in the forum, had 'multorum testimoniis' disproved the fact of the murder by the accused (6, 18). There may have been and probably was counter-evidence, and, as already pointed out, the reward given to a slave for the deed was not conclusive. It was indeed this conflict of evidence about the facts which had made the duumviral trial with its 'indicta causa' and compulsory condemnation such a scandalous violation of legal forms. In the case of Horatius the facts had been undisputed, and Caesar had either overlooked this essential point of difference, or had chosen to regard the murder as a matter of common knowledge. But it is obvious enough that the prosecution no more than the defence restricted itself to the strictly legal issues. Labienus was playing the part of 'tribunus popularis', and talked vaguely of liberty and the Porcian law. He even seems to have compared his own action to that of C. Gracchus in calling Popilius to account. We may be thankful to him for this, since it was in pointing the contrast between the true and false 'popularis' that Cicero tells us all we know of the *lex Sempronia de capite civium*.

At the conclusion of the third hearing Rabirius must have been condemned by Labienus, and would of course appeal, or be understood to appeal, to a *iudicium populi* in the form of the comitia centuriata. Both Suetonius and Dio know of the *provocatio*, but they both represent it as an appeal from the duumviral sentence, and Dio goes straight from the appeal to the final incident in the Campus Martius. We should not look for all the steps of this complicated case from either author, and I cannot regard the considerable gap left in the story by Dio as a serious objection to my theory of the case. The decision therefore came in the end before the comitia centuriata in the Campus Martius, but on appeal not from the duumviral sentence, but from that of Labienus. Rabirius might of course have saved himself, as so many had done before him, by voluntary exile, but Cicero no doubt had good hopes of a favourable result, and persuaded him to stand his ground. When the day came, Cicero delivered the speech which we possess. That it was delivered at the final stage and on the day when the votes of the people were to decide the fate of Rabirius, is an irresistible inference from the internal evidence of the speech itself. At the very outset and in the same sentence in which he emphasizes the capital nature of the charge, he calls upon his hearers 'ad absolvendum', a meaningless appeal unless a vote was to be given (1, 1). Soon after he declares that a greater or more critical matter has never been 'ad populum Romanum delatam' (2, 4), an unmistakable reference to a 'iudicium populi'. Before long, he prays the immortal gods 'ut hodiernum diem et ad huius salutem conservandam et ad rempublicam constituendam inluxisse patiantur' (2, 5), where the day on which he was speaking is beyond a doubt the final day of the whole proceedings. If more proof is needed, we get it in two decisive passages, both implying that it was by their actual votes, and by no less direct means, that the people were to save both Rabirius and the State: 'vita C. Rabiri . . . salus reipublicae vestris manibus suffragiisque permittitur' (2, 5): and 'non vos ad arma vocandos esse verum ad suffragia cohortandos . . . putavi' (12, 35). Yet another passage, as I interpret it, refers to the country voters, who rightly or wrongly were believed by Cicero to have come in to vote for Rabirius. What need to answer charges of cruelty in Apulia or Campania 'cum ad eius propulsandum periculum non modo homines sed prope regiones ipsae convenerint'? (2, 8). These passages are of course in themselves compatible with the view that the *iudicium populi* before which Cicero was assuredly speaking was the comitia tributa assembled to give its final decision on the *multae inrogatio* of Labienus. But apart from the overwhelming difficulty of finding a place for this supposed secondary *iudicium populi* either before or after the meeting of the centuries attested by Dio, the indications, already dealt with, that Cicero was speaking on a capital charge, are too strong to admit of this hypothesis. Nor is it conceivable that Cicero would have delivered his decisive speech on what, if we separate the *multae inrogatio* from the charge of *perduellio*, was a minor and subsidiary issue. I know of only one passage which can be interpreted so as to suggest that the proceedings against Rabirius had not reached their final stage. It is where Cicero concludes a vehement attack on the outrageous character of the duumviral court with the words 'liberum tempus nobis dabitur ad istam disceptationem' (5, 17). What does he mean by 'istam disceptationem'? Only a few sentences before had come the passage, already quoted, in which Cicero declares that by his means Labienus had been driven 'ex illa crudeli, importuna, non tribunicia actione sed regia'. He proceeds: 'Qua tu in actione quamquam omnia exempla maiorum, omnes leges, omnem auctoritatem senatus, omnes religiones atque auspiciorum publica iura neglexisti, tamen a me haec in hoc tam exiguo meo tempore non audies: liberum tempus nobis dabitur ad istam disceptationem.' Cicero therefore is alluding here solely to the 'iudicium perduellionis sublatum', to proceedings which, however illegal and unconstitutional, were things of the past and cancelled: 'so I shall not waste any of my miserably short half-hour by dwelling on them further. I shall have the opportunity as consul of bringing these matters forward later on.' I cannot doubt that this interpretation of the passage will be accepted. There may be a temptation to translate 'non audies' 'you refuse to hear', but it certainly means 'I shall not speak of'. Any steps which Cicero intended to take later in the year to call Labienus to account for his action were of course prevented by the more exciting events which followed.

Cicero's speech then was delivered before the comitia centuriata, in which the Roman people was hearing the appeal of Rabirius from the capital sentence not of the *duumviri* but of Labienus. With this supposition the internal evidence entirely accords. Whatever magistrate condemned Rabirius would have had, as we know from several cases in Livy, to have asked the praetor for a day, i. e. for leave to summon the centuries at the expiration of a *trinundinum*, and to preside at the meeting. He would there play the double part of president and 'accusator'. There would be a 'certatio' between him and the accused man or his advocate, just as there had been between Horatius and the *duumvir* who had pronounced sentence. It has always been an objection, and it seems to me a fatal though not the most fatal one, against Dio's representation of the *iudicium populi* as an appeal from the duumviral sentence, that Labienus, and not either C. or L. Caesar, was obviously presiding when Cicero made his speech. It is to Labienus that Cicero addresses himself again and again; it is Labienus who is 'accusator' (2, 6); and it is Labienus who decides how long Cicero is allowed to speak. It has been partly to escape this difficulty that the untenable suggestion has been made that the speech belongs to some stage of the 'multae inrogatio'. On the other hand it is no small support to my presentation of the whole case that in what is obviously a capital trial before the Quirites present to give their votes, it is beyond question Labienus who is presiding.

As to the termination of the *iudicium populi*, we are dependent on the account given by Dio Cassius. From this it appears that the proceedings were brought to an abrupt end through the lowering of the red flag, which by immemorial usage had to be kept hoisted on the Ianiculum while the Roman people met as the assembled army in the Campus Martius below. Dio explains in some detail the origin and meaning of this custom, but we are not here concerned with it. What we should be concerned with, if there were any way of answering the question, would be the motive which induced the praetor, Metellus Celer, to have recourse to this primitive piece of machinery. What Dio tells us is that after the appeal *πάντως ἂν καὶ παρὰ τῷ δήμῳ ἑάλω, εἰ μὴ ὁ Μέτελλος ὁ Κέλερ, οἰωνιστής τε ὢν καὶ στρατηγῶν, ἐνεπόδισεν* (xxxviii, 27). He adds, after explaining the means adopted, *οὕτω μὲν δὴ τότε ἥ τε ἐκκλησία, καθαιρεθέντος τοῦ σημείου, διελύθη καὶ ὁ Ῥαβίριος ἐσώθη. ἐξῆν μὲν γὰρ τῷ Λαβιήνῳ καὶ αὖθις δικάσασθαι, οὐ μέντοι ἐποίησεν αὐτό* (cap. 28). The last statement, if accepted, disposes of the view, also rendered untenable by internal evidence, that the 'multae inrogatio' was a second attack upon Rabirius made after the capital charge had collapsed. That this in itself would have been a possible course is not only implied by the words of Dio, but is illustrated by the case of Claudius Pulcher, who, when his condemnation by the centuries on a charge of *perduellio* was prevented by a storm, was heavily fined in a process before the comitia tributa (Val. Max. viii, 1, abs. 4, Cic. *de Nat. Deor.* ii, 7, *div.* ii, 71). According to Dio, Rabirius would certainly have been condemned but for the intervention of Metellus. On the whole I see no reason to reject this. Dio certainly does not give a clear or complete account of the affair, but he must have been following in a confused way a version more detailed than his own. He knew of the two struggles, *περὶ τοῦ δικαστηρίου* and *περὶ τῆς κρίσεως*; he knew something of the duumviral court and of objections to it, as not *κατὰ τὰ πάτρια*; and if we accept his knowledge of the act of Metellus, it is somewhat arbitrary to reject the reason assigned for it. It is sometimes held that the words of Suetonius favour the belief that the people would have acquitted Rabirius; 'ut ad populum provocanti nihil aeque ac iudicis acerbitas profuerit'. I think this means no more than that after the summary and barbarous sentence of the *duumviri*, some indignation and sympathy was evoked by these 'inusitata supplicia', manifestations, which perhaps encouraged Cicero in the step already described. What Cicero's speech for the defence was like we know, and how full of arguments not strictly relevant to the point at issue. The speeches for the prosecution we have not got, but apart from the initial error of judgement in reviving obsolete barbarities, Caesar's case would not be an ineffective one, and very likely Labienus made the best of it. We need not decide whether Cicero was privy to the contrivance by which, if things looked bad, his eloquence was to be supplemented, but there was something perhaps of retributive justice in the concluding incident. Caesar, who had opened the attack by the revival of obsolete judicial machinery, found himself checkmated by a less barbarous but more ridiculous revival of the same sort.

V

CAESAR'S COLONY AT NOVUM COMUM IN 59 B.C.

IN his work, *The Municipalities of the Roman Empire*, Prof. J. S. Reid speaks of Caesar having established a new Latin colony at Comum (p. 124). Neither for this, nor indeed for any other statement made in this valuable but very discursive book, is any reference or authority cited. It so happens, however, that this particular point was discussed by Prof. Reid in an interesting article contributed to the first number of the *Journal of Roman Studies* (pp. 69–77), entitled 'On some Questions of Roman Public Law'. As I am unable to accept the conclusions deduced from the evidence in this discussion as either satisfactory or convincing, and as the question has some bearing on Caesar's policy and the methods of his opponents, I shall venture to subject the evidence to a re-handling.

It will be convenient to prefix to my discussion the principal passages from the ancient authorities which bear upon the subject.

(*a*) Asconius, *in Pison.* p. 3: 'Neque illud dici potest, sic eam coloniam (Placentiam) esse deductam quemadmodum post plures aetates Cn. Pompeius Strabo, pater Cn. Pompeii Magni, Transpadanas colonias deduxerit. Pompeius enim non novis colonis eas constituit sed veteribus incolis manentibus ius dedit Latii, ut possent habere ius quod ceterae Latinae coloniae, id est ut petendo magistratus civitatem Romanam adipiscerentur. Placentiam autem sex milia hominum novi coloni deducti sunt. . . . Deducendi fuit causa ut opponerentur Gallis qui eam partem Italiae tenebant.'

(*b*) Suetonius, *Caes.* 8: 'Decedens ergo ante tempus colonias Latinas de petenda civitate agitantes adiit, et ad audendum aliquid concitasset, nisi consules conscriptas in Ciliciam legiones paulisper ob id ipsum retinuissent.' (67 B.C.)

(*c*) Sallust, *Cat.* 49: 'Nam uterque cum illo (Caesare) gravis inimicitias exercebant: Piso obpugnatus in iudicio pecuniarum repetundarum propter cuiusdam Transpadani supplicium iniustum, Catulus ex petitione pontificatus.' (Piso was one of the consuls mentioned in (*b*)).

(*d*) Dio Cassius, 37, 9: *ταῦτά τε ἐν ἐκείνῳ τῷ ἔτει συνέβη, καὶ οἱ τιμηταὶ περὶ τῶν ὑπὲρ τὸν Ἠριδανὸν οἰκούντων διενεχθέντες, (τῷ μὲν γὰρ ἐς τὴν πολιτείαν αὐτοὺς ἐσάγειν ἐδόκει, τῷ δὲ οὔ) οὐδὲν οὐδὲ τῶν ἄλλων ἔπραξαν, ἀλλὰ καὶ τὴν ἀρχὴν ἀπεῖπον.* (65 B.C.)

(*e*) Caesar, *Bell. Civ.* 3, 87: 'Hae copiae, quas videtis, ex dilectibus horum annorum in citeriore Gallia sunt refectae, et plerique sunt ex coloniis Transpadanis.'

(*f*) Cicero, *ad Attic.* 5, 2, 3: 'Nondum enim satis huc erat adlatum quo modo Caesar ferret de auctoritate perscripta, eratque rumor de Transpadanis eos esse iussos IIIIviros creare.' (Written in May 51 B.C.)

(*g*) Cic. *ad famil.* 8, 1, 2; 'Ut nunc est, nulla magno opere expectatio est. Nam et illi rumores de comitiis Transpadanorum Cumarum tenus caluerunt, Romam cum venissem, ne tenuissimam quidem auditionem de ea re accepi.' (Written in the last half of May 51 B.C.)

(*h*) Strabo, p. 213: *αὕτη δ' ἦν μὲν κατοικία μετρία, Πομπήιος δὲ Στράβων ὁ Μάγνου πατὴρ κακωθεῖσαν ὑπὸ τῶν ὑπερκειμένων Ῥαιτῶν συνῴκισεν· εἶτα Γάιος Σκιπίων τρισχιλίους προσέθηκεν· εἶτα ὁ θεὸς Καῖσαρ πεντακισχιλίους ἐπισυνῴκισεν, ὧν οἱ πεντακόσιοι τῶν Ἑλλήνων ὑπῆρξαν οἱ ἐπιφανέστατοι· τούτοις δὲ καὶ πολιτείαν ἔδωκε καὶ ἐνέγραψεν αὐτοὺς εἰς τοὺς συνοίκους· οὐ μέντοι ᾤκησαν αὐτόθι, ἀλλὰ καὶ τοὔνομά γε τῷ κτίσματι ἐκεῖνοι κατέλιπον· Νεοκωμῖται γὰρ ἐκλήθησαν ἅπαντες, τοῦτο δὲ μεθερμηνευθὲν Νοβουμκῶμουμ λέγεται.*

(*i*) Cic. *ad famil.* 13, 35, 1: 'C. Avianius Philoxenus antiquus est hospes meus et praeter hospitium valde etiam familiaris; quem Caesar meo beneficio in Novocomenses rettulit. Nomen autem Aviani secutus est quod homine nullo plus est usus quam Flacco Avianio.'

(*j*) Appian, *Bell. Civ.* 2, 26: *πόλιν δὲ Νεόκωμον ὁ Καῖσαρ ἐς Λατίου δίκαιον ἐπὶ τῶν Ἀλπέων ᾠκίκει, ὧν ὅσοι κατ' ἔτος ἦρχον ἐγίγνοντο Ῥωμαίων πολῖται, τόδε γὰρ ἰσχύει τὸ Λάτιον. τῶν οὖν*

Νεοκώμων τινά, ἄρχοντά τε αὐτοῖς γενόμενον καὶ παρὰ τοῦτο Ῥωμαῖον εἶναι νομιζόμενον ὁ Μάρκελλος ἐφ' ὕβρει τοῦ Καίσαρος ἔξηνε ῥάβδοις ἐφ' ὅτῳδη, οὐ πασχόντων τῶν Ῥωμαίων· καὶ τὸν νοῦν ἀνεκάλυπτε, τὰς πληγὰς εἶναι ξενίας σύμβολον καὶ φέρειν αὐτὰς ἐκέλευε καὶ δεικνύναι τῷ Καίσαρι.

(*k*) Plutarch, *Caes.* 29: Νεοκωμίτας γὰρ ἔναγχος ὑπὸ Καίσαρος ἐν Γαλατίᾳ κατῳκισμένους ἀφῃροῦντο [οἱ περὶ Μάρκελλον καὶ Λέντυλον] τῆς πολιτείας καὶ Μάρκελλος ὑπατεύων ἕνα τῶν ἐκεῖ βουλευτῶν ἐς Ῥώμην ἀφικόμενον ᾔκισто ῥάβδοις ἐπιλέγων ὡς ταῦτα τοῦ μὴ Ῥωμαῖον εἶναι παράσημα προστίθησιν αὐτῷ καὶ δεικνύειν Καίσαρι κελεύει.

(*l*) Suetonius, *Caes.* 28: 'Nec contentus Marcellus provincias Caesari et privilegium eripere, rettulit etiam ut colonis, quos rogatione Vatinia Novum Comum deduxisset, civitas adimeretur, quod per ambitionem et ultra praescriptum data esset.'

(*m*) Cicero, *ad Attic.* 5, 11, 2: 'Marcellus foede in Comensi. Etsi ille magistratum non gesserat, erat tamen Transpadanus. Ita mihi videtur non minus stomachi nostro quam Caesari fecisse. Sed hoc ipse viderit.' (Written from Athens in July 51 B.C.)

Practically, almost all our knowledge of the constitutional status of Cisalpine Gaul is either contained in or inferred from the passage of Asconius (*a*). From the fact that he speaks only of the Transpadane region as affected by the lex Pompeia, it seems a fair inference that the country south of the Po, afterwards comprised in the province of Cisalpine Gaul, was allowed, either at once or eventually, to benefit by the provisions of the lex Iulia. Accordingly, it is universally assumed that such Latin colonies as Placentia and Bononia became colonies of Roman citizens, that the civitates foederatae were raised to the rank of Roman municipalities, and that the same may have been true, as far as citizenship, if not complete municipal organization, was concerned, of the fora, conciliabula, and castella which had come into existence. That the Latin colonies of Cremona and Aquileia would be treated differently from all other Latin colonies, merely because they were north of the Po, it is impossible to believe, and their status too was no doubt settled by the lex Iulia, and they became Roman communities. It is in accordance with these assumptions that from this time forward the question of the civitas within the Italian peninsula only occurs in connexion with the Transpadani.

What was done with regard to the Transpadane region by Pompeius Strabo in 89 B.C. is clear from Asconius. The Italian municipal system was made general between the Po and the Alps, but in the form hitherto represented by the twelve later Latin colonies, of which Ariminum was the first and Aquileia the last. The towns within the whole region, many of them at any rate having hitherto been civitates foederatae, became in a loose sense of the term Latin colonies. They did not, with apparently at least one exception not noticed by Asconius, receive new citizens as colonists, but they had the status, privileges, and constitution of towns with the ius Latii as conferred since 268 B.C. It is impossible to doubt that this constitutional settlement was accompanied by an elaborate redistribution of the country into large territoria belonging to these urban centres. The country was still, however, essentially Celtic, and round these towns, especially in the north, there must have been many native civitates or pagi. These Celtic civitates were, as we know from Pliny, 'attributae municipiis lege Pompeia'. The work indeed of Pompeius Strabo was, mutatis mutandis, very similar to that of his greater son in Pontus and Bithynia.

Most historians have followed Mommsen in dating the establishment of the Cisalpine province from the time of Sulla's dictatorship. This may be so, though I do not feel sure that the province was not established by the elder Pompey. But whether it was or not, the lex Pompeia was to all intents and purposes the lex provinciae for Gallia Cisalpina.

For the next twenty-two years we have, as far as I am aware, no information about the Transpadane country, its provincial development, or the feelings and aspirations of its inhabitants. If the motive for making the north of Italy into a province was more adequate protection against the Alpine tribes, we should expect it to be garrisoned, but there is no evidence that any governor had legions earlier than 59 B.C. In 67 B.C., however, we get an important ray of light thrown by the statement of Suetonius (*b*). In that year the Latin colonies of the Transpadane district were 'de petenda civitate agitantes', and in some way Caesar, who was returning from his quaestorship in Spain, associated himself with their demands. The version that he countenanced something like an armed rising may be classed with the story current about him and Crassus in connexion with the conspiracy of two years later, and was no doubt the invention of his political opponents at a later time. The important point is that the Transpadani had clearly put forward their demand before Caesar appeared on the scene, and that he supported it. Whether it was in connexion with the action of the consuls on this occasion, as alluded to by Suetonius, that C. Piso, who was one of them, inflicted the 'supplicium iniustum' on a Transpadane mentioned by Sallust is doubtful. At any rate, a few years later Caesar again showed his championship of the Transpadani by making the act a serious count in Piso's trial for repetundae (*c*).

That the demand of the Transpadani for the Roman civitas was one of the acute questions of the day about this time is shown by the fact that it was at least one of the causes of such an estrangement between Crassus and Lutatius Catulus, the censors of 65 B.C., that they resigned office without completing the census. The words of Dio Cassius, quoted in (*d*), do not in my opinion bear out Mommsen's statement that 'Crassus as censor made arrangements to enrol the inhabitants directly in the burgess roll, . . . which was only frustrated by the resistance of his colleague' (*Rom. Hist.* iv, p. 158). It seems far more probable that some enfranchisement proposal *περὶ τῶν ὑπὲρ τὸν Ἠριδανὸν οἰκούντων* was in the air during 65 B.C., and that Caesar and Crassus, certainly in close co-operation that year in connexion with Egypt, were known to view the scheme favourably. If so, we can well understand that Catulus, the extreme optimate, might, as a protest, adopt mutatis mutandis the tactics of Bibulus in 59 B.C. and refuse to discharge the duties of his office. The fact that on the proposal of C. Papius all non-Italians were ejected from Rome at this time strongly points to some impending legislation in the comitia. *κἀν τούτῳ πάντες οἱ ἐν τῇ Ῥώμῃ διατρίβοντες πλὴν τῶν τὴν νῦν Ἰταλίαν οἰκούντων ἐξέπεσον, Γαΐου τινὸς Παπίου δημάρχου γνώμῃ* (Dio Cass. loc. cit.).

That a law so resolutely opposed by the conservative party at this time should have been staved off is not surprising when we remember the difficult position of the popular leaders during Pompey's command in the East. It is clear from the events of 63 B.C. that the Transpadani were in a dangerous frame of mind, and would not have hesitated to support a possible revolution, if by so doing they could secure the coveted civitas.

A more difficult question is raised, but not satisfactorily answered, by Professor. Reid in connexion with Caesar's consulship in 59 B.C. Why, when Caesar and Crassus, who had both pledged themselves on the question, were at one with Pompey, and in complete possession of the government, was there still no enfranchising law passed in favour of the Transpadani?

Professor Reid thinks the answer not difficult. He finds it in the fact that, by giving all the inhabitants of the region full burgess rights, 'the provincial organization of Gallia Cisalpina would not have been easy to maintain'. He adds that 'the position of the Cispadane region was already sufficiently anomalous, as was also that of the two or three towns to the north of the river, which had benefited by the lex Iulia' (p. 76).

In answer to the last point it may be asked, Why was the position of Cremona or Aquileia or Eporedia more anomalous in Cisalpine Gaul than that of the Roman colonies or municipia in such provinces as Narbonensis or Tarraconensis? But, apart from that, if the difficulty of maintaining the provincial organization was so great an objection to the enfranchisement of the country in 59 B.C., how was it that neither Caesar nor Crassus realized the difficulty in 67 and 65 B.C.? The continued interest of Caesar in the Transpadani can only have meant an interest in their enfranchisement. Besides, this particular difficulty existed as much in 49 as in 59 B.C., and yet it did not prevent Caesar from having the lex Roscia passed in the former year.

On the other hand, Mommsen would apparently explain the absence of legislation in 59 B.C. by supposing that Caesar regarded the Transpadani as already in some way legally entitled to the full civitas. This is the assumption underlying his interpretation of Crassus' action in 65 B.C. Caesar is represented during the whole of his ten years' command as 'adhering to the standpoint of his party which, instead of seeking to procure for the Transpadani the Roman franchise, rather regarded it as already legally belonging to them' (*Rom. Hist.* iv, p. 312). What is thought to favour this view is the undoubted fact that Caesar freely recruited his legions from the Transpadane part of his province. He himself reports Labienus as saying of his army in Epirus: that it had been raised during recent years from levies in Cisalpine Gaul, and that most of the soldiers came from the Transpadane colonies (*e*). This, however, is by no means conclusive. While I should demur to Professor Reid's assertion that Caesar allowed no precedent to stand in his way, there can be little doubt that in military matters he gave himself considerable latitude. The practice of admitting peregrini to the legions with the simultaneous conferment of the franchise was carried to excess during the civil wars, and was continued within limits under the Principate. It is probable that such enlistment could, perhaps with a little straining, be brought within the range of a governor's imperium, and that Caesar was the first to set an example of doing what was shamelessly abused by the Triumvirs. There was certainly a strong inducement for Caesar to do this, for the Transpadani were good material for soldiers, and had every reason to be loyal. It is possible, but not certain, that the Catonian party made this enlistment a charge against Caesar, and interpreted it as Mommsen does, but in the light of subsequent practice, such an interpretation seems to be uncalled for.

It seems indeed sufficiently clear that up to the spring of 51 B.C. nothing had taken place which implied with certainty any recognition of the Transpadani as Roman citizens. For it was in May of that year that Cicero in a letter to Atticus (*f*) alludes to a rumour current at the time to the effect that the Transpadane towns had been instructed by Caesar to elect IIIIviri. A remark in a letter of Coelius Rufus (*g*) makes it probable that the rumour was only local, and had no solid foundation in fact. The important point is that Cicero and his friends understood it to mean that Caesar was authorizing the Transpadane towns to adopt the constitution of full Roman municipalities instead of that proper to Latin colonies.[1] He expected too some grave consequences from the act. But if Mommsen's theory is correct, that it had

[1] It cannot on the evidence be maintained that the magistrates in all Roman towns were IIIIviri, but there is no evidence, as far as I am aware, of any Latin town possessing these magistrates. The Atestan fragment of the lex Rubria proves that the towns of Gallia Cisalpina, affected by the lex Roscia, had IIviri prior to that law.

been all along the standpoint of the popular party to regard the Transpadani as already entitled to the full franchise, it is inconceivable that Caesar would have allowed eight years to pass before taking this step, while Cicero, long familiarized with the situation, could not, as he evidently did, have looked on the matter as a new danger.

But surely if the standpoint of the popular party was what Mommsen believes, there must have been some reason for it. The arrangements of the lex Pompeia seem to have been very definite, and there is no indication that its validity was ever questioned. The popular party, even under its most violent leaders, did not ignore existing laws, and carried out its own programme by means of legislation. It is not to be supposed that either Crassus or Caesar regarded the Transpadani as Roman citizens merely on grounds of abstract justice. There must have been some legal basis for their attitude. Mommsen passes over this difficulty, and there seems absolutely no evidence for any invalidation of the lex Pompeia between 89 and 67 B.C. It might be suggested that a law was passed during the Cinnan régime giving the Transpadani full citizen rights. But if so, and if Appian is correct in attributing to Sulla the announcement that he would not interfere with the status of any new citizens, why was this supposed law inoperative? Or, if Sulla cancelled it, and the Cinnan arrangement was not restored by the legislation of 70 B.C., as the incident of 67 B.C. shows could not have been the case, on what legal basis could the popular leaders rely?

Perhaps a more plausible suggestion would be that Sulla treated all these Transpadane towns as he treated Volaterrae and deprived them of the citizenship through the constitutive powers of the lex Valeria. But if the decision of the jurisconsults could set aside the legality of Sulla's action in the case of Volaterrae, can we imagine that the ambiguity with regard to the Transpadani would have been allowed to linger on for 20 or 30 years?

But for all these possibilities there is no evidence, whereas on the other hand we have the undisputed fact that the Roman civitas was actually conferred upon the Transpadani by the lex Roscia in March 49 B.C. There may be some difficulty in explaining why such a law was not passed ten years earlier, but at least it disposes equally of Mommsen's contention that the popular party all along regarded the Transpadani as legally entitled to the franchise, and of Professor Reid's suggestion that the enfranchisement of the region was felt to be inconsistent with provincial organization.

It is easier, however, to show that these two explanations of Caesar's abstention from legislation on the subject of the Transpadani in 59 B.C. are untenable than to suggest one more convincing. In all probability agitation for the franchise on the part of the Transpadani dated from the first establishment of the Cisalpine province, whenever that was. Differences of status within a province were not of course unusual, but where two definitely separated portions of a province were fully and partially privileged as the Cispadane and Transpadane regions were, the contrast was bound to lead to discontent in the latter. Sulla would no doubt ignore this discontent, and maintain the *status quo* of the lex Pompeia. The coalition of 70 B.C. evidently did the same, either because optimatist feeling was already very strong on the subject, or conceivably because Pompey was reluctant to upset the arrangement made by his father. For some reason, which requires more explanation than the evidence affords, the conservative party looked with abhorrence on the desired enfranchisement. In no other way can we explain the impracticable resistance of Catulus in 65 B.C. or the passing of the lex Papia in the same year, or Cicero's fluster at the rumour about the IIIIviri, or the atrocious protest of Marcellus.

Caesar was of course strong enough in 59 B.C. to have enfranchised the country in spite of this optimatist feeling. But he was himself to be governor of Cisalpine Gaul for the next five years; he would have every opportunity of safeguarding the interests of the towns, and the confidence inspired by his position and his known sympathy would effectually stop the recent agitation in the country. He may even have thought that the Transpadani could be more depended upon while still expecting a favour than after receiving it. At any rate, there is sufficient evidence that Caesar, when he entered on his provincial command, was an avowed supporter of the claims of the Transpadani to receive full citizenship instead of the ius Latii which the lex Pompeia had granted them.

It remains now to consider the narrower question with the statement of which I commenced this paper—Was Caesar's colony of Novum Comum merely a Latin colony, or was it invested with the full privileges of the Roman civitas? I think it may fairly be contended, apart from the evidence which will have to be examined in detail, that an antecedent presumption in favour of the latter view is furnished by the fact that up to the date of his consulship Caesar had identified himself with the discontent of the Transpadani at the possession of merely Latin rights. To establish or even to re-establish a colony with this inferior status would have seemed like acquiescing in the *status quo*, perpetuating a condition of things which the country repudiated, and positively reversing his previously announced policy. To abstain from immediately carrying out that policy was one thing, to act in direct contravention of it was quite another.

If the only evidence at our disposal was the statement that Caesar founded a colony at Comum, I imagine that the weight of this consideration would be admitted, and that few would doubt the Roman character of the settlement. But there is other evidence, and I am compelled to believe that it points to a conclusion opposite to that which Professor Reid's handling of the passages in question suggests to him.

The few known and essential facts may be briefly stated. On taking possession of his province, Caesar settled 5,000 colonists at Comum, henceforth often called Novum Comum (*h*). More strictly he settled 4,500, since 500 of the number were Greeks of distinction, who were nominal and non-resident citizens of the colony. Caesar took this step, not 'on his own authority', as many, incautiously following Mommsen, have stated, but on the empowering authorization of a lex Vatinia passed in 59 B.C. (*l*). He may have acted without a colleague, but it is not necessary to assume this because no colleague's name is mentioned, any more than it is assumed in the case of Marius after the law of Saturninus. Eight years later Marcellus, consul in 51 B.C., had a citizen of Novum Comum scourged in Rome, an act which was in some way a manifesto against Caesar, and which raised the question of the status, whether Latin or Roman, of the colony. No solution of the problem can be satisfactory which does not give an intelligible explanation of this notorious outrage, testified to, as it is, by Cicero, Appian, and Plutarch. The theory that

Caesar gave his colony only Latin rights offers, as far as I can see, no explanation whatever.

The only direct statement that Novum Comum was a Latin colony is found in the words of Appian (*j*), that Caesar had colonized Novum Comum 'into the Latin right'—ἐς Λατίου δίκαιον ᾤκίκει. He goes on to explain correctly enough the relevant feature of the ius Latii, and then gives a manifestly erroneous version of the outrage, representing the victim to have been an ex-magistrate, and therefore a reputed Roman citizen, protected by law against scourging. He remarks, however, that the punishment was intended to be ξενίας σύμβολον, i. e. a mark of non-citizen status, without adding a word of explanation as to the grounds of the disqualification implied in the act.[1]

A close examination of the evidence will, I think, suggest that Appian only believed Novum Comum to be a Latin colony through a mistaken inference from his own erroneous version of the outrage. His version is of course an impossible one, for if the man had been a magistrate in a Latin colony, he would have been a Roman citizen, and neither Marcellus nor any one else would have dared openly and flagrantly to violate the lex Porcia.

Now in the first place, Appian's evidence is fatally vitiated at the outset by his ignorance of the fact that Comum had been a Latin colony long before the time of Caesar. He clearly regards Caesar's colonization as equivalent to the conferment of Latin rights upon the town. The passages, however, quoted from Asconius and Strabo (*a* and *h*), of course prove this to be a complete mistake. It appears from Strabo that in the case of Comum, Pompeius Strabo did not adopt the course, described by Asconius, of giving the place the rights of a Latin colony without planting new colonists there. On the contrary, for military purposes and as a protection against the Raeti, he made it a real and effective Latin colony on the model of Placentia or Aquileia.

[1] Professor Reid identifies ξενίας σύμβολον with 'tessera hospitalis'. Perhaps he is right, but the joke is somewhat elephantine, and apparently Plutarch did not see it, if indeed it is not Appian's *bon mot* rather than that of Marcellus. Apart from the possible *double entendre*, the phrase clearly means 'a mark of non-citizen status', and is in any case neater, if less precise, than Plutarch's τοῦ μὴ Ῥωμαῖον εἶναι παράσημα. A hospitalis tessera could of course be given to Romans or non-Romans, but the recipient was never an actual citizen of the community conferring the hospitium.

This exceptional treatment of Comum was of course due to its vulnerable situation, and it is impossible to doubt that the re-colonizations by Scipio and Caesar, where Strabo states the number of colonists, had the same military object.

Appian, however, is ignorant of all this. He knows that the colonist punished by Marcellus had some claim to be a Roman citizen, that the claim was disallowed, and that the disallowance was *ἐφ' ὕβρει τοῦ Καίσαρος*, i. e. in defiance of his colonization. He had also clearly found in his authorities some reference to the question whether or not a magistracy had been held. From these data it was fairly obvious to infer, (1) that the claim to citizenship was based on the tenure of a magistracy, and (2) the man being nevertheless scourged, that the Latinitas of the town was impugned, and (3) as it was Caesar's act which was impugned, that that act must have been the bestowal of Latin rights. But if Appian had known, as we do, that the man had not held a magistracy—that Comum had been a Latin colony for 30 years, he would perhaps have given more reliable information. The one point which his evidence seems to me to establish is that the person scourged claimed by virtue of some act of Caesar to be a Roman citizen.

From the passage of Strabo we get, if I mistake not, more positive indications that Caesar established a Roman and not a Latin colony. Strabo was himself perhaps, as Professor Reid suggests, not interested in the distinction. He describes in precisely the same way the settlements of Pompey, Scipio, and Caesar, and we might imagine that they only differed from one another in respect of the number of colonists. From one point of view the three acts of colonization did fall under the same category. Comum was peculiarly exposed to the incursions of the Raetian barbarians, and it was to protect this vulnerable point that Caesar, like the other two, planted colonists there. It was not, therefore, a step towards the enfranchisement of the Transpadani. He would hardly have begun such enfranchisement at so out-of-the-way a spot. The colony had a purely military object, and there is no evidence that the validity of the colony or of the franchise involved in it was questioned, until the Catonian party took up a position of open hostility to Caesar after Pompey's third consulship in 52 B. C.

With regard to the status of Caesar's colonists, Strabo tells us nothing directly. There is no indication whatever as to the class from which 4,500 of them were drawn. The interest and importance of the passage lies in the statement about the 500 illustrious Greeks whom Caesar made nominal citizens of the colony. I am compelled to differ entirely from Professor Reid in his treatment of these 500 Greeks. He supposes that Caesar was empowered by the lex Vatinia to settle Latin colonists, of course a fixed number, at Comum, and at the same time to grant the Roman citizenship to a prescribed number of 'aliens', who were to be non-resident citizens of the colony. He also suggests that Caesar would have taken these 'aliens' from the Transpadani, if he had felt himself able to do so. This suggestion seems wholly gratuitous and improbable, but it does not effect the main question.

I believe with Professor Reid that the clause in the lex Vatinia concerning the incorporation of 'aliens' has a precedent in the colonial law of Saturninus, in which Marius was empowered to incorporate 300 Italians in each colony founded by him.[1] I am not sure, however, that there is any justification for saying that 'this was a regular practice when the older burgess colonies were founded'. At any rate, and this is the relevant point, it was not the regular practice, and was quite inconsistent with the regular practice, when Latin colonies were founded. As Professor Reid himself admits, Roman citizens who joined a Latin colony themselves became Latins. It seems to me an entire misconception to suppose that the permission granted by the lex Apuleia or the lex Vatinia or by any other colonial law was first to create a certain number of Roman citizens, and then to incorporate them in this or that colony. It was rather a permission to incorporate certain peregrini in a Roman colony, provided for by the law, whereby they *ipso facto* became Roman citizens, like the other colonists. This was the indirect way in which Saturninus would have brought about the enfranchisement of a good many Italians. Appian alludes to this in his somewhat obscure phrase, *πλεονεκτούντων ἐν τῷ νόμῳ-τῶν Ἰταλιωτῶν* (i, 29). This too was probably what C. Gracchus did, when, with or without legal permission, he

[1] Surely Ihne must be right in reading 'trecenos' for 'ternos' in *pro Balbo*, 49.

tried to make up the number of colonists for Iunonia ἐξ ὅλης Ἰταλίας.

This, it seems to me, is what Caesar did in the matter of the 500 Greeks. I agree that Cicero's reference to one of their number, C. Avianius Philoxenus, 'quem Caesar . . . in Novocomenses rettulit' (*i*), makes it pretty certain that they became Roman citizens, but I entirely dissent from Professor Reid's contention that Strabo's words imply any difference of civic status between them and the other colonists or that he even directly states them to have been Roman citizens at all. He says indeed that they were more distinguished persons than the rest, and they were no doubt not mere soldiers, but men of learning or reputation or social rank in their own country. Beyond this, he only says that Caesar gave them citizenship in the colony, and enrolled their names in the colonial register. Professor Reid takes the words ἔδωκε πολιτείαν to mean that he gave them the Roman citizenship. I imagine that few will agree with him. Even if Strabo had written τὴν πολιτείαν, the context would have been against this interpretation, but the absence of the article surely makes it impossible. Presumably, if he had so desired, Caesar, with the strength of the coalition at his back, could have had a law passed authorizing the full enfranchisement of the 500 Greeks, and, if he had done this, he might perhaps have attached his new citizens to one of the urban tribes in Rome. But the fact that permission to create Roman citizens was contained in what is admitted to have been a colonial law, is, I venture to maintain, a conclusive proof that the citizenship was the result of incorporation in a colony, and that the colony must therefore have been a Roman colony.

This conclusion is quite independent of the answer to Professor Reid's question, 'Was it possible to create a new colony in which the colonists had not all the same legal status?' At the same time, I believe that the answer must be in the negative. At least, no one of the instances adduced justifies an affirmative answer. It is of course true that in every Latin town, while most of the citizens had Latin rights, there was always a minority of Roman citizens, who had gained the civitas through a magistracy. But this was obviously not a case of creating a new colony of composite status. It was an inevitable anomaly, arising out of the very nature of Latinitas, regulated and mitigated by the lex data, but never probably without its drawbacks and inconveniences. Still, every Latin colony, though not at its creation, yet in its development, was a composite community. The fact, however, that resident Roman citizens, belonging to some other community, had a restricted vote at elections is surely irrelevant, since the presence and voting of such incolae no more made the state a composite one than the presence and voting of Latins did in the comitia at Rome.

The citation from Livy, xxxiv, 42, is more to the point, though there was no new restriction placed upon Latins at that date, 193 B.C., but a new privilege then claimed by Latins and refused. 'Novum ius eo anno a Ferenatibus tentatum est, ut Latini qui in coloniam Romanam nomina dedissent cives Romani essent.' Some Latins had been accepted as colonists for Puteoli and other places, and, in accordance with this new claim, gave themselves out as Roman citizens, but 'senatus iudicavit non esse eos cives Romanos'. It is not clear, however, that this 'adscription' of Latins made the colony a composite one. More probably the Latins who joined it were constitutionally in the position of incolae. At any rate, the obvious inference from the story seems to be this, that if Latins did not become Roman citizens by joining a Roman colony, still less would Greeks become Roman citizens by joining a Latin colony.

I should myself be inclined to apply a somewhat similar explanation to the case of the Salassi at Augusta Praetoria, 'qui se initio in coloniam contulerunt'. I agree with Professor Reid that it is impossible to regard them as full citizens of the colony. I agree also that they probably received Latinitas, but it does not follow that they formed a class of inferior citizens in a composite community. There can be little doubt that they were 'attributed' to the colony with Latin rights, as the Carni and Catali were 'attributed' by Augustus to Tergeste, as some of the Anauni were 'attributed' to Tridentum, and as many other Gallic civitates had been 'attributed' to municipia by the lex Pompeia. Why Caesar in founding a military colony chose to add to it these nominal and non-resident citizens, is a question which cannot be answered. We know that, as dictator, he gave the citizenship to many Greek professors of the liberal arts, and it may have been the same feeling and motive which actuated him in 59 B.C. Or they may have been persons with whom Pompey had come in contact during his command in the East, and whom he was anxious to oblige. That Pompey had some special interest in the colony, we shall see when we consider our last passage from Cicero. It is certain that Cicero, and probable that Roman society in general, found no fault with the enfranchisement of these Greeks at the time, and it is unlikely that the objections afterwards made to Caesar's carrying out of the lex Vatinia, as being 'per ambitionem et ultra praescriptum', had any special reference to these Greeks. The passages from Plutarch and Suetonius (*k* and *l*) contain nothing inconsistent with one another, and, taken together, give an intelligible account of the whole story, though without any mention of the 500 Greeks. They are strongly in favour of the view that Novum Comum was a Roman colony, and Professor Reid's manipulation of them to get the opposite conclusion will not bear a close examination.

We learn from Suetonius that in 59 B.C. Caesar had planted colonists at the place on the authority of a lex Vatinia. It was the same year in which his lex agraria was carried, by which he was empowered to establish colonies in Italy, both on the ager Campanus and on purchased land in other parts. For any extra-Italian colony he would need the authorization of a special law, precisely as C. Gracchus had needed the lex Rubria as a preliminary to his colonial scheme of founding Iunonia. I have already expressed the opinion, which indeed is a necessary inference from Strabo, that the colony was intended by Caesar as a 'propugnaculum imperii', just as Eporedia was by Marius. Strabo does not tell us, and Professor Reid makes no suggestion on the point, from what class or classes of men the 4,500 effective colonists were drawn. They were very likely not all from the same class. I should conjecture that many of them may have been Pompeian veterans, for whom provision was certainly being made at the time. But it is not impossible that Transpadani, many or few, were included in the number. They were the men from whom Caesar chose to recruit his legions, and he may well have deemed them suited to the work required from the colony. There would have been no difficulty in getting the necessary permission to incorporate them, and it is in no way necessary to assume that

500 was the maximum number of those who might by the terms of the law receive the franchise on enrolment in the colony.

There is no indication that any objection was raised to any part of this colonial scheme either at the time or during the next eight years. Suetonius, Plutarch, and Cicero all agree that hostile action in the matter on the part of the optimates was taken in 51 B.C.[1]

Suetonius states that Marcellus took away the citizenship from the colonists whom Caesar had planted (deduxerat) at Novum Comum. Plutarch makes precisely the same statement. It is curious that Professor Reid seems to accept the statement when made by Suetonius, because he somehow finds in it a confirmation of 'the impression that Caesar's colonists at Novum Comum had not all the same legal status', but rejects it when made by Plutarch, because 'it indicates that he did not altogether understand the circumstances', the misunderstanding being that Plutarch believed it to be a Roman colony, whereas his critic has decided otherwise.

Suetonius proceeds to give the reason for the action of Marcellus, viz. that the citizenship had been given 'per ambitionem et ultra praescriptum'. Now it is obvious that these are manufactured reasons, invented eight years after the colony had been founded when a dead-set was being made against Caesar's particular acts and general position. It was within a very short time of the probably unfounded rumour that he had ordered the Transpadane towns to elect IIIIviri. The conservative party was encouraged by the anti-Caesarian symptoms in Pompey's sole consulship. It was also probably nervous and anxious as to Caesar's possible intentions. The report 'de comitiis Transpadanorum' (*g*) had evidently for the moment made a deep impression. Caesar was credited with the absurd design of carrying out now by a *coup de main* what he could easily have accomplished years ago by legislation. In this tension of feeling sinister motives were readily discerned in an act long past, and hitherto regarded as unobjectionable. The colonization of Comun was now repre-

[1] Plutarch, it is true, makes the perhaps pardonable mistake of confusing the three Marcelli, who were consuls in successive years (51 to 49 B. C.), and makes Lentulus Crus instead of Sulpicius Rufus the colleague of the Marcellus who took the leading part in what followed. It is not, however, a real mistake as to date, since Curio is spoken of as not yet tribune, and the slip does not in the least invalidate Plutarch's evidence on the main points.

sented as a bid for popularity among the Transpadani (per ambitionem). It was easy too to discover irregularities in its accomplishment. The words 'ultra praescriptum' are vague, and need not imply that the number of colonists fixed by the law had been exceeded. This, however, may well have been the case. Caesar would probably in choosing his 500 Greeks or his 4,500 military colonists not have been more careful not to exceed the legal number than C. Gracchus had shown himself in collecting colonists for Iunonia. If Caesar had allowed himself any laxity in this respect, we may be sure that Catonian precisionists would have been only too ready to declare the whole law invalid. This indeed, whatever the irregularity may have been, was probably the course adopted. It was clearly a theory among the constitutionalists that many of the laws both of Caesar and Vatinius passed in 59 B.C. were strictly null and void, as having been carried by force, or against the auspices, or in defiance of intercessio. Cicero, most unhappily for his own reputation, had ventured to act on this theory in 56 B.C. in connexion with the lex Iulia agraria, and it is quite likely that Marcellus and his Catonian friends took a similar course in 51 B.C. If so, it would mean the taking away of the Roman citizenship from all on whom it had been newly conferred, and in effect the degradation of the town to the rank of a Latin colony. This would even, I conceive, involve for any Pompeian veterans who might have been settled at Comum, except in the case of those who had held a magistracy, the loss of Roman citizenship, since by a rigid application of the old rule, they would be regarded and treated as Romans who had joined a Latin colony.

From the point of view therefore of Marcellus and the senatorial party Comum was again a Latin colony. It followed that those only of its citizens, whether old or recent, were Roman citizens who had held a magistracy. I cannot understand in what way the words of Suetonius imply a distinction of status among the colonists. There is nothing whatever to indicate that 'ultra praescriptum refers only or specially to the 500 Greeks, or that the citizenship was only taken away from these. On the contrary, it was taken away from the colonists whom Caesar had planted at Comum, and the word 'deduxerat' is not applicable to these non-residents. It would be most arbitrary to maintain that Suetonius is referring to one class of colonists who lost the civitas, and Plutarch to another, and the latter is beyond doubt referring to resident colonists, since the senator who was scourged was one of them.

There is indeed no part of Professor Reid's argument which is less convincing than his treatment of Plutarch's evidence. Plutarch begins by stating explicitly that Marcellus and his friends deprived of the citizenship those who had been settled as colonists at Novum Comum by Caesar. One of these, a senator of the colony, who happened to be in Rome, Marcellus caused to be scourged, as a practical indication that he was not a Roman citizen. The act was obviously perpetrated to prove in this brutal way that the disenfranchisement was real and effective. On this Professor Reid remarks, 'whereas Appian blundered in making the man a past magistrate and therefore a Roman, Plutarch presents him as only a member of the local senate, and no Roman. Therefore in Plutarch's view Novum Comum does not possess citizen rights.' Surely this is to argue in a circle. If Plutarch includes this senator, as he certainly does, among those deprived of the citizenship, he must, I presume, have regarded him as possessed of the citizenship up to the act of deprivation. After that act, Plutarch expresses no opinion of his own as to the man's status, but says that Marcellus scourged him to show that in his view he was no Roman.[1] Plutarch is clear, precise, and consistent, and the only conclusion to be drawn from his statement is that Novum Comum was a colony of Roman citizens. To assert that the statement as to the citizenship being taken away is a misunderstanding of the circumstances is simply to beg the whole question.

Suetonius and Plutarch therefore are in perfect agreement on the essential point. The citizenship which both represent as taken away from the colonists was the Roman citizenship, and

[1] Plutarch's statement that the man was a senator is not of course in itself inconsistent with that of Appian that he was a past magistrate. The senatorial album of Canusium shows that in that town as many as 68 out of the 100 decuriones were ex-magistrates. If Plutarch considered Comum a Roman town, there would be no occasion to allude to a magistracy, whether held or not held by the man. We know from Cicero's words that he had not held one. Besides, if he had, Marcellus, acting as he was on the theory that Comum was a Latin colony, could not possibly have disputed his Roman citizenship.

the particular colonist, scourged by Marcellus, claimed to be a Roman citizen, not, as Appian erroneously supposed, on the tenure of a magistracy in a Latin colony, but on belonging to a military burgess colony. From Plutarch and Suetonius together we can gather an intelligible story, and the only story which gives an intelligible sense to the last passage from Cicero (*m*).

Professor Reid asserts that 'this passage is unintelligible unless Novum Comum was a Latin colony. The reference to a magistracy would be meaningless.' I venture to think on the other hand that the passage is unintelligible on the supposition that Novum Comum was established as a Latin colony by Caesar. For in that case there would have been no motive for the outrageous action of Marcellus. The colonists of Comum would have been in the same legal position as all the other Transpadani, a position thoroughly acquiesced in by the constitutional party since the lex Pompeia. Any Transpadani included by Caesar among the 4,500 colonists would have had no better civic status than they had before, and there was no possible motive for outraging a Transpadane as such. Professor Reid himself suggests no motive, though, I suppose, he would contend that any insult to a Transpadane was an insult to Caesar. Such a pointless insult, however, is not what we should expect from a party engaged at this very time in employing such elaborate constitutional contrivances against Caesar.

To make the story intelligible, some definite motive is required, which the theory of Comum being only a Latin colony does not afford. This motive is supplied by both Appian and Plutarch. They both distinctly bring the insult to Caesar into connexion with his colonization of Comum. They both represent the man scourged as claiming to be a Roman citizen, and Marcellus as disallowing that claim. Appian wrongly supposes that the claim was merely based upon the tenure of a magistracy. Plutarch is aware that the man possessed the civitas in common with the other colonists. But they both assert in almost identical terms that the scourging was intended to signify that the claim to Roman status was disallowed. Why it was disallowed, Suetonius, as we have seen, tells us vaguely and imperfectly, but in a way which admits of intelligible explanation. Whatever was the precise form in which the deprivation of citizenship took place, and it was probably by a declaration of the senate that the lex Vatinia was invalid, the result was that, from the standpoint of Marcellus and his friends, Comum was merely the Latin colony it had been between 89 and 59 B.C. The question of the magistracy therefore was from this point of view all important. I am not sure, in spite of Cicero's epithets, that Marcellus was 'by no means a violent man', but in any case he would never have ventured to scourge an acknowledged Roman citizen. He had to make quite sure, and from Cicero's words he had made quite sure, that the man, though possibly a senator, had not been a magistrate. If Professor Reid had contented himself with saying that Cicero's reference to a magistracy was meaningless unless Marcellus regarded Comum as a Latin colony, the remark would have been unexceptionable. But the attitude of Marcellus was one thing, the status actually given to the colony by Caesar and the lex Vatinia was quite another.

Cicero severely condemns the action of Marcellus, not as illegal, for he no doubt accepted as valid the disenfranchisement of the colony, but as an outrage on humanity and as inconsistent with political expediency. Legally, it is probable that Latins, in spite of the proposal or law of the elder Livius Drusus, were liable to be scourged. But every year crowds of Latins by virtue of their Latinitas were becoming Romans as it were automatically and it was obviously monstrous to subject to such an indignity a man whom perhaps a year's magistracy alone separated from the citizenship. But the words 'erat tamen Transpadanus' were far more a protest against a political blunder. The Transpadani had long been a factor in Roman politics which could not be ignored. So far their demand for complete enfranchisement, which for some not very intelligible reason appeared intolerable to the conservatives, had been staved off. But such a practical exhibition of the disabilities involved in Latinitas would not only increase tenfold the devotion of the Transpadani to their champion, Caesar, but would make it impossible any longer for Caesar to postpone the grant of the franchise which would render such outrages impossible in future. The lex Roscia, passed in the very first months of the civil war, was Caesar's answer to this silly defiance of Marcellus.

Cicero's concluding words suggest that Pompey would be hardly better pleased with what had taken place than Caesar himself. This has usually been explained by the fact that the settlement of the Transpadane region had been the work of Pompey's father, and that he therefore took a special interest in these Latin communities. The suggestion is perhaps a little far-fetched, and there is at any rate no evidence that Pompey, like Caesar and even Crassus, had concerned himself about the Transpadani in the interval. It is possible that Pompeius Strabo may have settled in his colony at Comum some of the soldiers who had served under him in the Social war, and that on that account Pompey had a special interest in that particular town. I imagine that, when Caesar established his settlement at Comum with Roman rights, the act would carry with it the enfranchisement of any remaining colonists planted there by Pompey or Scipio. This of course was not absolutely necessary, but as in all the older colonies the assimilation between the settlers and the older inhabitants had long since been complete, Caesar, especially with his liberal views, would naturally have taken this course. I cannot believe that he would have tolerated any distinction between Comenses and Novocomenses, and I understand this to be Strabo's meaning, when he says, *Νεοκωμῖται γὰρ ἐκλήθησαν ἅπαντες*. In this way it is not impossible that the victim of Marcellus was a son or grandson of one of the original Pompeian settlers. But there remains the possibility that mutatis mutandis there was as close a connexion between the lex Vatinia and Caesar's agrarian laws as there was between the lex Rubria and the colonial scheme of C. Gracchus. In that case many if not most of the actual colonists may have been chosen from among Pompey's veterans for whom Caesar was certainly providing at the time. Marcellus in his desire to insult Caesar may have overlooked the slight to Pompey, or he may even have disregarded it, as it is clear from both Cicero and Plutarch that Pompey was at the time opposing him on the question of appointing a successor to Caesar. 'M. Marcello consuli finienti provincias Gallias Kalendarum Martiarum die restitit.' One or other of these possibilities[1] would, I think, give more point to Cicero's

[1] While there were very likely Pompeian veterans among the Novocomenses

words, 'videtur non minus stomachi nostro quam Caesari fecisse' than the usual explanation.

What is especially interesting about the question both as to the status of Comum and the treatment of its nameless citizen is that we happen to have so many statements bearing upon it, no one of which by itself is free from obscurities, but which, pieced and compared together, give us a fairly clear and consistent account of the whole episode. Caesar's colonization of Comum was not a purposeless act, taken on his own authority and in defiance of the senate, it was not a partial and indirect method of redeeming a pledge of enfranchisement to the Transpadani, which he was not strong enough to carry through directly. The number of new citizens created under the terms of the lex Vatinia was not a mere instance of the megalomania of the times. The step was one of a series of military precautions to protect a vulnerable point, no doubt all the more necessary at the moment in view of the disquieting rumours as to the intended movements of the Helvetii. What made it differ from the two previous acts of colonization was, partly the political agitation in the Transpadane region, which Caesar had favoured, and which prevented him from perpetuating the present state of things by founding a colony with merely Latin rights, partly perhaps the inclusion in the colony of Pompeian veterans, who could not be expected to accept the status of Latins. Caesar therefore made the town a burgess colony. The fact that, while the colony was established in 59 B.C., the protest against the citizenship of its members was not made till 51 B.C., shows conclusively that the objections urged by Marcellus and stated by Suetonius were an afterthought, got up at a time when Caesar's whole position was being attacked. Nevertheless, it was easy for the constitutional party, when startled by silly rumours as to Caesar's intentions, to find technical flaws either in the passing or carrying out of the lex Vatinia, and Marcellus was better supported in getting it invalidated than Cicero had been in a similar attempt in 56 B.C. His success meant, as Plutarch and Suetonius put it, that the Novocomenses

the statement of Suetonius that the civitas was 'given' to colonists settled there makes it practically certain that Transpadani were also included. On the whole, Cicero's marked use of the word 'Transpadanus' points to the man who was scourged being one of these.

were deprived of the Roman citizenship. Then followed the fortunate or unfortunate appearance in Rome of the senator from Comum, and his scourging as a *ξενίας σύμβολον*. The affair was perhaps crowded out of attention by more exciting events, but it was undoubtedly the cause of the rapid enactment of the lex Roscia almost within a month of Caesar's crossing of the Rubicon.

VI

CAESAR'S LEGAL POSITION IN GAUL FROM 52 TO 49 B.C.

IN a short article in the *Classical Quarterly* (Jan. 1916) Dr. Rice Holmes has reopened for English scholars the intensely interesting question as to the legal issues involved in the senatorial attack on Caesar between 52 and 49 B.C. It is to be supposed that the general acceptance in this country of the main conclusions arrived at nearly sixty years ago by Mommsen was due, not to the authority of his name, but to independent examination of the evidence which he adduced. It is at any rate somewhat surprising to one, who had accepted Mommsen's conclusion on the evidence, but had not followed more recent discussions on the subject, to learn, not only that an essentially different view, propounded by Hirschfeld, has meanwhile dominated the learned world for nearly ten years and has now been itself put out of court by a still more convincing theory on the part of Judeich, but that the few who still hold the earlier view are regarded as the mere devotees of a 'pious faith'.[1]

It is some consolation, however, to find among these devotees a scholar and historian of so much repute as Dr. Rice Holmes, and I regard his article as a valuable protest against the tendency to accept the latest German theories at their own valuation. My only regret is that he has been far too lenient and on the defensive with 'Hirschfeld and the rest',[2] and has contented himself with exposing the fallacious interpretation put upon certain crucial passages, instead of carrying the war into the enemies' country by a review of the evidence as a whole.

That is what I propose to attempt. Having read and re-read

[1] Mommsen's monograph *Die Rechtfrage zwischen Caesar und dem Senat*, published in 1857, is to be found in *Hist. Schrift.*, vol. i, pp. 92 to 145. Hirschfeld's articles are in *Klio*, iv, pp. 76–87 and v, pp. 236–40. That of Judeich is in *Rhein. Mus.* 1913, pp. 1 to 10.

[2] The phrase is quoted by Dr. Rice Holmes from 'the writers of the article on Latin Literature in *The Year's Work in Classical Studies* (1915)'. If Judeich stands for 'the rest', it might be shown, if it were worth while, that on every essential point the two confute one another. I cannot but feel that Dr. Rice

Hirschfeld's two articles and that of Judeich, I must confess myself unable to comprehend how their reasoning can have convinced any one conversant with the evidence and appreciative of the principles of constitutional law and procedure involved. Much of the evidence, not only of the later writers, but even of Cicero and Caelius, is wholly ignored, while the important passages on which the argument is concentrated are not only in some cases taken apart from their immediate context, but are not viewed in connexion with the situations to which they refer. In order to make my examination of the evidence as far as possible an independent contribution to the problem, I have refrained from consulting Mommsen's treatise, which I have not read for some twenty-five years, and I have not read the paper in which Holzapfel replied to Hirschfeld's first article in *Klio*.

With a view of making my paper, what is all I claim for it, a study of the evidence, I shall consider the questions involved under the following separate heads: (1) the evidence for the second *quinquennium*; (2) the question *de successione Caesaris*; (3) the second consulship of Caesar and the tribunician law of 52; (4) the evidence derived from Pompey's attitude; and (5) the legal position of Caesar after 52. I had better admit at once that this method will involve a certain amount of repetition. The same passages may have to be cited in different connexions, the same constitutional points will come to the front more than once, and even the same incidents in the chain of events cannot on this method be disposed of once for all. I am not, however, without hope that some cumulative weight will be added to my argument, the object of which is not historical exposition, but the sifting of evidence.

Standing out from many minor, though not unimportant points, the main question to be decided is, what was the legal period for which Caesar's provincial command was prorogued by the *lex Pompeia-Licinia* of 55? Was it extended, as Mommsen argued, for a full *quinquennium* from March 1, 54, and so to March 1, 49? Was it prolonged, as Hirschfeld maintains, with

Holmes seriously weakens his own position (1) by admitting that in *ad fam.* viii, 8, 4 and *ad Att.* viii, 3, 3 the 'Kalends of March' refer to 50, and (2) by the hesitating attitude which he takes up with regard to the 'Ides of November' in *ad fam.* viii, 11, 3. I deal with the points in their proper place.

no specified legal termination, the senate, however, being precluded from raising the question *de successione Caesaris* till March 1, 50? Or was it extended, as Judeich pretends, for a nominal *quinquennium*, shortened, however, by Caesar's own consent, to an actual period of four years and ten months, and so ending on Dec. 29, 50? Whichever of these three arrangements was agreed upon at the conference of Luca, it is not disputed that, but for the *lex Pompeia de iure magistratuum*, passed in 52, there would have been no legal or constitutional question at all, and Caesar, under the operation, as explained below, of the Sullan provincial system and the *lex Sempronia*, would have been entitled to retain his command till the end of 49.

I. THE EVIDENCE FOR THE SECOND *QUINQUENNIUM*

As against Hirschfeld's contention that the *lex Pompeia-Licinia* established no fixed termination of Caesar's command, this is of primary importance. I propose to examine the statements made with some care.

SUETONIUS. (*Iul.* 24 to 30.) In 56 Caesar, threatened by the candidature of Ahenobarbus and the expressed intention to recall himself, *Crassum Pompeiumque in urbem provinciae suae Lucam extractos compulit ut . . . consulatum alterum peterent, perfecitque per utrumque ut in quinquennium sibi imperium prorogaretur.*

Now Suetonius clearly believed that the command was to last till the end of 49. (*a*) In mentioning that Caesar started for his province soon after laying down his consulship (c. 23), he presumably takes this as the beginning of the first *quinquennium.* (*b*) In c. 25 he speaks of the nine years *quibus in imperio fuit*; i. e. to the end of 50, so that he must have regarded 49 as the tenth year. (*c*) When in 52 the tribunes wished to make Caesar Pompey's colleague, he urged them *id potius ad populum ferrent, absenti sibi, quandoque imperii tempus expleri coepisset, ut petitio secundi consulatus daretur, ne ea causa maturius decederet* (c. 26). As the *absentis ratio* was certainly, as we shall see, for the elections in 49, that was the time when the command was beginning to expire, and the privilege prevented it from being shortened by the last six months of the year (conf. *semenstre imperium*). (*d*) In c. 28 Marcellus, consul in 51, is said to have made two proposals: (1) *ut ei succederetur ante tempus*; (2) *ne absentis ratio comitiis haberetur, quando nec plebiscito Pompeius postea abrogasset* (i. e. since Pompey's subsequent action in 52 had not really cancelled the privilege). Suetonius evidently supposed that Caesar's recall would have taken place, if the proposal of Marcellus had been carried, about the time when he would make use of the tribunician law, i. e. in the first half of 49. This is consistent with Cicero's statement that Marcellus tried to terminate the command *Kalendarum Martiarum die* (*ad Att.* viii, 3, 3) and it would be *ante tempus*, if 49 was the tenth year of the command. If Marcellus had really thought, as Hirschfeld supposes, that Caesar could be recalled on March 1, 50, his second proposal would have been unnecessary, since conditions under which the *absentis ratio* could be exercised would have been extinguished for sixteen months before July 49. Suetonius did not make this blunder, though Hirschfeld's guide, Dio, makes a far worse one, but his statement is vitiated (*a*) by the false *terminus a quo*, 58 instead of 59, and (*b*) by the assumption that in any case a proposal could have been seriously considered for recalling Caesar before the expiration of his legal period. We may take it as absolutely certain that, whatever that period was, no attempt was made by the constitutionalist party to curtail it. We need not decide at this point whether the motion of Marcellus was wrecked by the veto of tribunes (c. 29) or by a vote of the senate (Hirt. *b. g.* viii, 53) or by the resistance of Pompey (*ad Att.* viii, 3, 3), while the exact meaning of the phrase *ut Caesari succederetur* will be discussed in the next section.

In c. 29 Suetonius distinctly says that in 50 C. Marcellus made the same attempt as his predecessor, i. e. to recall Caesar *ante tempus*. If so, it was certainly not, in the opinion of Suetonius, a proposal to recall Caesar at once after March 1, 50, as Hirschfeld contends, but in 49. Caesar's reply, according to Suetonius, was to demand *ne sibi beneficium populi adimeretur*. Whether the *beneficium* was the tribunician law, and not, as I am inclined to think, the law extending his command to the end of the year, it was virtually that extension which Caesar demanded, since only on that condition was the *absentis ratio* either applicable or of consequence. It appears therefore that the evidence of Suetonius, though needing correction, is not without method and consistency and deserves more attention than it has sometimes received.

APPIAN. In ii, 17 Appian states that it was arranged at Luca for Pompey and Crassus to be consuls in 55, and for Caesar's command to be extended for five years. In c. 18 we have the carrying out of this arrangement. *Αἱρεθέντες δ' οὖν ὕπατοι Κράσσος τε καὶ Πομπήιος Καίσαρι μέν, ὥσπερ ὑπέστησαν, τὴν ἑτέραν πενταετίαν προσεψηφίσαντο.* In c. 25 Caesar is said to have secured the passing of the tribunician law, because he feared *ὑπὸ τοῖς ἐχθροῖς ἰδιώτης γενέσθαι.* Appian goes on to say, clearly referring to the next year 51, that Caesar, wishing *ἐπὶ δυνάμεως εἶναι, μέχρι ὕπατος ἀποδειχθείη, καὶ τὴν βουλὴν ᾔτει χρόνον ἄλλον ὀλίγον ἐς τὴν παροῦσάν οἱ τῆς Γαλατίας ἡγεμονίαν ἐπιλαβεῖν,* but Marcellus prevented this. Appian therefore, like Suetonius, believed that the end of the command was in the same year as the consular elections for which the *absentis ratio* was required, i.e. 49. The short extension which Caesar begged for would be either from March 1 to July, or more probably till the end of the year. The action of Marcellus, which Suetonius represents as a motion *ne absentis ratio comitiis haberetur*, is, according to Appian, the refusal of a demand made by Caesar. It seems to me that this demand, made in 51, according to Appian, is the same as the letter sent, according to Suetonius, in 50. It is uncertain which, if either, is correct, but Appian seems to recognize, as Suetonius did not, that the legal term ended early in the year.

In c. 26 Appian agrees with Suetonius as to the proposal of Marcellus in 51 for superseding Caesar, though his phrase *προαφαιρῶν τοῦ χρόνου* is ambiguous. Pompey's opposition, coupled, however, with the declaration *ὅτι χρὴ μετὰ τὸν χρόνον παραλύειν τῆς ἀρχῆς αὐτίκα τὸν Καίσαρα* is in complete agreement with *ad Att.* viii, 3, 3 and *ad fam.* viii, 8, 4. Appian also agrees that C. Marcellus in 50 made exactly the same proposal at a date *ὡς ἔληγεν ὁ χρόνος*, words consistent enough with the command expiring on March 1, 49, but inconsistent with Hirschfeld's view that the *legis dies* had arrived when Marcellus made his proposal.

Lastly (c. 28), Appian says that Pompey, later in the year,

made a show of willingness to resign his command so as to create a prejudice against Caesar as οὐκ ἀποδιδόντος τὴν ἀρχὴν οὐδ' ἐν τῷ νενομισμένῳ χρόνῳ. Hirschfeld, strangely ignoring the tense of ἀποδιδόντος, takes these words as proving that Caesar's term had already expired, and, as this is inconsistent with the five year's extension, suggests that Appian is here inadvertently following the good authority of Asinius Pollio (*Klio*, iv, p. 81). On the contrary, Pompey's point, clear to every one but a German professor with a theory to establish, is that Caesar, with his claim to the *absentis ratio*, was not likely to resign even on the legal termination of his command. If these words come from Asinius Pollio, that historian proves that there was a fixed *legis dies* and that it had not arrived in the middle of 50.

LIVY. On the whole the evidence of the epitomator is in favour of the second *quinquennium*, though his statement is ambiguously worded and in one point incorrect. In *epit.* 105 mention is made of Cato's opposition to the law *qua provinciae consulibus in quinquennium, Pompeio Hispaniae, Crasso Syria . . . Caesari Gallia et Germania dabantur.* The mistake is that Caesar's extension is included in the Trebonian law; the ambiguity lies in the position of *in quinquennium*, which, as the sentence stands, does not with certainty apply to Caesar. I cannot doubt, however, that the order of the words is a mere inadvertency, for it is not likely that, if Livy had given different conditions of tenure to the two laws, the epitomator would have made the mistake of merging them in one. But we get an additional sidelight on the question in *epit.* 107, where, speaking of the *contentiones inter consules* (in 51) *de successore Caesari mittendo*, the epitomator says: *agente in senatu M. Marcello cos. ut Caesar in petitionem consulatus veniret, cum is lege lata in id tempus consulatus provinciam obtinere deberet.* This passage, added to those in Suetonius and Appian, establishes in my opinion the fact that the question of the *absentis ratio* came up in connexion with the termination of Caesar's command, which it could only have done if the command was to end in 49. I agree with Hirschfeld that the words *lege lata* must refer to the tribunician law, and not to the *lex Pompeia-Licinia.* The point is that, under the conditions existing when the former law was passed, Caesar had the right (*deberet*) to retain his provinces till entering on the consulship. On the assumption that he was to be consul in 48, nothing but the tribunician law could give him the last *semenstre imperium* in 49. The evidence therefore of the epitomator, when fairly examined, is in favour of the second *quinquennium*.

Of VELLEIUS (ii, 46) and PLUTARCH (*Pomp.* 51; *Caes.* 21; *Crass.* 15) I will only remark that the one is a comparatively early authority, who may well have followed Livy, while the other is at least explicit, and repeats his statement in three separate Lives.

But though the consensus of these historians is strong evidence, that of CICERO, if it is forthcoming, would of course be far more conclusive. Now there are four passages, which may be and have been interpreted in such a way as to confirm the historians. In contesting this interpretation, Hirschfeld is on the defensive, since, with one possible exception, there is nothing in any passage to suggest an extension shorter than five years.

1. *ad Att.* vii, 7, 5–6, written between Dec. 18 and 21, 50. In discussing whether any classes or orders deserve to be called 'good', Cicero asks: 'Do you think the senate "good",' *per quem provinciae sine imperio sunt; nunquam enim Curio sustinuisset, si cum eo agi coeptum esset, quam sententiam senatus sequi noluit; ex quo factum est ut Caesari non succederetur.* Taken as a whole, the sentence was no doubt intended to imply that, as the motion necessary for appointing Caesar's successors had been vetoed, and the veto had remained unchallenged, the Gallic provinces were *sine imperio.* But Cicero is clearly speaking loosely and inaccurately, for, as Caesar by Cicero's own admission had not been superseded, he still held the *imperium*, or, if that had really lapsed earlier in the year, what is the meaning of Cicero's own following phrase *annorum decem imperium?* All that Cicero can mean is that the future *imperium* of Gaul was still unfixed. If any province was *sine imperio*, it was Cilicia, but that was due not to the senate but to Cicero's abrupt desertion of it.

But Cicero goes on: *Quid ergo? exercitum retinentis cum legis dies transierit rationem haberi placet? Mihi vero ne absentis quidem, sed cum id datum est, illud una datum est. Annorum enim decem imperium et ita latum †placet? Placet igitur etiam me expulsum et agrum Campanum perisse . . . Sed horum omnium fons unus est. Imbecillo resistendum fuit; . . . Nunc legiones XI, etc. Cum hoc depugnandum est aut habenda e lege ratio.*

Hirschfeld maintains (*a*) that the words *cum legis dies transierit* prove that Caesar's legal tenure was already at an end; (*b*) that *annorum decem imperium* refers to the actual, not the legal length of the command. It seems to me that his first point is urged in defiance of both grammar and logic. Grammatically, the tense of *transierit* shows that the *legis dies* is still in the future, and this is perfectly consistent with its being March 1, 49. Logically, how on Hirschfeld's own view can Caesar's command have been legally terminated in Dec., 50? His own point is that March 1, 50 was the only time limit specified in the law, and that this limit was merely 'preclusive', or, as it became after 52, permissive. In other words, the law laid down no fixed termination of the command, but allowed the senate on or after March 1, 50 to take the necessary steps for Caesar's recall. The expiration therefore of the *legis dies* in Hirschfeld's 'preclusive' sense by no means implied any legal obligation on Caesar's part to lay down his command, unless the senate by effective decree or decrees had taken steps to send him a successor. Will Hirschfeld pretend that up to December it had done so? Do not Cicero's words *ex quo factum est ut Caesari non succederetur* prove that it had not?

As for the second point, Hirschfeld argues that the preceding sentence and the explanatory *enim* prove that *annorum decem imperium* is actual, not legal. But he naturally finds the words *et ita latum* inconvenient to his theory, as indeed they are fatal, and so he arbitrarily substitutes for them *ei ita datum*, and rejects *placet* at the mutilated end of the clause. It is usually a weak case which resorts to tampering with the text, and the force of *enim* is not difficult to detect. Cicero answers one question by asking another. 'Do I approve of the *absentis ratio*? How should I, for do I approve of the ten years' command conferred by such a law?' It is really an *a fortiori* argument; 'I disapproved of the ten years' command and of our weakness which made it possible; still more do I disapprove of the canvass in absence, which would be *cum legis dies transierit*.'[1]

[1] I cannot compliment Hirschfeld on his manipulation of this passage, which,

2. *ad Att.* vii, 9, 2–4, written between Dec. 24 and 27, 50. Cicero is discussing the situation created by Caesar's demand to be enabled to use the *absentis ratio*, and sets forth a number of possible alternatives. He agrees with Atticus that the best thing would be if Caesar could be persuaded to give up his provinces and canvass in person, though even so, his consulship would be a disaster. On the other hand, the worst thing would be *haberi rationem Caesaris, illo exercitum vel per senatum vel per tribunos obtinente*. (The last words evidently imply that the *tempus legis* would have passed, but that the senate, either voluntarily or prevented by *intercessio*, would not have effectively superseded Caesar.)

Remarking on the impudence of this demand, Cicero thus addresses the absent Caesar: *Tenuisti provinciam per annos decem, non tibi a senatu sed a te ipso per vim et per factionem datos* (this is merely the old grievance of an extraordinary law, instead of regular senatorial conferment); *praeteriit tempus non legis sed libidinis tuae, fac tamen legis; decernitur ut succedatur. Impedis et ais: 'habe rationem meam'; . . . Exercitum tu habeas diutius quam populus iussit invito senatu?*

Now this is the passage on which Hirschfeld chiefly relies as a demonstration that Caesar's command did not legally extend till March 1, 49, because, as a matter of fact, it had already expired before the date of Cicero's letter.[1] Let us see then in the first place whether there is the slightest difficulty in interpreting the address to Caesar on the assumption that the *tempus legis* was the end of a second *quinquennium*, i. e. March 1, 49. If it was, then the question of the *absentis ratio*, though already debated and already disturbing, would not become absolutely critical till that date arrived. That was the day on

with the ordinary text, he knows well to be fatal to his position. He therefore tampers with *latum*, and by rejecting *placet*, tries to discount the sentence by making it unintelligible. *Placet*, he declares, belongs to the next clause. No doubt, but that is no reason why the same word should not end the previous one, though a careless scribe might easily regard it as an accidental dittograph, and omit it. (See *Klio*, v, p. 237.)

[1] *Klio*, iv, p. 80; Judeich (*Rhein. Mus.* 1913, p. 5) takes the phrases *cum legis dies transierit* and *praeteriit tempus . . . legis* as proving that Caesar's legal term was expiring at or about the date of Cicero's words. I admit that the latter is not fatal to the term being Dec. 29, 50, but Judeich, who admits the second *quinquennium*, has to regard it as consisting really of only four years and ten months. My interpretation stands against his view as against that of Hirschfeld.

which all eyes were fixed, as indeed they had long been fixed; that was the day by which both Caesar and the senate must have determined on their course of action. Is it not clear that Cicero addresses Caesar from the standpoint of that critical day? 'When the day comes and Caesar gives effect to his impudent demand by staying in his province, this is what we shall say to him.' This simple explanation, suggested by the whole context of the letter, removes every difficulty, and we are no longer reduced to the grotesque expedient of understanding by *decem annos* 'nine years nine months and twenty-seven days'. I should have thought that in any case it was sufficiently obvious that *tenuisti provinciam per annos decem*[1] and *praeteriit tempus . . . legis* are intended to be two different ways of saying precisely the same thing. The *decem annos . . . a te ipso datos* correspond exactly with the *tempus non legis sed libidinis tuae, fac tamen legis.*

But Hirschfeld's assertion that the words *praeteriit tempus . . . legis* prove that Caesar's term had already expired, cannot be allowed to escape so easily. He avails himself, perhaps inadvertently, certainly illegitimately, of the ambiguity which he has himself imported into the meaning of *legis dies.* He declares that the only time limit specified in the *lex Pompeia-Licinia* was March 1, 50, but that this was merely a preclusive or permissive limit, on or after which day the senate was free to take steps for Caesar's recall. But the arrival of this date did not *ex hypothesi* terminate Caesar's legal tenure of his provinces, unless the senate was willing and able to use the permission given it, and to pass the decree or decrees necessary to bring about Caesar's supersession. Not until the senate had effectively taken these steps would the *legis dies* in the full and natural sense be reached. In Dec. 50 the *tempus . . . legis* in the first sense had of course long passed, but the present passage can only disprove, as Hirschfeld declares that it does, the full five years' extension, if *tempus . . . legis* is taken in the second sense. But the senate had all through the year been prevented from passing effective decrees,

[1] To get rid of *annorum decem imperium* by talking about round numbers is inadmissible where the point is precise and legal. On the other hand, round numbers are natural enough where the total length of the Gallic campaigns is summed up. It is in such a context that Suetonius (c. 25) and Caesar himself (*b. c.* 1, 7) speak of nine years, though Caesar was only eight years and nine months actually in Gaul.

and this very passage proves that it was still vainly trying to accomplish this end. How else does Hirschfeld propose to interpret the words, *ut succedatur decernitur; impedis?* 'Decrees for appointing your successors are under consideration: you block the way.' Perhaps some of the scholars, who regard Hirschfeld's arguments as convincing, will take the preliminary step of showing that they are not self-contradictory.

3. *ad Att.* vii, 6, 2. *Cur autem nunc primum ei resistamus?*

Οὐ γὰρ δὴ τόδε μεῖζον ἐπὶ κακόν

quam cum quinquennium prorogabamus, aut cum ut absentis ratio haberetur ferebamus?

4. *Phil.* ii, 10, 24. *Duo tamen tempora inciderunt quibus aliquid contra Caesarem Pompeio suaserim; . . . unum, ne quinquenni imperium Caesari prorogaret; alterum, ne pateretur ferri ut absentis eius ratio haberetur.*

It is obvious that neither of these passages is against the theory of a five years' extension; the only question is whether they positively favour it. Hirschfeld's assertion that *quinquenni imperium* can only be the five years of the *lex Vatinia* is far from settling the matter, and the context in both passages is against him. The extension of *imperium* is in both brought into close connexion with the *absentis ratio*, and the latter could only be of use to Caesar, and therefore a danger to his opponents, if the extension was a *quinquennium*. Besides, the words of *ad Att.* vii, 7, 6 show that what Cicero disapproved was not the prolongation in itself, but a prolongation constituting a *decem annorum imperium*.

DIO CASSIUS. Of all the ancient historians Dio alone disbelieves in the five years' extension, and Hirschfeld, in spite of his contempt for later writers, is not disinclined to find some support from this disbelief. The statements relied on are three.

1. In 39, 33, after mentioning five years' command secured for themselves by Pompey and Crassus, Dio says that they disarmed the opposition of Caesar's friends ὥστε τὴν ἡγεμονίαν καὶ ἐκείνῳ τρία ἔτη πλείω, ὥς γε τἀληθὲς εὑρίσκεται, μηκῦναι. This statement is supposed to be the more valuable, because it depends on Dio's own reasoning and not on mere tradition. 2. Consistently with this, Antony in his funeral speech is made

to say to the people in 44, 43, that they had granted to Caesar ὅπερ, ἀφ' οὗ ἐδημοκρατήθημεν, οὐδενὶ ἄλλῳ ὑπῆρχε, λέγω δὲ τὸ ὀκτὼ ἔτεσιν ὅλοις ἐφεξῆς ἡγεμονεῦσαι. 3. In 40, 59, Dio states that, when Marcellus in 51 proposed to send successors to Caesar even before the time, Pompey opposed, ἔπραττε δ' ὅπως, ὅταν τὸν δεδομένον οἱ χρόνον διαπράξῃ, τοῦτο δὲ οὐκ ἐς μακρὰν, ἀλλ' εὐθὺς ἐν τῷ ὑστέρῳ ἔτει γενήσεσθαι ἔμελλεν, τά τε ὅπλα κατάθηται, καὶ ἰδιωτεύσων οἴκαδε ἐπανέλθῃ.

Now the second statement is obviously a mere deduction from the first, and if the third can be regarded as a deduction from the other two, it is worthless, since the reasoning by which Dio infers the three years' extension is demonstrably false. If the eight years, ending in 50, were made up of a five years' period and a three years' period, then the five years must have ended in March 53, but the one point on which all scholars are agreed is that the first *quinquennium* ended on Feb. 28, 54, and therefore Dio's three years would have to end in 51. As a matter of fact, Dio has hopelessly vitiated the calculation, which Hirschfeld thinks so preferable to a conscientious following of authorities, by a false *terminus a quo*.

It seems to me, however, more likely that Dio's first two statements are deductions from the third. If so, it is important to ask whether the view that Caesar's command ended early in 50 was derived from some authority, or was, as I suspect, a too clever pre-Teutonic conjecture of his own.

It is clear from 40, 59 that in 51 Marcellus proposed *ut Caesari succederetur*, and that the *successio* was *ante tempus*. But Dio misunderstands both phrases. It is proved by *b. g.* 8, 53 (to be cited later) that *ante tempus* refers to the *relatio* of Marcellus and not to the date of the recall, while, as we shall see in the next section, the motion *ut Caesari succederetur* merely meant that Caesar's provinces should be fixed as consular or praetorian for some specified year. Dio thinks that it was a proposal for instant recall, and that Pompey opposed it on that ground. He does not state the proposal of C. Marcellus in 50, but he undoubtedly thought with Suetonius and Appian that it was the same proposal over again, i. e. in his view for instant recall in March 50. It is surprising that an historian of Hirschfeld's reputation should take the same view (*Klio*, iv, p. 86), especially as we know from the s. c. of Sept. 29, 51 that the motion to be made by Marcellus on March 1, 50 was *de provinciis consularibus* (*ad fam.* viii, 8, 5). Dio, however, believing the proposal in 50 to be for instant recall, and knowing that Pompey did not oppose it, supposed, in view of Pompey's declaration of the previous year, that this was because the legal term had now expired. The statement therefore that Caesar's command was to end in 50 seems to be a mistaken inference from phrases that were misunderstood. I would not lay too much stress on Dio's inconsistency in making Antony say that Caesar was actually brought back before his term had expired (44, 43), but I own to some surprise that Hirschfeld, who speaks with much superiority on the inability of other scholars to evaluate witnesses, should follow the speculations of an historian who throughout this section hopelessly misunderstands the relations of Caesar and Pompey. To establish this judgement, it is enough to point out that no allusion is made to the conference of Luca; that Pompey and Crassus are represented as seeking the consulship for 55 out of jealousy of Caesar; that their main object is to secure commands for themselves, and that the idea of extending Caesar's command is a pure afterthought occasioned by the hostility of Caesar's friends to their own schemes, an attitude which of course explains the short extension.

HIRTIUS. Hirschfeld finds some confirmation of Dio's statement that Caesar's command was to end in 50 in a passage of *b. g.* 8, 39, where Caesar is stated in the summer of 51 to have hastened forward the siege of Uxellodunum, *cum omnibus Gallis notum esse sciret reliquam esse unam aestatem suae provinciae, quam si sustinere potuissent, nullum ultra periculum vererentur.* Hirschfeld argues that *reliquam unam aestatem* must refer to the summer of 51, not of 50; (*a*) on Bardt's authority, who declares that *unam* can only mean 'this one', and (*b*) because, if Caesar had had the summer of 50 before him, there would have been no need so to hasten the siege. To both these points Dr. Rice Holmes's reply is irresistible. (*a*) It is clear from c. 46 that at the time of the siege only a small part of the summer of 51 was left, i. e. not *unam aestatem*, but *exiguam partem unius aestatis.* (*b*) An immediate success at Uxellodunum might leave Caesar's last year free for settlement and conciliation, and might shatter the Gallic hope of a last year's successful resistance.

But apart from this, what was there on Hirschfeld's theory for the Gauls to know in the summer of 51? Of course, if Dio is right, and Caesar's legal eight years were to end in 50, the Gauls might have known that. But Hirschfeld, while profiting by Dio's calculations, does not venture to accept his statement of facts. On his own theory there was nothing in the *lex Pompeia-Licinia* limiting Caesar's command except a clause disallowing discussion of it till March 1, 50. Was this what the Gauls knew, and, if they knew it, does Hirschfeld pretend that they also knew what the result of the discussion would be, when the time came? Or did they understand the highly technical reasons which, after Pompey's law of 52, had turned a clause originally favourable to Caesar into a possible weapon against him? They might have heard of the hostile attempt of Marcellus in the spring, but, if so, they would also have heard of its defeat. They certainly could not have known of the senatorial decrees, obviously hostile to Caesar, passed on Sept. 29, because the siege of Uxellodunum was earlier than that date. On the other hand, if the *lex Pompeia-Licinia* gave Caesar a second *quinquennium*, the Gauls would certainly have known this, and as the summer of 51 passed away, the knowledge would be a motive for more obstinate resistance with a view of getting through the approaching last year. (See *Klio*, iv, p. 82 and v, p. 237.)

II. DE SUCCESSIONE CAESARIS

The first question *de successione Caesaris* arose in 56, when Ahenobarbus openly threatened *se ei adempturum exercitum* (Suet. *Iul.* 24). What happened was a debate in the senate to fix the consular provinces for 54 according to the *lex Sempronia*. Caesar's opponents wished that one or both of the Gauls should be selected, so that he might be recalled. Cicero was ordered, as his παλινῳδία for the rash step taken earlier in the year, to defeat this scheme. It is by means of his arguments on this occasion that several important points can be proved.

1. Caesar's first five years ended on Feb. 29, 54, and therefore

must have begun on March 1, 59. How is it possible, Cicero asks, for a consul of 55 to succeed Caesar in 54? *Fuerit toto in consulatu sine provincia, cui ante quam designatus est decreta provincia. Sortietur an non? Nam et non sortiri absurdum est, ei quod sortitus sis non habere. Proficiscetur paludatus? Quo? quo pervenire ante certam diem non licebit. Ianuario Februario provinciam non habebit: Kal. denique Martiis nascetur repente provincia* (*de prov. cons.* 15, 37). This proves conclusively that Caesar was in possession till March 1, 54. 2. Provincial commands under existing Sullan arrangements were bound to begin on Jan. 1. *Mihi nihil videtur alienius a dignitate disciplinaque maiorum quam ut qui consul Kal. Ian. habere provinciam debet, is ut eam desponsam non decretam habere videatur.* 3. The only constitutional way of appointing a successor to a provincial governor, except by means of a special law, was to fix his province in advance as either consular or praetorian. How, for example, could Piso or Gabinius be recalled from Macedonia and Syria? *Faciam, inquit, illas praetorias, ut Pisoni et Gabinio succedatur statim* (i. e. in Jan. next year). But this might be stopped by tribunician *intercessio. Mihi credite; nunquam succedetur illis, nisi ea lege referetur qua intercedi de provinciis non licebit,* i. e. by making the provinces consular for 54 in accordance with the *lex Sempronia,* which prohibited *intercessio* (*de prov. cons.* 7, 17). 4. The phrase *ut Caesari succedatur* does not mean, therefore, that a successor shall be forthwith sent to replace Caesar, but that his provinces shall be fixed as consular or praetorian, with a view to a successor being sent at the proper time. This is of course all that Cicero means, when he writes in 56: *Nam . . . ne Caesari lege Sempronia succederetur facile perfectum est:* Caesar's provinces were not made consular for 54 in accordance with the *lex Sempronia* (*ad fam.* i, 7, 10). As we shall meet this phrase again, it is as well to note its meaning.

The question *de successione Caesaris* does not meet us again till 51, the *lex Pompeia-Licinia* having meanwhile been passed, extending Caesar's command and, whatever term it fixed, certainly forbidding any motion *de successione Caesaris* till March 1, 50. But the whole question *de provinciis* was now complicated by Pompey's law of 52 requiring a five years' interval between the consulship or praetorship and a provincial command. This put an end to the Sullan system of provincial succession, and at the least rendered uncertain the applicability of the *lex Sempronia* to consular provinces.

Now in dealing with the motion *de successione* made by M. Marcellus in 51, it must be insisted that, in spite of Suetonius and Dio, there could have been no question of recalling Caesar before the termination of his legal command. To admit that there could is to deny that there was any legal or constitutional question at all, and to make Pompey's law, admittedly directed against Caesar, irrelevant to the situation. The phrase *ante tempus* receives its full explanation from the statement of Hirtius (*b. g.* 8, 53), *Marcellus . . . cum impugnaret Caesaris dignitatem, contra legem Pompei et Crassi rettulit ante tempus de Caesaris provinciis.*

What then was his motion, and why did he make it *ante tempus*? No one will doubt that his proposal was, *ut Caesari succederetur*, rendered by Dio and Appian as διαδόχους πέμπειν τῷ Καίσαρι. We may further take it from Cicero's words (*ad Att.* viii, 3, 3), *M. Marcello consuli finienti provincias Gallias Kalendarum Martiarum die*, that the recall of Caesar was to be effective on March 1 in either 50 or 49. I may perhaps pause for a moment temporarily to dispose of Judeich, who by the way is discreetly silent about this proposal. Unless he rejects Cicero's evidence altogether, he is bound to take the date as March 1, 50, and as by his own theory Caesar's legal term did not end till Dec. 29 of that year, he is convicted of the irrational view that Marcellus, by a decree of the senate, tried to shorten Caesar's legal term by ten months.

Let us first on the strength of the evidence examined in section i take the motion *ut Caesari succederetur* to mean that one or both of the Gallic provinces were to be consular after March 1, 49. This would be taking advantage of Pompey's law, since on the older system a governorship could not begin on March 1, or on any date but Jan. 1, and, if carried, it would mean Caesar's recall on the lapse of his legal term.

It is usually assumed that the effect of the five years' interval was to abrogate the *lex Sempronia*, and no doubt on the principle *cessante legis ratione cessat ipsa lex*, this would be the case. But we do not know the wording of the law, and there may well have been some uncertainty on the point early in 51.[1] This would explain the precipitate motion of Marcellus, for, if the law was still in force, the only way of superseding Caesar in 49 was to fix his provinces as consular for that year before the elections in 51; and even if it was not in force it might well seem advisable to take immediate advantage of Pompey's law, while there was at least one consul to be depended upon. Of course the motion involved the violation of a *sanctio* in the *lex Pompeia-Licinia*, but there are many examples to show that there was a great difference between violating a law and disregarding sanctions in it intended to restrict the free actions of magistrates. It was at least worth trying, and, if Pompey's conscience had been less tender, the *optimates* might have carried their point.

On the other hand, the alternative view of Hirschfeld that Marcellus proposed *finire provincias Gallias* on March 1, 50, is full of difficulties. (*a*) The motion would not only be *contra legem Pompei et Crassi* (not a fatal objection), but by boldly treating the *lex Sempronia* as defunct, it laid itself open to tribunician *intercessio*,[2] and would not have had the smallest chance, even if Pompey had concurred. (*b*) Why should Marcellus have fixed upon March 1, 50, as the date on which the Gallic provinces were to become consular? On Dio's view we could understand it, but on Hirschfeld's, the date, being preclusive, had no significance, unless it was observed, and for Marcellus to make it the end of Caesar's command would have been nothing but an impudent advertisement of his own illegality. (*c*) Marcellus must have known, though Hirschfeld apparently forgets, that it was out of his power to make the Gallic provinces consular on March 1, 50, because the two consular provinces, Cilicia and Syria, held

[1] When later in the year it was decreed that the question *de provinciis consularibus* should be brought up on March 1, 50, it was assumed that the *lex Sempronia* was out of force, but to provide against possible illegality, the magistrates of this or the following year were instructed, *si quid de ea re ad populum pl.ve lato opus esset, . . . uti . . . ad populum pl.ve ferrent* (*ad fam.* viii, 8, 5). I am not aware that this passage has hitherto been so explained, but I have no doubt that this is the solution.

[2] This is proved by the passage in *de prov. cons.* 7, 17, quoted above. The proposal would have been so hopeless, owing to this liability, that it seems necessary to suppose that the *optimates* were so far upholding the *lex Sempronia*, just as long of course as it suited their purpose. If Suetonius is right that tribunes opposed Marcellus, it must have been to maintain the Pompeio-Licinian sanction. But probably a senatorial vote defeated him, as Hirtius declares (*b. g.* 8, 53).

by Cicero and Bibulus, would not be vacated till four or five months after that date, and it has been shown from *de prov. cons.* 7, 17, that there was no other way of superseding Caesar.

The defeat of Marcellus meant that the *successio Caesaris* would have to be postponed till next year. But this was now part of a wider question *de provinciis*, which Pompey's *lex de iure magistratuum* had rendered urgent and complicated. It is clear from Caelius that something was still expected from Marcellus, who was hanging back *non inertia sed . . . consilio* (*ad fam.* viii, 2, 2). A fruitless attempt was made to raise the question *de successione Caesaris hoc est de provinciis* in July (ib. viii, 4, 4), and it was believed that in August *aut transigetur aliquid aut turpiter intercedetur.*

The abolition of the Sullan system in 52 had thrown the whole *successio provinciarum* out of gear. We must assume that the consular provinces for 51, Syria and Cilicia, had been fixed in 53 in the usual way, but after Pompey's law it was impossible to assign them to the consuls of 52, and therefore, but not without a delay of some months, Bibulus and Cicero were sent out. As for the praetorian provinces, those for 51 may have been allotted in 52 before Pompey's law was passed, but quite possibly there was the same delay, and for the same reason, in sending out the governors. At any rate, it is clear that no allotment of praetorian provinces in 51 was attempted till the end of September. As there was probably some shortage of ex-consuls and ex-praetors qualified under the new law, and as there is reason to suppose that most provincial commands in 51 began, like the consular, later than usual, it would have seemed a natural course to retain in their provinces all governors, consular and praetorian, throughout 50, and to make all provincial appointments for 49. This was at any rate Caesar's view and it seems to have been adopted with modifications by the senate in September. But there were two methods of carrying out this arrangement. (*a*) All provinces, consular and praetorian, might be settled together at the date when the Gauls could legally be considered, i.e. on March 1, 50.[1] This was what Caesar wished, because it was still possible that

[1] As with the defeat of Marcellus the *lex Sempronia* must by common consent have been given up, there was no constitutional reason for dealing with the two groups of provinces separately.

in a general debate on the provinces one or both of his provinces might be left out of the settlement, and consular or praetorian selected from the rest. (*b*) The praetorian provinces might be settled at once, either for the second half of 50, as Cicero of course would have preferred,[1] or for 49. This was what the *optimates* wished, because it would be possible to make all provinces praetorian except those, e.g. the Gauls, which they intended to fix as consular on March 1, 50. It is, in my opinion, in the light of these two policies that the following passages of Caelius are to be explained. *Nosti enim haec tralaticia; de Galliis constituetur, erit qui intercedat; deinde alius existet qui, nisi libere liceat de omnibus provinciis decernere senatui, reliquas impediat* (ib. viii, 5, 2). *Ut video, causa haec integra in proximum annum transferetur; et quantum divino, relinquendus tibi erit qui provinciam obtineat* (because Cilicia is not likely to be made praetorian before 49). *Nam non expeditur successio, quoniam Galliae quae habent intercessorem in eandem condicionem quam ceterae provinciae vocantur* (viii, 9, 2).

At the end of September, after many postponements, caused partly by Caesar's threat of *intercessio*, partly by Pompey's uncertain attitude, the senatorial policy was embodied in several important decrees. (1) A meeting of the senate was to be called next year on March 1, by the consuls, C. Marcellus and Aemilius Paulus, to make a settlement *de provinciis consularibus*, which was to be debated day by day, and alone (*neve quid coniunctim*), i.e. without the praetorian. As this was the preclusive date fixed by the *lex Pompeia-Licinia*, the Gallic provinces would not be excluded from the debate, and it was no doubt intended to fix one or both of them as consular for 49, as M. Marcellus had vainly tried to do earlier in the year. As this was in perfect accordance with the agreement between Caesar and Pompey, no Caesarian tribune blocked this decree. But as the *lex Sempronia* was now assumed to be obsolete, and there might be some doubt about this, the magistrates of this or the following year were instructed *si quid de ea re lato opus esset*, to get the necessary

[1] Even if Cilicia and the eight praetorian provinces were to be filled from July 50 and not from Jan. 49, it would still be the case that the only provinces available as consular in 49 would be those not already fixed as praetorian. As a matter of fact, all existing governors had to remain till the beginning of 49.

sanction from the people.[1] (2) As the elimination of the *lex Sempronia* made the settlement of consular provinces liable to be blocked by *intercessio*, it was decreed that any tribune blocking the settlement to be arrived at next year would be treated as acting *contra rempublicam*, a decree which might have consequences, but was more likely to be futile. (3) Contrary to Caesar's wish, that all the provinces should be decided together, a decree was now made about the praetorian provinces. Such a decree was abnormal because, as things had worked out, instead of the praetorian provinces being automatically settled by the previous selection of the consular, they were now to be selected first, so that the consular would necessarily be those not made praetorian, and not *vice versa*. Again, ostensibly the praetorian provinces for 50 were being fixed, but owing to the confusion and uncertainty caused by the *lex Pompeia* probably all provincial governorships in 51 began, like Cilicia and Syria, late in the year, so that practically, if not formally, it was for 49 that praetorian provinces were now assigned. The decree passed was that Cilicia and the eight provinces held by ex-praetors should (i. e. when they fell vacant) be filled by ex-praetors of five, or, failing them, of four or three years' standing. The result would be that, when March 1 arrived, and the consular provinces for 49 had to be fixed, only Syria and Caesar's two provinces would be available, and all hope that the latter might be left out of the distribution would be gone. It is no wonder, therefore, that this decree was blocked by Pansa's *intercessio*.[2] But though the question of praetorian provinces was hung up, it was open to the senate, on the initiative of C. Marcellus and his colleague, to settle the consular provinces on March 1, 50, the preclusive date of the *lex Pompeia-Licinia*. Unfortunately Caelius does not describe the meeting, but we know, explicitly from Suetonius and Appian, constructively from Cicero and Caelius, that it

[1] See above, p. 166, n. 1. That this possible appeal to the people had reference to the present decree, and not to any decision to be made next year, is shown by the fact that the instruction is given primarily to the present magistrates, and only on their failure to act to those of next year.

[2] The decrees, with others less essential, are given in *ad fam.* viii, 8, 5–8. The blocking of the last decree made it certain that Cicero would not be relieved at the end of his year, and as a matter of fact no governors appointed in 51 were relieved till the beginning of 49 (Caes. *b. c.* 1, 6).

took place and that the contemplated decree was passed. What was it?

Appian (2, 27) says it was *πέμπειν Καίσαρι διαδόχους ἐπὶ τὰ ἔθνη· καὶ γὰρ ἔληγεν ὁ χρόνος*, but, as we have seen above, he did not understand this to mean immediate recall. Cicero (*ad Att.* vii, 7, 6) makes it clear that it was a decree *ut Caesari succederetur*, a decree which might have been made effective if M. Marcellus had been supported. The s. c. of Sept. 29 proves beyond doubt that the only question before the senate on March 1 could have been *de provinciis consularibus*. Lastly, as that s. c. was passed in consequence of Pompey's expressed wish, *eum post Kal. Mart. decedere*, the effect of the proposal made by Marcellus on March 1, 50, must have been for Caesar to be superseded on March 1, 49.[1] We have already seen that there was only one way of bringing this about, viz. by making his provinces consular on the date of his intended recall. This is what *ut Caesari succederetur* had meant in 56, and the conjunction now of the same phrase with *de provinciis consularibus* in the s. c. makes its meaning certain. The proposal, therefore, of C. Marcellus was that the consular provinces for 49 should be either the two Gauls from March 1 or Transalpine Gaul from that date and Syria from Jan. 1. In the latter case, Cisalpine Gaul would have been afterwards assigned with the praetorian provinces, though not available till March 1. If this decree had not been vetoed, and if the supplementary step of selecting qualified successors and sending them out had been taken, Caesar would have found himself a *privatus* on March 1, 49.

On the other hand, Hirschfeld (pp. 82 and 86) and apparently Judeich[2] regard the proposal of Marcellus *ut Caesari succederetur* as one for immediate recall on or shortly after March 1, 50. I shall come to closer grips with the latter in a later section, and I will only point out here that if Caesar's legal term extended till Dec. 29, 50, the only logical explanation of Marcellus' proposal is that it was to render possible in the proper way his actual supersession on that date. Judeich is cut off from

[1] I reserve a full examination of the phrase *post Kal. Mart. decedere* for the section on Pompey's attitude.

[2] The proposals of the two Marcelli, involving, as they both do, the inconvenient date, March 1, do not interest Judeich very much, and he steers clear of them as much as he can.

this explanation by his reference of *post Kal. Mart. decedere* to the year 50, so that he is compelled to adopt, as in the case of the proposal in 51, what I venture to call the irrational view that Marcellus proposed by senatorial decree to deprive Caesar of ten months' command legally conferred upon him by the people.

Hirschfeld's position is different, but hardly more logical. He does not pretend that March 1, 50, was the *legis dies* in the sense of being the legal termination of the command, but merely in the sense that it was the only time limit specified in the *lex Pompeia-Licinia.* Originally, as preclusive, it was in Caesar's interest, indirectly guaranteeing his position till the senate was allowed to discuss it. Moreover, as long as the *lex Sempronia* was in force, no decree resulting from the discussion could make Caesar's provinces consular before 48. But when Pompey's law had abrogated the *lex Sempronia,* the preclusive date became permissive in the sense that the senate, in the absence of any other legal limit, could at once supersede Caesar by sending out successors forthwith, this being the meaning of *ut Caesari succedatur.*

Now (1) the only way of superseding or 'succeeding' Caesar, whether there was a legal term or not, was to make his provinces consular (or perhaps praetorian) from a fixed date. (2) The only difference made by the abrogation of the *lex Sempronia* was that on March 1, 50, the senate could make Caesar's provinces either consular or praetorian for 49 instead of for 48. To suppose that with the passing of the *lex Pompeia* or the abrogation of the *lex Sempronia* all rule and custom with regard to provincial appointments were cancelled, and that provinces could be declared consular and filled on the same day, is preposterous and disproved in the case of praetorian provinces by the inoperative decree of Sept. 51. (3) Even if the course ascribed to Marcellus and the senate had been permissible, it would in the particular case have been impossible. Caesar's province could not be made consular on March 1, and he could not therefore be replaced by successors on that date, for the sufficient reason that there were already two consular provinces, Cilicia and Syria, which would not be vacant till June or July at the earliest.

Hirschfeld's whole position depends upon juggling with the phrases *tempus legis* and *festgesetzte Termin*; *denn dass sich ein solcher darin* (in the *lex Pompeia-Licinia*) *befand, ist an und für sich nicht zu bezweifeln* (pp. 83–4). If, when Cicero said in Dec. *praeteriit tempus legis*, he referred to March 1, 50, he must have regarded it as the legal termination of Caesar's command.[1] Hirschfeld does not pretend that it was.[2] It was only a preclusive or permissive date, and this could only be the actual termination if the senate was able to use the permission effectively on that day. The real *Termin* of the command, whether described as *legis dies* or not, would be the day on which the senate succeeded in doing this, and was therefore not a *festgesetzte Termin*.

We shall take it, therefore, that on March 1 or one of the following days the senate passed a decree declaring the Gallic provinces (or perhaps one of them, the other to be settled later) consular from March 1, 49, after which date Caesar would be *privatus*. This was not contrary to the *lex Pompeia-Licinia*, but it was a violation of the understanding made at Luca, which Caesar was still determined, if possible by constitutional means, to maintain. The *lex Sempronia* being out of force, there was no constitutional reason why Curio should not block the decree by his *intercessio*, and it is clear from *ad fam.* ix, 13, 2 and *ad Att.* vii, 7, 5 that he took this course. Provision had been made in Sept. against the possibility of this in the second of the decrees then passed, and the senate by bold action might, as Cicero believed, and as it actually did in the following Jan., have made its decree effective.[3] As a matter of fact, however, Curio maintained his *intercessio*, and threatened to use it against all compromises, so that the decree remained ineffective till the end of the year.

[1] Hirschfeld strangely overlooks the point that in Cicero's eyes *tempus libidinis tuae* was more correct than *tempus legis*. The *tempus legis* therefore was self-imposed by Caesar himself. I leave it to Hirschfeld's supporters to decide whether this suits best March 1, 50, or March 1, 49.

[2] If Hirschfeld is determined to make March 1, 50, the *legis dies*, I wonder that he does not more boldly adopt Dio's statement that the legal end was in 50, and explain it by making the second *quinquennium* date from the passing of *lex Pompeia-Licinia*, presumably on March 1, 55. This would mean the withdrawal of several ill-considered judgements, and would be vulnerable at many points, but it would at least be logical.

[3] The moves and counter moves of the year, including the compromise *ut Idibus Novembribus decedat*, I shall deal with in the section on Pompey's position. I am only concerned here with the technical question *de successione*.

At what point Curio first made his suggestion that Pompey and Caesar should resign together (i.e. as I understand it on March 1, 49) is not clear. In representing it as Curio's reply to the decree of March 1, Hirschfeld is following Appian (2, 24), one of those late writers, the acceptance of whose statements marks, in his opinion, incompetence to weigh evidence. At any rate, the daring proposal, carried, apparently late in the year, by a huge majority (App. 2, 30), was merely a piece of futile imbecility into which Curio trapped the senate, and as it contained no settlement with regard to either Caesar's provinces or Pompey's, it had no relation to the question *de successione*.

That question might have dawdled on, as Caelius wrote in 51 (viii, 5, 2), *plus biennium*, but for Caesar's ultimatum at the beginning of 49. The senate, realizing the alternative, *depugnandum est aut habenda e lege ratio*, replied by a decree, *uti ante certam diem Caesar exercitum dimittat; si non faciat, eum adversus rem publicam facturum videri* (*b.c.* 1, 1). This was not an act of *successio*, but a counter ultimatum, intended perhaps to clear the way for the only step by which Caesar could be formally superseded. It at any rate had that effect, for it provoked the *intercessio* of the Caesarean tribunes, who were then dealt with as Marcellus would have dealt with Curio ten months earlier. The last decree was passed, and the tribunes fled from Rome. Their departure removed the deadlock of the past ten months, and the senate in a subsequent meeting proceeded to the *successio provinciarum*, including those of Caesar. It was decreed that Further Gaul and Syria should be consular provinces, while Cisalpine Gaul was one of the praetorian, the respective governors being Ahenobarbus, Scipio, and Nonianus (*b.c.* 1, 6, *ad fam.* xvi, 12, 3). In one respect only were these decrees irregular, viz. that the provinces were fixed as consular and praetorian simultaneously or almost simultaneously[1] with the appointment and dispatch of the new governors, a course which I have argued could not have been taken in March 50. It was excused now by the emergencies of what was already practically a state of civil war. At the same time, unless Caesar acted as an enemy, his legal term was not to be cut short. The *certa dies* of the

[1] Apart from civil war, Caesar's successors would still not be sent out till March 1, but on crossing the Rubicon his status as governor was gone.

ultimatum was the real *festgesetzte Termin* the *legis dies*, March 1, and Ahenobarbus and Nonianus would only succeed on that date. Thus even after the crossing of the Rubicon, when negotiations for avoiding war were again pending, Caesar was required to return in *provinciam*, an indication that his term had not yet expired (*b. c.* 1, 11), and it is not till the late summer, when March 1 was a date of the past, that Caesar can talk of *abductum exercitum.*

III. CAESAR'S SECOND CONSULSHIP AND THE TRIBUNICIAN LAW

It was at Luca that arrangements were made for the second consulship of Pompey and Crassus and for the future position of Caesar. It may be regarded, therefore, as certain that his own second consulship was also provided for. The year fixed for it was 48, (*a*) because the five years' extension of his command made an earlier year impossible; and (*b*) because Caesar thought it convenient and advisable to conform to Sulla's law requiring an interval of ten years after his first consulship in 59. That he made a point and a merit of this conformity is shown by his own words in *b. c.* 1, 32: *docet se nullum extraordinarium honorem appetere, sed exspectato legitimo tempore consulatus eo fuisse contentum.* The same conclusion must be drawn from Dio, 40, 51, who says that the *absentis ratio* was to be allowed ὅταν ἐκ τῶν νόμων καθήκῃ. But if the consulship for 48 was agreed upon at Luca, it cannot be doubted that an understanding was also arrived at that Caesar should stand for it in his absence, and so be enabled to take advantage of the existing regulations, and retain his provinces till entering on the office, since it was well known that the *optimates* would impeach him for the irregular acts of his first consulship the moment he became a *privatus* (Suet. *Iul.* 30). No steps, however, were taken at once to secure this privilege, since there was plenty of time, and Caesar would naturally not wish to disclose his full hand.

But in 52, when Pompey was made sole consul, and his attitude towards Caesar had become at least ambiguous, we may assume that the latter claimed the carrying out of the understanding as to his canvass in absence. Pompey, who within his own limitations was a man of honour, allowed and perhaps even initiated the law of the ten tribunes. Among the many statements as to this law, the following of Cicero is as explicit as any. Pompey in his third consulship *contendit ut decem tribuni pl. ferrent ut absentis ratio haberetur, quod idem ipse sanxit lege quadam sua* (*ad Att.* viii, 3, 3; conf. ib. vii, 3, 4; Liv. *epit.* 107 and 108; Caes. *b. c.* 1, 9; Suet. *Iul.* 26, where the privilege is to be used *quandoque imperi tempus expleri coepisset*; App. 2, 20; D. C. 40, 51).

A question arises whether this exemption was still uncancelled at the end of 50, when it seemed likely to be of vital importance for Caesar's position. We know that it was jeopardized by Pompey's *lex de iure magistratuum*, which contained a clause, ostensibly perhaps tralatician, κελεύοντα τοὺς ἀρχήν τινα ἐπαγγέλλοντας ἐς τὴν ἐκκλησίαν πάντως ἀπαντᾶν ὥστε μηδένα ἀπόντα αἱρεῖσθαι (D. C. 40, 56). It appears, however, from Dio, Suetonius (c. 28), and Cicero (*ad Att.* viii, 3, 3) that Pompey had in some way, though according to Suetonius after his own law had been engraved, corrected the 'oversight' and legalized Caesar's right. Marcellus in 51 must have taken this view, since Suetonius says: *rettulit ne absentis ratio comitiis haberetur, . . . quando nec plebiscito Pompeius postea abrogasset.* The epitomator agrees with this: *agente in senatu M. Marcello ut Caesar in petitionem consulatus veniret, cum is lege lata in id tempus consulatus provinciam obtinere deberet.* Cicero too in several passages, but very forcibly in *ad fam.* vi, 6, 5, implies the continued validity of the law: *rationem absentis haberi non tam pugnavi ut liceret, quam ut, quoniam ipso consule pugnante populus iusserat, haberetur.*

It seems important to establish two points about this law. (1) It limited the privilege to a particular year, viz. 49, and could not have enabled Caesar to stand in his absence either before or after that year. This is not only indicated by the words of Dio Cassius already cited, ὅταν ἐκ τῶν νόμων καθήκῃ, but from Caesar's own words (*b. c.* 1, 9), *cuius absentis rationem haberi proximis comitiis populus iussisset.* It is indeed inconceivable either that such an exemption would have been granted for an undefined year, or that Pompey, who was in a sense responsible for the law, or Caelius Rufus, who knew all that was going on, would have been under any misapprehension on this point. Hirschfeld, however, strangely interprets several statements of Caelius as showing that both he and Pompey were under the impression that Caesar thought of standing at the elections in 50 for the consulship of 49 (*Klio*, v, p. 240). (*a*) Early in Sept. 51 Caelius writes (*ad fam.* viii, 9, 5) that Pompey will clearly not allow Caesar to retain his command and to be consul designate. (The reading is slightly corrupt, but the sense is clear.) He was, however, not prepared to recommend any decree on the matter at present. This only shows what is clear from other evidence, that the situation threatened in 49 was already occupying attention in 51. (*b*) In Oct. 51, after enumerating the decrees passed on Sept. 29, and recording Pompey's promise to take up a definite line against Caesar after March 1 next, Caelius adds (viii, 8, 9): *Itaque iam, ut video, alteram utram in condicionem descendere vult Caesar, ut aut maneat neque hoc anno ratio sua habeatur, aut, si designatus esse poterit, decedat.* Caelius is obviously making a forecast of his own as to Caesar's probable course, and he is certainly wrong in supposing that he would resign after being elected, since his one aim was to leave no interval in which he would be *privatus*. But Caelius could not be wrong about the year of Caesar's candidature. It was the year on which all eyes were centred the year which in particular he and Cicero were always discussing, as that in which Caesar's legal term would expire, and which could not but be specified in the tribunician law. Neither for Cicero nor for any one else could there be the smallest ambiguity as to the identity of *hoc anno*, and it speaks little for Hirschfeld's power of weighing evidence that he should seriously adduce the the *ipse dixit* of 'his friend, Bardt' as decisive that *hoc anno* can only be the electoral year in which Caelius was writing. (*c*) In a letter written in May 50 (*ad fam.* viii, 11, 3) Caelius, after mentioning a suggestion believed to be favoured by Pompey, that Caesar should be recalled 'on Nov. 13', concludes a passage, to be discussed elsewhere, by saying of Pompey: *valde autem non vult et plane timet Caesarem cos. design. prius quam exercitum et provinciam tradiderit.* Hirschfeld denies that this can refer to Nov. 49, because Pompey's dislike and fear of the *absentis ratio* is inconsistent with his allowing it by letting Caesar stay till Nov. But on the assumption that Pompey mistook the year of Caesar's intended *ratio*, precisely the same difficulty would arise on referring the Nov. to 50. When does Hirschfeld suppose that Pompey recognized the truth? He will hardly deny that he had done so in Sept. 50, when, according to Caelius, Pompey is using precisely the same language, two months after the elections of 50, as he had used a year before: *constituit Pompeius non pati Caesarem aliter consulem fieri, nisi exercitum et provincias tradiderit.* Hirschfeld's motive in attributing this mistake to Pompey and Caelius is obvious, for, if Caesar's legal term extended to March 49, they could never have been so simple as to believe that he would voluntarily curtail it.

(2) The second point to be established about the *absentis ratio* is its precise scope and effect. Its object was not to extend Caesar's command or to enable him to retain it after the legal term had expired. For it must be remembered that, when the tribunician law was passed, Caesar could already count on retaining his position till the end of 49 owing to the joint effect of the *lex Pompeia-Licinia*, the provincial regulations of Sulla, and the operation of the *lex Sempronia*. But Caesar desired more than this; he desired for the sake of his own safety to step direct from his provincial command into the consulship at the beginning of 48, and as a personal canvass in the summer of 49 would mean the relinquishment of his *imperium*, the *absentis ratio* was the indispensable condition of the last *semenstre imperium* of 49. When Caesar complains to the senate in Jan. 49 (*b. c.* 1, 9), *quod populi Romani beneficium sibi per contumeliam ab inimicis extorqueretur, ereptoque semenstri imperio ad urbem retraheretur, cuius absentis rationem haberi proximis comitiis populus iussisset*, and when the epitomator (108) says that he had the right *lege lata in tempus consulatus provinciam obtinere*, the reference is merely to the indirect result originally aimed at by the tribunician law. The law in itself said nothing of *imperium*, or army or provinces, but, as all the evidence shows, was merely *ut absentis ratio haberetur*.

That object was thwarted by the *lex Pompeia de iure magistratuum*, which, though it did not invalidate the tribunician law, might easily make it useless to Caesar. To assert with Hirschfeld (IV p. 85) that after 52 Caesar was compelled to fall back on the tribunician law, or with Rice Holmes (p. 50) that that law implied a right on Caesar's part to retain his province till at least July, is to misunderstand the situation. It was possible now to make Caesar a *privatus* after March 1, 49 (on Hirschfeld's view, much earlier), and if that was done, though he might still claim the *absentis ratio*, he would have to use it as a *privatus* and practically as an exile, and not as the governor of the Gallic provinces. I venture to lay it down as incontrovertible that whatever interval there was between the *legis dies*, whether March 1, 50, or Dec. 29, 50, or March 1, 49, and the consular elections, was incapable of being bridged by the tribunician law. An appeal is sometimes made to Cicero's words in *ad Att.* vii. 7, 6, as proving that the retention of the army was sanctioned by the grant of the *absentis ratio*. *Exercitum retinentis, cum legis dies transierit, rationem haberi placet? Mihi vero ne absentis quidem. Sed cum hoc datum est, illud una datum est.* But Cicero's point merely is that the danger should have been foreseen when the law was passed, since at that time the *absentis ratio* involved, as it was meant to do, the *exercitum retinentis ratio*.

But, it may be asked, how is the fact to be explained that at the close of 50 the struggle between Caesar and the senate seems to be concentrated round the privilege of the *absentis ratio*? Why does the former so insist upon it—*habe rationem meam*—and why are his opponents so outraged at his impudence in doing so? The answer is simple. Caesar had not given up the programme agreed upon at Luca, which was indeed more essential to his safety now than it had seemed then, of retaining his command till the end of 49, and only resigning it for the consulship. The retention of his command beyond March 1, though no longer secured by legal safeguards, might still be compassed without violating the constitution, but it would be a mere postponement of the danger without the consulship at the end, and this was as completely dependent now as before 52 on the *absentis ratio*. It was therefore a crucial point for Caesar, and if for Caesar, then for his adversaries also.

The privilege of canvassing in absence was not one which the senate could allow or withhold, since its legal conferment by the people was obviously not disputed, and if Caesar still found himself in possession of his provinces in July, nothing could prevent its exercise. But there was an awkward gap between

March 1, *cum legis dies transierit*, and the elections, and it was the question of this gap which agitated political circles at the end of Dec. 50. If the senate could effectively make Caesar's provinces consular or praetorian, and be ready to send out successors, Caesar would be *privatus* after March 1, and the *absentis ratio*, though not disallowed, would be useless to him. Up to Dec. he had prevented the necessary steps from being taken by the constitutional method of tribunician *intercessio*, and it was the possibility that he might maintain his position even after March 1, either by the same tactics or by diplomatic persuasion (*vel per senatum vel per tribunos*), which so excited Cicero in his letters to Atticus. As matters stood, there was only one way in which Caesar could be deprived of the *absentis ratio*, and that was by either compelling the withdrawal of the *intercessio*, or in the last resort quashing it by the last decree. Whether it would have taken this course, which, as Cicero realized, practically meant civil war, but for Caesar's unexpected ultimatum on Jan. 1, it is impossible to say, but at any rate, when it was taken, and the Gallic provinces duly assigned to successors after March 1, Caesar recognized that the *absentis ratio* was of no use to him, and it is this which explains his subsequent suggestion that, if Pompey would go to Spain, *ad consulatus petitionem se venturum, neque iam se velle absente se rationem haberi suam; se praesentem trinum nundinum petiturum* (*ad fam*. xvi, 12, 3).

One more point may be cleared up. It has been argued that even if Caesar had been allowed to remain (or more correctly, had succeeded through his obstruction in remaining) till July, and had been designated consul in his absence, he would have been no more entitled than before to remain till the end of the year. That is perfectly true, but Caesar's election, while still governor, being due to the want of vigorous action by the senate, would considerably strengthen his position, and weaken that of the senate, and continued obstruction during the last six months of the year would have been rendered easier by its success in the first six. Thus Caesar's chances of getting the last *semenstre imperium* would have been very favourable, since, as Caelius had said in 50, want of courage on the part of the senate would mean that *Caesar quoad volet manebit* (*ad fam*. viii, 11, 3).

IV. THE ATTITUDE OF POMPEY TOWARDS CAESAR'S COMMAND

As Hirschfeld and to a certain extent Judeich claim to find support for their theories as to the legal termination of Caesar's command in Pompey's attitude, as indicated both by the general situation and by certain passages in Cicero's correspondence, it will be as well to examine this aspect of the question with some minuteness.

It can hardly be denied that up to 56 Pompey's position in the coalition had been a secondary one, that his enforced activity in Rome was uncongenial, and that he was anxious for a position more commensurate with that of Caesar. In the first half of 56 two incidents, in neither of which Pompey was directly concerned, convinced Caesar that the security of his own position called for some reconstruction of the coalition. The first incident was the ill-advised attempt of Cicero to give effect to the view of strict constitutionalists that Caesar's agrarian law was a *lex vitiosa.* The second was the design to fix, in accordance with the *lex Sempronia,* one or both of the Gauls as consular provinces for 54, and when Caesar should thus have become a *privatus* at the end of his five years, to impeach him for the acts of his consulship (Suet. *Iul.* 24 and 30). These were the occasions for the conference of Luca, at which it is clear from Suetonius and Appian that Caesar was the dominant figure.[1]

That he had been the dominant partner in the coalition for the past three years and a half cannot be doubted, and there seems no reason why at this point he should have adopted the principle, attributed to him by Judeich, of 'equal rights for all'. But no doubt the immediate securities which he desired for his own position as well as future acquiescence in it on the part of his allies had to be purchased, and Caesar was prepared to relinquish the sole military headship of the coalition by conceding to both his partners a parallel provincial command. Hence it was agreed that Crassus should have a command in

[1] I have already alluded to Dio's demonstrably incorrect version, in which the meeting at Luca is ignored, and Pompey and Crassus are represented as acting independently of Caesar.

Syria and Pompey one in the two Spains for five years.[1] To carry out this arrangement, as well as to establish Caesar's own position, Pompey and Crassus were to hold the consulship in 55, thus disposing of the threatening and inconvenient candidature of Ahenobarbus.

The legal termination of Pompey's command of the Spanish provinces was not a factor in the problem presented at the end of 50, because by its uncovenanted extension in 52 it would have outlasted Caesar's, and even Caesar's second consulship, by several years. But at the conference of Luca it was not without its importance. According to Judeich (*Rhein. Mus.* 1913, p. 4) there can be no doubt that Pompey and Crassus entered on their provincial command in the normal way after their consulship, i. e. on Jan. 1, 54. I should have thought, on the contrary, remembering the precedent of the *lex Vatinia*, and the fact that Pompey and Crassus desired the consulship mainly as a means of securing their own military position, that the necessary laws would have been passed early in the year, and that their provincial *imperium* would have begun, like Caesar's, at once. This supposition is confirmed by the fact that Crassus not only collected his forces while still consul, but actually left Rome *paludatus* for the East in the middle of November (*ad Att.* iv, 13, 2). Judeich is anxious to show, as we shall see, that Pompey's command was timed to expire on Dec. 29, 50, but he seems to have overlooked the fact that his actual, though not his legal, term would end on that date, even if his five years began in March or April 55. As the Sullan regulations were still in force, no successor could take his place when the legal term ended, and he would remain in command, whether in Rome or in Spain, till two of the praetors of 50 succeeded him on Jan. 1, 49, this being the extreme limit of his *imperium*, as depending on the *lex Trebonia*.[2] Of course his own *lex de iure magistratuum* would

[1] The *quinquennium* of Pompey and Crassus depends on the same writers of the imperial age (with Dio thrown in) whose evidence as to Caesar's second five years Hirschfeld sweeps aside. It is curious, but characteristic, that he should only reject that part of their evidence which conflicts with his own preconceived hypothesis.

[2] Dr. Rice Holmes suggests that, as the *lex Sempronia* was in force, Pompey probably inserted in the *lex Trebonia* a clause similar to that in the *lex Pompeia-Licinia*, making it possible for him to retain his provinces till the end of 49. We have no right to assume this without evidence, and it seems to me unlikely. In the first place, it would mean the retention of his command

have made it possible to recall Pompey at the end of his legal term, but neither that law nor the extension of his command for a second *quinquennium* was foreseen at Luca.

But what were the arrangements made for Caesar's benefit? Their practical effect is not disputed by either Hirschfeld or Judeich. It was that Caesar should be enabled to retain his provinces till the end of 49. His two essential requirements were (*a*) ample time to complete his military and political work in Gaul, and (*b*) the avoidance of an interval during which, as *privatus*, he would be liable to the impeachment which men like Ahenobarbus and Cato openly threatened. His only goal of safety was a second consulship, and it cannot be doubted that this was arranged for him, but in accordance with the Sullan requirement of a ten years' interval, and therefore not till 48. The question is how the interval between March 1, 54, up to which the *lex Vatinia* secured him, and the end of 49 was guaranteed.

In the first place, we may assume that what was at the time a minor point, though circumstances lent it a factitious importance at a later stage, permission to stand for the consulship without abandoning his command by returning in the summer of 49, was arranged to be secured at the proper time. It was an essential part of the scheme, and could not possibly have been overlooked. Another point on which there is no dispute is that skilful use was made of the *lex Sempronia de provinciis consularibus*. It was certain that Transalpine Gaul at least, when vacated by Caesar, would have to be a consular province, and would therefore by the terms of this law definitely have to be fixed as such before the election of the consul who would hold it (Sall. *Iug.* 27). In order to make sure, therefore, that no ex-consul could be assigned to it or to Cisalpine Gaul before 48, steps were to be taken to make illegal the fixing of either of Caesar's provinces as consular before March 1, 50. Such a legal prohibition against applying the *lex Sempronia* to Caesar's *successio* till 50 meant that he could be superseded at the earliest by one of the consuls of 49 at the beginning of 48. But Caesar was

eighteen months at least after the legal term, whereas Caesar would only have had ten months extra. In the second place, it assumes that Pompey's provinces would be made, one or both, consular, whereas both the Spains, even the more important, Further Spain, were usually praetorian, and in that case Pompey could not expect to remain after the end of 50, when praetors of that year could succeed him.

not likely to be content with such negative protection. He naturally required a law definitely extending his command, and, as a matter of fact, this preclusive stipulation was to be nothing more than a clause in such a law.

It might of course have been arranged for this law to extend Caesar's command up to the end of 49, and this would have made his position legally unassailable. But such an unsymmetrical extension of five years and ten months would inevitably have disclosed what was almost certainly the secret arrangement, that Caesar was to step straight from his provincial post into a second consulship. Besides, it was not necessary, and the more obvious and regular course of granting a second *quinquennium*, i.e. to March 1, 49, would perfectly meet the case. For as long as the Sullan system was in force, even *cum legis dies transierit*, Caesar could not be replaced till the end of the year, there being the same obstacle to a consul of 50 succeeding him on March 1, 49 as, according to Cicero, there would have been to a consul of 55 succeeding him on March 1, 54.

In Caesar's interest therefore, and I insist that this was the dominant factor at Luca, a five years' extension was the sufficient and obvious course, since it carried with it an extension to the end of the year, an extension also guaranteed, for the sake of double security, by the non-applicability of the *lex Sempronia* to Caesar's provinces till March 1, 50. Now it is precisely such a five years' legal extension to which all the ancient authorities, as we have seen, except Dio Cassius testify, and few will disagree with the remark of Dr. Rice Holmes that in default of very strong counter-evidence their testimony must stand.

This at least is admitted by Judeich, who nevertheless for the flimsiest reasons argues that the legal termination of the second *quinquennium* was the last day of Dec. 50. His particular arguments, derived from passages of Cicero's correspondence written in that year, I postpone to their proper place, but the general justification of his position, based on his view of the situation at Luca, must be dealt with here.

Ignoring the evidence of Suetonius and Appian as to the antecedents of the conference, and taking no account of the threatened attack on Caesar's position by Cicero's motion on the Campanian land question, and by the plan for recalling him in 54, Judeich seems to regard the meeting at Luca as due to something like a revolt on the part of Pompey and Crassus. In accordance with this view, Caesar's primary aim is represented as, not the securing of an impregnable position for himself, but the conciliation of a discontented Pompey and a sulky Crassus by the concession of the principle 'equal rights for all'.[1] Not only so, but he was willing, no doubt in the hope of ultimate advantage to himself, to soothe Pompey's vanity by accepting less, as the result of immediate legislation, than he might have fairly claimed. According to the principle of 'equal rights for all', each of the three was to have a second consulship and a quinquennial command. But, while Pompey and Crassus were to have their consulship at once, Caesar was content to wait seven years for his. Again, while an extension of five years to his own command would mean its extension to March 1, 49, he was content to sacrifice two months of his command by allowing its legal termination to be fixed for Dec. 29, 50, because that was the date on which the five years of Pompey and Crassus would come to an end, and it would have given too much offence to allow his own term to extend beyond theirs.

This explanation, so far from being convincing, seems to me unsound at every point. (1) If it is a question of the legal termination of Caesar's command as compared with that of Pompey and Crassus, Judeich, as we have seen, has no right to assume that the precedent of the *lex Vatinia* was departed from, and that the *lex Trebonia* fixed the commencement of the commands not at once, but at the end of the year, an assumption made improbable by the fact that Crassus left Rome in the middle of November. It is far more likely that the five years for which Syria and the Spanish provinces were granted would legally terminate at some date in the first half of 50. (2) But, even if Caesar had consented to allow his *quinquennium* to be cut short by two months so as to coincide with the end of Pompey's term, would the latter have been so simple as to regard this as a case of equal rights as between himself and Caesar? Whether December 29, 50, was the legal end of his *quinquennium*,

[1] The view that Pompey and Crassus were in revolt against Caesar receives no support except from Dio, whose presentation of the situation is wholly vitiated by his ignorance that any conference was held at all.

or, as is more probable, the end of the year in which his *quinquennium* would expire, and so by the Sullan regulations the the actual limit of his command, it was in either case, in the absence of further legislation, a date beyond which no extension was possible. On the other hand, as Judeich himself admits, the sole object of the clause in the *lex Pompeia-Licinia*, prohibiting Caesar's *successio* till March 50, was to make it certain that his *quinquennium*, whenever ending, would be practically prolonged till the end of 49. Pompey therefore could have been under no illusions, and unless he already meditated the disloyalty of which he was afterwards guilty, he must at Luca have been prepared not only to see Caesar retain his command twelve months after his own had expired, but to face the possibilities of Caesar's second consulship in 48. (3) Judeich seems to overlook the fact that Caesar, in this vain attempt to conciliate or delude Pompey, would have sacrificed much more than two months of his full *quinquennium*. The full *quinquennium* would, under the existing Sullan system, have made it impossible for a successor to replace him before January 1, 48, whereas, if Judeich is right, he laid himself open to be superseded on January 1, 49. Is this what Judeich is thinking of when he declares that it was as a set-off to the sacrifice of two months that Caesar insisted on the clause already referred to being inserted in the *lex Pompeia-Licinia*? But (*a*) such a set-off would have been a flagrant violation of the supposed principle of 'equal rights for all', for instead of the two months sacrificed, it not only restored them in another form, but added the last ten months of the year as well. (*b*) The use made of the *lex Sempronia*, bound up as it was with the constitutional method of *successio*, could not have been a mere after-thought, but must have been an essential part of Caesar's scheme. With it and the full *quinquennium* he had a double security. By the former his provinces could not be assigned to the consuls of any year earlier than 49; by the latter, even if they were assigned to the consuls of 50, such assignment would be inoperative for the reasons given by Cicero, when the question arose in 56. If Caesar had voluntarily relinquished, as Judeich supposes, this second guarantee, he would have allowed his whole case to rest on the *sanctio* in the law of Pompey and Crassus, and if this had been disregarded, as similar 'sanctions' often were, and as Marcellus actually tried to disregard it in 51, he would have had to resign his provinces to the consuls of 50. Of course, as the result of the changed situation after 52, Caesar lost both guarantees, but that does not make it easier to believe with Judeich that at the very moment in 56, when he was realizing the bar offered by the Sullan system to his recall in March 54, he would of his own accord have renounced the similar advantage which the same system might give him in 49. If Judeich had been a little less anxious to establish a new theory independent alike of Mommsen and Hirschfeld, he might have examined the situation, as it presented itself at Luca, somewhat more carefully, instead of resting his whole position, as he virtually does, on a single phrase of Cicero, *praeteriit tempus legis*, written at the end of 50.[1]

A bolder, but not more logical, theory is put forward by Hirschfeld. Rejecting the consensus of authorities for a second *quinquennium*, he supposes that the arrangement made at Luca and carried out by the *lex Pompeia-Licinia* was that Caesar's command should be prorogued from March 1, 54, without any specified time limit, but should be indirectly confirmed up to March 1, 50, by a clause making it illegal to fix Caesar's provinces as consular before that date. But as, while the *lex Sempronia* was in force, no decision taken on that day by the senate could bring Caesar's command to a termination before the last day of 49, he could count on retaining his provinces up to that date. No real *legis dies* therefore was fixed either at Luca or by the *lex Pompeia-Licinia*, for March 1, 50, was merely the date on which the senate might take the preliminary step towards recalling Caesar, and even December 29, 49, could only be regarded as the *legis dies* conditionally on the senate taking that step.

With the inconsistencies in connexion with the phrase *legis dies* in which Hirschfeld's theory inevitably lands him, I have already dealt. The question here is whether such an arrangement could

[1] I have already dealt with this passage, and also pointed out that Judeich's theory is absolutely irreconcilable both with Pompey's view that Caesar should be recalled *post Kal. Martias* (*ad fam.* viii, 8, 4), and with Cicero's statement (*ad Att.* viii, 3, 3) that Marcellus wished to limit his command *Kalendarum Martiarum die*. If these dates refer to 50, Judeich is committed to the impossible view that Pompey and Marcellus thought of depriving Caesar of ten months' command legally conferred by the people. We shall see later that his interpretation of *ad fam.* viii, 11, 3 involves the same irrational hypothesis.

have commended itself to Caesar at Luca. Hirschfeld suggests that he would have preferred it to a definite five years' extension, because the latter would have implied that that time was likely to be required for the conquest of Gaul, while this arrangement might suggest a speedier termination of the war. (*Klio*, iv, p. 87.) This might have been so, if March 1, 50, could be regarded as even a possible termination of the command, but by a strange confusion of thought Hirschfeld forgets that even on his own theory it was only after Pompey's law of 52 and the consequent abrogation of the *lex Sempronia* that the possibility of ending it so soon could have presented itself, whereas he professes to be discussing Caesar's calculations in 56.

But a more important consideration is whether the vague arrangement supposed by Hirschfeld would have satisfied Caesar. It in fact gave him no security at all if the 'sanction' forbidding action by the senate till March 50 was disregarded. The *lex Pompeia-Licinia*, on Hirschfeld's view, simply continued Caesar's command till it was terminated by the senate's action as limited by the *lex Sempronia*, that action being prohibited till a certain date. But for a single prohibiting clause the senate might have taken action in the summer of 54 or of 53 or of 52, in which case Caesar might have been superseded at the beginning of 52 or 51 or 50. Caesar's whole position, in a word, would have hung on the observance of this one clause, an observance which the attempt of Marcellus in 51 proves to have been precarious.

Viewed, therefore, from the point of view of Caesar's interests at Luca and the relation in which Pompey stood to him in 56, the hypotheses both of Judeich and Hirschfeld fail to satisfy the conditions of a convincing explanation of the problem. We will therefore, in considering the landmarks of the question from this point, start from the assumption, favoured by the ancient historians, that a second *quinquennium* was to be granted to Caesar, and that it was to terminate on March 1, 49.

The programme was duly carried out by the legislation of 55, the *lex Pompeia-Licinia* containing the stipulated clause, that Caesar's provinces should not be discussed in connexion with the *lex Sempronia* before March 1, 50.[1] The proof of this last point

[1] On the supposition that both Gauls could have been made praetorian, Caesar was protected from being superseded in 49, not by the *lex Sempronia*,

is found in the fact that in 51 Marcellus acted *ante tempus* and *contra legem Pompei et Crassi*, taken in combination with Pompey's own statement made in Sept. of the same year, *se ante Kal. Mart. non posse sine iniuria de provinciis Caesaris statuere* (*ad fam.* viii, 8, 9). The public could of course draw its own inferences from this arrangement, but I suggest that Caesar's second consulship, and with it of course the *absentis ratio*, were for the present kept in the background. In the following years various causes produced a growing estrangement between Pompey and Caesar, the first discordant note being probably due to the fact of Pompey remaining in Rome instead of going out to Spain. That Caesar had resented this is indicated by his own words, *in se novi generis imperia constitui, ut idem ad portas urbanis praesideat rebus et duas bellicosissimas provincias absens tot annos obtineat* (*b.c.* 1, 85). Nothing critical, however, happened till 52, when Pompey, contrary to the *lex Cornelia*, carefully observed by Caesar, became consul for the third time, and without a colleague. As this irregular appointment was favoured by Cato and Bibulus, and as the senate had already in the previous year passed a decree providing for a five years' interval between a magistracy and a provincial command (Dio Cass. 40, 46), it seems probable that Pompey was pledged to the *optimates* to confirm this decree by legislation (id. 40, 56). At any rate Caesar thought it time definitely to pave the way for his second consulship as a direct continuation of his provincial position by securing legal permission to stand in the summer of 49 in his absence. The permission was granted by a tribunician law with Pompey's consent, a sure indication that it had been stipulated for at Luca. This law, as we have seen, in spite of Pompey's ambiguous action later in the year, and its attempted annulment by Marcellus in 51, was recognized by Cicero as still in force at the end of 50.

But the *lex Pompeia de iure magistratuum* changed the whole situation, and destroyed the continuity of Caesar's position, which it had been the object of the arrangements at Luca to secure. It did not indeed violate the letter of the *lex Pompeia-Licinia*, or

but only by the Sullan system of provincial succession. As a matter of fact, however, Transalpine Gaul was bound to be consular.

curtail the second *quinquennium* granted by that law. But it violated the spirit of the clause so often referred to, which, with the help of the *lex Sempronia*, had made it impossible for either of Caesar's provinces to become consular till 48. In the first place, on the principle *cessante legis ratione cessat ipsa lex*, it might be interpreted as abrogating the *lex Sempronia*, so that on March 1, 50, the senate could make Caesar's provinces, or one of them, consular not for 48 but for 49. In the second place, as the Sullan regulations, making January 1 the necessary commencement of a provincial command, were also annulled, no obstacle could, as in 54, be put in the way of a succesor replacing Caesar on March 1, so that on that date he could be made *privatus*. Caesar recognized how the ground was cut from beneath his feet when he complained, *in se iura magistratuum commutari ne ex praetura et consulatu ut semper sed per paucos electi et probati in provincias mittantur* (*b. c.* 1, 85). Only one constitutional chance still remained. If the *lex Sempronia* lapsed, so did the provision contained in it that tribunician *intercessio* was inapplicable against the settlement of consular provinces (*de prov. cons.* 7, 17). If by this means the senate could be prevented from completing the steps necessary for his recall till the summer of 49, it would be compelled to acquiesce in the carrying out of the tribunician law of 52, and by that acquiescence would perhaps be morally, if not legally, precluded from interfering with Caesar's *semenstre imperium* till the end of the year. Such was the constitutional position when the actual struggle began in 51.

It may be asserted with confidence that during the next two years the Catonian party, always probably a small minority in the senate, but which far more than Pompey was responsible for the new law, never swerved from their aim of making Caesar a *privatus* after March 1, 49, while Caesar on his side would refuse every compromise which would leave him a *privatus* for however short a space before entering on his second consulship. That the Catonian party determined to open the struggle in 51, and so to violate the sanction of the *lex Pompeia-Licinia*, can only be explained by two considerations. (1) If there was any chance that the *lex Sempronia* might still be appealed to in spite of Pompey's law, it would be too late to leave the matter till 50, and the *relatio ante tempus* must be risked. (2) The sanction might be, as other sanctions sometimes were, ignored with impunity, if only senators generally and Pompey in particular lent their moral support.

The proposal of Marcellus, as I have already argued, must have been that the two Gauls should be fixed as consular provinces after March 1, 49 (*provincias Gallias finienti Kalendarum Martiarum die; ad Att.* viii, 3, 3). There is no doubt that it was Pompey's resistance which prevented this proposal from being carried, as the evidence of Cicero (*loc. cit.*), Dio Cassius (40, 59), and Appian (2, 26) agrees on this point. But it is not clear whether it was defeated or withdrawn. Hirtius (*b. g.* 8, 53) definitely says that the senate rejected it, but the evidence of Caelius is against this version. On May 24 he writes: *Marcellus adhuc nihil rettulit de successione provinciarum Galliarum et in Kal. Jun., ut mihi ipse dixit, eam distulit relationem* (*ad fam.* ix, 1, 2). In June he says: *Marcelli impetus resederunt non inertia sed, ut mihi videtur, consilio* (*ib.* viii, 2, 2). It therefore is probable that Pompey, who was not prepared to repudiate the sanction of his own law, staved off the motion till after the consular elections, thereby making it necessary, if anything was to be done, to ignore the *lex Sempronia.*

We gather from Caelius (viii, 4, 4) that as late as August Pompey had not yet committed himself, and was anxious to avoid doing so, *de successione Caesaris hoc est de provinciis.* In the beginning of September Caelius, though not expecting any decisive action till next year, reports Pompey as making it plain (almost certainly in connexion with the attack of Marcellus on the *absentis ratio*, alluded to in Suet. c. 26 and Liv. *epit.* 108) that he was opposed to Caesar's election to the consulship while retaining his command, though he thought it premature to pass any decree on the subject. *Pompeius tuus aperte Caesarem et provinciam tenere cum exercitu et consul; ipse tamen hanc sententiam dixit, nullum hoc tempore senatus consultum faciendum* (*ad fam.* viii, 9, 3).

But later in the same month Pompey allowed his views to be still more unmistakably known, so unmistakably that the senate, no doubt on the initiative of Marcellus, was emboldened to pass several important decrees.

Pompey's view at this time is thus expressed by Caelius: *plane perspecta Cn. Pompei voluntate in eam partem ut eum decedere post Kal. Mart. placeret* (viii, 8, 4). This is of course a crucial passage, and Hirschfeld's theory stands or falls with his interpretation of it.

If the words *post Kal. Mart.* refer to 50,[1] then undoubtedly no second *quinquennium* was granted to Caesar, and both December 29, 50, and March 1, 49, are as legal terminations of Caesar's command ruled out. But on the other hand, if we assume, as the evidence already considered entitles us to do, a five years' extension, all difficulties in the way of referring the Kalends of March to 49 will disappear. For on that assumption (*a*) we get an intelligible explanation of the motion of Marcellus in 51, and (*b*) are able to confirm the statements of Suetonius and Appian that Marcellus in 50 made precisely the same proposal. Marcellus proposed to terminate Caesar's command (*provincias Gallias finire*) by recalling him at the end of the *quinquennium* (*Kalendarum Martiarum die*) by making his provinces consular from that date. Thus Caesar would have had *decedere post Kal. Mart.* Pompey had resisted this only on the ground that Marcellus had acted *ante tempus* and it was not till the following Sept. that he allowed it to be known that he wished Caesar *decedere post Kal. Mart.* As this was immediately followed by the decree of Sept. 29 directing the consuls of 50 to make a proposal on March 1 *de provinciis consularibus* (*ad fam.* viii, 8, 5) it is certain that that proposal was intended to give effect to Pompey's known wishes, viz. *ut eum decedere post Kal. Mart. placeret.* It is again only on the assumption that Caesar could legally retain his position till March 49 that we can explain the attack of Marcellus on the *absentis ratio*, and Pompey's expression of opinion on it as quoted above. For if, as Hirschfeld believes, it had been legally possible to get rid of Caesar in March 50, the question of the *absentis ratio*, demonstrably belonging to 49, could have had no critical importance in 51.

But, it may be asked, why, if Caelius was referring to 49, does

[1] I find it impossible to accept the suggestion of Dr. Rice Holmes that *post Kal. Mart.* refers to 50, but is to be taken with *placeret* and not with *decedere*. This would leave the date of Caesar's recall, on which everything depended, vague and indeterminate.

he not say so? Because, on the assumption that Caesar's command legally ended in March 49, it was not necessary. Neither to Caelius nor to Cicero, who were forecasting all this time what Caesar would do or would be obliged to do *cum legis dies transierit*, could there be any ambiguity. Their eyes were fixed on the year 49 and especially on March 1 of that year, and therefore such statements as 'Caesar must go on March 1', or 'Caesar may possibly not stand for the consulship "this year"', or 'Caesar may be allowed to stay till Nov. 13' would need no explanation. It would have been ridiculous for Caelius to have written *post Kal. Mart. secundas* or *Idibus Nov. secundis*, just as Cicero himself in *ad Att.* viii, 3, 3, leaves undated by its year the expression *Kalendarum Martiarum die*.

On the other hand, when the *senatus consultum* passed on September 29, 51, provides that the consuls designate should hold a meeting *de provinciis consularibus ex Kal. Mart.*, it would be clear, even without the addition of the words *quae in suo magistratu futurae essent*, that the next year, 50, is intended. Similarly, when Pompey's speech in support of this *senatus consultum* and in explanation of his own position is quoted, declaring that after March 1 he will have no objection to a decision on the subject of Caesar's provinces, it is obvious that he is referring to the same March 1 as that specified in the decree under consideration. For it is immediately after transcribing the senatorial decrees that Caelius proceeds: *Ea praeterea Cn. Pompei sunt animadversa . . . ut diceret* (these words show what follows to be a quotation from Pompey's speech) *se ante Kal. Mart. non posse sine iniuria de provinciis Caesaris statuere; post Kal. Mart. se non dubitaturum.* It seems to me therefore that, if we examine a little more carefully than Hirschfeld has felt it worth while to do, the context of the three passages in this letter where the Kalends of March are mentioned, no contradiction or inconsistency is involved in referring the first to 49, the other two to 50. I will even go further and say that the contradiction is involved in Hirschfeld's own interpretation.

For him the statement of Pompey's views *ut eum decedere post Kal. Mart. placeret*[1] and the quotation from his speech *post Kal.*

[1] As I have already pointed out, Judeich is discreetly silent about the two phrases *provincias Gallias Kalendarum Martiarum die finienti* and *eum decedere*

Mart. se non dubitaturum (*de provinciis Caesaris statuere*) mean exactly the same thing. But *statuere de provinciis Caesaris* can only mean to give a decided vote on the motion to be brought forward on March 1, 50, and we happen to know from the terms of the *senatus consultum* transcribed by Caelius what that motion was. It was technically not a proposal *de provinciis Caesaris* but raised the wider question *de provinciis consularibus*. The Gallic provinces, however, could in March 50 be legally discussed with the rest, and it was no doubt understood that one or both of these would be selected. If they were, it would be a motion, as we know from Cicero that it was, *ut Caesari succederetur* (*ad Att.* vii, 7, 5). As the *lex Sempronia* was regarded as out of force, it was clearly not the consular provinces for 48 that were to be selected, but, as by all precedent and analogy provinces were fixed in the year before they were to be held, the proposal concerned the consular provinces for 49. It follows that Pompey's promised vote could not have been for Caesar's immediate recall on March 1, 50, that not being the question before the senate, but it would be indirectly a vote for his recall on March 1, 49 (*eum decedere post Kal. Mart.*), since it would make his provinces consular as early in 49 as they were legally vacant.[1] If Hirschfeld had borne in mind the technical meaning of *successio provinciarum*, he would have seen that his view of the proposal made by Marcellus in 50 is wholly untenable.

We have no more evidence as to Pompey's attitude till the spring of 50, when the motion of Marcellus *de provinciis consularibus* had been voted upon, but had been blocked and hung up by the *intercessio* of Curio. That *intercessio* created so complete a deadlock in regard to what was undoubtedly the absorbing question of the hour, that possible means of removing it must at once have engaged the attention of the senate. The situation had been foreseen, and tentatively provided for by the declaration registered in the previous September, that any tribune blocking the contemplated decrees should be regarded as acting *contra*

post Kal. Mart. They are both obviously inconsistent with his hypothesis that Caesar's command legally ended on Dec. 29, 50.

[1] This is perfectly consistent with Appian (ii, 26), who says that Pompey in 51 *κῆλον ἐποίησεν ὅτι χρὴ μετὰ τὸν χρόνον παραλύειν τῆς ἀρχῆς αὐτίκα τὸν* Καίσαρα. That Appian did not place this term *μετὰ τὸν χρόνον* early in 50, I have already pointed out.

rem publicam. Probably the Catonian party were for taking extreme action (*omnibus rebus premere Curionem*) at once, but it was a serious step to take, and others besides Caelius might regard it as provoking civil war.

The situation at the end of April may be gathered from a letter of Caelius (*ad fam.* viii, 11, 3). *In unam causam omnis contentio coniecta est, de provinciis; in quam adhuc incubuisse cum senatu Pompeius videtur ut Caesar Id. Nov. decedat; Curio omnia potius subire constituit quam id pati . . . Nostri porro, quos tu bene nosti, ad extremum certamen rem deducere non audebant. Scaena rei totius haec: Pompeius, tanquam Caesarem non inpugnet sed quod illi aequum putet constituat, ait Curionem quaerere discordias, valde autem non vult et plane timet Caesarem† cos. desig. prius quam exercitum et provinciam tradiderit. Accipitur satis male a Curione et totus eius secundus consulatus exagitatur. Hoc tibi dico: si omnibus rebus prement Curionem, Caesar defendet intercessorem; si, quod videntur, reformidarint, Caesar, quoad volet, manebit.* It is clear from this that, in the hope of finding a way out which Curio would not block, and which the Catonians might accept, the senate, not without Pompey's adhesion, had suggested a compromise, intended to dispense with the necessity for extreme action. Caesar was to be allowed, *cum legis dies transierit,* not only to retain his command long enough to make use of the *absentis ratio,* but for four months longer still, to November 13. Why this date was chosen is not clear, but it was no doubt calculated so as not to prevent the Catonian extremists from bringing their threatened impeachment before the end of the year.

It was of course on the face of it a considerable concession to Caesar, since it allowed him more than eight months' grace after the expiration of his legal term, and its rejection might seem to put Curio and Caesar in the wrong. Curio, however, was quick to see the trap; he realized that to accept this specious compromise was to give up the one point vital to Caesar's safety, the avoidance of an interval, however short, during which, as a *privatus,* he would have to run the gauntlet of an impeachment at the hands of his enemies. To allow the *absentis ratio,* and with it election to the consulship in July, was to give with one hand what an impeachment between November 13 and the end of the year would take away with the other. It would in fact render more than precarious the second consulship; *totus eius secundus consulatus exagitatur*. Curio therefore announced his intention of risking the extremist pressure rather than leave this insidious proposal unblocked. Pompey of course ignored the real point, affected to be scandalized at Curio's contentious behaviour, *ait Curionem quaerere discordias*, and protested that the arrangement was not unfair to Caesar, obviously soothing his conscience with the palliating reflection that after all Caesar would get everything agreed upon at Luca except six short weeks. But, while protesting against the fuss made by Curio about so 'fair' a proposal, Pompey was really, Caelius seems to have thought, rather relieved, since he was strongly averse to and clearly afraid of the *absentis ratio*.[1]

At any rate, Curio's threatened opposition clearly put an end to the scheme, and we hear no more of it. By September we find that Pompey has reverted to the Catonian position as expressed in the proposal of Marcellus; *Cn. Pompeius constituit non pati C. Caesarem consulem aliter fieri nisi exercitum et provincias tradiderit* (viii, 14, 2). As a matter of fact, Caelius in his last sentence seems to sweep aside all thoughts of this futile compromise, and to sum up the situation as Curio's *intercessio* in March had left it. 'If they adopt the plan of putting the extreme pressure on Curio, it will mean civil war; if, as their previous conduct makes likely, they shrink from this, Caesar will remain till his second consulship and longer if he likes.'

It remains to notice how Hirschfeld and Judeich deal with this passage. The former, arguing that the Ides of November can only be those of 50, finds in the passage his strongest proof that Caesar's command did not legally continue till March 1, 49, for Pompey could never have represented it as fair to recall Caesar three months and a half before the expiration of his legal term (*Klio*, iv, p. 72; v, pp. 238–9).[2]

[1] That this is the force of *autem*, which Hirschfeld's interpretation wholly ignores, I cannot doubt.

[2] Hirschfeld justifies his hypothesis that the *lex Pompeia-Licinia* contained no *legis dies* other than the preclusive one, March 1, 50, by asserting that only in this way can we reconcile on the one hand the proposal of Marcellus for Caesar's instant recall in March 50, followed by the suggestion of a respite till November, and on the other, Caesar's own claim to remain till the end of 49. Several questions, however, are begged in this claim to have simplified the

His arguments for referring the Ides of November to 50 may be summarized thus. (1) If Caelius had meant the year 49, he would have said so, i.e. he would have inserted *secundis*. (2) In that case Curio's extreme opposition is inexplicable, since it would have been a concession of all the time claimed by Caesar minus six weeks. (3) As compared with the proposal of Marcellus in March, this suggestion might well be represented by Pompey as *aequum*. (4) If Pompey allowed Caesar to remain till November 49, he would concede the *absentis ratio*, but in that case, how could Caelius say that he was averse to and afraid of Caesar's election while still retaining his command?

I will reply to these points *seriatim*. (1) As I have argued in regard to *decedere post Kal. Mart.* and *hoc anno*, the whole attention of Caelius and Cicero was absorbed in the year 49, the critical year in which Caesar's command would end, in which the *absentis ratio* would be claimed, and in which civil war might become inevitable. In discussing these matters there was only one year for them, and to specify it was utterly unnecessary. (2) It is true that to allow Caesar to remain till November 49 would have been a retreat from the Catonian position and a concession of eight extra months, but, as already pointed out, to have accepted it would have jeopardized Caesar's whole position and might well have made the second consulship impossible. Nor is Hirschfeld correct in saying that Caesar himself later in the year offered terms more unfavourable to himself. He no doubt alludes to the statement of Suetonius (*Iul.* xxix) that Caesar offered to give up Transalpine Gaul on condition of retaining the Cisalpine with two legions, or even Illyricum with one *donec consul fieret*. The last words Hirschfeld interprets like Mommsen to mean 'until elected consul', i.e. in July 49, but Caesar could have made no such offer, since it would have relinquished the *semenstre imperium* so essential to his personal safety. Even Caelius as late as September realizes more clearly than he had done in the previous October Caesar's determination on this point: *Caesari persuasum est se salvum esse non posse, si ab exercitu recesserit* (viii, 14, 2). The obvious meaning of the offer was that Caesar might avoid being *privatus* till the end of 49,

problem. I hope I have shown that Marcellus made no such proposal, and if he did not, Hirschfeld's view as to the Ides of November must be abandoned.

and this object would have been effected by retaining a mere nominal command like Illyricum. If Caesar was ever to reach his second consulship, Curio had no alternative but *omnia subire quam id pati.* (3) As regards the assertion that the suggestion of Pompey and the senate was *aequum* as compared with the proposal of Marcellus, I have already dealt with Hirschfeld's inexcusable misunderstanding of this latter proposal. But it is no doubt true that, whether Marcellus was for recalling Caesar in March 50 or in March 49 an extension to November in either year was in a sense *aequum*, because it was a concession. The real question however is, whether it was *aequum* in view of Pompey's agreement with Caesar at Luca. Hirschfeld himself admits that that agreement was for Caesar to be safeguarded till the end of 49, and yet he argues that it might be called *aequum* to recall him fifteen months and a half before that time. I do not say that the suggestion, as affecting 49, was really *aequum*; but it at least allowed the specious, though hollow, plea that Caesar was after all losing only six weeks. (4) As to the inconsistency which Hirschfeld finds between Pompey's acceptance of the senatorial compromise conceding the *absentis ratio* and several months beyond it and his dislike and fear of Caesar's election while still retaining his army, the objection has been completely met by my interpretation of the passage. It was only in the vain hope of shaking off the iron grip of Curio's *intercessio* that he had agreed to the suggested extension, and his dislike and fear of Caesar's election remained. The word *autem* marks a strong contrast between his professed protest against Curio and his real feeling. If Hirschfeld had consulted 'his friend Bardt', he would perhaps have realized that his interpretation required *enim* and not *autem*.[1]

Judeich's explanation of this proposal to recall Caesar on November 13 need not detain us long. As, like Hirschfeld, he refers this date to the year 50, he has to explain how Pompey could possibly represent it as *aequum* to deprive Caesar of his command six weeks before its legal termination, as fixed, in Judeich's opinion, by the *lex Pompeia-Licinia*. He can only meet the difficulty by suggesting that Caelius is merely reporting

[1] If Hirschfeld believed that Pompey was still expecting the *absentis ratio* to be claimed in 50, his argument, as I have already shown, recoils upon himself.

vague rumours pointing to the vacillation of Pompey, who could not have openly supported such a plan, though he might allow it to be understood that in his own mind he was not averse to it.

The very fact that he tried to represent it as *aequum* is an indication, Judeich thinks, that his conscience was uneasy. This obviously does not meet the case even as regards Pompey, especially if Caelius is right in making him declare that Curio by his opposition was merely seeking a quarrel. But Judeich fails to see the real difficulty which stands in the way of his theory. Putting Pompey himself out of the question, we cannot reasonably doubt that the senate, not of course including the Catonian irreconcilables, seriously meditated Caesar's recall on November 13, and, as it is inconceivable that any responsible section in the senate would have put itself so hopelessly in the wrong as to curtail, even by six weeks, a legally fixed period, the Ides of November cannot have been those of 50, and must have been those of 49.

It seems to me that Dr. Rice Holmes is far too lenient in considering Judeich's explanation of this passage. He contents himself with pointing out that, even if this view of the proposal and of Pompey's part in it is accepted, it is as consistent with taking March 1, 49, as the legal term as it is with Judeich's own date, December 29, 50. The real point is that it is absolutely inconsistent with either date.

In the beginning of June, while Pompey was still indisposed at Naples, the Catonian party, led by M. Marcellus, attempted in accordance with the September decree to bring Curio to reason. Caelius describes what took place in viii, 13. *Voles, Cicero, Curionem nostrum lautum intercessionis de provinciis exitum habuisse; nam cum de intercessione referretur, quae relatio fiebat ex senatus consulto, primaque M. Marcelli sententia pronuntiata esset, qui agendum cum tribunis pl. censebat, frequens senatus in alia omnia iit. Stomacho est scilicet Pompeius Magnus ita languenti ut vix id quod sibi placeat reperiat. Transierant illuc rationem eius habendam qui neque exercitum neque provincias traderet. Quem ad modum Pompeius hoc laturus sit, cum cognoscam, quidnam rei publicae futurum sit, si †aut non curet, vos, senes divites, videritis.* Cicero believed that Curio would have given way if the senate had supported Marcellus; *nunquam enim Curio sustinuisset, si cum eo agi coeptum esset, quam sententiam senatus sequi noluit; ex quo factum est ut Caesari non succederetur* (*ad Att.* vii, 7, 5). At any rate, the senate shrank from the only means of making their decree of March effective, and Caelius describes it as a virtual change of front (*transierant illuc*, &c.), involving the unconditional surrender of the *absentis ratio*, so that, as Caelius put it, *Caesar, quoad volet, manebit.* Pompey was known to dislike the *absentis ratio*, though for a moment he had been ready to concede it, but what attitude he would take up in the face of this humiliating surrender, Caelius does not know. As a matter of fact, the attention of both senate and Pompey was distracted from the main issue by a new and adroit suggestion of Curio.

V. CAESAR'S LEGAL POSITION AFTER 52

Caesar's legal and constitutional position after the passing of Pompey's *lex de iure magistratuum* was by no means hopeless, and his claim to retain his command after its legal termination did not, as Hirschfeld maintains (*Klio*, iv, p. 85), depend wholly or mainly on the tribunician law allowing the *absentis ratio* in 49. That law had been intended from the first to answer an important object, but Caesar could only take advantage of it, if he could by some other means maintain his position in his provinces till the elections of 49 came on. In the first place, the new law left unchanged the term of Caesar's command, as fixed by the *lex Pompeia-Licinia*, so that he was secure at any rate till March 1, 49. But it cancelled the Sullan arrangements, so that, if the Gauls could be made consular provinces for 49, Caesar could now be superseded at once on that day, and would have no claim of any kind to remain longer. In the second place, by practically abrogating the *lex Sempronia* it made it possible for the senate on or after March 1, 50, to fix Caesar's provinces as consular for 49.

On what then could Caesar rely? On this at any rate, that the question *de successione Caesaris* could only come on as a proposal *de provinciis consularibus* (cf. the phrase of Caelius; *de successione Caesaris . . . hoc est de provinciis*, viii, 4, 4), and this again (*a*) would by all precedent have to be made in the year previous to the vacancy, (*b*) would, before being effective, have to be followed by the nomination of ex-consuls of proper standing.

and (*c*) would only affect him, if one or both of his provinces were selected.

After the failure of Marcellus in 51 *de provinciis Caesaris ante tempus referre*, the first struggle was on the third point. If all the provinces, consular and praetorian, for 49[1] were settled at the same time, there would be at least the chance that other provinces might be fixed as consular, and the two Gauls left alone. If, on the other hand, the praetorian provinces were settled first, things might be so arranged as to make all provinces praetorian except those which the senate wished to be consular. It is this consideration which explains the forecast of Caelius, written in 51 before the *senatus consulta* of September (viii, 5, 2). *Nosti haec tralaticia; de Galliis constituetur; erit qui intercedat; deinde alius exsistet qui, nisi libere liceat de omnibus provinciis decernere senatui, reliquas impediat.* Similarly in viii, 9, 2 he writes: *Quantum divino, relinquendus tibi erit qui provinciam obtineat* (i.e. Cilicia will not be made a praetorian province in time for you to leave it at the end of your year), *nam non expeditur successio, quoniam Galliae, quae habent intercessorem, in eandem conditionem quam ceterae provinciae vocantur.* On September 29 the Caesarian tribune, Pansa, blocked a proposal to settle the praetorian provinces on the line indicated above (viii, 8, 8), but on the other hand it was resolved to decide on the consular provinces without the praetorian (*neve quid coniunctim*) on March 1, 50. On that date, as we have already seen, the motion *de provinciis consularibus* must have been put by C. Marcellus, and one or both of Caesar's provinces must have been fixed as consular for 49,[2] i.e. after March 1 of that year. The senate was within its constitutional rights in taking this step and it rendered inoperative the tribunician law conceding the *absentis ratio*, since from March to July Caesar would be *privatus*, and could at best only claim the exemption as a virtual exile. But the motion of

[1] I have already pointed out that practically the provinces to be settled, both consular and praetorian, were for 49. Cilicia, e.g., which was to be praetorian, and Syria which was eventually consular, would not be vacant till July 50, and, as a matter of fact, it is certain that no decisions were effectively made about any provinces between September 51 and January 49.

[2] This decree was not vetoed, partly because it was in accordance with the *lex Pompeia-Licinia*, and partly because no *intercessio* was necessary till the Gauls were actually made consular, and as the praetorian province, as the result of Pansa's *intercessio*, would still be open, this might possibly be still staved off.

Marcellus presupposed the abrogation of the *lex Sempronia*, and with that law disappeared the prohibition against tribunician interference with the settlement of consular provinces (*de prov. cons.* vii, 17).[1]

There was therefore no legal obstacle in the way of Curio's *intercessio*, which, as we have seen, blocked and madc incffcctivc the decree, and which on grounds of equity Caesar could justify as the only means of meeting Pompey's gross breach of faith in passing his *lex de iure magistratuum.*

What Caesar wanted, and had wanted ever since Luca, was to retain his command till entering on the consulship without civil war, and without open disobedience to an effective decree of the senate. As long as Pompey had been loyal, there had been no difficulty; now everything depended on whether Curio's *intercessio* could be maintained through 50, and whether the *intercessio* of other tribunes could be secured through 49. If so, the prediction of Caelius in 51 might be verified: *Sic multum ac diu ludetur atqua ita diu ut plus biennium in his tricis moretur* (viii, 5, 2).

But the senate had at its disposal a possible counter-stroke which might or might not be justified by precedent. Its decree had been perfectly legitimate, and Curio's obstruction, however justifiable on grounds of equity (which after all concerned a personal understanding between Caesar and Pompey), might be regarded as politically inexcusable and seditious. If no lesser pressure availed, he might be declared, according to the decree of September 29, to have acted *contra rempublicam*, and might even find himself the object of the last decree. In this case he would probably leave Rome, his *intercessio* thereby lapsing, and the blocked decree would automatically become effective. This was certainly the course urged by M. Marcellus, and its rejection was the cause *ut Caesari non succederetur* (*ad Att.* vii, 7, 6). It was rejected because it would have meant civil war, since others besides Caelius could realize that *si omnibus rebus prement Curionem, Caesar defendet intercessorem.*

[1] In 56 Cicero met the idea of recalling Gabinius and Piso by making their provinces praetorian with the objection *tum enim tribunus intercedere poterit.* He goes on: *sed mihi credite; nunquam illis succedetur nisi cum ea lege referetur qua intercedi de provinciis non licebit*, i.e. by making their provinces consular in accordance with the *lex Sempronia.*

I am convinced that Hirschfeld is led into a wrong track by Appian, when he declares that the senatorial decree passed by Marcellus in March was met by Curio with the audacious proposal that Caesar and Pompey should resign together. It was rather an adroit manœuvre on the part of Curio and Caesar,[1] intended partly to delay action against his own *intercessio*, partly to embroil Pompey with the senate, and especially to embarrass both. It introduced a side issue quite irrelevant to the main question, which it only affected indirectly by hastening on the crisis at the end of the year.[2]

At what point it was first suggested, whether by Caesar or by Curio, is not clear,[3] but it is first alluded to by Caelius in September, when after stating Caesar's determination not to resign his army, he adds: *fert tamen illam conditionem ut ambo exercitus tradant* (viii, 14, 2). It had probably been hanging over Pompey and the senate for some time, and may have been an answer to the proposal about November 13, which looks like a less skilful attempt to put Caesar in the wrong.

Early in December a large majority of the senate passed a decree that Pompey and Caesar should resign together. By this it was no doubt intended that Caesar should become *privatus* on March 1, while Pompey, to whom a second *quinquennium* had been granted in 52 (App. ii, 26, and Dio Cass. xl, 56), was asked to abandon the last four years of his command. But (1) it was futile to order Caesar to resign while the decree making his provinces consular was still blocked, and (2) the senate had no

[1] Caesar claims the suggestion in *b. c.* i, 43: *patientiam proponit suam cum de exercitibus dimittendis ultro postulavisset*, and Hirtius confirms this (*b. g.* viii, 52).

[2] Judeich tries to read into Curio's proposal a revival of the principle 'equal rights for all', which he thinks Caesar had conceded at Luca. It was, however, in effect to call on Pompey to give up four years of his second *quinquennium*. Pompey had in appearance a great advantage over Caesar in still having four years of his command to run, but Caesar well knew that, if only he could reach the second consulship, the future would be in his hands.

[3] Appian (ii, 24) says that Curio supported the proposal of Marcellus, but added as a rider that Pompey should resign too. This leaves no room for the *intercessio* testified to by Caelius, and Hirtius (*b. g.* viii, 52) clearly puts the 'promise' made by Curio that both should resign in the latter half of the year after the consular elections. As to the passing of the resolution in the senate, Appian appears to place it shortly before the termination of Curio's office, and represents it as Curio's proposal after the consuls had tried to put the cases of Pompey and Caesar separately. On the other hand, Hirtius (c. 52 *ad fin.*) says that Curio was about to carry out his promise *per discessionem*, but that the consuls intervened and themselves brought the affair to a division.

right to curtail Pompey's legal term. It was apparently the disgust of the Catonian minority which led to the irregular action of Marcellus, the consul designate, in authorizing Pompey to raise troops, and to Pompey's acceptance of the commission. It was this which changed the whole situation, for Caesar, who had so far hoped to stave off effective senatorial action through 49 by means of tribunician obstruction, now realized that the initiative of war might come from his opponents, and that his plan of reaching his object by constitutional means might at any moment become unworkable.

It was becoming more and more clear that Caesar's opponents intended to prevent his second consulship. Cicero himself gives expression to the views of the senate when he writes, *nihil timendum magis quam ille consul*; while he attributes the same apprehension to Pompey: *eo consule certum est Pompeio esse in Hispania* (*ad Att.* vii, 9, 3). It is for this reason that in his letters to Atticus written in December, Cicero seems to represent the whole question as turning on the *absentis ratio*. He assumes that by the continued effect of tribunician obstruction Caesar will retain his command *cum legis dies transierit*, will thus be able to take advantage of the tribunician law, and in fact, as Caelius had put it, *quoad volet manebit*.[1]

Caesar's own eyes were equally fixed on the consulship, and with a view to it, on the *absentis ratio*. Cicero, in making him say *depugnes oportet nisi concedas* does not misrepresent his attitude. To make sure of the consulship, he was ready to make considerable sacrifices, though not to incur the risk of impeachment by running the gauntlet of however short an interval as *privatus*. *Caesari persuasum est se salvum esse non posse si ab exercitu recesserit*. But he made an offer towards the close of the year the acceptance of which would have secured his position. He professed himself willing to resign Transalpine Gaul with eight legions at the end of his legal term, if it was understood that he might retain Cisalpine Gaul with two legions,

[1] Cicero's apostrophe to Caesar in vii, 9 assumes that the senatorial decree will have been blocked from March 50 to March 49 and that the obstruction will be continued at least up to the elections. The words *ut tibi succedatur decernitur; impedis* describe the situation ever since the motion of Marcellus. I cannot agree with Dr. Rice Holmes that *decernitur* is equivalent to *decretum est*.

or even Illyricum with one legion *donec consul fieret* (Suet. *Iul.* xxix; App. ii, 32).[1] By this arrangement Caesar would at least have secured the *absentis ratio*, and would escape the necessity of becoming *privatus*. It was apparently the refusal of this offer, accentuated by the threatening attitude of the Catonian minority, which induced Caesar to send Curio with an ultimatum at the end of the year.

His demands, *minaces et acerbae* from the circumstances under which they were sent (*ad fam.* xvi, 11, 2), were probably a repetition of his claim to retain at least one of his provinces till the end of 49, and they confronted the senate with Cicero's alternative, *aut habenda e lege ratio aut depugnandum est.*[2] The answer of the senate, once more under the influence of the Catonian section, was a counter ultimatum: *uti ante certam diem Caesar exercitum dimitteret; si non faciat, eum adversus rem publicam facturum videri* (*b. c.* i, 1).[3] This of course was merely preliminary to the constitutional steps still necessary to supersede Caesar on March 1. It, however, answered its purpose, for the Caesarian tribunes interposed their veto, and the senate at last adopted the extreme course which M. Marcellus had urged against Curio. With the passing of the *senatus consultum ultimum* and the consequent flight of the tribunes from Rome Caesar's last constitutional support had broken down, and there was no longer any obstacle to his supersession in due form on March 1.

The settlement and assignment of all provinces had been blocked since the previous March, and it was impossible now to allow the usual intervals between the several steps. But except in this one point the normal course was taken. The status of all the provinces was discussed and settled; Transalpine Gaul and Syria were made consular, the latter immediately, the former

[1] The phrase *consul fieri* is ambiguous, and may equally well mean 'to be elected' or 'to become' consul. It must be interpreted by the context or by the situation. To interpret it in this passage as Mommsen and Hirschfeld do is to make Caesar stultify his whole position.

[2] Hirtius (viii, 54 *ad fin.*) correctly describes Caesar's attitude up to this time; *Caesar omnia patienda esse statuit quoad spes sibi aliqua relinqueretur iure potius disceptandi quam belli gerendi.*

[3] I disagree with Dr. Rice Holmes's view that *ante certam diem* refers to July 1. After Caesar's ultimatum there could be no more compromise, and it was clearly now the Catonian standpoint which was being taken up, viz. that Caesar should not have a day beyond his legal term.

from March 1, while Cisalpine Gaul, Cilicia, and the other eight provinces were made praetorian. At the same time, or immediately afterwards, governors were appointed, Scipio to Syria, Dom. Ahenobarbus to Transalpine Gaul, Nonianus to the Cisalpine. *Provinciae privatis decernuntur, duae consulares, reliquae praetoriae; Scipioni obvenit Syria, L. Domitio Gallia* (*b. c.* i, 6; cf. also *ad fam.* xvi, 12, 3). The result of these decrees and appointments, apart from the civil war which they inevitably foreshadowed, was, by making Caesar *privatus* after March 1, to nullify the grant of the *absentis ratio*, which had all along presupposed that he would be in possession of his provinces at the date of the elections. This was fully recognized by Caesar himself who, in his final offer (made of course because he knew that it would be refused) was ready, if the Italian levies were disbanded and Pompey went to Spain, to become *privatus* and to canvass in person. *Feruntur omnino conditiones ab illo, ut Pompeius eat in Hispaniam, dilectus qui sunt habiti . . . dimittantur; se ulteriorem Galliam Domitio, citeriorem Considio Noniano . . . traditurum* (i. e. on March 1)*; ad consulatus petitionem se venturum, neque iam se velle absente se rationem haberi suam; se praesentem trinum nundinum petiturum* (*ad fam.* xvi, 12, 3). Perfectly consistent too with the view taken above is the passage in *b. c.* i, 9: *doluisse se quod beneficium populi Romani per contumeliam ab inimicis extorqueretur, ereptoque semenstri imperio in urbem retraheretur, cuius absentis rationem haberi populus iussisset.* Caesar's complaint is that the action of his enemies, i. e. the law of Pompey and the decrees of January made possible by it, had made the *beneficium populi*, the grant of the *absentis ratio*, of no use to him; for, though it had been intended to secure him the last six months of the year,[1] he was being brought back to Rome superseded and *privatus.* The whole point is that the tribunician law, the validity of which

[1] As Hirschfeld has withdrawn his ill-considered contention that *semenstre imperium* means the first six months of 49 instead of the last six, I need not point out the contradictions involved in that view. If Caesar was to be consul in 48, the retention of his provincial command from July to December depended absolutely on the *absentis ratio*, since by coming home to canvass he would have laid down his *imperium.* But before Pompey's law it was certain that he could use the *beneficium*, after that law he could only use it if his supersession by the senate could be obstructed till July. (For Hirschfeld's argument and its withdrawal, see *Klio*, iv, pp. 85–6 n. 6, and v, p. 237 n. 4.)

was not disputed, had presupposed a condition, viz. Caesar's absence in Gaul during July, which his supersession on March 1 had cancelled. Caesar had exhausted all the constitutional means at his disposal, and the only alternative to his political annihilation was civil war.

VII

THE TABLE OF VELEIA OR THE *LEX RUBRIA*

THERE is in some quarters what I cannot but regard as a regrettable tendency to label, with implications of approval or depreciation, particular views relating to ancient history as progressive or conservative. Where a view, of however long standing, depends on evidence, direct or indirect, which has not been successfully assailed, the conservative would seem also to be the scientific attitude. On the other hand, where existing evidence can be proved insufficient, or is counterbalanced by new, or admits of convincing reinterpretation, real progress may result from the substitution of new views for old. I am led to draw attention to the point by recent criticisms on the part of certain continental scholars directed against the Caesarian date and authorship of two famous documents, the Table of Heraclea and the Table of Veleia, generally believed till the last fifteen years or so to contain portions of the *lex Iulia municipalis* of 45 and the *lex Rubria* of 49 B.C. In connexion with the Table of Heraclea I am dealing below[1] in considerable detail with the hypotheses of Dr. Henri Legras, who attempts to push back all its sections to the period of Sulla. As far as the Caesarian date is concerned, I have maintained the view generally accepted since Savigny and Mommsen, though I have rejected much of the latter's early conjecture as to the character and scope of the document, as well as all his later and unsettling changes of view. In the present paper I propose to discuss a somewhat similar attempt on the part of Mr. J. M. Nap to relegate the so-called *lex Rubria* back into Sulla's dictatorship.[2] In many respects this

[1] See Essay No. viii, p. 239.

[2] Mr. Nap's discussion of the so-called *lex Rubria* is contained in *Themis*, 1913, no. 2, pp. 194–207. The article is entitled *Het iudicium legitimum in de Romeinsche wetgeving*. The first section, pp. 182–93, deals with the *lex Valeria* of 86 B.C. The subject is continued in the next year's *Themis*, where the *lex Cornelia* and the *lex Aebutia* are discussed.

latter attempt to strike out a new path is more paradoxical, and deserves less serious consideration than that of Dr. Legras. But, as these progressive theories seem rather in the air across the water, and sometimes impress those who have not studied them carefully by their very audacity, it may be of interest and use to examine in a second instance the methods and reasoning in deference to which we are asked to accept these new and startling conclusions in place of those which have long held the field.

It will be convenient at the outset to summarize the salient points which it is necessary to bear in mind throughout the discussion of the law partly preserved on the Table of Veleia.[1] (1) It is concerned with the province of Gallia Cisalpina; (2) at most only one-fifth of the whole is extant, since the tablet is numbered iv, and closes with the opening lines of a chapter; (3) the surviving portion deals exclusively with questions of judicial procedure in suits for *damnum infectum*, *pecunia certa credita*, and claims for other than money liabilities;[2] (4) the judicial magistrates within the province are described as *IIviri IIIIviri praefectusve*; (5) the provincial communities are, like the Italian towns in the Table of Heraclea, *coloniae*, *municipia*, *praefecturae*, *fora*, *conciliabula*, though *vici* and *castella* are here added to the list; and (6) there is for certain cases and under certain conditions a *revocatio Romae* from the municipal jurisdiction.

Before directly approaching the question of date, it will be as well to recall the ground of Puchta's conjecture[3] that the Table contains part of a *lex Rubria*, a title which Mr. Nap, in accordance with his own theory that it is a *lex data* of Sulla, is of course bound to reject. He indeed calls it a feeble conjecture which has no firmer basis than the fact that a *lex Rubria* happens to be mentioned in the inscription. It appears from the opening words of cap. xx, *a quo in Gallia Cisalpina damnei infectei ex formula restipularei satisve accipere volet*, and from the subsequent directions, that cases of *damnum infectum* were the subject of a *legitimum iudicium* in the province, constituted in accordance with the praetor's *formula*, and that in normal cases the municipal magistrate was competent to set up and conduct such a

[1] Bruns, pp. 97 ff.

[2] The fragmentary chapters xix and xxiii need not enter into the discussion.

[3] *Kleine civilistische Schriften*, pp. 71, 518.

iudicium, the procedure adopted being no doubt that laid down in the praetorian edict. But, where the defendant absolutely refused to be party to a *stipulatio* or to give security, a special procedure, different from that adopted in such cases at Rome, is prescribed. Whereas in the praetor's court the matter would have been summarily dealt with by a *missio in possessionem*, in Gallia Cisalpina the magistrate is ordered to ignore the defendant's recusancy and to set up a *iudicium*, provided that, in appointing a *iudex*, he uses a specified form of words. Now within this form of words comes the clause: 'supposing that the defendant has refused to obey the decree of the magistrate, such decree being in accordance with the *lex Rubria* or the *plebiscitum* so entitled.' It seems a fair and even obvious inference from this that the *lex Rubria* was the general law regulating such points of procedure for Cisalpine Gaul. But, as the Table of Veleia is on the face of it part of such a general law, Puchta's suggestion that we have on the Table portions of this *lex Rubria*, so far from being a feeble conjecture, seems in the highest degree reasonable. When Mr. Nap objects that the same document could not possibly call itself at one time *haec lex*, and at another *lex Rubria*,[1] the answer is that it does nothing of the kind. It always describes itself as *haec lex*, but, where it is to be referred to by a magistrate in a prescribed form of words, it obviously cannot be *haec lex*, and can only be designated by its proper title.

Mr. Nap, however, has another objection to identifying the *lex Rubria* with the law on the Table, viz. that the former was a *plebiscitum* or *lex rogata*, whereas he agrees with Mommsen's[2] last pronouncement that the latter is a *lex data*. Of Mr. Nap's contention on this point, put forward at the outset on Mommsen's authority, though quite inconsistent with his reasoning, I shall have to speak later. But, as his view of the Table as a *lex data* was what mainly induced Mommsen to repudiate the title of *lex Rubria* as applied to it, I shall notice in a few words his revised account[3] of the law so entitled. He can only suggest that it was a law, otherwise unknown, dealing with the subject of *damnum infectum*. But surely, when the *formula* for *damnum*

[1] *Themis*, p. 195. [2] *Juristische Schriften*, i, 193.

[3] Mommsen's latest view on the subject is contained in the article on the *lex Municipii Tarentini*, *Juristische Schriften*, i, especially pp. 152 ff.

infectum or for any other matter made the subject of a *legitimum iudicium* came into existence, it was not by means of legislation, but by the administrative act of the praetor, who introduced it into his *album* and perpetuated it by his edict. In falling back upon this shadowy *lex Rubria de damno infecto*, I venture to think that Mommsen forgot his own valuable suggestion, that the law on the Table of Veleia was intended to make the principles and details of procedure embodied in the praetorian edict applicable with modifications to the municipal courts of Gallia Cisalpina.

We come now to the question of date which Mr. Nap professes to reach by the retrogressive method of establishing a series of *termini ante quem*, until he comes to a point beyond which it is impossible to recede. In accordance with this plan it is successively argued that the date of the Table is anterior (1) to 49 B.C.; (2) to 59 B.C.; (3) to 66 B.C.; (4) to 81 B.C.; while (5) Mr. Nap undertakes to establish the point that the *lex Rubria*, referred to in the Table, is no other than the colonial law of that name passed in 123 or 122 B.C. by a colleague of C. Gracchus.[1]

I. The first of Mr. Nap's *termini ante quem* is the year 49 B.C. This is indeed a crucial date, because hitherto by very general consent the law has actually been assigned to this year, and the whole discussion might be concentrated on this point. Obviously the earlier dates in the scheme of retrogression fall to the ground if this is not convincingly established. As Mr. Nap, however, is content to rest his case for an earlier date than 49 B.C. on a single argument, I shall confine myself at this stage to its refutation, returning subsequently to a somewhat fuller examination of the questions involved. Mr. Nap bases his argument on the *Fragmentum Atestinum*, which mentions, as a dividing-line in regard to judicial procedure, a law passed by L. Roscius on March 11. This Roscius is identified, beyond all doubt correctly, with the Roscius Fabatus known from Cicero to have been a praetor in 49 B.C., so that the date of the Fragment is fixed to this year. There is good reason to believe, as I shall show later, that the *lex Roscia* was the measure, referred to by Dio Cassius,[2] which conferred the Roman citizenship upon the Transpadane communities of Gallia Cisalpina. Mr. Nap, however, ignoring this

[1] *Op. cit.* p. 195. [2] xli, 36.

explanation, attributes to the law a far wider object and scope, which he makes no attempt to establish by evidence.[1] It must have been, he declares, a law conferring on Caesar the absolute power to make and unmake laws. In virtue of this empowering measure, Mr. Nap's argument proceeds, Caesar issued a *lex data*, of which the *Fragmentum Atestinum* is the sole surviving part, annexing Cisalpine Gaul to Italy, and presumably, though he is not explicit on this point, granting the Roman citizenship. It is from this point, therefore, the issue in 49 B.C. of Caesar's *lex data*, that Cisalpine Gaul ceased to be a province and became a part of Italy; but, since the Table of Veleia on the face of it belongs to a period in which it was still a province, its date is necessarily anterior to 49 B.C. Such is Mr. Nap's proof of his first *terminus ante quem*.

I fear that I must traverse every stage in it. (1) In the first place, there is no evidence for the view taken of the *lex Roscia*. It is indeed on general grounds unlikely that such powers were conferred on Caesar at this time, March 11 being before Pompey had left Italy, or Caesar had reached Rome. Besides, when he did reach Rome, *orat atque postulat* (*senatum*) *ut rempublicam secum administrent*, an attitude quite inconsistent with so extraordinary a position. It is true that with the dictatorship Caesar may have acquired the right of making (not of unmaking) laws, as Sulla had done (ἐπὶ θέσει νόμων ὧν αὐτὸς δοκίμασειε). But the dictatorship was not held till the end of the year, and then only for eleven days. (2) On the other hand, on the supposition that the *lex Roscia* was the enfranchising law of Dio Cassius, we can understand at once how it was a dividing-line between two juristic conditions of the province or of part of it. (3) Again, with regard to the Atestine Fragment, there is absolutely no indication in either of its two clauses which implies the incorporation of Cisalpine Gaul with Italy. The one and only novelty discoverable in it, and that obviously due to the *lex Roscia*, is that henceforth there is to be, under certain conditions not affecting suits commenced before the passing of the latter law, a

[1] The reference to Dio xli, 36 *ad fin.*, taken in its context, does not support Mr. Nap's view. The words πάντα γὰρ μετὰ ἀδείας ὅσα ἂν βουληθῇ πράττειν οἱ ἐπετράπη refer not to a law, but to a decree of the senate, and describe the military and not the political position of Caesar.

revocatio Romae from the municipal courts.[1] It is hard to believe that Mr. Nap regards this as a proof that the country was becoming part of Italy, because this very *revocatio Romae* was an essential feature of the Table of Veleia, which on the face of it belongs to the period when Cisalpine Gaul was still a province. (4) As Mr. Nap's whole argument so obviously collapses if Cisalpine Gaul did not cease to be a province in 49 B.C., it is surprising that he did not make sure of his ground by reflecting on the known history of the country in the following years. Cisalpine Gaul was one of the provinces for which Caesar fixed the governors before his death: it was in accordance with these arrangements that Dec. Brutus took possession of it; and it was because he refused to exchange it with Antony that the latter began the civil war which culminated in the battle of Mutina. I strongly suspect that Mr. Nap has been misled by a passage of Strabo,[2] in which, without specifying any date, he alludes to the conferment of the citizenship and the incorporation of Cisalpine Gaul with Italy in the same sentence: *ὀψὲ δέ ποτε, ἀφ' οὗ μετέδοσαν Ῥωμαῖοι τοῖς Ἰταλιώταις τὴν ἰσοπολιτείαν, ἔδοξε καὶ τοῖς ἐντὸς Ἄλπεων Γαλάταις τὴν αὐτὴν ἀπονεῖμαι τιμήν, προσαγορεῦσαι δὲ καὶ Ἰταλιώτας πάντας καὶ Ῥωμαίους.* If we had no other information, this might be ambiguous, but the known facts show that two different events are referred to, and Dio Cassius[3] clearly refers the absorption of the province in Italy to the time of Octavian, and apparently to 42 or 41 B.C.: *ἐκ τῆς Γαλατίας τῆς Τογάτης, ἣ καὶ ἐς τὸν τῆς Ἰταλίας ἤδη νομόν, ὥστε μηδένα ἄλλον προφάσει τῆς ἐνταῦθα ἀρχῆς στρατιώτας ἐντὸς τῶν Ἄλπεων τρέφειν, ἐσεγέγραπτο.*

II. Having thus argued that the Table of Veleia must be earlier in date than 49 B.C., Mr. Nap proceeds to show[4] that it must also be anterior to the passing of the *lex Iulia agraria* of 59 B.C. His arguments are two. (1) The *lex agraria* of 59 B.C., as appears from the third of its three extant chapters,[5] provided for the appointment of a *curator* with certain judicial functions in *coloniae, municipia, praefecturae*, &c., and as the Table of Veleia,

[1] The clause declares: 'It is not provided by this law that *revocatio Romae* shall be required in suits begun before *IIviri* (of Latin towns) prior to the *lex Roscia*.'

[2] v, 210. [3] xlviii, 12. [4] *Op. cit.* pp. 197 ff. [5] Bruns, p. 96.

which is also concerned with the same classes of towns, makes no reference whatever to any such *curator*, it is impossible to suppose that it was passed later than 59 B.C. Whether this *argumentum e silentio* is a sound or an unsound one depends on considerations into which Mr. Nap does not think it necessary to enter. A reference to the chapter of the *lex Iulia* shows that in colonies planted or *municipia* and *praefecturae* 'constituted' by the law the commissioners had to fix the boundary marks within the land of the community, and that any person removing such boundaries was liable to a fine of 5,000 sesterces. The official who in such cases had *iuris dictio*, *reciperatorum datio* and *addictio* was the *curator qui hac lege erit*, or, in the absence of such *curator*, the ordinary judicial magistrate. It appears, therefore, that this *curator* established by the *lex Iulia* was an official wholly concerned with jurisdiction in agrarian matters, and, as all the extant portions of the Table of Veleia deal with matters other than agrarian, we should hardly expect to find such an official alluded to, even if the Table was later than the *lex agraria* of 59 B.C.

(2) But what Mr. Nap regards as a more important argument is that, if the law on the Table of Veleia had been later than 59 B.C., it must have made some reference to the general colonial law passed in that year, viz. the *lex Iulia agraria*. The *lex coloniae Iuliae Genetivae* of 44 B.C. does make such reference in cap. 97, and even incorporates in cap. 104 one of the clauses of this general law. The Table of Veleia on the contrary, so far as it bases any of its directions on an earlier law, refers to a *lex Rubria*, which is to be identified with the colonial law of 123 or 122 B.C. This argument, therefore, like the previous one, is very largely an *argumentum e silentio*. Now not only are there several serious misconceptions involved in this way of presenting the case, but, as an argument to prove the Table of Veleia anterior to 59 B.C., it involves at more than one point a *petitio principii*. The *lex Iulia agraria* was a general colonial law only in the sense that an indefinite number of colonies were to be founded under its provisions, in addition probably to a few which were specified. Beyond this we may, I think, admit from the evidence of the surviving chapters and from caps. 97 and 104 of the *lex Ursonensis*, (*a*) that it laid down certain general directions

for the *deductores* of colonies, at any rate for the agrarian arrangements to be incorporated in the colonial charters; and (*b*) that it in some way affected the *constitutio* of existing *municipia* and *praefecturae*. This last point seems to follow from the phrase, *qui hac lege . . . municipium praefecturam . . . constituerit*, but the precise meaning of this is uncertain, and it may quite possibly refer only to agrarian arrangements. At any rate, there is no indication that the provisions of the law were applicable to any colonies founded before its date, or that they had any reference to judicial matters or to the general government of colonies. It is hard to see, therefore, in what connexion the Table of Veleia, if passed later than 59 B.C., could be expected to refer to the *lex agraria* of that year, since it deals only with Gallia Cisalpina, and the colonies in that province were older than, and therefore outside the range of, Caesar's law. But it is far harder still to understand why such reference should be looked for in the extant chapters of the Table, concerned as they are exclusively with juristic questions. To find, indeed, any plausibility in Mr. Nap's line of argument at this point, it is necessary implicitly to assume three propositions: (*a*) that the scope of the *lex Iulia agraria* was not only the foundation of future colonies, but the government and constitution of all colonies both in Italy and in Gallia Cisalpina; (*b*) that the *lex Rubria* of 122 B.C. had been a law of precisely similar scope, and was still in operation when the law on the Table of Veleia was passed; and (*c*) that the law on the Table was a general *lex provinciae* for Cisalpine Gaul, and dealt with all its relations, juristic, agrarian, and constitutional. Of these propositions, (*a*) is assumed without discussion or citation of evidence; while for proposition (*b*) arguments (of the flimsiest character) are indeed adduced at a later stage, but as a step in the reasoning at the present point it is neither explained nor justified. But to rely on proposition (*c*) is to beg the whole question of date, since, if the Table contained the general *lex provinciae*, it of course goes back to the time of Sulla or earlier, a result which Mr. Nap professes to reach as the conclusion of a retrogressive concatenation of reasoning. The year 59 B.C. therefore, as a *terminus ante quem*, is a date in the air, and does not mark any real advance towards Mr. Nap's objective.

III. Even more imaginary and hypothetical is the next

terminus in our retrogression. In 67 B.C. Mr. Nap points out,[1] the Latin colonies are described by Suetonius [2] as *de petenda civitate agitantes.* From this he strangely infers that the *lex data*, drawn up by or for Sulla, had not given proper facilities to the Latin citizens of the province to exercise their right of voting in the Roman *comitia* in some tribe assigned to them by lot. Discontent with this disability to vote in the *comitia* was the cause, according to Mr. Nap, of revolutionary agitation, and must, he argues, have led to a modification of the *lex data* in the interval between 67 and 65 B.C., by which this right was fully assured to the Cisalpini.[3] What convinces him that the *lex data* must have been altered about 66 B.C. is the remark of Cicero written in July 65 B.C.: *videtur in suffragiis multum posse Gallia.*[4] This is taken to show that the Cisalpini were no longer subject to the disability complained of in 67 B.C. From 66 B.C. onward, the argument assumes, the *lex data* of the province would be the modified law of that year, and would necessarily contain some reference to the change then introduced. But the Table of Veleia, so far from dealing with the vital matters agitated about in 67 B.C., is concerned solely with *damnum infectum*, *condictio certi*, and the like, and this fact proves it to belong to the unmodified *lex data* anterior to 66 B.C.

Apart from more special objections to this remarkable line of argument, I would point out that the reasoning *e silentio* is singularly weak. The law admittedly occupied at least five tablets, and we have the contents of only one. How does Mr. Nap know that on one of the others there was no reference to this question of voting in the Roman *comitia*? Not only, therefore, is the supposed remodelling of the *lex data* a matter of pure conjecture, but the argument based upon it wholly collapses, since the extant fragment might equally belong to the revised or unrevised edition of the law. But the inference as to the need for modifying the *lex data*, drawn from the two passages of Suetonius and Cicero, is wholly fallacious, since they refer to two different

[1] *Op. cit.* pp. 198 ff. [2] *Iul.* viii.

[3] Mr. Nap holds that, whenever our authorities speak of the 'Transpadani', they really mean the 'Cisalpini', i.e. the inhabitants of Cisalpine Gaul generally, since the legal position of Transpadani and Cispadani was identical. I have exposed the fallacy of this view above, Essay No. ii, p. 44.

[4] *ad. Att.* i, 1, 2.

sections of the Cisalpini. The inhabitants of the Latin colonies were not Roman citizens, but they were agitating, according to Suetonius, to obtain the citizenship. So far was the cause of this agitation from being removed by any step taken in 66 B.C., that in 65 B.C., within a month or two of Cicero's utterance, we find parties in Rome violently divided on the question of admitting or not admitting the Transpadani εἰς τὴν πολιτείαν.[1] Whether the Latins of Cisalpine Gaul retained the old privilege of voting, when in Rome, in an allotted tribe, is uncertain, but at any rate their influence in the *comitia* would have been so small that it would not have been worth a journey to Rome in order to exercise it. It is quite certain that Cicero's words do not imply that they did so exercise it. He is alluding to a meditated canvassing tour in Cisalpine Gaul, where the voters to be canvassed would of course be found not in the Latin colonies spoken of by Suetonius, but in the important Roman colonies in the Cispadane part of the province, such as Mutina, Parma, Placentia, Bononia, and Cremona. I may add that, even if Mr. Nap's interpretation of Suetonius were correct, and if the Latin provincials had complained of their inability to vote in Rome, no modification of the *lex data* would have relieved them. The right of voting, as long as it existed, was part of the *ius Latii*, and these colonies possessed that status. If this particular right was no longer included in it, no *lex provinciae* could restore it; if it was, then its exercise was a mere matter of travelling expenses and personal convenience. From these considerations it is not, I think, unfair to assert that the argument concerned with the year 66 B.C. throws absolutely no light on the date of the Table of Veleia.

IV. But, having brought the Table back to the period prior to 66 B.C., Mr. Nap proceeds to argue from the legal procedure implied by it that it must also be anterior to the passing of the *lex Cornelia iudiciaria* of 81 B.C.[2] In dealing with these points, I do not profess to be an expert in Roman law, and far less to have solved the many difficult problems presented by this much-discussed document, but it seems to me that in more than one respect Mr. Nap has seriously misunderstood his authorities, or unjustifiably interpreted passages apart from their context, and

[1] Dio Cass. xxxvii, 9.

[2] *Op. cit.* pp. 200–4.

it is the validity of his reasoning rather than the correctness of his law which I venture to impugn. The two chapters of the Table, with which this discussion is concerned, are xxi and xxii, the one dealing with claims for *pecunia certa credita*, the other with claims for services or obligations other than money.

With regard to the former (cap. xxi), Mr. Nap is no doubt right in maintaining that they were in Rome the subject of a *legitimum iudicium*,[1] dependent on a praetorian *formula*. Not only so: but he successfully shows that this *legitimum iudicium* was applicable in the municipal courts of Gallia Cisalpina. The words *ex iudicieis dateis iudicareve recte iusseis iure lege damnatus* prove the point, which is, however, clear enough without them. In normal cases, where the defendant took the ordinary course, the proceedings in Gallia Cisalpina would be the same as those in Rome, though after condemnation and *ductio* the debtor, if insolvent or obstinate, would have to be handed over to the praetor's court before *missio in possessionem* or *proscriptio* could be applied to him, since these were distinctly acts of *imperium*. Where, however, before the magistrate *in iure*, he confessed, but refused to pay, or refused to answer to the claim, or declined to enter into a *sponsio*, and in a word would not *se sponsione aut iudicio defendere*, judgement was to be given against him by default, and he was to be treated as *ex iudicieis dateis iudicareve recte iusseis iure lege damnatus*.

Mr. Nap argues that this chapter must be earlier than the *lex Cornelia iudiciaria* of 81 B. C., because in it claims are only made by way of *sponsio*, whereas the *lex Cornelia* allowed them equally to be made by way of *fidepromissio* and *fideiussio*. This argument rests upon a complete misunderstanding. (*a*) Claims made against the sureties of the defendant, whether they were *sponsores* or *fidepromissores* or *fideiussores*, would belong to the normal proceedings, which, as already pointed out, were not contained in this chapter, because they were blocked by the defendant's contumacy. Their omission, therefore, from this chapter is no proof whatever that at the time of this law *sponsio* was the only recognized form of surety in cases of *certa pecunia*. But (*b*) Mr. Nap entirely misapprehends the passage of Gaius, iii, 124, on which he relies. After pointing out in cap. 123 that a *lex*

[1] See the passage from *pro Rosc. Com.* iv, 10, quoted below, p. 218.

Pompeia had eased in certain respects the position of *sponsores* and *fidepromissores*, Gaius notices that *fideiussores* are not specified by the law; *sed beneficium legis Corneliae,* he goes on, *omnibus commune est; qua lege idem pro eodem aput eundem eodem anno vetatur in ampliorem summam obligari pecuniae creditae quam in XX milia.* The *lex Cornelia* therefore merely placed a limitation on the legal obligations of *sponsores, fidepromissores,* and *fideiussores*, and did not, as Mr. Nap asserts, for the first time allow claims for *pecunia certa* to be made through all three kinds of surety. (*c*) Apart, however, from this misunderstanding of the reference in Gaius to *fidepromissores* and the others, the *sponsio*, alluded to in caps. xxi and xxii, is clearly part of the actual procedure in the *iudicium* (or rather in the *in iure* preparation for it) and not surety for the money borrowed, i. e. the guarantee of a *sponsor*, which was of course a transaction antecedent to the trial. That the *sponsio* mentioned in these chapters is not the engagement of a surety, who has rendered himself liable to a summons, but a method of defence expected and required from the debtor in the course of the proceedings, is proved by the recurrence of the phrase *se sponsione et iudicio utei oportebit defendere.* It is in fact the *sponsio tertiae partis*, a mutual engagement between the parties, by which each agrees to risk the third part of the amount claimed in case of defeat. *Periculosa est actio certae creditae pecuniae propter sponsionem qua periculatur reus, si temere neget, et restipulationem qua periculatur actor, si non debitum petat.*[1] That this was in force in Cicero's time appears from *pro Rosc. Com.* iv, 10 *pecunia tibi debebatur certa, quae nunc petitur per iudicem, in qua legitimae partis sponsio facta est.*[2] We may therefore safely say that so far Mr. Nap has shown no reason for placing the Table of Veleia before the *lex Cornelia.* Indeed, underlying the line of argument just examined are two fatal objections to his view which he has overlooked. They are that neither a *legitimum iudicium* nor a *sponsio* was applicable except where all the parties concerned were Roman citizens. But it is certain that in Gallia Cisalpina at the date of the *lex Cornelia* Roman citizens were in a minority, being mainly confined to the

[1] Gaius, iv, 13.

[2] Cf. *pro Rosc. Com.* v, 14 *pecunia petita est certa, cuius tertia parte sponsio facta est.*

colonies in the Cispadane region. The Table of Veleia, however, as Mr. Nap himself insists and as is obvious, treats all the communities in the province as on the same legal footing, and their inhabitants as being all equally capable of being parties to a *sponsio*, or playing the parts of claimant or defendant in a *legitimum iudicium*. These conditions, as will be shown later, were not realized earlier than 49 B.C.

Hitherto there has only been occasion to refer to cap. xxi of the Table, but Mr. Nap bases another series of arguments for the priority of the Table to the *lex Cornelia* on the internal evidence which he discovers in cap. xxii. His contention is that the *lex Cornelia* put actions for the recovery of debts or the enforcement of obligations not strictly pecuniary on the same footing, as regards procedure, as suits for the recovery of *certa pecunia*, whereas a comparison of caps. xxi and xxii of the Table shows that the cases respectively dealt with are not on the same footing; that the directions given to the municipal magistrates are different; that the position of the defendant resulting from the absence of a proper defence is different in the two cases; and that, in a word, while cap. xxi implies the existence of a *legitimum iudicium*, cap. xxii implies some other basis for the procedure.

For his interpretation of the *lex Cornelia* Mr. Nap relies upon a continuation of the same passage of Gaius,[1] and again, as it appears to me, misapprehends its import. There seems no evidence that this law had so wide a range as to justify its citation as the *lex Cornelia iudiciaria*, but at any rate Gaius only deals with it under the section concerned with *sponsores*, *fidepromissores*, and *fideiussores*. After mentioning the limitation as to the amount for which they might render themselves liable as sureties for any one person, &c., Gaius proceeds:

> Pecuniam autem creditam dicimus non solum eam quam credendi causa damus, sed omnem quam tunc, cum contrahitur obligatio, certum est debitum iri . . . appellatione autem pecuniae omnes res in ea lege significantur; itaque si vinum vel frumentum, et si fundum vel hominem stipulemur, haec lex observanda est.

I should have thought it obvious that the provision of the law here cited lays down nothing in respect to the procedure to be

[1] iii, 124.

adopted, or the *formula* to be employed in cases where money or money's worth are respectively claimed, but simply extends the limitation of liability, imposed on or conceded to sureties, to both kinds of action alike.

But, while a correct appreciation of the passage of Gaius disposes of the *lex Cornelia* as a *terminus ante quem* for determining the date of our Table, I am not disposed to let Mr. Nap's assertion pass unchallenged, that caps. xxi and xxii imply essentially different forms of procedure. If, indeed, the difference between the two sets of claims coincided with that between suits for *certa* and *incerta pecunia*, I should not, of course, deny that the procedure was different, for we know from Cicero, *pro Rosc. Com.* iv, 10, that in the one case there was a *iudicium*, resulting from the praetor's *formula*, and in the other an *arbitrium* emanating from his *imperium*. But the claims dealt with in cap. xxii did not technically fall under those for *incerta pecunia*, and yet on the other hand, while standing outside the strict *formula* for *certa pecunia*, they might nevertheless be claims for money's worth, capable of provisional specification as to amount, but requiring more elastic treatment, and probably reassessment of value. To these claims were not only applied the special limitations as to sureties fixed by the *lex Cornelia*, but an analogous, though naturally not identical, *formula* with a consequent *legitimum iudicium*.

That this *formula* and *iudicium* were in existence before Sulla's dictatorship is probable, but in any case there can be no question that the directions contained on the Table of Veleia presuppose them. For I entirely dispute Mr. Nap's assertion that any differences of phraseology in the two chapters or the difference in the treatment of the defendant in the one case and the other point to any essential difference of process, or show that the one implied a *legitimum iudicium*, and the other did not. As a matter of fact, neither chapter throws much light on the actual procedure, for the simple reason that they both deal with certain obstructions at the stage *in iure*, which prevented the actual process or *iudicium* from taking place at all, and then lay down a course to be adopted, which in these abnormal cases is a substitute for a *iudicium*, and not the result of one.

In both cases, i. e. in claims for *certa pecunia* and for matters, services, or restitutions other than *certa pecunia*, the defendant, who may or may not have already provided himself with a *sponsor* or *fidepromissor* or *fideiussor*, is summoned before the municipal magistrate *in iure*. But both chapters assume that there may be obstacles in the way of a *iudicium* being set up. In cap. xxi the assumed difficulty is: *sei eam pecuniam in iure dare oportere debereve se confessus erit . . . neque id quod confessus erit solvet satisve faciet.* Precisely the same difficulty is assumed in cap. xxii, but it naturally has to be expressed somewhat differently: *sei eam rem . . . in iure . . . dare facere praestare restituereve oportere, aut se debere eiusve eam rem esse, . . . confessus erit deixerit, neque de ea re satis utei oportebit faciet.* Again, cap. xxi goes on: *aut (sei) se sponsione iudiciove, uteive oportebit, non defendet,* where the *sponsio tertiae partis* is assumed, as we have seen to be the case, to be part of the procedure for *certa pecunia.* On the other hand, cap. xxii puts it differently: *aut, sei sponsionem fierei oportebit, sponsionem non faciet, aut non restituet, neque iudicio utei oportebit se non defendet.* Both chapters therefore agree that the proper course is a *iudicium*, and both assume the *sponsio tertiae partis* where circumstances admit of it. In cases of *certa pecunia* they always do, and so *sponsione iudiciove* are coupled together; in the other cases they may or may not. Where a commodity is in dispute, like a farm or a slave, its money value is provisionally assessable, and a third part may be staked in a *sponsio*; but where it is some service that has to be rendered, a *sponsio* may obviously be out of place, so that the wording is modified: *sei sponsionem fierei oportebit.* Once more the two chapters proceed in almost identical terms, except in the matter of the *sponsio*, as already explained. Cap. xxi: *sei is ibei de ea re in iure non responderit, neque de ea re sponsionem faciet, neque iudicio, utei oportebit, se defendet;* cap. xxii: *aut sei de ea re in iure nihil responderit, neque de ea re iudicio, utei oportebit, se defendet.* So far the two chapters seem to be on all fours; in neither is the *iudicium* reached, but in both it is contemplated, and in both, from all that appears, as the result of a *formula*, though naturally this *formula* is not identical, when the conditions of the claim are different.

But as proving that caps. xxi and xxii put the two sets of claims on a different legal footing, and therefore belong to a law earlier than the *lex Cornelia*, Mr. Nap insists most strongly on the difference of treatment accorded to the contumacious defendant in the two cases. In both his refusal to make his confession effective, or to plead, or to make a *sponsio*, or to accept a *iudex*, prevents a *iudicium* from being set up. Cap. xxi directs: *siremps res ius lex causaque . . . esto*, exactly as if the defendant *ex iudicieis dateis iudicareve recte iusseis iure lege damnatus esset.* I fully admit with Mr. Nap that the phrase is equivalent to condemnation in a *legitimum iudicium*, though it is not necessary to add the words 'at Rome', for the decision of a *legitimum iudicium*, wherever lawfully constituted, had the same binding force. On the other hand, cap. xxii directs: *siremps lex res ius causaque . . . esto*, exactly as if the defendant had adopted this contumacious attitude *de ieis rebus Romae apud praetorem.* Mr. Nap regards this latter direction as proving, from the absence of the words *iure lege damnatus*, that the municipal court had not been a *legitimum iudicium*, and that the defendant is placed on an essentially different footing in the two cases.

It seems to me, on the contrary, that the defendant in cap. xxii is put in exactly the same position, though, owing to the different circumstances of the case, he is dealt with differently and by different authorities. Where *certa pecunia* is concerned, the only question for the *iudicium* is whether the specified sum is to be paid or not, and therefore not only may the maxim *confessus pro iudicato* be safely applied, but the magistrate is empowered to proceed himself to the seizure (*ductio*) of the condemned person. But from the silence of the law we must infer that he has no power beyond the *ductio*, and that therefore, in case of further obstinacy or insolvency, recourse may ultimately be had to the praetor for *missio in possessionem* and *proscriptio bonorum*. But in cases of money's worth or compensation for acts committed or omitted, the *iudicium* has more complicated decisions to make, and therefore the magistrate is not allowed himself to decide what the *iudicium* ought to have decided. Accordingly, the defendant is not treated by the municipal court as if he were *ex iudicieis dateis iudicareve recte iusseis iure lege damnatus.* But this is not to be explained, as Mr. Nap explains it, on the ground that there was no *legitimum iudicium* to adjudicate on such claims. It was rather due to the circumstance that no such *iudicium* had been held, and that the magistrate was not in this case, as in the other, allowed to dispense with it. Eventually the defendant in cap. xxii is put exactly on the same footing as the defendant in cap. xxi, and becomes as fully *iure lege damnatus*. But there has in the meantime to be a *revocatio Romae*, and it is the praetor and not the municipal magistrate who puts him in this position. For cap. xxii goes on: *praetorque isve quei de eis rebus Romae iure deicundo praerit in eum et in heredem eius de eis rebus omnibus ita ius deicito decernito, eosque duci, bona eorum possideri proscribeive veneireque iubeto.* The praetor in this case, and not the magistrate, dispenses with the *legitimum iudicium*, but I submit that in doing so he treats the defendant as *ex iudicieis dateis iudicareve recte iusseis iure lege damnatus*, exactly as the municipal magistrate is allowed to treat the defendant in cap. xxi, though, unlike the magistrate, he can carry the proceedings to their final conclusion.

I hope that the preceding discussion will have made it clear (1) that there is no essential difference of procedure implied in caps. xxi and xxii, and (2) that, even if there were, the fact would not prove the Table of Veleia to be older than the *lex Cornelia*, since there is no evidence that, so far as procedure went, that law made any change in actions for *certa pecunia*, or for claims in respect of liabilities other than money.

A brief notice will suffice of Mr. Nap's final attempt to prove from internal evidence the priority of the Table to the Sullan judicial legislation. It appears from *In Verrem*[1] that in 70 B.C. tribunician *intercessio* was not allowed to obstruct the praetor's civil jurisdiction, and Mr. Nap may be right, though I doubt it, in attributing the rule to Sulla's anti-democratic policy. At any rate, in the Table of Veleia, while there is no prohibition of *intercessio* in caps. xxi and xxii, the concluding words of cap. xx run: *neive quis magistratus prove magistratu neive quis pro quo imperio potestateve erit, intercedito neive aliud quid facito quo minus de ea re iudicium detur iudiceturve.* From this supposed unevenness of treatment Mr. Nap infers that, at the time when the law on the Table was passed, the principle of prohibiting *intercessio* was not yet established, and the prohibition only applied in isolated cases. A reference to the context of the

[1] ii, 1, 60, 155; ii, 2, 12, 30.

provision shows that this argument is wholly irrelevant. The words quoted above are in strict continuation of what has preceded, and receive their explanation from it. The prescribed form of words to be used by the magistrate in appointing a *iudex* contains certain exemplary proper and place names, e. g. Licinius, Seius, Mutina, and it is regarded as conceivable that a case may be capriciously stopped by a magistrate or even by the proconsul on the ground that through some clerical error these fanciful names were employed instead of the actual ones. It is merely as a precaution against such a possible miscarriage of justice that the words in question are added. They have nothing to do with tribunician *intercessio*, and there was no necessity for them in the two following chapters.

V. I now come to Mr. Nap's somewhat audacious identification of the *lex Rubria* mentioned on the Table with the colonial law of that name passed by a colleague of C. Gracchus, an identification assumed, as we have seen, in the argument to prove the Table earlier than the *lex Iulia agraria*.[1] As to the *lex Rubria* of the Table, what appears on the surface is that it contained directions applicable to cases of *damnum infectum*, though, as we have seen, there is little to be said for Mommsen's latest view that it was confined to such cases. It may well have had a wider scope, and been, as Puchta held, a general law regulating judicial procedure for Gallia Cisalpina. Was it of still wider applicability, dealing not only with juristic, but with agrarian and constitutional relations for all Roman communities within the Italian peninsula? This is Mr. Nap's view, and he seeks to establish it by arguing that the *lex Rubria* of 122 B.C. was a wide and general law of this character.

Now with regard to this latter law, one thing is certain, that in two out of the three passages where the law of Rubrius is alluded to, it is in special connexion with the colony to be founded in 122 B.C. on the site of Carthage. Thus Plutarch says: Ῥουβρίου τῶν συναρχόντων ἑνὸς οἰκίζεσθαι Καρχηδόνα γράψαντος;[2] while the *lex agraria* of 111 B.C. (l. 59) mentions a *lex Rubria* in connexion with land in Africa which had been assigned to colonists. But Mr. Nap refuses to accept this limitation of the law to the colony of Iunonia, and maintains that it

[1] *Op. cit.* pp. 204–7. [2] *C. Gracch.* x.

was probably the law by which all the Gracchan colonies (Neptunia, Minervia, &c.) were authorized. To have passed a separate law for each colony, he argues, would have been useless repetition, and, as a matter of fact, we know that Livius Drusus in 122 B.C. and Caesar in 59 B.C. passed single laws providing generally for a number of colonies; in the former case for as many as twelve. This last point is of course true, and he might have added the law of Saturninus and the proposal of Rullus, though it is curious that he should include among general colonial laws the *lex agraria* of 111 B.C., which did not provide for the foundation of any colonies, but only for the confirmation in their lands of any colonists already sent out under previous laws. I will even furnish Mr. Nap with another point, prima facie perhaps in his favour. It is clear from the *lex Acilia* (l. 22) that in the beginning of 122 B.C. the only commissioners in existence under agrarian or colonial laws were the Gracchan *IIIvirei agreis dandeis adsignandeis* and those *quei l. Rubria IIIvirei col. ded. creati fuerant.* Mr. Nap may read in the latter phrase *coloniis deducendis*, and ask triumphantly where are the commissioners for the other colonies, if the *lex Rubria* only concerned Iunonia.

I draw attention to this question, though Mr. Nap does not himself put it, because the answer to it affects more laws than the *lex Rubria.* It seems to me clear from the *lex agraria* (especially ll. 3 and 22) that the foundation of the colonies in Italy belonged to the *IIIvirei agreis dandeis adsignandeis*, acting under the agrarian law of C. Gracchus. In l. 22 we have: *in quo agro loco IIIvir id oppidum coloniamve ex lege plebeive scito constituit deduxitve conlocavitve.* Almost as clearly in l. 3 it runs: *quem agrum locum quoiusque de eo agro loco ex lege plebeive scito IIIvir sortito* (i. e. as a colonist) *civei Romano dedit adsignavit.* Now, as the title *IIIvir* occurs repeatedly in the Italian part of the law without the amplification *agreis dandeis adsignandeis*, and yet, as the context shows, in connexion with the Gracchan law, which has in most cases just been mentioned, it is reasonable to assume the same connexion in these cases where colonies are concerned. Fortunately, however, we have one crucial passage proving beyond a doubt that this is so. In l. 15, after the usual reference to the public land available in 133 B.C., we get the words: *eius agri IIvir agreis dandeis adsignandeis ex lege plebeive scito sortito* (as a colonist) *quoi civei Romano agrum dedit adsignavit.* It follows from these passages that the *lex Rubria* and the commissioners acting under it had nothing to do with the colonies in Italy, which must have been provided for by the re-enacted and enlarged agrarian law of Caius, and founded by the *IIvirei agreis dandeis adsignandeis* of that law.

Had then a general agrarian or colonial law to be supplemented by a special law for each particular colony, or would this, as Mr. Nap puts it, have been useless repetition? It must be remembered that the *lex Rubria* does not stand alone as a law providing for a particular colony. Mr. Nap declares that the *lex Iulia agraria* was the general law sanctioning all Caesarian colonies, and that it was applicable in Gallia Cisalpina. But even in the same year in which that general law was passed, a special *lex Vatinia* was required, as we know from Suetonius,[1] for the foundation of a colony at Comum. Again, Mr. Nap cites cap. 97 of the *lex Ursonensis*[2] as proving that the colony was based upon the authorization of the general *lex Iulia*, but he omits all reference to the *lex Antonia* mentioned in cap. 104 of the same charter, where lands are spoken of as given and assigned to the colony *iussu C. Caesaris dictatoris . . . et lege Antonia.* A comparison of the two chapters shows that the *lex Iulia* provided generally that for all colonies founded on its authority some person should be appointed to distribute lands, and that he should be *ex officio* a *patronus* of the colony; while this particular colony was established by the *lex Antonia*, which among other things specified the lands to be distributed, and named the person to distribute them.

I think we should be safe in laying it down that no colony could be planted which had not been specifically provided for or sanctioned by a law, and that therefore a purely general colonial law, providing for the foundation of colonies, and even fixing their number, would, unless the names of the colonies were also specified, have to be supplemented by special laws for each of the colonies actually planted. It is probable, however, that most agrarian or colonial laws added to their general clauses, providing for colonies of a certain character, the specification and

[1] *Iul.* xxviii.

[2] Bruns, p. 122.

names of particular colonies, which might therefore be proceeded with at once without further legislation. I am especially led to this view by the proposal of Rullus, which was a general law for colonies, most of which were necessarily unspecified, since they were to be on purchased lands, the site of which was still unknown. But we find from *de leg. agr.* ii, 35, 96 that one colony at least, viz. Capua, was specified, and that even such details as the number of colonists, the number of *decuriones*, and even the number of *pontifices* were specified in it. May we not equally assume that the general Gracchan law, whether it was, as I suggest, the re-enacted *lex agraria*, or a distinctly colonial law, specified certain colonies, including Tarentum, to be founded forthwith, and provided more vaguely for others each of which, when the site was settled, would require the authorization of a special law? Precisely in the same way the *lex Iulia agraria* of 59 B.C. no doubt specified Capua and perhaps other colonies, but not Comum, so that for the latter a special law, the *lex Vatinia*, was required.

The *lex Rubria*, therefore, was not the general colonial law, at least for Italian colonies.[1] But even if it had been, why should this Gracchan colonial law have been referred to in what Mr. Nap regards as Sulla's *lex data* for Cisalpine Gaul, as a guide for magistrates in matters of civil procedure? Mr. Nap's answer seems to be that it was not only a law providing for the foundation of colonies, but also a law regulating the government of colonies, and regulating them so minutely as to cover the procedure in cases of *damnum infectum*. If this width of scope attributed to an agrarian or colonial law were regarded as applicable only to the constitutional, agrarian, or juristic relations within the colonies founded under its provisions, the conjecture, though very uncertain, might not be wholly inadmissible, and perhaps receives some support from the extant chapters of the *lex Iulia agraria*.[2]

[1] I do not deny that the *lex Rubria* may possibly have been a general law for transmarine colonies, though specifying only Iunonia. Sallust (*Iug.* xlii) speaks of Gracchus as *triumvir coloniis deducendis*, while the *lex agraria* (l. 59) has *IIIvirei coloniae deducendae*, but the words almost immediately following, *in coloniam coloniasve deduci*, perhaps make the scope of the law doubtful. It is not necessary to discuss the point, as the operation of the law was cut short by its repeal. See below, pp. 229–30.

[2] Bruns, p. 96.

Mr. Nap, however, regards the *lex Rubria* as in operation for Gallia Cisalpina in Sulla's dictatorship, though he cannot pretend that there was or had been any design of founding new colonies there under its provisions. Nor can he deny that the colonies in Cisalpine Gaul had been founded long before the passing of the *lex Rubria*, and it therefore follows that the law could only have been applicable to the government and juristic arrangements in that country, if we adopt the wholly gratuitous supposition that Gracchus caused the law to be retrospective, and even made it equivalent to a general municipal law, affecting not only existing colonies, but, as cap. xx of the Table shows, *municipia* and *praefecturae* as well.

But it is hardly surprising that Mr. Nap is imperturbable in the face of these difficulties, when we find him extending the operation of the *lex Rubria* to the arrangements of *civitates foederatae* in the eastern provinces. He has no hesitation in identifying it with a 'law of Rubrius and Acilius' mentioned on a Greek inscription belonging to the year 105 B.C.[1] The inscription contains part of an *aequum foedus* made in that year with Astypalaia, and the *foedus* is preceded by a decree of the senate. The decree speaks of the renewal of friendship and alliance between Rome and Astypalaia, and among other things directs that the Astypalaean envoy shall receive at the hands of the quaestor, on the instructions of the consul, ξένια and permission to sacrifice on the Capitol κατὰ τὸν νόμον τὸν Ῥουβρίου καὶ Ἀκιλίου. I do not pretend to follow Mr. Nap into the reasoning which convinces him that there was a colony at Astypalaia and land purchased by Rome, and that the sacrifice on the Capitol was in some way symbolic of this. It is possible that my translation of his article has done his argument less than justice. But at any rate, he has no doubt that this law of Rubrius and Acilius is the *lex Rubria* of Plutarch, the *lex Acilia*, and the *lex agraria*, as cited above; and that it was in active operation not only in Italy and Cisalpine Gaul, but in the East as late as 105 B.C. I content myself with pointing out (*a*) that the official description of the law in the *senatus consultum* as the law of Rubrius and Acilius is not consistent with the repeated description in the two laws referred to of the colonial law as the *lex*

[1] *Inscr. Gr.* xii, 3, 173.

Rubria; and (*b*) that we can only accept the identification, if we regard the *lex Rubria* as not only providing generally for the foundation of colonies and their government, but as concerned with even the minor privileges of *civitates foederatae*; (*c*) as to the real nature of the law testified to by the inscription as passed in 122 B. C. by Rubrius and Acilius, there is little to go upon, but, as the *senatus consultum* speaks of the 'renewal of friendship' with Astypalaia, it seems possible that this law settled the first relations between Rome and Astypalaia, perhaps, like the *lex Antonia de Termessibus*, constituting it a *libera civitas*, and that this privileged position was renewed and guaranteed by a *foedus* in 105 B. C.

I have so far treated Mr. Nap's view as to the scope of the *lex Rubria* and as to its continued operation down to 81 B. C. as arguable, though untenable, because some points of interest seem to arise out of its consideration. But, as a matter of fact, I might have blocked it at the outset by the contention that the *lex Rubria* was repealed, probably in 121 B. C., certainly before 111 B. C. It is clear from the authorities that a deliberate attempt was made by Minucius Rufus, one of the tribunes of 121 B. C., to repeal some or all of the Gracchan laws,[1] and that it was to counteract this attempt that Gracchus and Fulvius took the steps which called down the *senatus consultum ultimum*. That the attempt of Minucius was finally stopped by the disturbance which for the moment interrupted it, is improbable, and, though the historians do not mention the actual repeal of laws, and though most of the *leges Semproniae* were certainly not repealed,[2]

[1] Oros. v, 12; *de Vir. illustr.* 60; Plut. *C. Gracch.* 13.

[2] It may be asked why in the Italian section of the *lex agraria* it is considered necessary for the lands of colonists in Italy to be confirmed to them (*lex agraria*, l. 3), unless, as was certainly not the case, the Sempronian *lex agraria* was repealed. It seems to me that the answer is obvious and unassailable. The abolition of the *IIIviri a.d.a.* in 118 B. C. by the *lex Thoria* might be interpreted by the opponents of the Gracchan legislation as rendering ambiguous the validity of their work. To obviate any such doubt, the law of 111 B. C. definitely confirms the legal position, not only of all colonists already planted, but also of all the smallholders, who had not taken advantage of the law of 121 B. C. permitting the sale of their holdings. It might also be suggested that, owing to the difficulty of getting sufficient adjacent land, some of the colonies had not yet been fully constituted at the time when the land-commissioners were abolished, though the colonists may have been duly selected (*sortiti*), and some actually settled on land. At any rate, the abolition of the commissioners for Italian colonies before their work was done might produce

we happen to know from Appian[1] that the prohibition against the sale of small holdings was set aside in this year. Against the *lex Rubria* there were special objections. We can hardly doubt that Velleius[2] reflects conservative tradition, when he calls this law the most pernicious of the Gracchan measures, and attributes the feeling against it to jealousy of a revived Carthage. There were also the technical objections that the curse laid upon the site by Scipio had been disregarded, and that the number of colonists prescribed by the law had been exceeded. That no *colonia Iunonia* was permanently established is proved by the implications or silence of the authorities, but the conclusive proof that the law was repealed or cancelled is found in the *lex agraria* of 111 B. C. This law carefully provides that all colonists sent out to Africa shall be fully confirmed in their lands by the *IIvir* created by it, a provision unnecessary if the *lex Rubria* was still in operation, and goes out of its way to describe that law as *lex Rubria quae fuit* (*lex agr.* l. 59). This unanswerable phrase seems to have escaped Mr. Nap's attention, but I am not aware that any scholar has thrown doubt on its obvious implication. Unless he is prepared to do so, the whole of his contention about the *lex Rubria*, and in particular his detection of a reference to it in the Table of Veleia, falls to the ground.

We have examined the method by which the date of the Table of Veleia has been pushed back to a point anterior to the *lex Cornelia* of 81 B. C. As the Table presupposes the existence of the province, and as Mr. Nap accepts Mommsen's 'proof' that it was created by Sulla as dictator, we seem to have reached the backward limit. It will be seen presently that this is the case, but Mr. Nap thinks it necessary to prove that the date must be later than the *lex Valeria* of 88 B. C.,[3] and, as his argument is characteristic, I shall devote a paragraph to its examination. What we know of the law of Valerius Flaccus (mainly from Sall. *Cat.* xxxiii) is that it was a temporary expedient for dealing with an acute phase of the debt problem, by which a large percentage of existing debts were cancelled. Mr. Nap, after calling it a law *de pecunia credita*, a title which is misleading if it suggests a

the same kind of uncertainty in Italy as the repeal of the *lex Rubria* produced in Africa.

[1] i, 27. [2] ii, 7, 7. [3] *Op. cit.* p. 200.

connexion with the process of *certa pecunia credita*, proceeds arbitrarily to identify it with a *lex Vallia* mentioned in Gaius, iv, 25. This law he regards as having introduced certain novelties into the procedure in cases of *certa pecunia*, which he finds reflected in cap. xxi of the Veleian Table.

As to the identification of the two laws, it seems to me reckless and uncritical in the extreme, depending upon the single fact that both are concerned with debt. But, while the *lex Valeria* deals with the cancelling of debt, the *lex Vallia* is concerned with a special method of recovering it. Nor, strange to say, has this method of recovery any point of contact whatever with the process for which directions are given in cap. xxi of the Table. While that chapter, as Mr. Nap rightly insists, presupposes a *legitimum iudicium* based upon the praetor's *formula*, a reference to Gaius will show that the *lex Vallia* is cited as making certain modifications in that form of *legis actio* known as *manus iniectio*. This is obviously fatal to Mr. Nap's argument, since no modifications in the *legis actio* could have any relation to the formulary process for *certa pecunia*.

He declares that the *lex Valeria* (*Vallia*) allowed a defendant to enter into a *sponsio* on his own account, and in his own name, without employing a third party as *sponsor*. But the Table presents us with a defendant refusing to enter into a *sponsio* with the claimant, the context showing that no third party was required. Therefore, it is argued, the Table must be later than the *lex Valeria*. There are two misconceptions in this argument. In the first place, the *sponsio* of the Table, as already pointed out, is the *sponsio tertiae partis* to which by its very nature there can only be two parties. In the second place, the *lex Vallia* has nothing to do with a *sponsio* of any kind, but with the formalities of *manus iniectio*. Gaius has explained that, when this *legis actio* is employed, a debtor could escape arrest by finding a substantial *vindex*, who becomes his representative before the court. *Sed postea lege Vallia, excepto iudicato et eo pro quo depositum est, ceteris omnibus, cum quibus per manus iniectionem agebatur, permissum est sibi manum depellere et pro se agere.* It would be irrelevant to my present purpose to follow Mr. Nap into his elaborate discussion of this supposed *lex Valeria*.[1] This point I

[1] *Op. cit.* pp. 182–94.

have mentioned is the only one by which he seeks to fix the date of the Table of Veleia, and I hope I have shown that, even if the *lex Vallia* is the *lex Valeria*, it is based upon an astounding misconception of the passage in Gaius.

Having by means of the preceding *termini post* and *ante quem* placed our law, admittedly concerned with Cisalpine Gaul, between 86 and 81 B.C., and at the same time accepting Mommsen's 'proof'[1] that Sulla created the province in his dictatorship, Mr. Nap argues that the Table can have been no other than Sulla's *lex data* or *lex provinciae*. As an additional support for this view, he cites the words of Licinianus: *data erat et Sullae provincia Gallia Cisalpina.*[2] With regard to this last point, I will only notice that, though the words of Licinianus are mutilated and have no immediate context, they clearly refer to a date before the dictatorship, and are therefore so far against Mommsen's view. Apart from this, if the single word *data* is sufficient to convince Mr. Nap that the province was entrusted to Sulla for the purpose of receiving a *lex data*, it seems useless to argue the point.

As to the creation of the province by Sulla, I am not satisfied with Mommsen's conjecture, and I argue above[3] that it was more probably created immediately after the Social War, and that the *lex Pompeia* of 89 B. C. was the *lex provinciae*. At any rate, whether the province was due to Sulla or not, there are fatal objections to accepting the Table of Veleia as part of his *lex data* for it. (1) Directions for procedure in the case of abnormal behaviour on the part of defendants in civil suits are not what we should expect to find in the *lex data* of a newly constituted province. (2) The communities in the province, to which the law applies, do not correspond with the conditions of the country in 82 or 81 B.C.; when apart from minor and only half-urban places, practically all the towns were either Roman or Latin colonies, the latter being in a great majority. (3) As there were no *municipia*, so there were no *IIIIviri* in Sulla's time, nor, as we know from Cicero,[4] as late as 51 B. C.; and accordingly the titles of magistrates found in the Table, *IIviri IIIIviri prae-*

[1] For Mommsen's and other views on the creation of the province, see Marquardt, *Staatsverwalt.* i, pp. 218, 219.
[2] Licin., p. 32, ed. Teubner. [3] See Essay No. ii, p. 46 ff. [4] *Ad. Att.* v, 2, 3.

fective, are equally out of place in a document of the Sullan period. (4) The civil procedure of Roman law, implied by the Table as applicable to the whole province, was not necessarily adopted by Latin towns, which, though they possessed the *ius commercii*, were not likely to be all *fundi* of Roman law. (5) The Table shows that there was for all the communities of the province, under certain conditions, a *revocatio Romae* to the praetor's supreme court, whereas it is certain, and is proved by the Atestine Fragment, that the judicial competence of the Latin *IIviri* was subject to no such limitation. (6) There is nothing in the conditions of the province in Sulla's day to explain why the proconsul is wholly ignored in these judicial matters, and why the local courts are brought into direct relation and subordination to the praetor in Rome. (7) I will add, as a not unfair *argumentum ad hominem*, that if, as Mr. Nap contends, the *lex Cornelia* of 81 B.C. introduced changes of procedure into suits for *certa pecunia* and claims other than money, it is strange that he should have perpetuated for the new province what within a few months were to become obsolete forms.

Although I have scrupulously followed Mr. Nap through his somewhat artificial *termini ante quem*, I declared at the outset that the really crucial date to be considered was the year 49 B.C. To that year undoubtedly belong (*a*) the enfranchisement, recorded by Dio Cassius (xli, 36), of all still unenfranchised communities of Cisalpine Gaul, and (*b*) the document known as the *Fragmentum Atestinum*.[1] That the two are intimately connected is certain, for the Fragment refers to the enfranchising law, 'the law or plebiscite passed by L. Roscius on March 11', and makes it a dividing-line as regards at least one point of judicial procedure. We may even go further and assert that the law of which the Fragment is a part, is a corollary, or, if Mommsen prefers the term, a *lex secutoria* to the enfranchising measure. They were both therefore—and Mr. Nap admits this—virtually Caesarian laws, though why the latter should be described as the first *lex Iulia iudiciaria* is one of the peculiarities of Mr. Nap's system, which is never made to cohere with its context.[2]

[1] Bruns, p. 101.
[2] Mr. Nap regards it (*a*) as a *lex data*; (*b*) as concerned with Cisalpine Gaul.

But the question about the Atestine Fragment which makes it essential to the present argument is whether with its fixed and certain date it does not by itself preclude any earlier date for the Table of Veleia than 49 B. C. This would obviously be the case if it could be shown that both the larger and the smaller fragments belong to the same law. There are not wanting strong indications that they do. (1) Both laws are concerned with judicial procedure in municipal courts. (2) Both are concerned with these courts as existing in Gallia Cisalpina. This is of course explicit in the case of the Table of Veleia, but is a safe inference in regard to the smaller document; (*a*) from the fact of its having been found at Ateste, an indication very strong, though of course not conclusive; (*b*) from the fact that it makes the *lex Roscia* a dividing-line in judicial procedure, and that that law by common consent concerned Cisalpine Gaul. (3) Both are concerned with the *revocatio Romae* of certain suits and actions from the competence of the municipal magistrates.

This last point comes out in the following ways:

(*a*) Suits for money or other debts involving more than 15,000 sesterces have to be tried in Rome (Tab. of Vel., caps. xxi and xxii). (*b*) In certain cases a *vadimonium* to appear in Rome has to be entered into before a municipal magistrate (Tab. of Vel., cap. xx, *ad fin.*). (*c*) In some abnormal cases *ductio, missio in possessionem*, and *proscriptio* are applied by the Roman praetor to municipal defendants (Tab. of Vel., cap. xxii). (*d*) Cases of delict, involving *infamia*, have to be tried in Rome, except where, in minor claims involving less than 10,000 sesterces,[1] the defendant expressly demands trial in a municipal court (*Frag. Atest.*, cap. A). (*e*) *Revocatio Romae* is expressly disallowed, whatever the amount claimed, in all cases initiated before the passing of the *lex Roscia*, a provision implying that henceforth it would under certain conditions be resorted to (*Frag. Atest.*, cap. B).

(4) On the matter of date, we may point out (*a*) the certainty that the Atestine Fragment belongs to 49 B.C., and (*b*) certain considerations which make for the Table of Veleia an earlier date

But (*a*) by all analogy a *lex iudiciaria* would be a *lex rogata*, and (*b*) a *lex iudiciaria* would by its very nature be a general law, not one dealing with a particular province.

[1] There is no serious inconsistency between the maximum of 15,000 sesterces in the Table and 10,000 sesterces in the Fragment, since the former referred to purely civil suits, the latter to cases of delict.

than 49 B.C. impossible. Thus its provisions apply without discrimination to the whole province of Cisalpine Gaul, and the communities of the province are described, with the trifling exception that *vici* and *castella* are added, exactly as the admittedly enfranchised communities of Italy are described in the Table of Heraclea: *municipia coloniae praefecturae fora conciliabula*.[1] Not only so, but the highest magistrate in these communities is *IIvir IIIIvir praefectusve* (cap. xx, l. 39), just as in the Table of Heraclea (l. 83) they are *IIvirei IIIIvirei*. All this points to the Table not being earlier than 49 B.C., the date of the enfranchisement, especially as from *ad. Att.* ii, 5, 3 it is clear that as late as 51 B.C. there were as yet no *IIIIviri*, at any rate in the Transpadane district, and almost certainly not in the province at all, since the magistrates in the Latin colonies would be *IIviri*. Equally conclusive is the fact that the Table not only treats all the communities of the province as *fundi* of Roman civil law, and their magistrates as entitled to set up a *legitimum iudicium*, but makes them all subject under certain conditions to a *revocatio Romae*, an arrangement proved to be inapplicable to Latin communities by the Atestine Fragment (cap. B).

I quote the last citation as very instructively marking the transition produced by the *lex Roscia*:

Quoius rei in quoque municipio colonia praefectura quoiusve IIviri eiusve qui ibei lege foedere plebeive scito senatusve consulto institutove[2] iure dicundo praefuit, ante legem seive illud plebeiscitum est, quod L. Roscius a. d. V eid. Mart. populum plebemve rogavit, quod privatim ambigetur, iuris dictio, iudicis arbitri reciperatorum datio addictiove fuit, quantaeve rei

[1] In the Fragment only *municipia coloniae* and *praefecturae* are mentioned, perhaps because they alone possessed magistrates with the highest judicial authority. In the Table the list of communities is a longer one, because the inhabitants of every community could be plaintiffs before the appropriate court in such matters as *damnum infectum*, &c.

[2] It does not belong to my present argument to inquire who the judicial magistrates were, apparently not entitled *IIviri*. I will only make the following suggestions: (*a*) The *civitates foederatae* made Latin towns by the *lex Pompeia* would naturally adopt the usual title, *IIviri*. But a few may exceptionally have been allowed to give their magistrates the old titles in accordance with the original treaty, *foedere*. (*b*) Perhaps a few towns other than *civitates foederatae* were made Latin by Pompeius, and also allowed the same privilege, as a concession to custom, *instituto*. (*c*) Lastly, other smaller towns, passed over in 89 B.C., and subsequently made Latin either by law or senatorial decree, *lege plebiscito senatus consulto*, may have similarly retained their old magistrates.

pecuniaeve fuit [i. e. if over 15,000 sesterces], eius rei pecuniaeve quo magis privato Romae revocatio sit . . . ex hac lege nihil rogatur.

Prior therefore to the *lex Roscia* we have a state of things in which the *IIviri iure dicundo* of the Latin colonies had the right of *iurisdictio* and *iudicum datio* in matters involving any amount of money, with no necessity for a *revocatio Romae.* But this point is by itself absolutely fatal to Mr. Nap's whole scheme of throwing back the Table of Veleia into Sulla's period, for in that Table we clearly have the state of things subsequent to the *lex Roscia*—communities with titles appropriate to Roman towns, magistrates who are *IIviri* or *IIIIviri*, and a regular system of *revocatio Romae* under specified conditions.

In view of the preceding considerations, we can again turn to the question whether these two documents can be regarded as belonging to the same law. Is it likely that two laws were passed between March 49 and 42 or 41 B. C., when the province ceased to exist, not only both dealing with Cisalpine Gaul, but with judicial matters in it, and especially with local competence? Only one answer seems possible, viz. that the Atestine Fragment comes from one of the four lost tablets of the law partially preserved on the Table of Veleia. Or the probabilities of the case may be put in this way. The Table of Veleia could not have been later than 41 B. C., since in that or the preceding year Cisalpine Gaul ceased to be a province. Its contents imply political and juristic relations within the province which could not have been present prior to the enfranchising law of 49 B. C. But that enfranchising law would naturally and properly be followed by some legal determination and readjustment, whether by *lex data* or *lex rogata,* of municipal competence and procedure in judicial matters. On this indirect evidence it has seemed permissible to many to regard the law as a corollary to the enfranchisement, and therefore as belonging, if not to 49 B. C., at least to the period of Caesarian ascendancy. This view is confirmed by the Atestine Fragment, which on incontrovertible internal evidence is part of a law passed in 49 B. C. as a sequel to the *lex Roscia,* and which deals with precisely the same kind of juristic readjustment as the Veleian Table. Unless therefore we are prepared to argue that two separate laws dealing with these subjects were passed within at most a year or two of one another, we must accept the two fragments as portions of the same law.

At the risk therefore of having my view of the law described as conservative, I reject the attempt to relegate it to the pre-Caesarian period, and I regard it as a natural sequel to the complete enfranchisement of the province. The urban communities were now roughly, as in Italy, *municipia coloniae* and *praefecturae*; they were necessarily all *fundi* of Roman law, and of course had their own local jurisdiction in general accordance with it. That for Italian municipalities there had either grown up by custom, or had been established by statute law, some delimitation of competence between the local magistrates and the Roman praetor, can hardly be doubted. We may fairly assume, too, that Caesar, who had long favoured the removal of all political inequality between the province and Italy, would also insist on equal juristic treatment. But this policy necessitated legislation, since without it the local courts, as belonging to provincial municipalities, would be subject to the higher jurisdiction, not of the praetor, but of the proconsul. It seems to me that, as long as the country remained a province, nothing short of a special law could attain what I conceive to have been Caesar's object.

No doubt the law so called for was in a sense a *lex provinciae*, though it only concerned judicial relations. But it does not follow that it was a *lex data*. As a matter of fact, the institution of *leges datae* was simply a convenient time-saving expedient. When a province had to be regulated, usually at a distance from Italy, and full of complicated local conditions, it was simpler to empower the man or men on the spot to draw up the necessary arrangements in the form of a *lex data* than to insist on their being brought before the *comitia*. Similarly, when charters were to be framed for Italian towns, it would have been useless repetition and waste of labour to pass separate laws, and therefore commissioners were authorized to draw up *leges datae*, guided either by custom or by some general law. But where the province was almost a part of Italy, where the conditions were all but identical, where differences of status were non-existent, and where the only matters requiring regulation were technical and juristic, the natural course was surely to proceed by means of a *lex rogata*, just as for cognate reasons Caesar proceeded a few years later in his *lex municipalis*. Mommsen argued that the *lex Roscia* was a *mater lex*, giving birth to the law on the Veleian Table, a *filia lex*, just as the *lex municipii Tarentini* was a daughter law to the *lex Iulia de civitate* of 90 B. C.[1] The parallel is illogical and misleading. The only *filiae leges* to which the *lex Roscia* could give birth would be the various *leges datae* framed for the newly enfranchised *municipia fundana* of Cisalpine Gaul. Why again should the *lex Roscia*, *qua* enfranchising law, call into being a general judicial *lex data*, if the *lex Iulia* (of 90 B. C.), equally an enfranchising law, had done nothing of the kind? After all, the closest parallel between the *lex Roscia* and the law under discussion is that between the *lex Iulia* of 90 B. C. and the municipal law partly preserved on the Table of Heraclea. In both cases the *lex secutoria* was a logical consequence of its predecessor, and as the municipal law was admittedly a *lex rogata*, there seems no reason for placing our present law in a different category. The *lex Rubria* mentioned in the Table was a *plebiscitum* or *lex rogata*, and as it was manifestly a law binding on the municipal magistrates of Gallia Cisalpina, and concerned with judicial procedure, Puchta's conjecture that this was the actual title of the law on the Table seems to me, in spite of Mommsen's change of view, still to hold the field.

[1] See *Juristische Schriften*, i, 152 ff.

VIII

THE TABLE OF HERACLEA AND THE *LEX IULIA MUNICIPALIS*

PART I. RECENT THEORIES OF PRE-CAESARIAN AUTHORSHIP

FOR many years the controversy as to the nature of this mysterious document,[1] though not entirely extinct, was rendered almost dormant by the general acceptance of the famous hypothesis of Savigny and Mommsen. It was, they suggested, the concluding portion of a comprehensive law, entitled the lex Iulia Municipalis, by which Caesar in 45 B.C. regulated municipal institutions, not only in all communities of Roman citizens within the Italian peninsula, but partly at least in Rome herself, as after all merely the foremost municipality of the empire. It is idle to deny that the hypothesis, so stated, rests upon a somewhat slender basis of established fact. Only two general municipal regulations are contained in the Table, one with certainty, the other with great probability attributable to Caesar. It has to be assumed, therefore, that only an insignificant part of the whole law has been preserved. As for the reason suggested for including provisions about Rome in such a municipal law, Prof. Reid's dictum can hardly be gainsaid that never was so profound an idea presented in a more trivial form.

But in one of his last papers, written in 1903, Mommsen, who had accepted Savigny's views in the main, explicitly withdrew the theory that there was or had been any general law regulating the constitutions or the administrative arrangements of either Roman or Latin towns.[2] The occasion for this remarkable

[1] The text of the Table has often been edited since it was found in 1732–5 near Heraclea. It may be seen conveniently in Bruns, *Fontes* (ed. 7, 1909), p. 102, in Dessau, *Inscr. Selectae* (1902), No. 6085, and (with an English translation) in the author's *Roman Laws and Charters*, pp. 136 ff.

[2] In his edition of the lex municipii Tarentini, *Ephem. epigr.* ix, pp. 5, 6 (*Ges. Schriften*, i, 152, 153).

recantation of what had come to be 'the classical theory' was the discovery of a fragment of the 'lex data' framed for Tarentum, and attributed to the period of the free republic. It is assumed by some recent writers that this discovery necessitated Mommsen's change of view, and that the existence of a 'lex data' at Tarentum, and by inference in other towns as well, is incompatible with a general municipal law, whether passed by Cinna, or Sulla, or Caesar. I do not believe that Mommsen recognized any such incompatibility, or that it exists. It did not need the law of Tarentum to reveal the fact virtually established by the last clause of the Table, that all enfranchised towns received constitutions from commissioners. It was surmised as far back as Mazochi (1754), recognized by almost all succeeding commentators, and by none of them was it judged inconsistent with a general law. Mommsen makes the briefest allusion to the fact that he has changed his view, and enters on no explanation as to why he has done so. It seems probable that he had long been conscious of weak points in Savigny's original hypothesis, and took the opportunity presented by the new find of reconsidering his position.[1] I shall argue in the course of this paper against the necessity of his negative conclusion, stated at least as uncompromisingly as he states it.

As a matter of fact, there are two problems suggested by this document: (1) What light does it throw on the legislation or other procedure necessitated by the enfranchisement of Italy? (2) What is the explanation of its being at Heraclea? Mommsen, perhaps over hastily, considered that both questions could be answered by the same hypothesis, that a general municipal law was passed by Caesar, and that a copy of it was set up in Italian towns, the Table being a fragment of the copy set up at Heraclea. But while the answer to the first question is not incompatible with the existence of separate 'leges datae' for the towns, the answer to the second question undoubtedly is. If Heraclea had a 'lex data' of its own, there was no possible reason why a copy of the general law should be set up there. The general law was intended to guide the commissioners, not to be directly obligatory on the towns. I imagine that it was the recognition of this fatal

[1] Objections to Savigny's view had been brought by Hackel, *Festheft Bormann* (in *Wiener Studien*, xxiv), 1902, p. 320, and others.

objection which induced Mommsen to withdraw his hypothesis. I am not convinced that he need have abandoned the first part of it, and it is unfortunate that he has left us with no answer of any kind to the second of the two questions.

It was inevitable that the discovery of the Tarentine law, with its striking coincidences with parts of the Spanish charters, would lead to re-examination of the Heraclean Table, and it was equally inevitable that Mommsen's recantation would open the door to new speculation. The whole question indeed seems to be in the melting pot; 'mysterious and insoluble document' are the terms now most often applied to what a generation ago was confidently spoken of as the lex Iulia Municipalis. As far as I can see, the only point on which scholars of to-day are fairly well agreed is the negative one, that the document, when complete, was not the copy of a general municipal law. It almost of necessity follows that the Table is a composite document, made up of different measures. Questions at once arise as to the date, bearing, and authorship of each. It is possible to abandon the lex Iulia Municipalis, and yet to maintain the Caesarian date and authorship of all the different sections. Or it may be maintained with Prof. Reid and others that there was a lex Iulia Municipalis, but that only one clause of the Table belongs to it, while other sections date from the end of the Social war. Or the Caesarian authorship of any part of the document may be denied, and a return may be attempted to theories like those in vogue before Savigny.

By far the most dangerous attack on the Caesarian date of the Table, as well as on the theory in any form of a general municipal law, is contained in *La Table latine d'Héraclée, la prétendue lex Iulia Municipalis* (Paris, 1907), by Dr. Henri Legras. I do not know how widely the book is known in this country, but it has excited considerable attention abroad, and from its ability, learning, and controversial vigour it constitutes the most notable contribution to the discussion since Mommsen's article in 1903. For myself, I have recently read the book with extreme admiration for its boldness and ingenuity, though without being convinced of the soundness of its conclusions. At the same time I feel strongly that so thorough-going and concentrated an attack on the Caesarian character of these enactments must be met by those who are not prepared to give up the whole position. If Legras has failed to eliminate Caesar from the Table of Heraclea, I doubt whether any other scholar can hope to be more successful. I do not feel myself particularly well equipped to become his critic. But, like many better scholars, I have expressed my adherence to Mommsen's hypothesis, and, though I am not prepared to reaffirm it as a whole, I should like to make an attempt to vindicate not only the Caesarian authorship of the document, but some part of the theory of a general law. The former object will be best attained by an examination and criticism of Legras' theories as to the several sections of the Table in order. To reach a conclusion with regard to the second point, I shall have to attempt something approaching a constructive theory, and I recognize with Legras that no solution of the problem can claim to be even provisionally complete, which leaves unanswered the questions: why was the document engraved at Heraclea, and in what relation does it stand to the 'lex data' of that town?

The Table falls into the following sections: (I) lines 1 to 19, the commencement of the provision having been contained on another bronze. (II) lines 20 to 82. (IIIa) lines 83 to 141. (IIIb) lines 142 to 158. (IIIc) lines 159 to 163.

I. It is admitted by all that lines 1–19 belong to a section of the Table of which the beginning is missing. Certain persons have to make a declaration, not only of their names but of other matters, to specified magistrates, either in person, or, if absent from Rome, through agents, or, if minors or women under legal wardship, through their guardians. The names and statements of these persons are to be entered in the 'tabulae publicae', and also put up at the place where corn is distributed. Any official giving corn to any person on this list of 'professi' is to be heavily fined. The fragment in itself contains no clue as to who these 'professi' were, or what they had to declare, or why they were excluded from the corn distributions. It is not even clear whether the declaration was primarily with a view to the frumentations, or had some other object which led to the concluding prohibition. It is an apparent objection to the first view that, though the declarations seem to be voluntary, they are attended not by a privilege but by a disability. This led to the conjecture of Dirksen and Puchta that 'non' has fallen out of the text, and that the prohibition affects those whose names are *not* on the list. It is not necessary to discuss any explanation based upon this conjecture, since it is covered by no canon of legitimate textual criticism.

Far more attractive is the suggestion of Hirschfeld, who brings these regulations into connexion with two of Caesar's measures. To prevent any undue reduction of the city population, he prohibited all between the ages of 20 and 40 from leaving Italy for more than three years, except on military service.[1] This would necessitate a declaration being made by those intending to leave Rome, and a list being preserved. But as some of these absentees might be on Caesar's reduced list of corn-recipients, it was necessary to guard against their corn being claimed by unqualified persons in their name. It was for this reason that their names were to be exposed at the place of distribution. But (1) though all these declarants would be entered in the 'tabulae publicae', it would only have been necessary to expose in the forum the names of those who were on the list of corn-recipients; (2) even this would be unnecessary, as the obvious course would be to strike their names off the corn-list; (3) the mention of 'pupilli' and 'pupillae' is inexplicable on this theory; (4) this interpretation would increase the difficulty of explaining the Table as a document related somehow to Heraclea.

Mommsen's interpretation, in the light of Suet. *Caes.* xli, as I intend to reaffirm it, will more conveniently be considered later with Legras' criticisms. In Legras' view it has been the attempt to connect this section with Caesar's legislation that has obscured its real meaning. He goes back to Sulla's first consulship in 88 B.C. The lex Iulia had been passed, and crowds of new citizens, belonging to the towns, which by accepting its offer had become 'fundi' of the law, were eager to use their new privileges. But a necessary preliminary was registration in the Roman tribes, and to effect this was the function of the censors. The censors of 89 had not been able to accomplish the task, and besides, fresh states were, one after another, becoming 'fundi' of the lex Iulia. It was therefore impossible to make the new citizens wait for the next censors, and Sulla passed this law empowering the consuls,

[1] Suet. *Caes.* xlii.

or in default of them other magistrates, to receive the declarations of the Italians. As a supplement to this provision, with a view of preventing a possible shortage of corn for the old citizens, and to remove an inducement for flocking to Rome, the clause was appended excluding all these declarants from the distributions.

This hypothesis is ingenious, but there is absolutely nothing to verify it, and there are several objections which seem to me fatal. (1) The list of names in the forum was clearly put up for purposes of the frumentations. Why then were the names of 'pupilli' and 'pupillae' included, whose ineligibility is one of Legras' chief arguments against Mommsen's view? His point that, though incapable of political rights, they required registration in order to secure the private rights of citizens, is irrelevant, since, though it might explain their inclusion in the 'tabulae publicae', it would not account for their entry in the forum list. (2) A list containing such a multitude of names as this theory implies, would have been unmanageable and useless to the distributing magistrate, and it was unnecessary. In the absence of a register of recipients, which Legras is probably right in assuming for this period, certain tests would have to be applied and certain questions asked by the magistrate. If these had been sufficient up to this time to exclude the host of non-citizens in Rome, they would presumably have met also the case of these supposed Italian claimants. (3) It seems certain that only citizens domiciled in Rome could claim the corn distributions. If, therefore, the Italians came merely to register their names, they had no claim; if on the other hand they came to stay, by what possible right could they be excluded from the privileges of other domiciled citizens? (4) In 88 B.C. the new citizens were still limited to eight of the thirty-five tribes, and their voting power was a mere farce. Under these circumstances they would hardly be so impatient for registration and its political consequences as not to wait for the next censors. But (5) a far more serious objection is that the lex Iulia conferred the citizenship not on individual Italians, but *en bloc* on whole communities. It is inconceivable that every member of every enfranchised town would have to register himself in Rome individually, either in person or through an agent. Under the lex Plautia-Papiria no doubt the case was different, but by that law registration was to be made before the praetor urbanus, not before the magistrates here specified. It may safely be assumed that the lex Iulia provided for the due registration of new citizens in each enfranchised town through the local magistrates. No other plan can be imagined as workable.

Legras' theory, though wholly unsupported by evidence, at least does not involve tampering with any text. That of Prof. Nap, as I gather it from an article by M. Besnier,[1] is far less legitimate. Dio Cassius (xxxvii, 9), after mentioning the dispute between the two censors in 65 B.C. about the enfranchisement of the Transpadani, speaks of a law being passed by a tribune named Papius, expelling from Rome certain aliens, vaguely and certainly incorrectly described as *πάντες, οἱ ἐν τῇ Ῥώμῃ διατρίβοντες πλὴν τῶν τὴν νῦν Ἰταλίαν οἰκούντων*. From the context it seems probable that the expelled persons were Transpadani. At any rate, Prof. Nap not only reconstructs the law of Papius so as to make it one requiring registration from all 'peregrini' in Rome and excluding them from the corn-distributions, but supposes that two other 'leges Papiae' were passed not only in the same year, but on the same day. One of these regulated aedilician duties, and the other dealt with municipal senates and the municipal census. I do not criticize this theory in detail, because I have not seen its author's own presentation of it. But, as it invents a purely fictitious situation for 65 B.C. by re-writing a passage of Dio, it can hardly claim serious consideration.

I will once more attempt an explanation in the light of Suetonius (*Caes.* xli). We are told that Caesar effected a 'recensus' of the people with a view to the corn-distributions, that it was carried out by the help of the owners of 'insulae' in the various 'vici', and that its result was the reduction of recipients from 320,000 to 150,000. How the latter number was arrived at, we do not know, but there must have been an official list of them, and those on this list were 'recensi'. This last point is placed beyond doubt by Suetonius' next statement: 'ne qui novi coetus recensionis causa (for the sake of getting on the list of recensi) moveri possent, instituit ut quotannis in demortuorum locum ex iis qui recensi non essent subsortitio a praetore fieret.' But it is obvious that this system necessitated a second

[1] In the *Revue des Études Anciennes*, tome xiv, no. 1.

list made out each year, to which the lot was to be applied. To get on to this preliminary list, application in person or by proxy would be necessary, and this would naturally take the form of a definite 'professio' before specified magistrates. It is equally clear that an official copy of this list of 'professi' would have to be kept in the 'tabulae publicae' to be used for the 'subsortitio' at the end of the year. But that there might be no suspicion of unfair dealing, and to give opportunities for checking and exposing false statements, a second copy was put up in the forum. Legras declares that the system of two lists, one of recipients and one of 'professi', was so cumbrous and maladroit as to be unworthy of Caesar. That is because he misunderstands the object of the list in the forum. It was intended merely to secure publicity and confidence, not to guide the distributing magistrate. If the latter found the name of an applicant on his list of 'recensi' he would not trouble to make sure that it was not on the public list. Legras curiously argues, and apparently thinks it a *coup de grâce* to Mommsen's view, that there could not have been two lists because vacancies were to be filled 'ex iis qui recensi non essent'. If the 'recensi' were the 150,000, the words are no argument against a second list. If they were not, who in his opinion were they?

Now the concluding portion of the first section of the Table, contained in lines 1–19, fits in perfectly, as far as it goes, with the scheme described by Suetonius. The 'professi' are the applicants placed on the preliminary list, whose names at the end of the year are to be subjected by the praetor to the subsortitio. It is admitted that we have only the end of the provision, and it would be easy to suggest an arrangement of the earlier part which would make the extant clauses appear the natural and intelligible conclusion. The opening words of line 1 prove that 'professio' before a consul had already been dealt with, and in connexion with it would naturally have come in all the arrangements leading up to and including the 'subsortitio'. The last clauses merely add some details in the matter of the 'professio', and remove possible difficulties and obstacles in particular cases. The law ends with what was perhaps a reaffirmation of the principle, in which lay the essential point of the reform, that a large number of present recipients were in future to be excluded.

The distributing magistrate needed to be reminded emphatically that he was to proceed on an entirely new system.

Legras contends that in a list drawn up in connexion with the frumentations, 'pupilli' and 'pupillae' could not have been included. But even if the passages cited by him establish this point, which appears to me doubtful, I have already shown that his own explanation is open to exactly the same objection. It may well be argued that, even if before and after Caesar the privilege of receiving corn was confined to adult male citizens, the dictator's law may have introduced an innovation which did not survive. As his object was to transform a political bribe into a means of poor-relief, it is conceivable that a widow or a son still under wardship may have been allowed to receive corn for a family. It seems to me, therefore, that Mommsen's identification of these lines with the conclusion of Caesar's 'lex frumentaria' still holds the field, and that Legras and Nap have both failed in their attempts at a pre-Caesarian explanation.

II. The second section (lines 20–82), whatever may be its relation to the other parts of the Table, has primary reference to no other municipality than that of Rome. It describes itself more than once as a 'lex', and it lays down regulations with regard to the roads and footpaths within the city, vehicular traffic during the day, and the keeping clear from obstruction of open spaces and porticoes. It is clear that all these regulations would fall under the competence of the curule and plebeian aediles, although these magistrates are only directed to take special action in connexion with the 'maintenance' of roads. If this section is merely an extract from a larger law, dealing with the municipal administration of Rome, it may have been preceded or followed by similar regulations with regard to such other aedilician duties as the charge of the markets and the prevention or extinction of fires. On the other hand, if we regard the Table as the fragment of a single law, whether a 'lex satura' or not, the fact that the clauses preceding and following this section are not concerned with aedilician functions seems to necessitate the view that the other duties of the aediles were not dealt with. It can hardly be said that such a conclusion is favourable to Mommsen's hypothesis of a general law including the administration of Rome. As far as I can see, the only way of meeting the objection would be the suggestion, which I am not prepared to make, that lines 1–19 are the concluding part of a section which began with the duties of the two new 'aediles Cereales', who might even conceivably have been created by the law.

But whether the law, of which this section formed a part or the whole, was concerned merely with the aedilician superintendence of roads, traffic, and open spaces, or with the municipal administration of Rome generally, the immediate question is, to what date must it or can it be assigned. We may eliminate Sulla's first consulship (88 B.C.) as a year of political excitement utterly unsuited to domestic reforms of this kind. Legras himself admits that there is no reason to connect it with Sulla's dictatorship, while the mention of the censor (l. 73) is inconsistent with a régime in which there were to be no censors. He suggests two periods as suitable to reforms in the police surveillance of roads, traffic, and public places, the period supervening on the second Punic war, when Rome first became 'une grande ville', and the dictatorship of Caesar. To accept the latter would be wholly inconsistent with his interpretation of all the other sections of the Table, and Legras also finds some positive reasons for preferring the former.

During the first half of the second century B.C. there is evidence that at least ten public porticoes and basilicae were erected, and it was therefore especially appropriate that the attention of the aediles should be drawn by the legislator to their duty of keeping them open to the public. But even if we admit that this consideration points to the beginnings of legislation on the subject of protecting public places from encroachment, it is irrelevant to the date of the clauses on the Table, because from l. 72 it appears that there had already been a number of laws or plebiscita or decrees of the senate on the subject of these spaces.

Another somewhat more concrete argument for the early date of the regulation as to roads is found by Legras in the statement of Livy (xli, 27), that in 174 B.C. 'censores vias sternendas silice in urbe, glarea extra urbem substruendas marginandasque primi omnium locaverunt'. He assumes, arbitrarily as it seems to me, that the footpaths were not paved at this time by the censors, but that no long interval can be supposed between the paving of the roads and the paving of the footpaths. Otherwise Rome would have been more backward than Aletrium, where footpaths were paved in the time of the Gracchi.[1] Now l. 52 of the Table deals with footpaths, and, speaking of the householder and the path before his house, says: 'is eam semitam . . . constratam recte habeto.' Legras interprets this to mean that the paving of footpaths was first introduced by this law, and that it fell upon the householder. The latter point seems very improbable, and I interpret the injunction to mean that the householder is to keep the path properly paved, and, if repairs are necessary, to repair it in the manner specified. It is clear from l. 52 that the provisions about roads, like that about public places, had been preceded by various laws, plebiscita, or decrees of the senate on the same subject.

But what Legras seems chiefly to rely upon in assigning this section to the second century, is the fact that in his view it was copied from a Greek source. Portions of a very interesting law, dealing with the duties of the *ἀστυνόμοι* at Pergamum, were discovered in 1901,[2] and there are resemblances between some of its regulations and the provisions about roads and public places in the Table of Heraclea, which appear to Legras too striking to be independent of each other. The inscription dates from Trajan's time, but is the copy of a *βασιλικὸς νόμος*. This would seem to make the date of the law earlier than 133 B.C. when the last of the Attalid kings died and left his kingdom to the Roman people. The law is far more comprehensive than the provisions of the Table, since in its four extant columns it contains regulations as to the removal of obstructions from public places, the maintenance of roads by householders, their duties in respect to the removal of dirt or refuse, the prevention of obstructions hindering circulation in the roads, the oversight of edifices in respect of walls and partitions and their proper upkeep, and the charge of fountains, wells, and water-conduits.

Some of these regulations stand outside the Latin law and

[1] *C.I.L.* i, 1166, does not prove that footpaths in Aletrium were paved, but only that they were made.

[2] Hitzig, *Zeitschrift der Savigny-Stiftung, roman. Abteilung*, xxvi, 433; brief account in Haverfield, *Ancient Town-planning*, pp. 53–5.

need not be considered, but others, namely, those about roads and public places, coincide in object, and if they are to be taken as the archetypes of the latter, or used in fixing its date, some comparison of them is necessary.

In the matter of roads the Table lays it down that every householder shall maintain (*tueri*) the road opposite his house, and that the aedile to whom that part of the city belongs, shall see that he does so, and that no standing water is allowed to impede traffic. The aedile is clearly responsible for the repair, paving, and maintenance of the roads in his district, and it is only the last of these duties which he is to impose on the householder (ll. 38–41). If a householder neglects this duty, the aedile is to contract, through the agency of the quaestor urbanus, for the maintenance of the road, giving ten days' notice, and all particulars of his intention. As part of the contract, the delinquent was made the legal debtor of the contractor for the cost of the work, and if he did not pay it within thirty days, he was proceeded against by a civil iudicium for half as much again, all of which went to the contractor. Then follows the regulation already alluded to with regard to footpaths, but without any instructions as to the course to be pursued in case of neglect. Lastly, with regard to all the roads in Rome, restrictions are laid down on traffic in the daytime, except under certain specified conditions.

Now the clause in the Pergamene law with regard to the maintenance of roads is as follows (col. i, l. 63): *Παρεχέτωσαν δὲ καθαροὺς καὶ πορευσίμους τὰς ὁδοὺς οἱ τὰ κτήματα κεκτημένοι παρὰ τὰς οἰκίας καὶ τὴν γειτνίασιν ἕως σταδίων . . . συνεισφέροντες καὶ συνεπισκευάζοντες. καὶ ἐὰν ἀπειθῶσιν, ἐνεχυραζέτωσαν αὐτοὺς οἱ ἀστυνόμοι.* It would appear from this that, while, as in Rome, the 'maintenance' of the roads fell upon the householders, neglect was followed not by a semi-penal 'locatio', but merely by the seizure of pledges. Probably, however, the householders contracted among themselves for the work to be done (*συνεισφέροντες*). That they did so in the matter of cleansing the footpaths (*ἄμφοδοι*) from refuse, I gather from col. ii, l. 57, &c., which orders that, if any fail to pay their share to the contractor, pledges are similarly to be seized and, if necessary, sold. The Roman law makes no allusion to common action on the part of householders, though, of course, it would be natural.

But the penal 'locatio' does come into another interesting provision about roads, which, however, has itself no counterpart in the Latin law. Column ii, l. 38, &c., runs: *Ἐάν τινες ἐν ταῖς ὁδοῖς χοῦν ὀρύσσωσιν ἢ λίθους πῆλον ποιῶσιν . . . κωλυέτωσαν αὐτοὺς οἱ ἀμφοδάρχαι. Ἐὰν δὲ μὴ πείθωνται, ἐπαγγελέτωσαν τοῖς ἀστυνόμοις. Οὗτοι δὲ ζημιούτωσαν τὸν ἀπειθοῦντα καθ' ἕκαστόν ἀτάκτημα δραχμαῖς πέντε καὶ ἀναγκαζέτωσαν τά τε ἄλλα ἀποκαθιστάναι ἐς τὰ ἐξ ἀρχῆς. . . . Ἐὰν δὲ μήδ' οὕτως πειθαρχῶσιν οἱ ἰδιῶται, ἔκδοσιν ποιεισθῶσιν ἐν ἡμέραις δέκα καὶ τὸ γενόμενον ἀνάλωμα πραξάτωσαν παρὰ τῶν ἀπειθούντων ἡμιόλιον.* There are thus three points in common with the Table, a 'locatio' by the magistrate, the interval of ten days, and the super-tax of half the cost of the work. But on the other hand, these particular obstructions to traffic are not mentioned in the latter; the delinquents at Pergamum are not made legal debtors to the contractor, and exaction of payment is made by the magistrate. As appears from the clause quoted below, it is the magistrate who pays the contractor, and, otherwise than in Rome, he pays him not the whole sum exacted, but only the cost of the work, while the extra half goes into the Treasury. Not only so, but at Pergamum the extra half is exacted at once and in all cases, while at Rome the delinquent only becomes liable to it if he fails to pay the contractor within thirty days. As regards the limitation of traffic in the daytime, there is nothing on the subject in the extant part of the Greek law.

In the matter of public spaces the prohibitions in the Table are brief, while the cases where they do not apply are more in evidence. No building materials or soil are to be left in such places; they are not to be occupied or blocked against the public. No penalty and no means of compulsion is specified. In the Greek law obstructions of some kind in public places are clearly dealt with in the mutilated beginning of col. i. In case of disobedience the *στρατηγοί* are to inflict a fine; *οἱ δὲ ἀστυνόμοι ἔκδοσιν ποιησάμενοι τῆς ἀποκαταστάσεως τοῦ τόπου εἰς τὰ ἐξ ἀρχῆς ἐν ἡμέραις δέκα τὸ διαφόρον πράξαντες ἡμιόλιον παρὰ τῶν ἀπειθούντων ἀποκαταστησάτωσαν τοῖς μὲν ἠργολαβηκόσιν τὸ ἐπίβαλλον τὸ δὲ λοιπὸν τοῖς ταμίαις.* Public spaces are again dealt with in the mutilated beginning of col. ii, where persons who have thrown out refuse on to them are compelled to undertake the work of cleansing, or, in default, to pay to the ἀστυνόμοι half as much again as they have agreed with a contractor.

It seems to me that a comparison of the two laws on the only points where they at all coincide, regulations as to roads and public places, reveals more differences than resemblances. All great cities, Greek or Roman, were bound to have such regulations, and in Rome, at any rate, there had clearly been laws on these subjects earlier than that on the Table. Legras, however, mainly relies on two general resemblances, that between the ἔκδοσις at Pergamum and the 'locatio' at Rome, and the topographical division of functions among the ἀστυνόμοι and aediles. In the latter he sees such a serious departure from the principle of collegiality that it could only have come from a Greek source, since in Greece collegiality in its technical sense was unknown. But in the first place, the strict collegiate principle was modified in various points at the end of the Republic, and this particular modification, so obviously convenient, was just what we should expect from Caesar. Besides, the most essential element in collegiality, that each member of a college could by himself exercise its full 'potestas', was not impaired. In the second place, there is absolutely no evidence that this local distribution of duties existed among the ἀστυνόμοι at Pergamum. The ἀστυνόμοι are throughout represented as acting collectively. Legras relies on a single expression in col. iv, l. 59, where it is said that 'as many of the ἀστυνύμοι as have failed to draw up a list of wells are liable to a penalty'. It seems hardly necessary to point out how flimsy this foundation is for the inference drawn from it. With regard to 'locatio' and ἔκδοσις Legras can hardly be serious in suggesting that the former was copied from the latter. Long before the Gracchi and earlier than the second century there is ample evidence that the Roman government contracted for the carrying out of public works and undertakings of all kinds. No doubt the system existed in Greek lands too, though it is less in evidence. The curious survival of compulsory personal labour in the colonia Genetiva, alluded to by Legras, is obviously irrelevant. It may be true, though I am not sure that it is, that the penal 'locatio' of the Table is found nowhere else. But it is equally true that neither is the penal ἔκδοσις of the βασιλικὸς νόμος. The preservation of these two fragments of municipal laws is an interesting coincidence, but the 'startling resemblances' between them have been exaggerated, and there is no reason to regard one as a systematic copy of the other.

So clear does this seem that I do not think it necessary to do more than suggest a doubt as to the meaning of the phrase βασιλικὸς νόμος. Legras, arguing that its date must be well before 133 B.C., places this section of the Table, first in the second century, and finally in the tribunate of C. Gracchus, a curious example of the tendency, which he deplores in others, of attributing nameless laws to famous statesmen. Considering the frequency with which the title βασιλεύς was applied in the East, both to Caesar and Augustus, I do not feel sure that the law may not have belonged to the reorganization of Asia, by either one or the other of these two. I do not think it necessary to my argument to press this possibility, but if there is evidence to support it, Legras would perhaps be less certain that one law was copied from the other.

If the evidence for the second-century date of this section is unconvincing, it must also be admitted that the reasons for assigning it to Caesar's dictatorship are not conclusive. Still, such as they are, they are rather strengthened than weakened by Legras' criticisms. He admits that this was one of the two periods in which such police regulations for Rome might be looked for, and that is obviously true. It is certain that Caesar did much for Rome. Perhaps he municipalized it; at any rate, he added much to the conveniences of its population. It is not necessary here to insist on the new forum and the commencement of a new basilica, since it will be admitted that improvements of various kinds in Rome were in keeping with Caesar's policy.

With regard to internal indications, Mommsen long since pointed out that the descriptions of two magistrates point to impending or possible changes. The magistrate who is to effect the 'locatio' is 'quaestor urbanus queive aerario praerit'. The magistrate who may have leased out the use of public places is 'censor aliusve quis magistratus'. Now with regard to the quaestor urbanus Legras admits that there is not the smallest indication that any one thought of removing from him the charge of the aerarium, either in Sulla's time or in the second century. He explains the phrase as an instance of the extreme caution used by Roman legislators and intended to cover any unforeseen constitutional changes. But, if so, why was the quaestor urbanus described in the lex Acilia, at the very date to which this section of the Table is assigned, as 'quaestor quei aerarium provinciam optinebit'?[1] As a matter of fact, the only parallel cases which Legras can cite come from Caesarian laws. There was never any idea, it is argued, of replacing the praetor urbanus by another official, and yet in the lex Rubria[2] we have 'ex decreto eius quei ibei (in Rome) iuredicundo praerit'. The vagueness of the phrase was not due to mere unnecessary caution. At the time when this law was passed, the elections for the next year had not been held, and as both consuls were absent, it was not clear how they were to be held, and some such cautious phrase was imperative. That it was called for, is shown by what happened in 45 B.C. when 'praefecti' actually discharged the duties of the praetors.[3] But on the supposition that this law was passed in 45, there was a more immediate reason for caution in describing the presidents of the aerarium, since Dio Cassius[4] states that in that year it was under the charge of *δύο τῶν πολιανομούντων* instead of quaestors. In view of this fact, it is irrelevant to argue that Caesar did not intend the change to be permanent, and that no definite change was made before Augustus. The fact that, for however short a time, the aerarium had been under an official who was not 'quaestor urbanus' would necessitate the phrase in the text or some equivalent.

With regard to the censor we have, both in this section and in that dealing with the municipal census,[5] 'censor aliusve quis magistratus'. The identity of the phrase is curious, if, as Legras holds, one section belongs to the Gracchan period and the other to Sulla's first consulship. It is also curious that he explains it differently in the two cases. It is used in the earlier section, he says, because, in the intervals between two sets of censors, other magistrates might lease out the use of public places, and in the later because, by the end of the Social war, censorships were already beginning to be irregular. Mere irregularity in the sequence of censorships, however, obviously does not explain the phrase, and there was no suggestion of displacing the censors till

[1] l. 69. [2] Cap. xxi. [3] Suet. *Caes.* lxxvi.
[4] xliii, 48. [5] ll. 73 and 144.

Sulla's dictatorship. On the other hand, the phrase seems quite appropriate to the last two years of Caesar's life, when the constitution was almost in the melting-pot, and when the dictator himself had assumed the office of censor under the title of 'praefectus morum'.

These indications of Caesarian authorship for this section are of course not conclusive, but they make it probable. The regulations are not necessarily new, but they relate to matters which had probably been much neglected during recent years, and were essential to the more orderly city which the new régime contemplated. The question whether this section was part of a general municipal law, or, if it was a purely Roman law, whether this was a part or the whole, will be more conveniently discussed later on. Another question, too, will then have to be faced; how came these regulations to be engraved on the Table of Heraclea?

III. The third section of the Table confronts us with a law, or parts of a law, or several laws, concerned with municipal affairs. It falls into three divisions: provisions with regard to municipal senates, regulations concerning the municipal census, and a clause providing for the correction of existing municipal charters within a specified time. These three provisions will have to be considered separately, but they have this point in common, that they are, on the face of them, general laws or parts of general laws, referring respectively (i) to 'coloniae, municipia, praefecturae, fora, conciliabula', (ii) to 'coloniae, municipia, praefecturae in Italia', and (iii) to 'municipia fundana'.

(a) The first sub-section is concerned with the decurions or 'conscripti' in the above-mentioned communities of Roman citizens. It is, however, only concerned with them in one point, namely, that it excludes certain categories of persons, as incapable of being elected to the senate or to any magistracy qualifying for the senate. There is no reference to the functions of the senate, or to its importance in local government, but it is not to contain certain undesirable elements. This in itself gives no indication of date, but Legras makes it apply to the period immediately following the Social war, and finds in it a reflexion of the aristocratic policy of Sulla. It was unconnected with any attempt to establish a common form of constitution for the newly enfranchised towns, but it insisted on what past experience had shown to be essential, if the towns were to remain loyal, that the senate, as the governing body in each, should be taken from the best and most respectable classes, so that the Italian towns, like Rome herself, should be aristocracies. It is obvious, however, that, apart from the cases of 'praecones' and 'libitinarii', the exclusions aimed at securing not an aristocratic but a morally respectable senate; nor is there anything to ensure that the senate should be the governing body. For this it would have been necessary to define the privileges and functions of the senate, to limit the magistrates to their proper rôle, and to specify the matters for which the comitia were competent. Whatever Sulla's views may have been as to the position of municipal senates, we have enough of the charter of Urso to be sure that Caesar intended them to control the urban government. This object was, no doubt, secured at Urso by means of the 'lex data', and Legras argues that such constitutional arrangements, after the enfranchisement, were carried out by the various commissioners. But, if Sulla's object was to secure aristocratic governments in the towns, can we suppose that his general law, having, according to Legras, this very end, would have merely insisted on the respectability of the senate, while leaving its political position to the discretion of commissioners? Unless this theory goes too far in attributing this aim to Sulla, it ought to go further, and credit him with a complete municipal law.

There are, however, several points of internal evidence which make the attribution of this provision about the senates to Sulla impossible:

(1) A crucial point is the insertion among the excluded persons of 'quei ob caput civis Romanei referundum pecuniam . . . cepit ceperit'. If this is rightly referred to Sulla's agents in the proscriptions of 82 B.C. it not only rules out the first consulship and the dictatorship of Sulla, but makes it impossible to date the provision earlier than the year 64, when for the first time certain steps were taken against these men.[1] Legras is fully alive to the crucial nature of this point, and attempts to maintain an untenable position with much ingenuity.

[1] Suet. *Caes.* xi.

(*a*) The words 'cepit ceperit' are against the usual interpretation. The act of Sulla's agents, supposed to be made a disqualification, belonged to a past situation, definitely closed and not likely to recur, whereas 'ceperit' implies precautions against similar acts in future. Legras apparently forgets his own insistence on the extreme caution of Roman legislators, who use phrases intended to cover all possible eventualities. The provision was *ex hypothesi* intended to keep senates select, not only for the moment but in future, by the exclusion of a particularly disgraceful class of men. The situation was one quite likely to recur. Cicero indeed in 49 imagined it to be imminent, and foresaw in the victory of either Caesar or Pompey nothing but 'proscriptio et caedes bonorum'. If the law belonged to Caesar or the Caesarian time, it would have been insanity in the legislator to have omitted 'ceperit'.

(*b*) If Sulla's agents were alluded to, the phrase employed would have been 'ob caput relatum' and not 'ob caput referundum', since the former implies that the deed was actually done, while the latter is only consistent with the price having been paid in advance. The point seems to me not only hypercritical, but erroneous. 'Referundum' is not the future participle passive, but the gerundive. The two phrases mean the same thing, but in view of the general character of the exclusion, marked by 'ceperit', the phrase used is the more appropriate.

(*c*) Suetonius[1] states: 'in exercenda de sicariis quaestione eos quoque sicariorum numero habuit, qui proscriptione ob relata civium Romanorum capita pecunias ex aerario receperant, quamquam exceptos Corneliis legibus'. Therefore, as Legras argues, the separate mention of the Sullan agents was unnecessary, since they would be included under the heading of those 'publico iudicio condemnati'. But it by no means follows, because they could be proceeded against under the lex Cornelia de sicariis, that they all of them would be. There were probably a good many of these men still living in the towns where Sulla had planted them, and though some had been accused and condemned, the majority would be let alone. At any rate, from the unique atrocity of their act, they formed so specially despicable a class as to call for special exclusion.

[1] *Caes.* xi.

(*d*) If Sulla's agents had been intended, it would have been necessary to narrow down the description of the class by the insertion of the word 'proscriptione', since the wording of the law would cover many loyal and respectable citizens. Legras proceeds somewhat laboriously to argue that, in the absence of a public prosecutor or prefect of police, the only way in which the capital sentence of 'aquae et igni interdictio' or even 'senatus consultum ultimum' could be made effective was by the action of loyal citizens. This action could only be counted on by the offer of rewards to those who killed persons breaking their ban, or declared public enemies, or those sheltering them. There must therefore, he argues, have been many citizens who had received rewards 'ob relata capita', and no legislator of Caesar's time would have been so maladroit as to word his provision in such a way as to include these worthy and respectable persons. It is difficult to treat this argument seriously or even respectfully. It will be time enough to do so when a single instance has been adduced of an interdicted person having been put to death in this way, or of a reward being offered for such an act, or of a head having been brought in as proof of an execution, except in the Sullan proscriptions. As far as the evidence serves us, the act of Sulla's agents stood alone; down to Caesar's time it marked out these wretches as a peculiarly odious section of the not too popular 'Sullani homines', so that the wording of the law would leave no possible doubt as to the class of persons excluded.

If these were not Sulla's agents, who were they? Legras replies that they were the hired assassins, who between the Gracchi and Caesar had virtually become a professional class. Among them were the murderers of Scipio Aemilianus and Livius Drusus, the intending assassin of Roscius, and the ruffians of Clodius and Milo. But never, he thinks, were they so much in evidence as after the Social war in the years 87 and 86 B.C., when Marius and Cinna perpetrated their massacres not by any semi-legal form of 'proscriptio' but by hired assassins. As we know of nothing in 88 B.C. calling for special notice of these men, Legras, though it is inconsistent with the date to which he finally assigns this provision about the senates, suggests that it was the Marian assassins and their likes in the future whom Sulla in his dictatorship excluded from municipal senates. It was not necessary that they should all have actually murdered a citizen or brought in his head, but they had been paid in advance (Legras' inference from 'ob caput referundum'), or belonged to a class habitually paid in advance, for doing such acts, and the actual accomplishment was immaterial. But (1) people would not go on hiring assassins if they never performed their contract. Is there a single instance of any such assassin having brought in the head of his victim?[1] (2) How would these men be identified, since contracts for private assassination would presumably be made secretly? (3) What would these obscure and sordid ruffians be doing in the Italian towns as likely candidates for the senate? (4) What about the loyal and respectable citizens, who would be equally affected whether Caesar or Sulla was the author of the maladroit wording? (5) For Sulla 'imbecile' would be a fitter term than 'maladroit'. For, if his clause affected those who had taken money for bringing in heads, whether they had done it or not, a fortiori it would affect his own creatures who had done this thing in the sight of all.[2] I am bound to say that Legras' interpretation of this disability is so fanciful and ill-considered as hardly to deserve the serious examination to which I have subjected it, especially as he tacitly withdraws it all, when he assigns this as well as the provision about the census to the year 88, and actually holds that all these sections were on the Table and set up at Heraclea by 83 B.C.

(2) Among the 'iudicia turpia', condemnation in which is a cause of exclusion from the senate, is that 'de dolo malo' (l. 111). Now the establishment of this 'iudicium' is usually assigned to the praetorship of Aquilius Gallus in 66 B.C. on the strength of Cic. *de Off.* iii, 11, and *de Nat. Deor.* iii, 30. In the former, Cicero speaks of Aquilius as 'collega meus', and says: 'nondum de dolo malo protulerat formulas.' In the latter he speaks of the 'iudicium de dolo malo quod C. Aquilius . . . protulit'.[3] If the

[1] The case in *pro Roscio Amer.* is not an instance. To show the blood and the weapon is not to bring in the head, a phrase which Legras himself admits must be taken literally.

[2] Legras attempts to fortify his contention that the excluded class was a profession and not mere perpetrators of a particular atrocity, by pointing to its place in the list, where it is followed by professional *cinaedi* and *lanistae* and *lenones*. Curiously, however, he ignores the fact that it is immediately preceded by persons cashiered from the army and condemned by a public *iudicium*.

[3] The fact that the discussion in the *de Nat. Deor.* is supposed to have taken

'iudicium' dates from the praetorship of Aquilius, as these passages seem to imply, it cannot figure in a law passed in 88 B.C., and accordingly Legras will not accept the ordinary view. He argues that Aquilius had had a long career as jurisconsult before 66, being spoken of by Cicero in 69[1] as having had a high reputation for many years, and having acted as 'unus iudex' as early as 81 in the case of Quinctius. As jurisconsult, he may well have met the cases of certain clients by suggesting a formula, which so commended itself as soon to be inserted by some praetor in his album. This is not impossible in itself, and the phrase in the *de Off.* 'de dolo malo protulerat formulas' might, apart from the words 'collega meus', be taken in this sense. But the phrase in the *de Nat. Deor.* 'de dolo malo iudicium protulit', is decisive against it, for only a praetor could establish a 'iudicium'. Besides, in order to leave time for the insertion of the formula in the album by 88, Aquilius must have invented it at least as early as 91 or 92, and this would mean that by the year of his praetorship he was 55 or 56. This is in the highest degree improbable, and in spite of Legras' clever special pleading, the appearance of this action in the law seems fatal to his dating of it.

(3) But he is prepared to carry the war into the enemy's country by pointing to the omission of two 'turpia iudicia', contained in the Digest list (iii, 2, 1), as inconsistent with the Caesarian authorship of the law. The two actions omitted are 'de deposito' and 'vi raptorum bonorum'. Now the former is not contained in any of the three lists of such actions given by Cicero.[2] It is first alluded to by certain jurisconsults who were contemporaries of Caesar. But, as Legras admits, these all survived till the time of Augustus, and therefore their allusions do not prove that the action was in existence in 45 B.C. But he argues from a somewhat ambiguous passage of Ulpian[3] that an 'actio commodati', involving 'infamia' to those condemned under it, was in existence before 82, and that an action so similar as that 'de deposito' must necessarily have been introduced not long after. This very 'circumstantial' evidence is, however, much

place in 76 B.C. seems irrelevant, since there are no indications that Cicero was careful about the unities of time and place in such matters.

[1] *pro Caec.* xxvii, 77.

[2] *de Nat. Deor.* iii, 30, 74; *de Off.* iii, 17, 70; *Topic.* 10, 42, and 17, 66.

[3] *Dig.* 13, 6, 5, §§ 6, 10, 11.

weakened by the fact that this 'actio commodati' is not only omitted from Cicero's lists, but is not contained in the Digest list. With regard to the action 'vi raptorum bonorum' Legras declares that it was created by M. Lucullus, praetor peregrinus in 76 B.C., and that C. Antonius was visited with 'infamia' in consequence of the new action. Unfortunately, the passage of Asconius (p. 84) which he relies on for all this, does not prove any of it. Antonius had plundered many persons in Achaia, who summoned him before the praetor peregrinus. The praetor, after hearing the matter *in iure*, 'decreed what the provincials demanded', Antonius appealed to the tribunes, and nothing happened to him for six years. Then the censors of 70 removed him from the senate, not because he had incurred 'infamia' (how could he, having never been tried?), but 'quod socios diripuerit, quod iudicium recusarit' and because he had fallen into debt and had to sell his estates. Whatever 'iudicium' it was which the praetor decreed and Antonius with the help of the tribunes refused, it clearly related to provincials, and had nothing to do with the 'actio vi raptorum bonorum' of *Dig.* iii, 2, 1. There is no evidence that this latter existed in Caesar's time.

(4) There remains what has been claimed, and what I still claim, to be the decisive argument, not only against the Sullan date of this section, but for its having been passed by Caesar in 45 B.C. Cicero, writing from Rome to Lepta in January of that year, says, in a passage often quoted:[1] 'Simul atque accepi a Seleuco tuo litteras, statim quaesivi e Balbo per codicillos quid esset in lege. Rescripsit eos, qui facerent praeconium, vetari esse in decurionibus; qui fecissent, non vetari. Qua re bono animo sint et tui et mei familiares; neque enim erat ferendum, cum qui hodie haruspicinam facerent, in senatum Romae legerentur, eos qui aliquando praeconium fecissent in municipiis decuriones esse non licere.' In the Table (ll. 94–5) it is enacted: 'Neve quis quei praeconium dissignationem libitinamve faciet, dum eorum quid faciet, in municipio colonia praefectura . . . senator neve decurio neve conscriptus esto.' The inference seems irresistible that at the beginning of 45, while Caesar was in Spain, there were rumours of a law being prepared dealing with the qualifications for local senates, that Seleucus or

[1] *ad Fam.* vi, 18.

Lepta had friends whom this particular disqualification might affect, that Cicero on their behalf had consulted Balbus, Caesar's agent and confidant, and received a reply which was verified by the clause of the law published later in the same year.

Legras attempts to escape from this inference by declaring that Cicero is inquiring of Balbus, not about some projected law in preparation, but about some old law, the details of which both Lepta and Cicero had forgotten. Lepta, however, at least knew that there was a law dealing with this matter, and, as it was of consequence to some of his Italian friends, he applied to Cicero. It is argued that the past tense 'esset' instead of 'futurum sit' is in favour of this view; so, too, is the use of 'lex' rather than 'rogatio'. How was Lepta, a Pompeian, likely to have known anything about Caesar's intended legislation, and was Balbus likely to betray Caesar's confidence even to Cicero? It is obvious that all these points are of the weakest. 'Esset' is far more natural than a future tense; 'lex' is constantly used of a law not passed; we should expect rumours about coming laws, and the trifling matter inquired about was no state secret which Balbus would scruple to disclose.

Let us note a few other points which seem to have escaped Legras. What was this old law? It can obviously have been none other than that of which this section of the Table was a copy. That law, according to Legras, was passed by Sulla in 88, and had an important object, namely, to secure aristocratic senates. It was so important, according to him, that, probably in 83, Sulla caused it to be set up with other laws, at Heraclea in lieu of an ordinary 'lex data'. It was on the face of it to apply to all Italian towns, and would presumably have been reflected in their charters. How was it that the details of such a law were unknown not only to Cicero, but to his municipal friends? What adds to the difficulty of Legras' suggestion is the fact that, though unknown, the law could not have been obsolete, or Lepta's friends would not have been so anxious. Again, if Cicero wanted information about this old law, why did he not go and consult it at the aerarium? The suggestion that he did not wish to attract notice is futile. Or, if he had to inquire of another person, why did he choose Balbus? Balbus was the obvious person to consult about a measure of Caesar, but he was less likely than

Cicero himself to be acquainted with Sulla's laws or with previous Roman legislation. Legras seems curiously to consider that the whole force of the argument from this letter is destroyed, if there was no complete and comprehensive lex Iulia municipalis. But we are not concerned at present with the question of a comprehensive law, but with the dating of this section of the Table, which, whether part of a general law or not, is a general provision, and, as lines 159–63 prove, is to be reflected in particular charters.

Legras is apparently not unprepared for the rejection of his first suggestion, for he is ready with a second. If the law, about which Cicero inquires, is to be regarded as not yet promulgated, then it can only refer to some 'lex data' which Caesar was preparing, probably for one of the Spanish colonies founded at this time. The supposition seems quite gratuitous. I am not aware that 'lex' is ever used for 'lex data', except where the context makes the limitation of meaning unmistakable. The words 'in municipiis' are against this explanation, and why should Lepta or Seleucus be interested in Spanish colonies? Legras seems partly conscious of this last point, for he is quite ready to substitute Greek ones, because Seleucus was a Greek. But he must be kept to the logical consequences of his own theories. If this 'lex data' for a Spanish or Greek colony contained this regulation about 'praecones', it was obviously based on the principle laid down in the general law of Sulla's first consulship. Caesar had, at any rate, not forgotten the details of that ancient law. Must it not have been applied to all the 'leges datae' of Italian towns since Sulla? Legras himself implies that it was a necessary part of all such laws by making it a necessary part of the Table of Heraclea, which was there to take the place of a 'lex data'. But in that case, the ignorance of Lepta and his friends is inexplicable. It implies that Sulla's law had been a dead-letter, while Caesar's insertion of this detail in his supposed 'lex data' implies that it was still being observed. I submit that Legras' case has utterly broken down.

IIIb. The second sub-section of the third division of the Table, lines 142–58, gives directions to the highest magistrates in all Italian municipia, coloniae, and praefecturae to hold a census of Roman citizens within sixty days of the announcement of a census in Rome, and to send in the results to Rome within sixty days of the completion of the Roman census. Legras believes, and Professor Reid agrees with him, that the necessity of such a provision could not possibly have been postponed till the time of Caesar, and must belong to the period immediately following the Social war. It could hardly, indeed, have been postponed till the dictatorship of Sulla, and the mention of the censor, though qualified by the phrase 'aliusve quis magistratus', is against that date. It is therefore assigned, like the previous provision, to the year 88. It should be noted, however, that the uncertainty about the censor is very marked in this provision. Not only is the one mention of that magistrate accompanied by an alternative description, but in several other places the title is avoided altogether, and replaced by 'queiquomque Romae censum aget'. As far, therefore, as this point is concerned, the dictatorship of Sulla or that of Caesar would seem more appropriate than the first consulship of Sulla. There are, indeed, great difficulties in the way of attributing any organic legislation concerning the new citizens, let alone this vast scheme of a simultaneous census, to such a troubled and even revolutionary year as 88. It is admitted that, though 'quinquennales' are found in a few Italian towns, and censors were irregularly created after 70, there is no trace whatever of any synchronism between the municipal and the Roman census. Legras declares that it was Sulla himself who rendered impossible the working of his own scheme by destroying with the censorship its necessary machinery. But if Sulla had really thought the matter so important as to spare time for a law in 88, it is inconceivable that he would not have provided new machinery in 81, and, as a matter of fact, the provision on the Table is so worded as to make censors in the technical sense unnecessary. This is, indeed, an argument against the earlier date, but it protects Sulla from this criticism.

As to the assertion of Legras and Professor Reid that a municipal census must have been introduced long before Caesar, there are two things to be remembered: (1) Whenever a general law provided for it, it was, as Legras himself points out, not a new departure, but the confirmation of a partially established custom. Even before the Social war there is considerable evidence of the census in Italy; compare the law on the Bantine Table, and the passages in Livy cited by Legras. This custom may have taken sufficiently firm hold to be continued after the Social war, and may well have been reinforced by the agency of such commissioners as were sent out, whether these were directed by a general law or not. If they were not, Caesar may well have deemed it advisable to frame a general provision. If they were, it could not have been by the provision on the Table, because (2) the essential point of that provision is not the establishment of a municipal census, but its synchronism with that held in Rome. Such a regulation might well have been left till Caesar's time. Indeed a scheme which involved such combination, such elaborate machinery, and such unsparing labour as a simultaneous census of all Italy, was exactly suited to the character and genius of Caesar. The scheme was probably still-born, as Legras for a different reason conceives that of Sulla to have been. There is no trace of any such synchronism under the Principate. At first anarchy and civil war would prevent its working, and later it was no doubt replaced by some plan, which, though less theoretically perfect, was more workable. Legras regards the words 'in Italia' as indicating that, at the date when this provision was drawn up, there were no towns of Roman citizens outside Italy. I should have thought that they implied exactly the reverse. But to have included in the Roman census all provincial communities of Roman right, existing or to be created, was beyond even Caesar's horizon.

A still greater importance is apparently given to these words 'in Italia' by Professor Nap, if his view is correctly represented by Besnier.[1] The censors of 65 were at variance on the question of including the Transpadani in the census. The censors in the next year were also at variance, but not quite on the same point.[2] Therefore (he thinks) a law must have been passed in the interval, settling the cause of dispute, and that law was our provision (ll. 142–58), laying it down that only those are to be included in the census who are 'in Italia'. This hypothesis is so much in the air, and is so vitiated by the assumption that the Transpadani had already received the franchise by the lex Pompeia, and were only excluded from the census because they were provincials,

[1] See above, in Essay II.

[2] As a matter of fact, they were actually opposed on the same point, as the words διὰ τοῦτο καί prove, though other complications were added.

that I mention it merely as an instance of the random way in which this difficult document is being treated by some scholars.

I do not claim that the reasons in favour of attributing this provision to Caesar are conclusive, but, if its essential point is, as I believe, the synchronism, and not the first establishment of a municipal census, the strongest argument for an earlier date is met. Besides, it may be fairly claimed that it is a provision of the same law as that in which qualification for local senates is limited, and for that there is the strongest evidence of Caesarian authorship.

IIIc. The last paragraph of the Table is so important and crucial that it will be convenient to prefix its text to my discussion of it:

Quei lege plebeive scito permissus est fuit, utei leges in municipio fundano municipibusve eius municipi daret, sei quid is post h. l. rogatam in eo anno proxumo quo h. l. populus iuserit, ad eas leges [addiderit commutaverit conrexerit][1] municipis fundanos item teneto, utei oporteret, sei eae res ab eo tum, quom primum leges eis municipibus lege plebeive scito dedit, ad eas leges additae commutatae conrectae essent; . . . .

It seems to me that 'municipia fundana' are all those Italian towns, whether Latin or federate, which, by becoming 'fundi' of an enfranchising law, became ipso facto 'fundi' of Roman laws generally. They became at once 'municipia civium Romanorum', with all the public and private rights of the civitas, but until they were 'constituted', i. e. until their constitutions were revised and embodied in a 'lex data' by a commissioner appointed by the Roman people, they were technically and juridically 'fundana'.

Legras holds, on the contrary, that the towns accepting the civitas through the lex Iulia were allowed to retain their own systems of private law, and only became 'fundi' either of Roman laws generally or of particular laws, if they chose to do so. If they so decided, it would be the function of the commissioner sent out to 'constitute' their political arrangements and also to frame a code of civil law, containing those Roman laws of which they desired to become 'fundi'. He supposes that in this clause

[1] This supplement of Mazochi seems absolutely certain, and is generally accepted, though the last edition of Bruns mentions it only in a footnote. Many far more doubtful supplements are inserted.

'leges dare municipio' means to give a constitution to a town, while 'dare leges municipibus' is to draw up a civil code for its citizens. The suggestion is ingenious but untenable. The whole theory is based upon a definition of Aulus Gellius,[1] 'Municipes sunt cives Romani e municipiis, legibus suis et suo iure utentes, muneris tantum cum populo Romano honorarii participes a quo munere capessendo appellati videntur, nullis aliis necessitatibus neque ulla populi Romani lege adstricti, nisi in quam populus eorum fundus factus esset'. I have no hesitation in saying that this definition, as it stands, is an impossible one. The only class, coming under the shifting term 'municipes', and marked clearly enough by the words (omitted in Legras' citation) 'muneris tantum cum p. R. . . . participes', to which it applies, were not cives Romani.[2] That all municipia after the Social war were 'fundi' of Roman law is proved by (1) Cicero:[3] 'ipsa denique Iulia, qua lege civitas est sociis et Latinis data, qui fundi populi facti non essent civitatem non haberent. . . . Postremo haec vis est istius et iuris et verbi ut fundi populi beneficio nostro non suo iure fiant;' (2) what seems to have been the whole object and meaning of the lex Rubria; (3) the fact that the majority of disqualifications for the municipal senates imply the validity of Roman law in Italian towns; (4) the position of Roman citizens in Salpensa, who are unable to manumit a slave before the local duovir, as Latin citizens could.

To return to the provision on the Table. It is obviously the concluding part of some 'lex rogata', under which (it seems impossible to doubt) were included at least the two previous provisions of the Table. The words 'permissus est, fuit' show that some commissioners were still engaged in 'constituting' towns, and that others had done this in the past. All of them are empowered to make certain additions, alterations, and corrections in their charters within a year of the passing of the present law. The last words seem irresistibly to suggest that the changes are to be made in pursuance of what is contained in the present law. If we interpret the clause in this way, it is impossible to ascribe

[1] xvi, 13.

[2] I was relieved, after writing the sentence in the text, to see Mommsen's estimate of this definition as 'ein wahres Meisterstück historisch-juristischer Confusion und der Vermengung des alten und des neuen Sprachgebrauchs'.

[3] *pro Balb.* vii, 21.

it to the first years after the Social war, for that leaves no time for the earlier commissioners, and does not account for the changes and additions. By ascribing it to the dictatorship of Sulla we should escape this difficulty, but we should have to assume a lex Cornelia containing the points to be inserted, and, as we have already seen, we cannot make the two previous provisions parts of such a lex Cornelia. Legras, however, has made up his mind that this, like the two other provisions, must be made to fit in with the year 88, and he does not shrink from the necessary manipulation of the text. The clause has got to be not 'une mesure de circonstance', rendered necessary by supervening reforms, but a general regulation, fixing procedure for the future. In short, it is an enactment that all commissioners, appointed or to be appointed, are to complete their work within a year from the date of the law appointing them. He gives no explanation of any kind of what obviously is the central point of the clause, the binding force of additions made to charters. The point is simply ignored. But apart from this, he has to alter the text. 'Permissus est fuit' is on the flimsiest grounds changed to 'permissus est erit', and as the words 'quo h. l. populus iuserit' can only refer to the law copied on the Table, we are asked to believe that the engraver of the bronze was so used to writing 'h. l.' that he wrote it when he ought to have written 'illam legem plebeive scitum'. With these alterations, the provision no doubt says what it is required to say. But if the classical theory of Savigny and Mommsen can only be exploded by expedients like this, I make bold to predict for it a long future.

Turning aside, therefore, from these illegitimate methods of tampering with the text of the document, we seem compelled to admit that all commissioners comprised under the phrase 'quei ... permissus est fuit' were to make certain additions and corrections to charters already framed or being framed. But the only possible reason why all commissioners should have to make changes in their charters at the same time must surely be that these changes were necessitated by some provision or provisions applying to all Italian towns. This conclusion is confirmed by the fact that this clause is immediately preceded on the Table by two provisions precisely of this character. This consideration seems already to have carried us some way towards answering the question whether commissioners were directed by general laws in their task of framing 'leges datae'. If they were so directed in correcting their charters, it would seem reasonable to suppose that they had some similar guidance in first drawing them up. Throughout his book Legras seems to me to have done less than justice to the theory of a general municipal law, by identifying it with the particular form in which it was originally stated. This, however, is a question which will have to be faced later on.

Professor Reid argues, in favour of assigning to this clause a date not long after the Social war, that it seems to refer to all the commissioners as still alive, whereas by Caesar's time many of the earlier ones must have died. Even Savigny's theory that, the 'municipia fundana' being the Transpadane towns, the commissioners would have been appointed after 49, does not entirely escape this difficulty, and it is this more than anything else which has emboldened Legras to take the drastic course already described. I cannot regard the difficulty as very serious. It must often have happened that a commissioner died before his task was completed, and there was no doubt a tralatician method of meeting such cases. The words 'quei permissus est' imply that commissioners had been recently appointed, and they may well have included, in certain cases, successors to those deceased. I shall argue in the sequel that the number of commissioners sent out before 59 was probably not very large.

There is one more point which I cannot but regard as strongly in favour of a Caesarian rather than a Sullan date for this concluding provision. If we reject Legras' suggested alteration of the text, no appointment of commissioners seems to be contemplated for the future. Yet it is quite impossible to suppose that by Sulla's dictatorship, let alone his first consulship, commissioners had been appointed for all enfranchised towns. On the other hand, it would seem that, as a result of Caesar's lex agraria (to be referred to below), there had been considerable activity in 'constituting' municipia, and nothing is more likely than that Caesar substituted for the desultory methods of the twenty years since Sulla a more vigorous policy of giving effect to the logical consequences of the enfranchisement of Italy. The very fact that all charters are to be corrected and completed within a year after the passing of this law, strongly suggests to me that Caesar looked forward to that date as marking the completion of the municipal organization of Italy, and perhaps of Cisalpine Gaul.

I therefore regard the whole section of the Table from line 83 to the end as belonging to a law passed by Caesar towards the end of 45, containing certain general provisions for Italian municipalities, which, if not already embodied in their charters, were to be added to them by a fixed date. It is, of course, possible that before Caesar's time the commissioners had not been directed by a general law at all, but had followed with local variations a merely customary form, and that Caesar's law was the formulation and disengagement of customary regulations into a definite and precise statute, with, however, certain innovations, the incorporation of which is prescribed by the last clause. On the other hand, there may have been an earlier general law, possibly even more than one, guiding the commissioners, though not tying them down in all details, and the law of 45 may merely have added some new regulations. On the latter view it would still remain a question whether there were other additions besides the two on the Table, and, if so, whether they were probably contained in the missing portion of the document.

Before discussing these possibilities, and facing directly the perplexing problem presented by the discovery of this composite document at Heraclea, it will clear the way to deal with Legras' constructive solution of it. In his view, as we have seen, there are as many as five distinct measures. (1) A law expediting the registration of the new citizens in 88 B.C. (2) A law partly copied from *βασιλικὸς νόμος* at Pergamum, and dating, perhaps from C. Gracchus, certainly from the second century. (3) and (4) Two laws immediately following the Social war, dealing with important municipal arrangements. (5) A law providing that all commissioners, present and future, shall complete their work within a year from their nomination by the people.

Rejecting the theories both of a comprehensive municipal law and of a 'lex satura' as the originals of which the Table is a copy, he attempts to solve the problem by looking to the history and circumstances of Heraclea itself. Heraclea was a Greek town, probably retaining to some extent the Greek language and some

Greek institutions, though Strabo does not include it with Tarentum, Rhegium, and Neapolis in his list of Greek towns which had escaped Romanization (p. 213). It was always loyal to Rome, and it enjoyed a peculiarly favourable treaty. When the lex Iulia was passed in 90 B. C. we know from Cicero[1] that both Heraclea and Neapolis preferred the liberty involved in their treaties, and declined to become 'fundi' of the law. Neapolis was certainly a municipium by 64 B. C. and had probably accepted the civitas after no long delay. As to the date of Heraclea's acceptance there is no evidence, but, as Archias obtained the civitas under the lex Plautia-Papiria, it must have been postponed some little time. With regard to Naples, Strabo testifies to its non-Romanization, its inscriptions are mostly Greek, and the titles of its magistrates and other details of administrative machinery follow those of a Greek πόλις. From these points Legras argues that on accepting the civitas and becoming a municipium, Neapolis was not compelled to receive a 'lex data' from a commisioner, but retained its old constitution intact. But the inference is by no means necessary. Tarentum, like Neapolis, was, according to Strabo, non-Romanized, and yet had a 'lex data'. As a matter of fact, some of the magistrates at Naples were binominal, and after all, diversity in respect to titles is not incompatible with a general uniformity of function. Probably 'leges datae' allowed much latitude in detail, but would insist on such general principles as the functions, position, and mutual relations of senate, magistrates, and assemblies. That these were not insisted on at Naples, there is no evidence. But for Heraclea there is no evidence at all. It is not mentioned by Strabo as non-Romanized, and, as Legras laments, there are at present no inscriptions throwing any light on its government in Roman times. There is merely the fact that like Naples, and for the same reason, namely, party divisions in the town, Heraclea at first declined the civitas.

However, as a conjecture based upon what is itself a dubious inference, Legras assumes that, unlike Tarentum, Heraclea received no 'lex data' modifying its political institutions, and in fact that it was by this concession that both Neapolis and Heraclea were induced to accept the civitas. But there were

[1] *pro Balb.* 21–2.

certain Roman laws, or parts of them, which in ordinary cases commissioners would be expected to work into their charters, and the principles of which Rome was compelled to insist upon in all Italian towns. Of these a compilation, without preambles, was made—perhaps by a commissioner, perhaps without one—and set up in public at Heraclea. The document was not a 'lex data', but it was a substitute for one, putting no constraint upon the community, but guiding its magistrates, to whom was left the duty of putting these principles into practice. No doubt the same course was adopted at Neapolis, and in both cases, Legras believes, Sulla made this conciliatory settlement in the course of 83 B. C.

Could we, even if we accepted Legras' dating and explanation of the various laws, regard this as a satisfactory solution of the riddle of the Table? Was the observance of these laws by the local magistrates compulsory or not? If not, the settlement was a farce. If it was, surely the obvious course would have been for a commissioner to frame a 'lex data' containing just those regulations and no more, which represented the minimum of conformity required by Rome. The suggestion that Heraclea would have prided itself 'quasi effigies parva simulacrumque' of the capital, on the ground that Roman laws were set up in its market-place, or exulted over its rival Tarentum, which had the usual 'lex data', is far from convincing. There is no evidence that the towns were averse to the work of commissioners, who were probably selected, like Labienus in the case of Cingulum and perhaps the commissioner at Arpinum in 46 B. C., on account of some interest in the municipia.

A more serious objection to Legras' hypothesis is that the contents of the Table seem quite inappropriate to the object at which it is supposed to aim. The provision about the census would no doubt figure in such a document as he supposes. The regulations, too, as to the senate are intelligible, but only, it seems to me, on the assumption that they were accompanied by other provisions making the senate, as we know that other 'leges datae' did, the governing body of the town. Similarly, with regard to the aedilician functions, we can well understand that Rome might wish her own rules to be included in the municipal charters, which, as we know, contained all sorts of kindred details.

But why they should have been included in what is supposed to be the irreducible minimum of requirements, Legras in my opinion fails entirely to show.

But what are we to say of the first and last provisions on the Table? The first, giving directions for the registration of new citizens, might no doubt be notified at Heraclea, but it was obviously ephemeral, and would become obsolete as soon as the registration was effected. What place could such a provision have in a document intended to take the place of a 'lex data'? Besides, does Legras suppose that a 'lex data' was given to a town before its citizens were enrolled in the tribes? Yet here, a clause in what is virtually a 'lex data' gives directions for the registration as a future event. The last clause, interpreted as providing that all commissioners shall complete their 'leges datae' within a year, seems singularly out of place in a document the very existence of which meant that Heraclea was not to have a 'lex data' at all. Legras suggests that it was inserted as a notification to the town that it might, if it chose, renounce all or any of its traditional institutions and laws, and as a direction how to proceed in such a case. Both the notification and the direction were unnecessary, and it requires a lively imagination to detect either of them in this clause. What the first and missing part of the document may have contained we do not know, but the extant parts of it seem wholly inappropriate to play the part assigned to them by Legras. And his solution of the problem is hardly more satisfactory than Nipperdey's theory of a private collector of Roman laws.

I shall attempt, in the second part of this essay mainly in the light of the final paragraph of the document, the real import of which Legras has so totally obscured, to give at least tentative answers to what I suppose are the two most important questions suggested by the Table. In the first place, I shall venture on a new explanation as to why this document, containing laws or parts of laws, some relating to Rome alone, others to municipalities in general, was engraved, and, as it seems, publicly set up at Heraclea. In the second place, I shall consider whether, in spite of Mommsen's recantation, the hypothesis of a general municipal law, or, it may be, of more than one such law, need be entirely abandoned. A part no doubt of Mommsen's theory, as originally stated, will have to be thrown overboard, but my conclusion will be that there was after all a lex Iulia municipalis, and that, though not all parts of the Table of Heraclea belonged to it, the latter half of the inscription probably did. But it does not follow that Caesar's was the first or only municipal law, any more than that the lex Iulia repetundarum was not preceded by a lex Cornelia or a lex Acilia on the same subject.

PART II. THE MEANING OF THE TABLE AND THE QUESTION OF A GENERAL MUNICIPAL LAW

In the first part of this essay I examined some recent theories, especially that of Legras, for which the door was thrown open by Mommsen's somewhat abrupt abandonment of the 'classical theory' of a general municipal law. But I have so far dealt mainly with the question of date and authorship, endeavouring to show that the arguments adduced by Legras and others for assigning the various sections of the Table to a pre-Caesarian period will not bear detailed criticism. The general conclusion at which I arrived was that, apart from the question of a general law, there is a preponderance of probability throughout, and in many points a preponderance of actual evidence, in favour of attributing every provision contained in the inscription to the legislation of Caesar's dictatorship.

I shall, therefore, take as the basis for the remaining portion of my argument the hypothesis, rendered, I hope, at least probable by the previous discussion, that Caesar, and not Sulla or any other republican statesman, was the author of these provisions, and was also responsible in some way for their being set up at Heraclea. But it must be admitted at the outset that these different provisions cannot be regarded as forming parts of the same law. Such a law would obviously have to receive its designation from the contents of its second half, and would, in fact, be a general municipal law. (1) There could be no possible reason why a copy of a general municipal law should be set up in Heraclea, the political institutions of which must have been determined by its own 'lex data'. (2) The supposition that regulations concerned with the corn distribution and the duties of the aediles in Rome could form parts of a municipal law, is one for which nothing less than the spell of Mommsen's reputation could have secured credit, and which may now be safely pronounced outside the range of discussion. The latter difficulty might perhaps be eluded, if we contended that the document belongs to the copy of a 'lex satura'. But there was no reason why Caesar should make use of such a contrivance; the 'lex frumentaria' is clearly implied by Suetonius to have been a separate measure, and above all, there was no reason why a 'lex satura', even though it contained municipal provisions, should be copied in a town regulated by its own 'lex data'.

Why then were three laws or portions of three laws engraved together, apparently for public exhibition, at Heraclea, two out of the three measures being concerned only with Rome?

It seems to me that an answer may possibly be found by a consideration of what is implied in the last paragraph of the Table. It is clear that certain changes and additions to 'leges datae' are contemplated, to be made by commissioners within a year of the passing of the law of which this is the concluding clause. The clause would not have been set up at Heraclea unless it had had an application to that town. Heraclea, therefore, must have already received a 'lex data', and its commissioner was one of those empowered to add, or change, or correct certain points. Primarily, these changes would be made in the light of the new law, of which, as I have already argued, lines 83–158 form two of the provisions. But it does not follow that commissioners were limited to such changes. In framing charters they would have, notwithstanding the guidance of a general law or of a common form, some discretion in matters of detail, and I imagine that they would have the same discretion in the task of revision. If, therefore, any recent legislation in Rome, affecting the municipal affairs of the capital, struck a commissioner as applicable or useful to his town, it would be open to him to embody their effect, *mutatis mutandis*, in his revised 'lex data'. As to the method adopted by commissioners in revising their charters, there was again, perhaps, some discretion. But a commissioner may well have thought it fit, as changes were to be introduced, to give a public notification to the town of the alterations or reforms which he proposed to make. To effect this, there was no better way than to publish in full, not only the new provisions of the municipal law, but all those parts of any Roman laws from which he intended to borrow in his revised charter. It does not follow that all commissioners adopted this course, or that, apart from the contents of the municipal law, they all made the same changes. But I suggest that this was what the commissioner did at Heraclea, and that the mysterious Table with its mixture of Roman and municipal matters is a fragment of this public notification of intended changes in the 'lex data' of the town.

As to the applicability of the two Roman laws, we have nothing but conjecture to go upon. It seems to me by no means improbable that, when so many Roman institutions were copied from the capital, there should have been distributions of corn in some of the Italian towns. If so, the same abuses might be expected, and Caesar's reform of the system in Rome might well be an object lesson to enlightened commissioners. With regard to the maintenance of roads and the protection of public places, no doubt these and other aedilician duties had been attended to, though with varying adequacy, in many Italian towns long before the time of Caesar. Nevertheless, the fact that Caesar, in spite of previous laws on such subjects, had recently deemed it advisable to legislate on roads and open spaces in the capital, makes the action of a commissioner in attending to the same things at Heraclea intelligible. From their place on the Table we must infer that no other aedilician duties were at this time dealt with, but it may well have been that Caesar's law was much wider than the few provisions which alone the commissioner thought fit to embody in his charter.

It has already been suggested that the two provisions respecting the senates and the census belong to a municipal law passed by Caesar in 45, and that the concluding paragraph of the Table is the last clause of that law. That it is also the end of the document set up at Heraclea is indicated by the fact that there is an appreciable space between it and the bottom of the bronze. On the other hand, the extant beginning at the top of the bronze is admittedly not the beginning of the document. There was, therefore, at least one other preceding tablet, forming part of this same document. That this was of exactly the same size as the one preserved we cannot be sure, since the fourth-century Greek inscription on the front side of the Table is complete, and needed no second bronze. But in spite of the fact that the public archives of Heraclea are said to have been destroyed in the Social war, there were no doubt other obsolete Greek laws like the one preserved in *I.G.* 14,645, and we may fairly assume that the commissioner would have selected two, or more, of about the same size. If we allow 50 or 60 lines at the end of the first tablet for the beginning of the 'lex frumentaria', there would still remain about 100 for other matter. What this was it is idle to speculate, but the commissioner would be limited to no particular order in his notification of changes to be made, and there may have been other provisions from Caesar's new law. It is tempting to suggest, though there is no solid ground for the suggestion, that a clause prohibiting the dismantling of houses may have been one of them. We find it in the charter of the Caesarian colony of Urso (cap. 75), and in the 'lex data' of Tarentum (ll. 32–35), and there is no reason why the latter should not be a revision rather than the original charter of that town.

But a far more important question than that as to the nature and further contents of the particular document found at Heraclea must be raised concerning the municipal law which constitutes the third of its extant sections. That it was a municipal law, and a general municipal law, is obvious from its own description of its sphere of applicability. But was it, besides being general in its applicability, general in the sense of dealing comprehensively with all parts of municipal constitutions and municipal administration?

If we are to accept the position finally taken up by Mommsen, and still more emphatically supported by Legras, we shall have to answer this question in the negative. The whole theory of a scheme on Caesar's part for a more thorough and consistent organization of municipal affairs is given up by Mommsen, when he writes: 'legem populi Romani nego ullam exstitisse, quae statum municipiorum et coloniarum, sive civium Romanorum sive Latinorum, generaliter ordinaret.'[1]

It is unfortunate that Mommsen had never very thoroughly

[1] *Jurist. Schriften*, vol. i, p. 153.

developed his view as to how practical effect was given to the logical consequences of the lex Iulia de civitate in the years which followed it. He had suggested in his Roman History[1] that the beginnings of an Italian municipal system belonged to the Sullan epoch, and even admitted the possibility that its details may have been arranged either by the lex Iulia itself or by some law of Sulla. This possibility is now denied. The procedure adopted is now represented as a mere continuance of earlier custom. Upon the way in which a customary and normal type of constitution had gradually been developed by the date of the Social war, Legras throws valuable light by his careful treatment of the evidence. There can be little doubt that the primitive Romano-Latin constitution had perpetuated itself in the various Latin colonies, and not least in the twelve founded after 268 B.C., of which Ariminum was the first and Aquileia the last. Many of the details of this constitution we may with confidence infer from the charters of Salpensa and Malaca. It was undoubtedly on the lines of this normal type that in 95 B.C. Claudius Pulcher 'leges Halaesinis dedit'.[2] Among the earlier Roman colonies and municipia there were probably far greater shades of difference than between Latin towns, but we may accept from both Mommsen and Legras the fruitful suggestion that the type of constitution allowed must have gained a considerable amount of fixity after the foundation of the large and important Roman colonies at the beginning of the second century. Legras points out with reason that the less favoured, both of the colonies and municipia, would have strong claims to be put on the same level with these later foundations. In the light of these considerations, therefore, we may well believe with Mommsen that by the date of the Social war there had grown up a 'communis forma', allowing room within it, however, for certain distinctions between Roman colonies and municipia, and towns of Latin right. We may perhaps even go further, and argue that the constitutions of many of the 'civitates foederatae' had already been influenced by this 'communis forma'. This would, however, have been due more to spontaneous imitation of Rome than to any interference on the part of the predominant city. Clear traces of this imitation are found on the Bantine

[1] iii, pp. 376, 377 (Engl. trans.). [2] Cic. *in Verr.* ii, 49, 122.

Table, and the new capital of Italy to have been established by the allies in the Social war would apparently in constitutional matters have been a replica of Rome. Up to this point, therefore, Mommsen's summing up of the process may certainly be accepted: 'Mihi semper visum est Romanos in constituendis oppidis suae nationis linguaeque secutos esse formam communem, diversam eatenus, quatenus differt colonia a municipio itemque quatenus differunt ius civium et Latinorum, praeterea per tempora ampliatam et imminutam, sed ut fundamentum maneret.' Colonies of course, whether Roman or Latin, had had their 'deductores' and, we may safely assume, their 'leges datae', and probably Legras is justified in supposing that every municipium recognized as a 'respublica' also had a 'lex data'. It would seem, therefore, that by the beginning of the first century B.C. a uniform type of constitution had grown up without a general law, though of course each 'lex data' was 'secutoria', as Mommsen puts it, to a 'lex rogata', determining the category, whether colony or municipium or Latin community, to which the new constitution had to conform, the details being left to the discretion of the 'deductores' and commissioners. It does not follow that exactly the same course would be adopted after the enfranchisement of all Italy, when perhaps hundreds of towns became 'municipia fundana', and needed, some more, some less, to be reconstituted. It is all very well to argue that the Roman constitution grew up by adaptation and the influence of the 'mos majorum', not by means of general laws, but the lex Iulia was itself a general law of vast importance, and necessitating readjustments, both complex and far-reaching. As to the method by which the necessary readjustments would be carried out in particular cases, it did not need the discovery of the law of Tarentum to convince us, as Legras sometimes seems curiously to assume, that commissioners would have to be appointed sooner or later to frame 'leges datae' for each of the enfranchised towns. The question is whether the general and even sweeping character of the lex Iulia would not of necessity have involved more general and systematic instructions to the commissioners than had been requisite in the preceding centuries. Mommsen's objection to the doctrine of a general law seems to be the lack of evidence for it, and especially the 'altum silentium' of the later jurists as to any such law. But Legras is not content with this negative position. He argues that there is an absolute inconsistency between the existence of a general law and the method of reconstituting towns by special 'leges datae', the work of particular commissioners. It is in his view even repugnant to common sense to believe on the one hand that there was a vast municipal code, fixing the constitutional and administrative machinery of all Italian towns, and on the other that each town had its own charter. Why should Tarentum and Urso and Malaca have all had clauses in their charters prohibiting the demolition of houses if there had been a general law prohibiting this? Besides, if there had been a general law, the only function remaining for the charters would have been to fill up gaps in it, or to guarantee certain special and local privileges accorded to this or that town. That, however, Legras points out, is not the character of the 'leges datae' of which we possess extant portions. On the contrary, they seem to be exhaustive documents, dealing minutely with all the details of administration, and even assigning to the chief magistrates their judicial functions, which, if anything, would surely emanate from the general law.

Nor is it only the general incompatibility of two different systems of solving the municipal problem which troubles Legras. He finds in the differences revealed by inscriptions between the arrangements, and especially between the titles of magistrates in different towns, insuperable obstacles in the way of believing in the existence of a general law. Not only is it not true that 'IIIIviri' and 'IIviri' are limited respectively to municipia and colonies, but all sorts of survivals and irregularities are found, both before and after the date of Caesar's dictatorship. The irregularity is, of course, undoubted, and Legras' list with references of the various towns with dictators, consuls, praetors, or aediles for highest magistrates is a very useful and instructive one. He claims to make a palpable hit when he points out that even in some foundations of Caesar himself, the reputed author of the general law, 'suffetes' are tolerated in Africa and praetors even in some of his Latin colonies in Narbonensis.

Now it seems to me that, whether right or wrong, Mommsen's position, that there was never any general law, is not in the slightest degree reinforced by the arguments of Legras. To take his last point first. If irregularity or the absence of uniformity in the titles of the chief magistrates is an argument against a general law, how is it that, in the two extant general provisions of what is clearly a municipal law of some kind, the wording is so carefully framed as to cover every irregularity adduced by Legras? In line 83 the chief magistrates of 'municipia, coloniae, praefecturae', &c., are: 'queiquomque . . . IIvirei IIIIvirei erunt, aliove quo nomine magistratum potestatemve . . . habebunt.' In line 130 of the same provision we have 'quei . . . maximam potestatem habebit', while in line 142 the census is to be taken not necessarily by a censor or 'quinquennalis', but by the official with whatever title, 'quei . . . maximum magistratum maximamve potestatem habebit'. It is curious that Legras does not perceive that these broad and vague descriptions of the highest municipal magistrates make wholly irrelevant, as arguments against a general law, irregularities even more striking than any that he has adduced. It deserves, too, to be noticed that the number of towns in which these anomalies are found is small, compared with the total number of Italian towns, and that comparatively few instances come from those enfranchised after the Social war. When, too, Legras speaks of praetors in Caesar's Latin colonies in Gaul, it is not impertinent to ask whether he can cite any instance except that of Carcaso.[1]

But, after all, what is the inconsistency so repugnant to common sense between a general law and particular 'leges datae'? Legras himself admits that commissioners may have received direction and guidance, both from 'leges de civitate', such as the lex Iulia or the lex Roscia, and from laws which, though not amounting to general municipal codes, nevertheless contained provisions of general applicability. Even if he had not admitted this, we happen to have in the latter half of the Table of Heraclea conclusive proof that it was so. It is obvious that the additions and corrections which commissioners are to make in their charters are unintelligible, except on the supposition that they are to be made in the light of some general directions, whether those contained in the preceding provisions of the Table or not. Legras' own theory as to the nature of the document

[1] *C.I.L.* xii, 5371.

implies this. Its contents would in ordinary cases have been embodied by the commissioner in his 'lex data', and the very point of the concession made to Heraclea is that in the case of that town this is not done. But, if it is not repugnant to common sense to admit that in certain points commissioners were instructed by general provisions, there seems no reason why the remaining contents of the charters should not also have been dependent on general laws. Legras and others contend that the whole question as to the possibility of a general law has to be reconsidered owing to the discovery of the Tarentine Fragment. To me it seems that the discovery leaves the question exactly where it was. If it is asked why the charters of Tarentum, Urso, and Malaca all contained prohibitions against the demolition of houses, when there was a general law prohibiting it, the answer is simple. The 'leges datae' were the constitutional and administrative statutes which were immediately obligatory on the municipal magistrates and their townsmen. The general law was intended to fix the 'forma communis', to bind the commissioners in respect to principles, and to afford them guidance, though naturally with greater laxity, in matters of detail. Its provisions only became obligatory on the towns mediately, by being incorporated in their charters. Strangely enough, Legras himself emphasizes this very point, and declares that the chapter of Caesar's lex agraria, cited by the Gromatici, only became obligatory on Urso, when it took its place as cap. 104 of its 'lex data'.

Legras persists in speaking of a general law as a vast code of municipal law which he apparently regards as too unwieldy to be of practical use. The force of this objection is not very obvious. Roman laws tended to be lengthy documents, and he himself insists that the 'leges datae' were long and exhaustive. But a consideration which seems to have escaped Legras, and which I desire to emphasize, is that, if these local statutes were long, complex, and detailed, if there was a large number of them, sometimes two being framed simultaneously, and if they can be shown to have agreed with one another even in some matters of detail, the necessity of assuming a general law behind them is proportionately increased. It seems futile to speak of commissioners, simultaneously at work, 'copying one another'.

No such unsystematic contrivance would meet the case. Nor will Mommsen's 'forma communis' meet the case any better unless it was a written form. As far as I can understand him, Mommsen regards it as at least having come to be a written form, since he attributes the inconsistency in the description of the highest magistrates at Tarentum to the fact that 'in forma communi a qua pendet (lex) juxta nominabantur IIIIviri et IIviri'. But a written 'forma communis' containing such constitutional points as the titulature of magistrates, and such administrative details as the maintenance of private houses, was to all intents and purposes a 'lex generalis', and indeed, to be an effective rule for commissioners, would have to be sanctioned by statute.

As to the historical steps by which practical effect with all its logical consequences was given to the lex Iulia of 89 B.C. we have very little that is certain to go upon. No doubt the operation of the lex Iulia, originally restricted to the communities which had either not revolted or laid down arms at once, was gradually extended to all, as they submitted, and we may perhaps assume that by the end of the civil war there were few Italian towns which were not 'municipia fundana'. That either the lex Iulia itself contained any general constitutional enactments, or that it was accompanied by another law which did so, seems in the highest degree improbable. The object of the law was simply to limit the area of the war, and the government had no leisure for constitutional precautions. Nor was Sulla's first consulship likely to be marked by any municipal legislation. The year was disturbed and revolutionary, and even the preliminary question as to the principle on which the new citizens were to be distributed among the tribes was not yet settled. Sulla's legislation was to all appearance limited to the situation in Rome itself, and even if it had not been, Legras should not forget the ἀνατροπαὶ τῶν ἐπὶ Σύλλα τεθέντων νόμων which, according to Appian, followed his departure from Italy (i, 73). There are, of course, not the same objections to the hypothesis of a lex Cornelia municipalis belonging to the dictatorship, though it could not have contained any of the provisions on the Table of Heraclea. But, as far as the evidence goes, Sulla's activity in Italy, if we except the establishment of his military colonies, was more punitive than constructive. Indeed, his treatment of Volaterrae and other towns shows that even his general pledge to accept *faits accomplis* in regard to the recent enfranchisement was subject to serious reservations. Legras supposes that after the Social war the character of the 'lex data' granted to each town was determined by a kind of bargaining between them and Rome, each striving to retain as much as possible of its ancient constitution. He thinks that much of this diplomatic settlement is to be ascribed to Sulla in the course of 83 and 82, and that he owed his success in the civil war as much to diplomatic concessions as to military achievements. In this way, it is suggested, favourable 'leges datae' were given or promised to perhaps a considerable number of Italian towns. It was at this time that Heraclea was won over by the singular document given to it in lieu of a 'lex data'. It was at this time that Petelia in Bruttium was constituted by a charter called the lex Cornelia (see below), and that Suessa was made the 'lautissimum oppidum nunc municipium', as Cicero, writing after Caesar's death, calls it.

Now for this bargaining on the nature of the 'leges datae', either generally or in the time of Sulla, there is absolutely no evidence, and, as it seems to me, very little probability. It is at any rate quite inconsistent with Mommsen's doctrine of the 'forma communis'. As for Sulla, he was not in an official position till the end of 82, and he had neither the right to give Heraclea a substitute for a 'lex data', nor to frame a lex Cornelia for Petelia. With regard to Suessa, we only know that it was the first Campanian town to join Sulla,[1] and that the town set up an honorary dedication to him before the dictatorship.[2] That 'leges datae' must have been framed by Sulla or his 'deductores' for the seventeen colonial foundations, of which there is evidence, seems certain from the nature of the case, but the conditions in such towns as Arretium and Nola, where two or even more separate communities existed side by side, were exceptional and complicated, and we cannot be sure whether the charters only affected the new colonists, or comprised a reconstitution of the old communities as well. At any rate, the necessary regulation of his colonies does not involve a municipal reorganization of Italy on the part of Sulla. Quite as little connected with any

[1] App. i, 85. [2] Dess. 870.

inauguration of a municipal system for Italy would seem to have been Sulla's action in regard to Puteoli.[1] Puteoli was a colony of long standing, and as we know from the 'lex parieti faciendo'[2] had 'duoviri' in the second century B.C. Plutarch says that Sulla, ten days before his death, and so while a 'privatus', νόμον ἔγραψεν καθ' ὃν πολιτεύσονται. He also states that the step was taken to reconcile factions within the town, while Valerius Maximus alludes to Sulla's indignation with the colony. It can hardly be doubted that for a reason and in a capacity not to be ascertained, Sulla revised the 'lex data' of the town, but the incident throws no light on his municipal policy.

It seems to me that, if the new situation created by the lex Iulia almost of necessity involved a general municipal law of some kind, there is more to be said for attributing it to Cinna than to Sulla. The democratic leaders had always on the whole been more interested in the enfranchisement of Italy than their opponents, and in particular had taken up the principle of a fair distribution of the new citizens among the tribes. Till that was settled, there could have been no question of legislation, but its settlement under the Cinnan régime would be the natural starting-point for some new development. The 'mos majorum' certainly, and possibly a more strictly juridical necessity, called for the sending out of commissioners to the numerous new municipia, and though there was very likely already a 'forma communis', the number of towns to which it was now to be almost simultaneously applied would make general directions, and therefore a general law, almost inevitable. This would be all the more the case if anything was to be at this time added to the 'forma communis'. Now there is some indication that an innovation was introduced at this time in respect to the titles of magistrates. For the period before the Social war there is the smallest evidence of uniformity in this matter. Duoviri were probably the highest magistrates in burgess colonies; they may have existed in some Latin colonies, though, I think, there is no proof of it. But for the 'civitates foederatae' and even for the municipia, there would seem to have been infinite variety. As for 'IIIIviri', I believe I am right in saying that there is no instance of them before 90 B.C. It has already been conceded

[1] Val. Max. ix, 3, and Plut. *Sull.* xxxvii. [2] Bruns, p. 374.

to Legras that in many cases the old heterogeneous titles are still found in the following period. But it seems nevertheless true tha the normal title in municipia has come to be 'IIIIviri'. The evidence for this is, if not overwhelming, at least sufficient. (1) The 'lex data' of Tarentum, a municipium, speaks of the highest magistrates as 'IIIIviri', though in one clause the two colleges within the board are duoviri and aediles. This may serve as evidence for the decade 70 to 60 B.C. and if these magistrates appear in a town which was imperfectly Romanized, a fortiori we should expect them in the towns of central and northern Italy. (2) There was a rumour in 51 B.C. that the Transpadane towns had been incited by Caesar to elect 'IIIIviri'.[1] Cicero understood this to mean that they were to elect magistrates as if they were Roman municipia rather than as Latin towns. (3) The Atestine Fragment, probably belonging to the lex Rubria, implies that the magistrates in the Transpadane towns had been 'duoviri' up to the passing of the lex Roscia, whereas the title of the highest judicial magistrate in the lex Rubria is 'duovir quattuorvir praefectusve' (i. e. or his temporary substitute). There was probably far more uniformity in this region, where since 89 the 'ius Latii' had been universal, and where, accordingly, 'IIviri' were regularly replaced by 'IIIIviri'. (4) The wording of the Table of Heraclea, 'queiquomque ... IIvirei IIIIvirei ... aliove quo nomine', &c., clearly shows that, though room was left for survivals, 'IIviri' and 'IIIIviri' were the normal and recognized titles.

Now we have one clear piece of evidence that this innovation, which I argue would almost of necessity involve legislation, goes back further than to the dictatorship of Sulla. Speaking of the accuser of Cluentius, and clearly referring to the last year of the civil war, Cicero says: 'per illam L. Sullae vim atque victoriam Larinum in summo timore omnium cum armatis advolavit; quattuorviros quos municipes fecerant sustulit; se a Sulla et alios praeterea tris factos esse dixit'.[2] It appears from this that 'IIIIviri' had been elected at Larinum previous to 82, and that Sulla recognized the system, though he may have connived

[1] Cic. *ad Att.* v, 2, 3.

[2] *pro Cluent.* viii, 25. I am indebted to Mr. Strachan-Davidson, both for the reference to *pro Cluent.* and for the first suggestion that Cinna must have done something for municipal organization.

at these irregular proceedings. On these grounds I think it probable that after settling the position of the new burgess communities in the tribes, Cinna may have passed a lex Cornelia, probably fixing the general features of the 'forma communis' already arrived at, and in particular defining the normal titles of municipal magistrates, though no doubt leaving room for local varieties in certain cases. It is this law, in my opinion, and not a supposed 'lex data' of Sulla, which best explains the inscription of Petelia, in which a man is described as 'aedilis IIIIvir lege Cornelia'.[1] It is, of course, conceivable that the 'lex data' of a town, like a 'lex provinciae', might be called after the commissioner who framed it, but there is no certain instance of it, and as commissioners were so numerous, the practice would have been confusing. Besides, when a town had once received its charter, its magistrates would, as a matter of course, bear titles in accordance with it, and there could be no possible object in adding the words 'lege Cornelia', or 'lege Iulia'. On the other hand, a town, which had become 'fundus' of the lex Iulia, but had not yet received a charter, might, of its own accord and in anticipation, conform to some or all of the contents of such a general law as I suppose, and if it did so, the title 'IIIIvir lege Cornelia' would be natural and intelligible. The inscription from Patavium, to be noticed below, would, of course, have to be explained in the same way.

Whether the 'IIIIviri' at Larinum were also appointed in anticipation of a 'lex data', we do not know, but we may suspect that Petelia was far from standing alone in having to wait for its commissioner. The civil war was not favourable to the working out of any scheme of municipal organization, and, as we have seen, there is no evidence that Sulla in any way encouraged it. The 'lex data' of Tarentum may possibly date from soon after Sulla's death, but I cannot agree that 62 B.C. is a *terminus ante quem*, because Cicero speaks of Tarentum as a municipium in that year. It is impossible to say that commissioners were not being sent out between 80 and 59, but not a single instance is known. That the towns were averse to 'leges datae', or suspicious of commissioners, or wedded to antiquated institutions, as Legras assumes, there is not the slightest evidence. With the

[1] *C.I.L.* x, 113 and 114.

possible exception of a few Greek towns, they must, most of them, already have assimilated the essential features of the 'forma communis', and the commissioners were probably, as a rule, men with local knowledge and local sympathy like Labienus. But the government of the time was lethargic, and perhaps had little leisure for municipal organization.

It appears to me that the next landmark in the history of municipal organization in Italy is to be looked for in the year 59 B.C. It was Caesar's first consulship, and one of its most important legislative acts was the lex Iulia agraria. Now the latter portion of a chapter, cited as belonging to the 'lex agraria quam C. Caesar tulit', is given in *Dig*. xlvii, 21, 3. The same chapter in its entirety, together with two others, is contained in the *Corpus Gromaticorum Scriptorum*, under the title 'lex Mamilia Roscia Peducaea Alliena Fabia'. The second of these three chapters is found as cap. 104 of the lex col. Gen., while it appears from cap. 97 of that charter that lands in that colony had been distributed 'e lege Iulia'. From these data Mommsen has inferred that all three chapters in the Gromatici[1] belong to Caesar's agrarian law of 59 B.C. and that some of its provisions were sufficiently general to be applied to colonies founded in the provinces fifteen years later.[2] But if we accept this inference, we must ascribe to the law a more far-reaching character than we have hitherto done.

The first and third of the extant chapters begin respectively thus: 'Quae colonia hac lege deducta quodve municipium praefectura forum conciliabulum constitutum erit,' and 'Qui hac lege coloniam deduxerit municipium praefecturam forum conciliabulum constituerit.' From this only one inference is possible, namely, that not only was a considerable 'deductio' of colonies contemplated by the law, but the 'constitution' of municipia. I cannot doubt that Prof. Reid is right in insisting that to

[1] Bruns, p. 95.

[2] The five names attached to this law seem to present a problem even more insoluble than that of the Table of Heraclea itself. I do not attempt to solve it, but it is curious that a Roscius and a Peducaeus were praetors in 49, and that the former is known to have passed an important law for Caesar in that year, while Peducaeus and Allienus were respectively a few years later made governors of Sardinia and Sicily by Caesar (App. ii, 48). I cannot see my way to any hypothesis from these coincidences, though I have sometimes wondered whether this agrarian law may not belong to a later period of Caesar's life than 59.

'constitute' a town was to reconstitute it, in the sense of giving it a 'lex data'. To 'constitute' a 'forum' or 'conciliabulum' was to give these places a municipal constitution, so that in future, while retaining the old names, they would be in effect municipia, with 'decuriones' and 'IIIIviri' and even their own jurisdiction. The Table of Heraclea, which gives exactly the same list of towns, refers to them at a stage when they have been constituted, and regards them as all on the same footing, except that apparently for census purposes the 'fora' and 'conciliabula' are included in wider districts. It would seem, therefore, that provision was made in this law of Caesar for the sending out of a considerable number of commissioners. If the work of constituting the enfranchised towns had been performed, or nearly performed, in the years immediately following the Social war, as Legras assumes, such phrases as I have quoted would be inexplicable in a law of 59. It is clear that much, perhaps most, of the work still remained to be done, and that Caesar, among the preoccupations of his consulship, determined that the desultory way in which practical and juridical effect had so far been given to the lex Iulia and the lex Cornelia should be replaced by steps more prompt and logical. The wording of the law in referring to the 'deductores' and commissioners suggests very strongly to my mind that the 'constitution' was to be conducted in conformity with general directions contained in the law, and if it were not for the explicit description of it as a 'lex agraria', I should have little doubt that Caesar virtually re-enacted, probably with amplifications, the general municipal law, whether Cinna's or Sulla's, which had so far existed but been inoperative. That even an agrarian law might contain the outlines at least which a 'lex data' would fill in, is clear from *de leg. agr.* ii, 35, 96, which shows that the law of Rullus had at least mapped out the constitution destined for the new colony of Capua. But we are baffled by the mysterious five names prefixed to the law in the *Corpus Gromaticorum*. The names must have had some bearing, either upon the chapters cited or perhaps on some others, and the conjecture cannot be suppressed, though it cannot be verified, that the 'lex agraria' was supplemented by other legislation, which somehow constituted a fresh stage in the municipal organization of Italy. It is, of course, impossible to say, in the absence of all evidence on the subject, how many commissioners were now sent out, or to what towns, though we may be pretty sure that the 'constitution' of Cingulum by Labienus, referred to by Caesar himself,[1] belongs to the period after 59. The word 'constituere' was evidently used in so technical and recognized a sense that Legras is clearly right in drawing attention to the case of Arpinum, referred to by Cicero.[2] He writes: 'nam constituendi municipii causa hoc anno (46 B.C.) aedilem filium meum fieri volui et fratris filium et M. Caesium, . . . is enim magistratus in nostro municipio nec alius ullus creari solet.' Arpinum was, of course, not one of the towns enfranchised after the Social war, since it had received the full civitas in 188 B.C.[3] But, though its constitution no doubt agreed generally with the 'forma communis' as arrived at in the previous century, it was clearly behind the times in certain points, and a commissioner must have been at work there in the year 46. Legras, however, cannot be right in regarding Cicero's son as the commissioner, for he is merely mentioned as one of three aediles whose election Cicero had brought about. But in such cases the commissioner and the magistrates would naturally work together, and this sufficiently explains Cicero's solicitude in the matter.

We now come to Caesar's municipal law of 45 B.C., the existence of which I regard as established by Cicero's letter to Lepta. But there had been very important legislation four years previously in connexion with Gallia Cisalpina. In March, 49, the citizenship had been conferred on all the Latin communities of the Transpadane country by the lex Roscia. This had been followed later in the same year by the lex Rubria, dealing at any rate among other things with the relations between the municipal courts and the jurisdiction of the Roman praetor. Undoubtedly the lex Roscia, like the lex Iulia of 90, involved as its logical consequence the sending out of commissioners and the framing of 'leges datae' for this fresh batch of 'municipia fundana'. We can hardly doubt that the necessary preliminary steps were taken, though it is quite probable that little progress was made during the civil war and Caesar's absence from Italy. The constitutional changes involved in the transition from the 'ius

[1] *Bell. Civ.* i, 15. [2] *ad Fam.* xiii, 11, 3. [3] Liv. xxxviii, 36.

Latii' to the Roman 'civitas' would be small and could wait. But all the towns became at once 'fundi' of Roman civil law, and under the circumstances of the case, there was, I apprehend, cause for immediate legislation on this point.

It is impossible to avoid the conclusion that the effect of the lex Rubria was merely to apply to a province now composed of burgess communities rules and principles already obligatory on similar communities in Italy. It does not follow that there was a special law on the subject for Italy, but if there was not, these rules and principles, too precise to depend on mere custom, must have been either contained in a general municipal law, such as I attribute to Cinna, or perhaps dependent on the praetor's edict. They may have been ultimately incorporated in the 'leges datae', but their binding force could not be postponed and would commence as soon as a town became 'fundus' of a 'lex de civitate'. In the case of Cisalpine Gaul, we may assume that Caesar's object was to place its inhabitants on the same political and juridical footing as the rest of the peninsula. But in the latter respect as provincials they were subject to the proconsul, and if, like the other Italians, they were to be directly subject to the praetor, in cases where the local courts were not competent, they could only be made so by means of a special law. It is in this way that I should explain the necessity for the lex Rubria, which I still regard as a 'lex rogata'.[1]

What are we to say as to the extent of Caesar's municipal law of 45? We may assume as very probable that, though commissioners may have been appointed, many of the Transpadane towns and some in Italy were still waiting for the completion of their 'leges datae'. Further, we may take it as certain, from the concluding part of the Table, that there were certain new provisions which were to be added to, or substituted for, parts of all charters existing or being prepared. Did the new law consist entirely of these new provisions? Was it a mere rider to some earlier general law? It may have been so, but in my opinion that was not the course most consonant with the spirit of Roman legislation. For the lex Acilia was substituted the lex Servilia, for that the lex Cornelia, while this in its turn gave way to the lex Iulia. The groundwork of all these laws was probably the

[1] *Six Rom. Laws*, pp. 164–5.

same, but additions and corrections were incorporated at each stage. Circumstances had changed since 59: Caesar was in a different position, a new system of imperial government seemed beginning, and there might be much work for commissioners and 'deductores' in future. My hypothesis, therefore, is that the law which was in preparation in the early months of 45 was not the first formulation of a general municipal law, but a revision and re-enactment of earlier laws, together with certain new provisions, of which two are preserved on the Table of Heraclea, and of which some others were probably contained on the first and missing portion of that document. It need not, as far as I can see, have been 'a vast code', and it certainly did not include municipal ordinances for Rome itself, but it marked the close of one period of municipal development, and perhaps the beginning of another. Even though it was not all new, it may have been the development of Caesar's own earlier work, and, if its nature was what I have suggested, there could be no fitter title for it than 'lex Iulia municipalis'. Of course, the theory of a general law so entitled is as much an hypothesis to-day as when Savigny first presented it, but the probabilities in favour of it have not grown less. No new inscriptions have weakened it, and the fact that we now cut out the first half of the Table as not belonging to the municipal law, strengthens rather than weakens the evidence of the last half.

I still regard the inscription of Patavium, on which a magistrate of the town is described as 'IIIIvir aediliciae potestatis e lege Iulia municipali',[1] as giving us the official title of Caesar's law. With all deference to Karlowa, Mommsen, and Legras, I submit that 'lex Iulia municipalis' cannot be a description of the 'lex data' of Patavium. (1) There is no evidence and little probability that each 'lex data' bore the name of the commissioner who framed it. (2) In an official description of a law, as this clearly is, 'municipalis' can only have the general sense 'relating to municipia'.[2] A 'lex data' could only be 'lex de municipio' with the name attached. (3) When a town had received its charter,

[1] *C.I.L.* v, 2864.

[2] The use of 'lex municipalis' in the jurists for 'the charter of each particular town' stands on a different footing, and presents no analogy with the present case.

it followed as a matter of course that its magistrates would bear titles in accordance with it, and there was no point in specifying this on an inscription. It is clear that this inscription and that from Petelia (see above) must be interpreted in the same way, and I again suggest that a town might modify its constitution in anticipation of a 'lex data', and that in such cases it was perfectly natural to do so on the strength of the general law in force for the time being. This inscription may well date from the beginning of 44, after Caesar's law was passed, but before the lex data of Patavium was completed. If the Transpadane towns in 51 had really elected 'IIIIviri', as rumour had it they were ordered to do by Caesar, they would all of them, I imagine, have been 'IIIIviri' in accordance with the municipal law, whatever its title may have been, of 59.

The theory of a general lex Iulia municipalis, which in a sense I have attempted to rehabilitate, is therefore not exactly a reaffirmation of the 'classical theory' which Legras claims to have demolished. The law was, in my view, not the initiation, but the completion, as far at least as Italy was concerned, of a legalized system of municipal organization. Nor do I intend to reaffirm Mommsen's earlier view that this law is referred to in certain passages in the works of the jurists as the 'lex municipalis'. I believe that that expression is sufficiently explained in all cases as either the charter of this or that particular town, or the legal principles disengaged or summarized from the totality of charters and virtually forming a special department of law, lending itself to special commentary.[1]

[1] I cannot leave unnoticed Legras' insistence on the inconsistency between line 150 of the Table, where a mere majority, 'major pars decurionum', is required, and Ulpian's statement (*Dig*. l, 9, 3), 'lege autem municipali cavetur ut ordo non aliter habeatur quam duabus partibus adhibitis'. (1) The election of the 'legati' to carry the census papers to Rome was so trivial a matter that the provision accepting the election of a bare majority might well be an exception to a more general clause in another part of the law, requiring a quorum either for all or for the most important business. (2) The compiler of this part of the *Digest* has so isolated this excerpt from Ulpian's 'de appellationibus', as perhaps to give a false impression of its purport. In the case of an 'appellatio' from a municipality the town would be represented by an actor or syndicus elected by the decuriones. There may have been a praetorian edict, afterwards incorporated in the 'leges datae', to the effect that in such cases two-thirds of the decuriones were required, and to this Ulpian may be alluding. This is rendered the more probable, because both Ulpian and Paulus in their commentary on the edict, and in special reference

I am inclined to acquiesce in Mommsen's assertion that there is 'altum silentium' about this law in the writings of the jurists, but I am not sure that this need altogether surprise us. No municipal law could be final or complete. Conditions were bound to vary and develop even in Italy and in the same town, to say nothing of the multifarious conditions in the provinces, where municipal questions in the future were sure to be most numerous and most difficult. Naturally the provisions of Caesar's law would be reflected in future 'leges datae', and, indeed, there is an obvious allusion in the charter of Malaca (c. 54) to the list of disqualifications for admission to the senate. But local conditions and special developments or deteriorations would necessitate the intervention of some authority other than the general law. Even at Urso the 'deductor' must have received instructions not to disallow the election of freedmen into the senate, while at Malaca special provisions have to be introduced to meet the growing reluctance of candidates for magistracies. But the most important point of all [1] is that under the empire imperial constitutions and rescripts and edicts had taken the place of statutory enactments. No person had now the right to frame 'leges datae' but the emperor himself. All 'leges datae' emanated from his imperium, and accordingly the 'lex municipalis' which disengaged itself from a vast collection of charters, came in course of time to be quite independent of, and often even at variance with, any general municipal law of earlier days. This was not the course of development which came, or could have come, within the range of Caesar's political vision when he summed up the municipal organization of his day in a general municipal law, but it appears to me sufficiently to explain the 'altum silentium' which seems more than anything else to have been responsible for Mommsen's famous recantation.

to the election of actores, specify precisely this quorum as necessary (*Dig.* iii, 4, 34). There were no 'actores civitatis' in the technical sense at first, but it deserves notice that when officials with somewhat analogous duties have to be elected at Malaca, it is again this quorum of decuriones which is required (lex Mal. c. 63). For most of these points I am indebted to Legras himself, who seems unconscious that they dispose of one of his own arguments against identifying lines 83–158 of the Table with part of a general municipal law.

[1] An example of how far this was the case is found in the decision of Ulpian that an edict of Hadrian prohibiting burial within a town would override a 'lex data' allowing it.

IX

ON THE *LEX IULIA MUNICIPALIS*

PROF. REID'S recent article on 'the so-called Lex Iulia Municipalis' (*J. R. S.* vol. v, part 2) had been looked forward to with some interest. He was known to have regarded the inscription as an enigmatical document, but there was always the chance that, out of the special study he was devoting to it, he would evolve some conclusions, more or less definite, on the most essential questions which require answers. It cannot be said that these anticipations have been fulfilled. With the exception of a new hypothesis as to the identity of the *professi* in the opening lines of the Table, Prof. Reid's conclusions are all negative or destructive. If he found the document enigmatical, he has left it a disconnected medley. Apart from the opening section, to which a probable date may be assigned, we have, it appears, to deal with incoherent extracts, often abominably reproduced, from undatable laws or projects of law. No connexion and no common purpose is to be detected in these *disiecta membra*, no one throws any ray of light upon any other, and the question, why they are all found together on a tablet discovered at Heraclea, is regarded as too insoluble to be approached at all.

I may frankly explain why I am desirous of dealing briefly with some of Prof. Reid's main points. If they are accepted, or allowed to pass unchallenged, all the more constructive portion of my own article (see preceding Essay, No. VIII), always courteously referred to by him, would fall to the ground. I was of course never sanguine enough to expect any wide acceptance of my conclusions in a region littered with shattered or obsolete hypotheses, but I am reluctant to allow Prof. Reid's unqualified verdict of 'unacceptable' to go forth against them without some criticism of the arguments on which that verdict rests. I shall therefore, without any unnecessary re-statement of my own position, make an attempt to disarm the fresh objections made to it, and then ask the perhaps very small public, sufficiently interested in the discussion, to re-examine my paper in the light of criticisms made and replies offered.

THE PROFESSI.

With regard to the first section of the Table, and especially its relation to Caesar's reform of the *frumentationes*, I may perhaps be allowed to refer to a re-statement of my own interpretation in the *Classical Quarterly* (Jan. 1917) in connexion with a theory put forward by Prof. Jefferson Elmore (*J. R. S.* vol. v, part 1). I am glad to find that Prof. Reid rejects that theory on grounds which do not differ essentially from those used by me. As far as its bearing upon the nature of the whole document is concerned, I should be well content with the hypothesis which Prof. Reid substitutes for that which we both reject, for, if I understand him rightly, he regards lines 1–19 as forming part of the law in accordance with which Caesar's *recensus* and corn reforms were carried out. That is also my view. But I cannot agree with the hypothesis, now for the first time put forward, as to the persons who are to make the *professio*, and whose names and declarations are to be recorded in the public archives and posted up in the forum.

According to Prof. Reid they were the *domini insularum*, through whose agency Caesar is said by Suetonius (*Iul.* xli) to have effected the *recensus populi* in the city district by district (*vicatim*).[1] I quite agree that the selection of the *domini insularum* to carry out the *recensus* is a proof that for the future there were to be no recipients of corn outside the tenants in the *insulae*. Accordingly, we are told, the first step in Caesar's reform was to disqualify from the receipt of corn all owners of house property in Rome, as well as all those who, as occupants of separate houses, could have no equitable claim on the score of narrow means (p. 218). I do not discuss the question here whether the legal

[1] It will perhaps be convenient to quote the passage of Suetonius. *Recensum populi nec more nec loco solito sed vicatim per dominos insularum egit atque ex viginti trecentisque milibus accipientium frumentum e publico ad centum quinquaginta retraxit; ac ne qui novi coetus recensionis causa moveri quandoque possent, instituit, quotannis in demortuorum locum ex iis, qui recensi non essent, subsortitio a praetore fieret.*

disqualification of these classes was necessary, or whether the *frumentationes* had always been for the poor alone, since Prof. Reid admits that the well-to-do had all along been practically excluded by considerations of social respectability and pride.

It was, therefore, to the inhabitants of the *insulae* only that the *recensus* was applied, but instead of the persons affected having to present themselves before a magistrate, Prof. Reid believes that the owners of the *insulae* were required to make a *professio* of all their tenants who were Roman citizens domiciled in Rome, the aliens and minors being omitted from the returns. Any owners of *insulae* absent from Rome, when the returns had to be made, could make their declarations through business agents, while those still in the position of *pupilli* or *pupillae* could make them through their legal guardians. In this way the passage of Suetonius is brought into connexion with the Table. The *professi* of the latter are the *domini insularum* making returns of their tenants, while all those persons, whose names are thus returned, are the *recensi* of Suetonius. I will merely note at this point that, if this explanation takes full account of the words *per dominos insularum*, it seems to ignore the word *vicatim*. If that word means anything, it must mean that the *domini* made their returns locally, that is, in each *vicus* where they had property, whereas the *professiones* of the Table are clearly all made to the same central magistrates.

Putting this, however, on one side, we are told that the most radical part of Caesar's reform was the reduction of this total number of persons enumerated (*recensi*) or returned to a fixed maximum of 150,000. But this reduction, according to Prof. Reid, followed upon, and formed no part of the *recensus*. The latter was a mere enumeration of those returned by the *domini*, while the former, he argues, must have been effected by a *sortitio*. This method would involve the least break with the hitherto accepted principle of equal claims for all, and is also indicated by the use of the term *subsortitio* in connexion with the annual maintenance of the number. Again, the *recensus* and the *sortitio* which followed it were, in Prof. Reid's view, processes which took place once and once only. All the *recensi* were so far on an equality that they were all admitted to the *sortitio*, but those failing to secure a place among the 150,000 would remain permanently excluded, for there was no reason why any citizen should have more than his one chance. Vacancies in the list of recipients, caused by death or removal, were to be annually filled up by means of a *subsortitio*, applied solely to persons who had not been enumerated at all, *ex iis qui recensi non essent.* At first sight it might seem difficult to find such persons, and the difficulty, as I have shown, is fatal to Prof. Elmore's system, but Prof. Reid declares them to have been those who had either become adult, or had domiciled themselves in Rome during the current year. These persons, like the original tenants in the *insulae*, we must suppose to have been presented to the praetor who managed the *subsortitio* through a *professio* made by the *domini insularum*, but somewhat arbitrarily we are forbidden to regard them as *recensi.* Presumably, too, the principle of one chance only would be applied to these annual applicants for a place on the list. The various hypotheses involved in this explanation not only, it is contended, bring the statement of Suetonius into intelligible relation to the Table, but get rid of three great stumbling-blocks, the penalization of the *professi* by exclusion from the *frumentationes*, the mention of *pupilli* and *pupillae*, who are seen to be, not would-be corn recipients, but owners of *insulae*, and the necessity, involved in some other explanations,[1] of supposing something like 170,000 names to have been posted up in the forum.

That this explanation is a great improvement on Prof. Elmore's, with which, however, it has more than one point in common, I do not deny. But it is not only, as its author admits, unsupported by evidence, but, while introducing fresh difficulties of its own, is not consistent with a satisfactory interpretation of Suetonius. According to this theory, Caesar's reform, resulting in the restricted list of 150,000 recipients of corn, consisted of three stages: (1) the preliminary disqualification of all owners of house property and all occupiers of separate houses, (2) the enumeration (*recensus*) with the help of the *domini* of all citizens domiciled in Rome and living in *insulae*, and (3) the application of a *sortitio* to these *recensi*, involving the permanent exclusion of all save the prearranged number of 150,000 on whom the lot fell. Now this

[1] This difficulty is inherent in Prof. Elmore's view, but not, as Prof. Reid seems to assume, in mine. This will appear below.

view obviously depends on the assumption that the *recensus* was pure enumeration, with no element of selection, and therefore not what Dio calls it, an ἐξέτασις, and further, that both the *recensus* and the *recensi* dropped out of all relation to the *frumentationes* when once the supposed *sortitio* had taken place.

But why should a *recensus* any more than a *census* signify a mere counting of heads? Why should it not connote a process first of reaching a total by means of enumeration, and then of reducing it by some selective method to a smaller total? Surely Prof. Reid cuts the ground from under his own feet by first declaring that there is no difference between *recensus* and *recensio*, and then admitting that the latter can be used to describe the censorial register. In every passage where the word *recensus* is used (Suet. *Iul.* xli; *Aug.* xlii; Liv. *epit.* cxv)[1] it is not only in connexion with the corn distributions, but is closely associated, if not identified, with the reduction in the number of recipients. That the *recensus* and the reduction were not only parts of the same scheme, but involved one another, seems to me certain from the first sentence quoted above from Suetonius. Again, if Caesar adopted the method of selective exclusion in the case of the owners of *domus* and *insulae* (and Prof. Reid says that he did), is it not reasonable to assume that he would have adopted some analogous method with the 320,000, found by the *recensus* to be present recipients? Or are we to assume that the differences between comfortable and straitened means within that number were so slight as to be negligible? But, if we are justified in giving this wider scope to the *recensus*, and in regarding it as really an ἐξέτασις, and not a mere enumeration, then it would seem far more natural to understand by the term *recensi* not the first list gained by counting, but the reduced list of 150,000 persons, which after all was the final cause of the whole process.

Nor is there any validity in the inference from the use of the term *subsortitio* that there must have been a previous *sortitio*. The word simply means the appointment of substitutes by lot, and is therefore exactly appropriate, where it is not the creation of a list *de novo* that is in question, but the filling up of gaps in a list already existing, however that list was originally formed. I may add that the attempt to link up the *subsortitio* with a

[1] I have discussed the passages fully in the *Classical Quarterly*.

preceding *sortitio* is peculiarly unfortunate on Prof. Reid's theory, because the two processes are applied to essentially different categories, the persons submitted to the *sortitio* being absolutely ineligible for the *subsortitio*.

Once more, if the *recensus* was over and done with as soon as the total of 320,000 *recensi* was arrived at, how was it that Caesar foresaw in future years the possibility of disorderly assemblies *recensionis causa*? This phrase, which Prof. Reid only notices in remarking that *recensus* and *recensio* are identical, is really fatal to his theory. It proves that the *recensus* was not a process which took place once and once only, since the *subsortitio* is represented as a contrivance for making the *recensio* in future years more orderly. The passage also proves that those *qui recensi non essent* were eager to become *recensi*, and if so, the *recensi* must have been something more than a mere enumerated total; they must have been a select class with privileges attached to it.

I may notice here that Prof. Reid never makes it clear whether in his view the 320,000 persons of Suetonius represent the total of all burgesses domiciled in Rome (i.e. for him, the total of potential recipients) or merely the total of those dwelling in the *insulae* (a total practically co-extensive with actual recipients). If the former, his *recensi*, to whom the supposed *sortitio* was applied, would be appreciably less than 320,000. If the latter, there would have been no need to disqualify the *domini insularum* &c., since they were already outside the total which Suetonius declares to have been that of recipients up to the time of the *recensus*.

But apart from what seems to me the misinterpretation of *recensus*, *recensi*, *recensionis causa*, and *subsortitio*, let us see whether the identification of the *professi* with the *domini insularum* makes the first section of the Table easier to understand. The names of the *professi* as well as the contents of their declarations (*ea quae professus erit*) are not only to be preserved in the public archives, but also posted up legibly in the forum at the place where corn is distributed. We know that in the fourth century A.D. there were in Rome over 44,000 *insulae*, but it is obvious that no safe inference can be drawn from this as to the number of *domini insularum* in Caesar's time. Indeed, though we may have some misgivings, there is little to be said for or against Prof. Reid's contention that their number was sufficiently small for the list to be manageable and of practical utility. But a much greater difficulty lies in the fact that along with the names of the *domini insularum* (if these were the *professi*) there had to be published the contents of their returns, *ea quae professus erit*. This would mean, if Prof. Reid's view of the *recensus* is correct, that each *dominus* would have to return at least the names, if no other details, of all the eligible tenants in his *insula* or *insulae*, so that even if the number of *domini* was manageable, the list would have to include the names of 320,000 tenants. Prof. Reid admits that the magistrate would be obliged to have these names for the purpose of the *sortitio*, and of course the complete list might well be placed in the *tabularium*. But how could they be contained on a notice-board in the forum so as to be legible to the public? To meet this, Prof. Reid, disregarding the provision of the Table that the lists in the archives and in the forum were to be duplicates, suggests that the latter was a mere summary, containing the names of the *domini*, and under each the number of those returned by him in this or that *insula*. Even if we were justified in taking such a liberty of interpretation, it is difficult to see how such information would interest the public, for whom the notice was clearly intended. What the people would be anxious to know was not how many tenants each *dominus* had, but whether their own names were duly submitted to the *sortitio*. Nor is the clause excluding the *professi* from the *frumentationes* more but less intelligible on this hypothesis. For not only does it assume that the *domini insularum* as well as occupants of separate houses have already been specifically disqualified, but, even if they had not been, the nature of the *professio* made by the former so clearly put them outside the ranks of the *recensi*, who alone were entitled to the *sortitio*, that this additional safeguard, as Prof. Reid calls it, would be quite unnecessary.

With regard to the stumbling-block caused by the mention among the *professi* of *pupilli* and *pupillae*, Prof. Reid surmounts it neither more nor less successfully than Prof. Elmore. If these minors were not applicants for the *frumentationes*, but either owners of tenement houses registering their tenants, or owners of property making an annual return of it, it is of course natural that their names and statements should be lodged in the *tabularium*, but why, if as minors they were ineligible for the corn distributions, should they appear in the forum list, and share in a prohibition, which in their case was *ex hypothesi* superfluous?

In dealing with the *subsortitio*, Prof. Reid has his own explanation of the statement of Suetonius that it was applied each year to those *qui recensi non essent*. The *recensi*, i.e. those enumerated in the *recensus*, had all had their chance in the *sortitio*, and all but 150,000 had lost it, and lost it permanently. However many vacancies occurred in the privileged list, they were hopelessly left out in the cold. This is what Prof. Reid regards as a system involving the least possible break with the older régime, in which all citizens had been on an equality. But each year saw minors becoming adult, and fresh citizens domiciled in Rome from outside, and these were the *non recensi* to whom the *subsortitio* was applied. If Prof. Reid thinks that such an arrangement would have prevented the disorderly assemblies which, according to Suetonius, Caesar hoped to prevent by the *subsortitio*, I cannot agree with him. Would the older citizens, many of whom had shared in the corn doles for years, and perhaps needed them no less than those favoured by the lot, be content quietly to stand aside and see the coveted vacancies filled by these youths and interlopers, or can we ascribe to Caesar an arrangement so inequitable and so provocative?

Prof. Reid finds in Suetonius a clear implication that the persons admitted to the *subsortitio* were few in number. I fail myself to discover this implication. But, if, as I believe, the *recensus* was the whole process by which the list of 150,000, the *recensi*, came into existence, not by lot, but by some sifting and ἐξέτασις, it is not necessary to suppose that all the excluded, *qui recensi non essent*, perhaps something like 170,000 in number, were allowed to register themselves as candidates for the *subsortitio*. The *recensus* would have revealed, and perhaps classified, degrees of poverty, and the same selective method, which had marked out the 150,000, would also decide each year, taking account of the number of vacancies, how many and who might properly make the *professio* as candidates for the *subsortitio*. That the number of *professi* was somehow limited, is shown by the phrase in line 1—*quem profiterei oportebit.* As probably most of those whose names appeared in the forum had received corn in the past, and all had equal hopes of a lucky draw, there might be a risk that careless magistrates might anticipate the *subsortitio*, and it was to meet this risk that the prohibiting clause was inserted. On the whole, it seems to me that this new hypothesis, though in some respects preferable to that of Prof. Elmore, is not in harmony with the evidence, and creates more difficulties than it solves.

The questions involved in the second section of the Table in connexion with certain aedilician duties it is not necessary to reopen, as I find myself in substantial agreement with all that Prof. Reid says. He does not indeed accept the very slight positive indications of Caesarian date, but he admits, I think, that no period was more appropriate to such regulations.

It is when we come to the three divisions of the third section, dealing (*a*) with qualifications and disqualifications for municipal office, (*b*) with the municipal *census* in Italy, and (*c*) with instructions to commissioners sent to *municipia fundana*, that Prof. Reid finds my position unacceptable.

SECTION III (*a*).

I confess that I find it hard to discover any positive conclusion at all, or the solution of any difficulty in Prof. Reid's treatment of this division of the Table. He starts with the assumption that in this, as in the following sub-section, we are dealing with 'extracts from laws or contemplated laws dealing with municipal affairs in Italy', but declines to regard the two sets of provisions as belonging to the same law, or to accept for either any indication of date except the reference to the Sullan murder agents, which points for sub-section (*a*) to a date later than 64 B.C. He is, however, clearly averse to the Caesarian date, especially for sub-section (*b*), and therefore, we must assume, would place both the original laws between 64 or 62 B.C. and the opening of the civil war.[1] I must point out at once, though I may have

[1] It is inferred that sub-section (*a*) is later than 64 because it was in that year that Sulla's exemption of his agents from the charge of murder was ignored by Caesar (Suet. *Iul.* xi). With regard to the census regulations, it is inferred from *pro Arch.* xi that they were probably later than 62.

to return to it, a noticeable inconsistency in Prof. Reid's position as to the treatment of Italian municipalities after the Social war. On the one hand, he is explicit in holding that no general obligatory law was ever passed interfering with the internal affairs of the Italian cities which accepted the *lex Iulia*, while he reiterates his assertion that it was by spontaneous assimilation, and not by legislative compulsion, that municipal institutions were developed. On the other hand, it appears that, even before we come to the legislative activity of Caesar, there are extracts from at least two general obligatory laws[1] interfering very drastically with the internal arrangements of Italian towns, and enforcing their regulations with severe sanctions. I do not know whether it is a consciousness of this contradiction that presently induces Prof. Reid to withdraw his assumption, at least as far as sub-section (*a*) is concerned, that it is an extract from an actual law.[2] 'The category of circumstances, presented in the *Tabula*, which shut out men from municipal honours, bears in its front no sign of having been extracted from a statute, but rather the opposite' (p. 235). What leads to this conclusion is the unexampled slovenliness of the document, which points to the production of an amateur, not of an expert legislator. This slovenliness is illustrated in several ways. (*a*) By surplusage of expression, of which, however, only three doubtful instances are given. In l. 132 we have *comitiis conciliove*; in l. 98 *comitiis* alone. Prof. Reid cannot explain *concilio*, therefore it is otiose. In l. 107 we have *neque dicere neve ferre sententiam*, and he gives reasons, perhaps good ones, against the usual distinction drawn between these phrases. In l. 122 we have in connexion with rewards received by Sulla's agents *qui cepit ceperit*, and it is argued, with no point that I can see, that, as provision against the repetition of such an act would be futile, the engraver must have inadvertently, through familiarity with the collocation of the two tenses, inserted the word *ceperit*.[3] (*b*) Clauses seem

[1] That they were both general laws in the sense of binding all Italian communities, is sufficiently obvious. As both sub-sections are 'extracts', there is a presumption that both laws contained other compulsory provisions.

[2] The hypothesis of a contemplated law seems unjustifiable, unless it can be suggested how an extract from an abortive law found its way on to a bronze at Heraclea.

[3] I do not understand why so much importance is attached to this point, or why I am so pointedly reproved for expressing a confident opinion which

occasionally to be omitted. Only a single instance, however, in this sub-section is given, though another is suggested in the census regulations after l. 156. Very much the same matter is dealt with in ll. 98–107 and 126–34, and yet the sanction, which concludes the former provisions, is absent in the latter. Surely such points, even if there were more of them, are negligible as arguments to show that we are not dealing with 'a certified copy from an original source'. (*c*) A good deal more puzzling is the fact that, while in ll. 83–8 and 108–25 the restrictions and prohibitions apply to *municipia*, *coloniae*, *praefecturae*, *fora*, and *conciliabula*, the intervening lines 89–107 omit the two last classes, so that, as the document stands, there was no reason why a *praeco* should not be a *decurio* in a *forum* or *conciliabulum*.[1] I will only say with regard to this somewhat striking inconsistency that, if it is due to slovenliness, the fault is more likely to have lain with the engraver than with an amateur draftsman, while, if the variation is intentional, however the reason for it may elude us, it points to more method about the composition of the document than Prof. Reid allows for. (*d*) But what he lays most stress upon is 'the chaotic character of the disqualifications in lines 108–25'. It is impossible to believe them drawn up by a Roman legislator, or passed into law by the *comitia*, since 'as they appear on the *Tabula*, they bear the guise of a collection of notes jotted down as the framer chanced to think of them, or had come across them in study or experience'. I think that any one who takes the trouble to refer to

unfortunately differs from his own. At any rate, his reasons for rejecting *ceperit* seem wholly irrelevant. 'It is difficult to believe that any legislation would be directed against a repetition of the horrors consequent upon the Sullan edict'; and 'to enact a penalty in anticipation of such an event would be obviously futile' (p. 233). But the object of the legislation on the Table was not to prevent the repetition of any of the moral or legal delinquencies enumerated, nor to enact penalties for them. It simply declared that persons who had done certain things, or should do them in future, were ineligible for municipal senates. If *ceperit* were omitted, the receivers of blood money in future proscriptions would not be affected, and as proscriptions were admittedly in the air, no legislator, least of all Caesar, would have neglected the eventuality.

[1] Prof. Reid regards this as a *reductio ad absurdum*, but may it not suggest a possible clue to the difficulty? The restrictions on *adlectio* (ll. 83–8) and the disqualifications on moral grounds (ll. 108–25) apply to all communities, large and small. But the restrictions as to age and occupation are tacitly left more elastic in the smaller places, where a narrower circle would be available for municipal office. This would be somewhat analogous to the exceptional eligibility of freedmen in the *colonia Iulia Genetiva*.

the list, will agree with me that the absence of order is much exaggerated. No doubt we should have expected to find condemnation in criminal courts placed along with the other cases of conviction at the beginning of the list, while taking the gladiatorial oath is curiously sandwiched in between disqualifications of quite another character. But with these exceptions there is a certain method and order, and even if there had been less, the person responsible for the document was more likely to have been carelessly citing or copying an original than inserting his own random notes in what at least purported to be a legal provision. This last point is proved by the opening words of the clause immediately following the list of disqualifications: *Quod hac lege in municipio colonia praefectura foro conciliabulo senatorem . . . esse . . . non licebit*, &c. (l. 126).

But it is not only the chaotic classification of the disqualifications that Prof. Reid depends on. He argues, if I understand him rightly, that legal disqualifications to office were in themselves contrary to Roman usage. According to that usage, the admission or rejection of candidates at elections was a matter not of law but of custom, being left to the discretion of the presiding magistrate, who might, if he thought fit, ask the advice of the senate. This is of course true, and if the clauses in question had purported to affect Rome, the objection would have been to the point. But what was left to magisterial, and especially censorial, discretion at Rome might well be reinforced by legal sanctions in Italian towns, where there were no censors, and where the magistrates had no authority comparable with that of the holders of *imperium* in the capital.[1]

[1] Another argument used by Prof. Reid illustrates the danger of quoting from memory. He declares (p. 233) that a clause in the *lex Malacitana* (c. 54) provides that disqualifications are to be as at Rome, no special enactment being mentioned. This last point, it is argued, would be inconceivable, if a law so important as a *lex Iulia* had been in existence, specifying the disqualifications. In the first place, the *lex Iulia municipalis* did not affect Rome at all, and therefore on Prof. Reid's citation of the passage, we should not expect it to be mentioned. But, as a matter of fact, the clause in the *lex Malac.* says nothing about Rome, but declares candidates to be ineligible, in whose case there is any impediment *propter quam, si civis Romanus esset, in numero decurionum conscriptorumve esse non liceret.* This certainly points to a general and compulsory rule being in force in Domitian's time with regard to the senates of burgess communities in Italy or the provinces. This need not of course have been the *lex Iulia municipalis*, which under the imperial system had

But even where Prof. Reid, contrary, I think, to his real view, speaks of this sub-section as if it were an extract from an actual law, he still maintains that there is no indication of date, and that the only reason for assigning it to Caesar's time is the fact that other provisions on the Table may reasonably be referred to that period. This brings us to Cicero's letter to Lepta (*ad fam.* vi, 18), written at the beginning of 45 B.C., which I have argued, as against Legras, to be conclusively in favour not only of Caesarian date, but of Caesarian authorship. Prof. Reid sweeps away the inference, which so many scholars have held and hold to be irresistible, with an off-hand and arbitrary pronouncement that though there is evidence in the letter that Caesar drafted a law bearing on qualifications for local senates, and some presumption that such a law was passed, 'it affords no proof whatever that this portion of the *Tabula* was extracted from the law'. The disability of *praecones* was of long standing, as proved by the regulations made by Claudius Pulcher for Halesa in 95 B.C. (*in Verr.* ii, 49, 122).

Cicero's words prove nothing except that Caesar's projected law was to make no change in this respect. But is Prof. Reid sure that the disability, as stated on the Table, i.e. limited to those actually carrying on the trade of a *praeco*, was of long standing? He may have grounds for his statement which he does not produce, but the words *de quaestu quem qui fecisset ne legeretur* show that at Halesa at any rate the disability was not so limited. When therefore Prof. Reid talks of Caesar's projected law making no change, he is begging the whole question, viz. the identity or non-identity of the provision on the Table with Caesar's provision, for he assumes that the provision on the Table was earlier than Caesar, and that he merely repeated it in his law. It is obvious that he can only escape from this dilemma by proving that this carefully defined disability was older than Caesar. On his view, Seleucus, a *praeco* or *ex-praeco*, must have known of the existing regulation, that *praecones* were ineligible only till they relinquished the trade, but feared that the new law might make the disability more stringent. In view of Caesar's well-known policy with regard to admission

probably long since become obsolete, but the disqualifications alluded to may for all that have owed their origin to that law.

to the Roman senate this seems improbable. If Caesar contemplated changes, all would expect not greater stringency but great liberality. Seleucus, it seems to me, must have heard rumours that the old disability was to be modified, and it was his anxiety to get first-hand evidence on the point which led up to Cicero's letter to Lepta. If we take into account all the indications available, the balance inclines to the view that Caesar's provision, as reported by Balbus to Cicero, was a change and a concession, and not, as Prof. Reid thinks, the retention of an old rule. If so, the coincidence, so often insisted upon, between the information given by Balbus and line 94 of the Table is far too striking to be other than conclusive.

But there is more to be said. If the provision on the Table was in existence before Caesar's dictatorship, why should he have legislated on the subject, and if he did pass a law about the qualifications of *decuriones in municipiis*, what title was more appropriate to such a law than *lex Iulia municipalis*? Prof. Reid can only answer these questions by putting forward an hypothesis for which there is no solid basis whatever. There is nothing to show, he declares, that the projected law of Caesar was of a general character, i.e. like the clauses on the Table, applicable to all Italian towns. Even from this I fear I must dissent, for the antithesis between *in senatum Romae legerentur* and *in municipiis decuriones esse* surely marks the latter as a generic phrase. But, it is urged, Seleucus is a Greek name, and we know from Strabo that 500 distinguished Greeks received the nominal citizenship of Novum Comum in 59 B.C. Therefore Seleucus probably belonged to Novum Comum, and Caesar's projected law may have been one of a series of special enactments for Cisalpine Gaul, such as the *lex Rubria* and the *Fragmentum Atestinum*. The only thing to be said for this hypothesis is that, if accepted, it would get Prof. Reid out of a difficulty. I will merely point out, (1) that the distinguished Greeks, who had received the citizenship of Novum Comum fourteen years before, were non-resident, and would therefore have no interest in these disqualifications; (2) that, if Seleucus was a *praeco*, he could not have been one of the distinguished Greeks specially honoured by Caesar in 59; and (3) that there is no evidence whatever for a series of special laws for Cisalpine Gaul in addition to the *lex Rubria*, the *Fragmentum Atestinum* being almost certainly part of the latter law;[1] (4) that, if qualifications and disqualifications for office were not likely to be defined by legislation in Italians towns, there seems no reason why the case should have been different in the towns of Cisalpine Gaul.

As the result of the foregoing considerations, I cannot accept Prof. Reid's two main conclusions with regard to this sub-section; (1) that in all probability it is not an extract from any law actually passed; and (2) that, even if such a law was passed, there is no indication, either in the letter of Cicero or elsewhere, that it was passed by Caesar, or in the Caesarian period.

SECTION III (*b*).

This sub-section, which provides for a census of Roman citizens in all *municipia*, *coloniae*, and *praefecturae* of Italy, whenever a census is held in Rome, need not detain us long. Prof. Reid regards it as an extract from a law or contemplated law, but not from the same law as that which contained the previous sub-section, and he insists that there is no point of connexion or coherence between these two parts of the Table. I do not see that this consideration has any weight, for, though I assume both chapters to belong to the same law, I do not suppose them to be consecutive chapters, and therefore we need not look for more logical connexion between them than between any other two parts of the Table.

I had ventured to lay down three points about the census scheme of the Table, (1) that its object was to secure the simultaneous census of all Italy, (2) that the amount of labour, combination, and organization involved in it would have been such that few statesmen besides Caesar would have faced it, and (3) that even Caesar stopped short at Italy, and shrank from the task of co-ordinating in one vast simultaneous census all the Roman citizens domiciled in colonies, *municipia*, and Latin communities throughout the empire. Prof. Reid does not like any of these suggestions. (1) The object was not a simultaneous census, for 'that was already provided by the system

[1] On this point I may be allowed to refer to my essay on the *lex Rubria* above, No. vii. On the hypothesis that the last paragraph of the Table refers to *municipia fundana* in Cisalpine Gaul only, see below.

which required all burgessess to be registered at Rome. Its purpose was rather decentralization' and is comparable with the plan of Augustus for allowing the Italian colonies to send their votes to Rome at elections instead of attending the *comitia.* I agree with all this except the statement that a simultaneous census was already provided for. It was probably just because the *frequentia Italiae*, carried out for the last time in 70, had proved impracticable that decentralization by means of a simultaneous census was resorted to. (2) It is argued that the simultaneous census, even if it had extended to the provinces, would have been far less complex than the republican practice, and that it is therefore not necessary to postulate as its author a statesman of Caesar's calibre. I reply that it was the difference between a cumbrous, unworkable method with no system, no guarantee of complete registration, and no adequate organization, and a systematic and thorough handling of the problem which, though involving innumerable officials and immense labour, was calculated to achieve its object. To what statesman after 62 B.C. other than Caesar would Prof. Reid attribute so wide-reaching a measure, and if it was Caesar's law, was any date so probable as during the dictatorship?[1] (3) But 'it is strange that Caesar, if he was the author of the scheme, should have confined it to Italy. He was the first Roman leader who carried out on a large scale the policy of multiplying Roman communities abroad, and for these decentralization was more important than for Italian cities.' Undoubtedly the scheme on the Table took no account of Roman citizens domiciled in urban communities outside Italy, and would therefore not produce an exhaustive census. But neither would it have produced an exhaustive census if it had belonged to the period between 62 and 49 B.C., for not only would one or two Spanish colonies and Narbo in Gaul have been omitted, but the important burgess colonies in Cisalpine Gaul, and the ever-increasing number of Roman citizens domiciled in the Latin towns of the Transpadane country. As for the far more numerous Roman colonies, Latin

[1] The theory of the careless engraver is surely pushed to its extreme limit, when the significant phrase *censor aliusve quis magistratus* is eluded by the suggestion that it is 'a mere mechanical and inaccurate imitation' of the same phrase used in the second section of the Table. I merely note the suggestion which, as an argument, can convince no one.

colonies, and *municipia civium Romanorum* in Caesar's time, there may have been several reasons why he did not include them in his simultaneous census. Not the least would be, as I suggested, the greatly increased labour and organization required, if the returns from Gaul, Spain, Africa, and even remote colonies in the East had to reach the censor at or about some fixed date. No doubt decentralization would be essential, but its method might vary from that adopted within Italy. It would be more natural for the governor of each province to be made responsible for the census being carried out, and ultimately to forward the returns received by him and his staff to Rome. It would be easier in this way to make allowances for differences in distance and means of communication. If Prof. Reid thinks that the regulations on the Table could have been supplemented by the addition of a few words so as to make them applicable to the provinces, I fancy that an attempt to draft such a supplement would convince him of his mistake. As a matter of fact, Caesar's scheme for extra-Italian colonization was perhaps only in its infancy in 45 B.C., and he may well have intended to wait for its further development before making the simultaneous census universal and imperial instead of Italian.

SECTION III (*c*).

The last sub-section, evidently forming the conclusion of the Table, contains a provision that commissioners, who have been empowered to frame *leges datae* for *municipia fundana,* may within a year after the passing of the law make additions, changes, and corrections in their charters. Prof. Reid considers this, as I do, to be the most important portion of the Table, but he apparently only means by this that it raises the most important and perplexing questions. To the clause itself no importance whatever seems to be assigned, and no explanation of its object is suggested.

The first of these questions is concerned with the meaning of the term *municipia fundana,* but though the discussion raises some interesting points, it throws little light upon the clause in the Table, because it is contended that the term, as employed in it, has some special and exceptional meaning which no attempt is made to determine. Apart from this special sense, whatever it may be, and as applied to Italian towns, the term would seem to denote either towns which had accepted or become *fundi* to the *lex Iulia de civitate*, or towns which had accepted the whole of the Roman *ius civile*. I prefer the latter interpretation, though the former would not upset my conclusions as to the document as a whole. Prof. Reid apparently at one time took the same view himself, for he says in the Municipalities of the Roman Empire (p. 113) that a *municipium fundanum* was 'a town not originally Roman, which had accepted the Roman franchise and a Roman form of law'. He has now, however, come to the conclusion, contrary to what he admits to be the almost universal belief, that Italian towns, on accepting the *lex Iulia* and becoming communities of Roman citizens, did not commit themselves to the necessity of substituting Roman law for 'the law by which they had been previously governed', and that more probably the acceptance of the *lex Iulia* left their internal codes untouched. A couple of quotations will make his conception sufficiently clear. 'To me the idea that a great number of communities first had their laws made identical with those of the Romans, and then that the function of the *lex data* was to introduce differences, such as certainly existed at a later date, seems unnatural' (p. 239). Again, in remarking on my suggestion that probably there was not much activity in sending out commissioners earlier than 59 B.C., he asks what was the position of the towns up to that date. 'Were they tightly bound to Roman law for the thirty years between 89 and 59 B.C., and then did the commissioners introduce relaxation? Did laws passed at Rome during those thirty years become automatically part of the local code, or was it still needful for the communities to give express assent to them? Did the acceptance of the *lex Iulia* put an end to the freedom of legislation within the local communities?' (p. 240). I venture to think that all the difficulties and anomalies which these passages conjure up are purely imaginary, and are wholly due to the confusion between 'Roman law' and 'Roman laws', and to the loose use of the term 'codes'.

When I say that Italian towns, on accepting the franchise, became *fundi* to Roman law, I mean that, as communities of

Roman citizens, they naturally and *ipso facto* adopted the whole body of the Roman *ius civile*, and became subject in the last resort to the praetor's supreme jurisdiction. In the sense that there could be no option about this adoption of Roman law by Romans, the change was compulsory, but the *innumerabiles de civili iure leges* already voluntarily adopted, and the manifest advantages of the adoption both to individuals and communities,[1] would make the obligatory aspect fade out of sight. The towns then were, if Prof. Reid likes the phrase, tightly bound to Roman law (not from any yearning for uniformity, but from the inherent conception of a common citizenship), and the commissioners with their *leges datae* introduced no differences, and made no relaxation in this respect. The *leges datae* were not municipal codes of law, but municipal charters, regulating the political constitution and preserving or creating a miscellaneous collection of local administrative by-laws, in which, while there was probably general uniformity, there was room for many differences of detail. The position of a town, therefore, before a commissioner was sent to it was one in which, while subject of course to the *ius civile*, and to any new *leges de civili iure*, it was free to retain, if it chose, its existing ordinance, political and municipal. As for new laws, other than those *de civili iure*, potentially the *municipia fundana* would be bound by them, that is, as far as the scope of the law affected them, but I should doubt the propriety of saying that these laws became part of the municipal codes. Where laws affected national or imperial interests, *de nostra republica*, *de nostro imperio*, *de nostris bellis*, *de victoria*, *de salute*, there had never been, even before the enfranchisement, any option of accepting or rejecting them (*pro Balb.* xxii).[2]

Though it did not appear to me to be open to any doubt that all burgess communities would be *ipso facto* subject to the

[1] A few Greek cities might prefer the *libertatem foederis* (a phrase surely implying the alternative of compulsion), but there is no other indication of reluctance to accept either the franchise or Roman law. The point of law at Arpinum diverging from Roman usage is surely one of the exceptions that prove the rule. Cato would never have mentioned it if it had not been exceptional.

[2] As for what Prof. Reid calls 'the freedom of legislation within each community', it appears from extant *leges datae* that whatever corresponded to legislation was in the hands of the *decuriones*, and that it still continued within the limits set by the charter.

Roman *ius civile*, I indicated four incidental proofs of it. Prof. Reid's treatment of these calls for some reply. (1) I cited Cicero's words (*pro Balb.* xxi) *ipsa denique Iulia, qua lege civitas est sociis et Latinis data, qui fundi populi facti non essent, civitatem non haberent.* He denies their relevancy on the ground that *fundi* has no wider application than to the *lex Iulia* itself. As a matter of fact, the words quoted are inconclusive apart from their context, and I now rest my position not on them so much as on their place in Cicero's whole argument in sections 19 to 22. It would be out of proportion to discuss here at length what for my present object is a minor point, but the whole passage of the *pro Balbo* will be found fully discussed in the following essay (No. X). I will only note, as emerging from the argument, (*a*) that only federate states (*Latini et socii*), and not burgess communities, are spoken of as becoming *fundi* to Roman laws, the reason being surely that the latter were already subject to them. (*b*) The essence of the term *fundus fieri* is voluntary adoption, a point ignored by such expressions as 'tightly bound to Roman law', and 'having their laws made identical with those of the Romans'. (*c*) The reluctance of Heraclea and Naples to accept the citizenship is unintelligible, if its acceptance 'merely entitled the cities to the privileges of Roman citizens, and left their internal codes untouched' (p. 239).

(2) I declared that the whole meaning and object of the *lex Rubria* implies that the enfranchised towns of Gallia Cisalpina had adopted the Roman *ius civile.* Prof. Reid's question—if the complete Roman code had been accepted, why pass the *lex Rubria*?—makes me wonder what his conception of the *lex Rubria* can possibly be. My own is to be found fully stated in Essay No. VII above. If I am asked how the law indicates that the Transpadane cities, on becoming Roman, adopted the entire Roman code, I adduce the following points. (*a*) The directions for judicial procedure contained in it are applicable in all the communities of the enfranchised province. (*b*) The magistrates may set up a *iudicium* for *damnum infectum*, a process of Roman civil law, applying a formula from the praetor's *album.* (*c*) They may also conduct a *legitimum iudicium*, possible only between Roman citizens, for *certa pecunia credita*, an action notoriously peculiar to Roman law. (*d*) There is under specified

conditions, e.g. if more than the sum of 15,000 sesterces is at stake, provision for a *revocatio Romae.* (*e*) This *revocatio Romae* is shown by the *Fragmentum Atestinum* to have been non-existent before the enfranchising *lex Roscia* of 49 B.C., which is obviously the dividing-line between two different juristic systems. (*f*) The fact that such extreme steps as *ductio, missio in possessionem*, and *proscriptio bonorum* are reserved for the praetor, is inconsistent with the supposition that the towns retained their own internal codes. (*g*) It is provided in the *Fragmentum Atestinum* that certain cases of delict are to be tried in Rome, except where in cases involving less than 10,000 sesterces the defendant desires the case to be tried in the municipal court.

(3) I argued that many of the disqualifications for admission to municipal senates imply the validity of Roman law in Italian towns. Prof. Reid is not able to deny this, but he cryptically replies that this is not sufficient, since there should have been complete identity. I am quite at a loss to understand his point unless he means that nothing short of what logicians call induction by complete enumeration would justify the inference I have drawn.

(4) Apparently very much the same fallacy underlies his answer to my last instance. I cite the case of the Roman citizen at Salpensa, who is unable to manumit a slave, as the Latin citizen can, before the municipal *IIvir*, and has to go before the proconsul. I regard this as an indication that the Roman citizens lived under Roman law, while for the Latins there was their own municipal code. To object that this does not prove an identical form of manumission for all Roman colonies, and that even if it did, the proof relates to one process of law only, seems to me irrelevant.

Another proposition which Prof. Reid is very reluctant to accept is that the newly enfranchised towns of Italy, the *municipia fundana*, were compelled to receive *leges datae*, charters, or as he prefers to call them, municipal codes, at the hands of official commissioners. 'I do not believe in the generally accepted notion that every Italian community, on agreeing to become Roman, received from Rome a legislator, who drew up for it a *lex data* or new municipal code' (p. 241). Three classes of Italian towns are distinguished, the colonies, the small units raised to full municipal honours, and the old-established states which became parts of the Roman body politic. For the first two classes it is here admitted that *leges datae* were necessary. It is also admitted that, owing to special conditions, the newly enfranchised towns of Cisalpine Gaul, and the burgess and Latin communities in the Western provinces, would also have commissioners and *leges datae*. These admissions certainly clear the ground, and leave only the long-established states in Italy. For these, he declares, apparently quite unconscious that he is begging the question, there was no need for commissioners or *leges datae*, because their machinery was long-established. At the same time he guards himself against awkward instances by suggesting that in the event of internal dissensions, they might voluntarily call in an arbitrator to play the part, it might be, of an official commissioner.[1]

Presumably Prof. Reid would include under this class the cities which accepted the franchise under the *lex Iulia*, but there was surely a great difference between their case and that of states like Arpinum which had one by one become *municipia civium Romanorum*. The latter were comparatively few, entered the Roman body politic at different times, and, if they had not all passed through the intermediate stage of imperfect *municipia*, had probably more or less thoroughly already assimilated Roman forms. In these circumstances and at that period, the absence of system, in which Prof. Reid sees so much merit, may have been in place. But the *lex Iulia* marked a new epoch for Italy, and one that may well have called for greater uniformity. In the enfranchised communities the process of assimilation to Roman forms had reached very various stages; in some probably it had hardly begun at all. But the new conception of a *communis patria* and an *Italia tributim discripta* would call for something like a general acceptance of a *forma communis* in municipal government and administration. To bring this about, the system of *leges datae*, long since applied, as Prof. Reid

[1] In the case of Puteoli there was probably no official *lex data*, but, if he intends to apply his hypothesis of mere internal reform to Tarentum and Heraclea, or even to Arpinum, he has nothing tangible to support him, and in the case of Tarentum positive evidence against him.

admits, to important categories of towns, would seem the natural means. There is no need to assume that the system involved coercion or compulsion, since so much indulgence was shown to local anomalies and *consuetudo* that there was no motive for resistance, and there is no shred of evidence that the commissioners were unwelcome. He himself suggests that Heraclea and Naples came in by a vote of the majority of citizens.

It is of course true that of particular and actual *leges datae* between Sulla and Caesar there is little evidence. I call attention, however, to three points which in one way or another he evades. (1) The phrase in what the Digest calls the *lex agraria* of Caesar *qui h. l. coloniam deduxerit municipium praefecturam forum conciliabulum constituerit*, whether the law was passed in 59 or not, points to *leges datae* being at least contemplated not only for colonies, but for the other communities enumerated as well. He gives no explanation of, and indeed ignores, the point entirely. (2) The last paragraph of the Table implies that commissioners had been sent to draw up *leges datae* for *municipia fundana*. Prof. Reid, as we shall see below, escapes the natural inference by arbitrarily relegating the *municipia* to Cisalpine Gaul. (3) We have evidence of primary importance in the fragment of the Tarentine law. It is surely remarkable that in an article of 41 pages on the *lex Iulia municipalis* this document is only mentioned in two lines of a foot-note. The remark made on it is still more extraordinary: 'The *lex Tarenti* is in Latin, but that is no cogent reason for supposing it to be a "*lex data*".' I think, if my readers will refer to l. 9, they will find in the words *in diebus XX proximeis . . . post h. l. datam* a sufficiently cogent reason for the supposition.

The question as to the object and necessity of a general municipal law I do not propose to reopen. Prof. Reid energetically restates Mommsen's latest view, but as he does not think it worth while to notice my arguments as against both Mommsen and Legras, I will leave my readers, if they will, to weigh them for themselves. Any hint of compulsion or system in Roman law or administration is anathema to Prof. Reid, and from his standpoint it seems surprising that the Romans should have bound either themselves or others by any laws at all. With regard to my suggestion that Cinna may have passed a general law to embody the *forma communis*, and to serve as a guide to commissioners, I admit that his criticism has deprived it of all reasonable support from the inscription of Poetelia. I still think, however, that the presence of *quattuorviri* at Larinum before Sulla's dictatorship is significant, and I entirely disagree with the pronouncement that Cicero's virtual identification of the enfranchisement of Transpadane towns with their election of *IIIIviri* has little bearing on the matter. He declares it to be most improbable that enfranchised communities 'were required to use particular titles for their magistracies'. He has so keen a scent for compulsion that he finds it in words of mine which he has actually just quoted, and which were carefully framed to exclude the idea of compulsion; 'defining the normal titles of magistrates, but no doubt leaving room for local varieties in certain cases'. That the titles *IIviri* and *IIIIviri* were recognized by legislation as normal, it is futile to deny in the face of the *lex Tarenti*, the *lex Rubria*, and the Table of Heraclea. In view of the discretionary varieties which I assume, it is not a very successful point to object that in creating praetors in the short-lived colony at Capua, Cinna's friends overrode his law. Prof. Reid promises some further consideration of topics arising out of the Table. May we hope that he will include a fuller discussion of the chapters assigned in the *Corpus Gromaticorum* to a *lex Mamilia Roscia Peducaea Alliena Fabia*, and by a passage in the Digest to an agrarian law of Caesar? The problem of the five names I did not attempt to solve, but I suggested that, if the phrase *qui hac lege coloniam deduxerit, municipium praefecturam forum conciliabulum constituerit* really occurred in Caesar's agrarian law, that law must have contained provisions for the 'constitution' of Italian towns by means of commissioners and *leges datae*. He rejects this with much contempt, but makes no attempt whatever to explain the phrases in question, nor does he throw any light on the identity of the *lex Iulia* referred to in cap. 97 of the *lex Ursonensis*. It is certain that the three caps. preserved in the *Corp. Grom.* are extracted from some law dealing on general lines with matters appropriate to a *lex data*, and that it gives instructions to commissioners to see to these matters.[1] Does he believe that it was a Caesarian law, and if

[1] It seems to me futile to argue that cap. 104 of the *lex Ursonensis* need not

so, what sort of law was it, and when passed? I cannot think that the views expressed on p. 247 as to the agrarian law of 59 are well considered. I do not go into the question whether there were two laws or only one, though I think the evidence is against the latter view, but in any case Cicero's conversational phrase *Campana lex* must either mean the provision in the law about the Campanian land, or, if it does mean a law limited to that land, we must suppose that Caesar's main and general law was the first, and that the second law, alone alluded to by Cicero, was for the immediate appropriation and division of the *ager Campanus.* The admission that Caesar's law contained a provision affecting the lands of Volaterrae and Arretium is at once fatal to the contention that the agrarian legislation of the year was limited to the *ager Campanus.* Is it conceivable that, after two such comprehensive schemes of land purchase and Italian colonization as those of Rullus and Flavius, the former containing the design of Caesar himself, the programme of the coalition would have thrown overboard everything but the Campanian land? It would have been far more in keeping with the situation if the legislation was much wider in space, time, and content than any previous measure.

It is unfortunate, considering the importance which he assigns to the concluding paragraph of the Table, that Prof. Reid's treatment of it should be the least convincing portion of his article. In the first place, unless his contention that commissioners were not sent to the enfranchised towns of Italy after the *lex Iulia* is to be given up, it is necessary to attach some limited application to *municipia fundana*, and above all, to exclude them from Italy. What this limited application may be, or why it is assumed for a term which is ἅπαξ λεγόμενον, we are not told; but what seems to him the most probable account of the law to which this provision belongs is that it was one of a series of special measures by which Caesar dealt with the peculiar conditions of Cisalpine Gaul. Now for this series of special measures there is no evidence whatever. The three principal reasons

have been copied from the *lex Iulia,* because rules about boundaries were of such long standing as to have become traditional. Why then were the rules embodied in a chapter of a general law, and when they were so embodied, how could they be made applicable to particular communities except by means of its *lex data*?

which, it is argued, called for special legislation as well as for the sending of commissioners with *leges datae* were (*a*) the fact that so many communities were newly enfranchised (a fact not calling in the case of Italy, according to Prof. Reid, for either general legislation or *leges datae*), (*b*) the large size of the Transpadane *territoria* requiring special delimitation (a matter which had probably been attended to by the *lex Pompeia*), and (*c*) the system of 'attributed' tribes within the territories of many communities. One piece of special legislation of course there was, the *lex Rubria*, but it had nothing to do with the size of *territoria*, and Prof. Reid goes out of his way to say that the *attributae regiones* were not regarded by it. Another piece of special legislation, gratuitously suggested for Cisalpine Gaul, is the projected law dealing with qualifications of *decuriones*. I have already dealt with this hypothesis, and I will only ask whether this provision would have a place in the *leges datae* of the Cisalpine *municipia fundana*. Prof. Reid could hardly deny that it would, and is therefore committed to the position that a general municipal provision is made applicable to individual towns by means of their *leges datae*, precisely the situation I argue for in Italy.

So far there is surely no reason worth serious consideration for referring this last paragraph of the Table to Cisalpine Gaul. But, as Prof. Reid points out, the commissioners alluded to are *functi officio*, and are called upon after an interval to resume their work. But, as there is no provision in the clause for replacing any commissioners who might have died during the interval, the space between the original *lex data* and its proposed revision must have been a very brief one. On this ground he rejects my suggestion that perhaps most of these commissioners had been sent out in 59 and the following years, and gets a much shorter interval by taking the enfranchisement of Cisalpine Gaul in 49 as the occasion. I do not myself think the difficulty of the longer interval very serious, but, as my reasons are not acceptable to Prof. Reid, I will not repeat them. I must point out, however, that his own theory is open to precisely the same difficulty, since commissioners appointed in 49 may have died before 45, and though such cases might be fewer, we should equally expect to find them provided against.

If 'it would have been easy to provide by a few words for replacing the commissioners' who may have died, I do not see why the carelessness of the engraver should not be called to the rescue once more.[1]

But surely if these commissioners had drawn up their *leges datae* after the enfranchisement of Cisalpine Gaul in March 49, there must have been some special reason why they were called upon to revise them four years later. What sort of additions, changes, and corrections were to be made? To this question Prof. Reid has no answer; he can only admit that the omission of the purport of the ordinance is most extraordinary, as is also the contrast between its vagueness and the detail of the preceding clauses of the Table. If so much has to be admitted, I think it is pertinent to ask where is the importance attributed to this concluding paragraph. It seems in Prof. Reid's hands to throw no light on anything, least of all on the connexion of the Table with Heraclea.

We are told that the solution of this last point 'unless further relevant ancient material should come to light . . . must for ever elude the grasp of scholars' (p. 248). Nevertheless scholars will probably go on suggesting solutions, and Prof. Reid himself has been unable to resist the temptation of adding another hypothesis. I shall conclude this article by briefly comparing it with my own explanation which is declared to be 'most unacceptable'. Though the grounds of this disapproval are not stated, I imagine that it is mainly directed against the assumption that commissioners were sent to the enfranchised towns of Italy, and were not confined to those regions outside Italy which, like Cisalpine Gaul and subsequently other provinces in the West, presented special and exceptional problems. My own theory is, that the last paragraph of the Table, so far from standing out of all relation, and even in strong contrast to, the other sections (being confined to Cisalpine Gaul, while they refer to Rome or Italy) is not only organically connected with the two

[1] Prof. Reid says that a few words would have been enough to provide for the replacing of a deceased commissioner by a substitute. If this is so, I suggest that the few words may have been inscribed in the law, but omitted in the Table, not through the carelessness of the engraver, but because at Heraclea the original commissioner, being still alive, did not think it necessary to insert them.

sets of provisions immediately preceding it, but gives the clue to the whole document. I assume it to be the concluding clause of the same general municipal law to which the clauses on municipal honours and the Italian census belonged.[1] It implies that commissioners had been authorized at certain unspecified dates in the past to frame *leges datae* for a number, unspecified again, of Italian towns, and they are now instructed to make within the next year certain changes and additions. I suggest that these would be primarily any innovations contained in the municipal law itself, such as the two inscribed on the Table, and perhaps others contained in the lost portion of it, but there might also be included other arrangements, which the commissioners in their discretion might deem it advisable to introduce.

Now assuming, what seems not improbable, that Heraclea received a *lex data* in the same period in which Tarentum received one, I suggest that, when Caesar's municipal law was passed, with the novelties as to qualifications for office and the census, which with perhaps other changes were to be inserted in municipal charters within the next year, the commissioner of Heraclea, whether the person originally appointed or some one to replace him, decided to give a public notification to the town of the changes and additions to be made in the local charter. He therefore caused to be engraved on the back of an obsolete bronze tablet the two provisions from the municipal law together with the clause on the authority of which he was acting, and quite possibly other provisions from the same law, now lost with the bronze containing the earlier part of the document. In addition to this, he may have thought it appropriate to the circumstances of Heraclea to incorporate certain parts of Caesar's recent legislation for Rome, especially the new system of *frumentationes* and the new regulations as to streets, traffic, and open spaces.

I claim for this theory that it at least supplies a reasonable explanation of the facts. If the document is what I suggest, its heterogeneous character is accounted for, since we should not

[1] In these clauses the towns, as already 'constituted', are *municipia, praefecturae*, &c. In the last clause, as communities for whom *leges datae* were prepared, they are generically *municipia fundana*. Quite possibly there was a separate clause providing that the additions and changes should be made also in the *leges datae* of colonies.

expect to find 'linked together into an organic whole' a set of ordinances merely intended to amend or fill up gaps in an existing charter. At the same time, it does connect organically the concluding clause with the rest of the document, and in doing so, makes concrete and specific the 'additions, changes, and corrections' which it enjoins. When Prof. Reid declares that these changes 'touch on affairs which would certainly have been left to the discretion of the municipalities', he strangely forgets that by his own admission the provisions as to municipal office and as to the Italian census were extracts, if not from actual, at least from contemplated laws, while there are several provisions in the brief fragment of the Tarentine law closely analogous to those on the aedilician duties.[1]

Let us now turn to the explanation which Prof. Reid considers 'far easier, though not free from difficulties'. He agrees with me, it seems after all, in thinking that the document may have been a notification to the people of Heraclea of certain proposed reforms. But in his opinion it was a scheme of internal reform, and the person responsible for the Table was presumably either a party leader in Heraclea, or an arbitrator called in by the citizens; at any rate he was not a commissioner *lege plebeive scito permissus*. Though there is no evidence, and no analogy, except possibly at Puteoli, to support this hypothesis, it works smoothly enough, so long as we look only to the first two sections. But then Prof. Reid's difficulties begin, though he is apparently not conscious of them till he reaches the final clause. After remarking that the regulations at Rome in connexion with corn distributions and the policing of the streets might well be voluntarily adopted by Heraclea, he declares that the same may be said of the rules for municipal office and membership in the senate. Yet there is this difference, which seems to be overlooked, that the latter rules, as published at Heraclea, purport to be part of a legal enactment, already binding upon Heraclea as a *municipium*. How can a measure, by which Heraclea was already bound, belong to a programme

[1] As Prof. Reid, in spite of the words *post hanc legem datam* (was this too an addition of the engraver?), refuses to accept the Tarentine law as a *lex data*, I should be content to cite the provision which it has in common with the *lex Ursonensis* and the *lex Malacitana*, on the dismantling of houses.

of internal reform subsequent to 46 B.C.?[1] It will not help Prof. Reid much to call the provision an extract from a contemplated law, for how did such an extract from an abortive scheme of pre-Caesarian date reach the Heraclean reformer in 45 B.C.?[2] It hardly looks as if there was much feeling in Italian towns against compulsory legislation, when Heraclea, a more than usually non-Romanized town, is supposed to go out of its way to adopt coercive regulations abandoned by the central government.

As to the provision for a simultaneous Italian census, which Prof. Reid thinks may have been in the air at the time when the Table was engraved, he may take his choice of regarding the law as passed or only contemplated. If it was passed, we have the absurdity of supposing a compulsory administrative law, binding on all Italy, belonging to a programme of voluntary reform at Heraclea. If it was not passed, we have the still greater absurdity of a reformer making elaborate provision for his town to take part in a scheme, which was not only non-existent, but had been abandoned by its promotors.[3]

'The last paragraph about *municipia fundana* is the hardest to account for on the hypothesis of internal reform.' It certainly needs some ingenuity to explain why, in a city which had never had either a commissioner or a *lex data*, this vague and isolated extract from a law dealing with special conditions in Cisalpine Gaul should have been brought before the notice of the public, together with certain proposals of internal reform. Nothing is conveyed as to the matters originally dealt with by the *leges datae* to be revised, nor is there the slightest indication as to the nature of the revision. How hard put to it Prof. Reid finds himself, is shown by the following perplexing suggestion: 'What interested the person who ordered the inscription to be

[1] It must have been subsequent to 46, since clauses dealing with the reform of the *frumentationes* appear in the same notice.

[2] He has definitely rejected the Caesarian date for the provision, and must therefore place it, whether contemplated or passed, before that time.

[3] I do not understand how the census scheme could have been in the air in 45, unless Caesar was about, or was believed to be about, to propose it. But Prof. Reid definitely declines to regard the scheme as Caesar's, so that its contemplation and failure to pass must have been some appreciable time earlier than 45, when, we are told, it was in the air. It seems to me that this part of his hypothesis has been very imperfectly thought out.

engraved seems to have been the mere fact that certain towns were undergoing a fresh revision of their statutes after a very short interval, not the purpose of the fresh revision. This fact, even if, as I think, it concerned only Cisalpine Gaul, might have its use as an argument in a party conflict within the town, if a section of the citizens were urging changes of importance a little while after other changes of importance had been made.' I am content to leave this network of hypotheses within hypotheses to speak for itself, only remarking that it deprives the clause, which Professor Reid declares to be the most important, of all weight or meaning as part of the inscription, without throwing light on its meaning for Cisalpine Gaul. At any rate, in pronouncing Professor Reid's solution of the enigma to be 'unacceptable', I have felt it incumbent on me to examine it in detail, and I leave it to my readers to prefer his or mine, or to reject both.

X

CICERO'S ARGUMENT IN *PRO BALBO*, 8. 19–22

I ARGUED in the course of my essay on the *lex Iulia Municipalis* (see above, No. VIII) that the words in sect. 21, 'ipsa denique Iulia, qua lege civitas est sociis et Latinis data, qui fundi populi facti non essent, civitatem non haberent', prove Italian communities, on being enfranchised, to have become subject or *fundi* to Roman law. Prof. Reid (*J. R. S.*, vol. v, pt. 2, p. 239) denies the validity of this inference and declares that the words refer only to allied states, which had not become *fundi* to the *lex Iulia* itself. The words should not have been interpreted by either of us apart from their context, and my conclusion at any rate depends on a consideration of Cicero's argument as a whole. I shall therefore try briefly to bring out its salient points. He traces the case of Balbus back to the consular *lex Gellia-Cornelia* of 72 B.C., which legalized the enfranchisement of those persons, 'quos Cn. Pompeius de consili sententia civitate donaverit'. There was evidence that Balbus was among these, and 'accusator fatetur, sed negat ex foederato populo quemquam potuisse, nisi is populus fundus factus esset, in hanc civitatem venire'. In other words, it was contended that Gades, as a *civitas foederata*, could render the *lex Gellia-Cornelia* inoperative, as far as Balbus was concerned, by refusing or neglecting to adopt or become *fundus* to it. Such a pretension certainly seems preposterous, and the accuser must either have been misled, or must have tried to mislead the court by the analogy of the *lex Iulia*[1] as he perhaps understood it. Cicero's

[1] This is no doubt what Prof. Reid means when he represents the argument as being, 'just as the Gaditani could not be made Roman citizens collectively, unless Gades adopted the enfranchising law, so neither could Balbus unless the *lex Gellia-Cornelia* was adopted'. I am not aware that the former proposition can be established, unless it is by the statement in sect. 21 about the *lex Iulia*.

contemptuous apostrophe, therefore, *O praeclarum interpretem iuris*, &c., is not undeserved, but it cannot be said that he makes his point of view precise or clear in continuing, 'qui hanc poenam foederibus adscribat, ut omnium praemiorum beneficiorumque expertes faciat foederatos. Quid enim potuit dici imperitius quam foederatos populos fieri fundos oportere?' What of course Cicero means is that, if the accuser's assertion was correct, individual members of federate states would be liable to lose a well-deserved honour owing to the non-acceptance by their own communities of the law conferring it, and that it was ridiculous to affirm that federate states were bound formally to adopt these laws, if they wished their members to benefit by them. But he says neither of these things, for *poenam foederibus adscribere* implies prejudice to the federate states, and not to the individuals, while the words *fieri fundos oportere* are so vague and general as to conceal the point intended. In a later passage (sect. 54) Cicero very pertinently illustrates his position by the case of Latins who had gained the citizenship through securing a conviction under the *lex Servilia repetundarum*, and asks, 'num fundos igitur populos Latinos factos arbitramur aut Serviliae legi aut ceteris quibus Latinis erat propositum aliqua ex re praemium civitatis?' He might have added with even greater effect the case of those enfranchised under the *lex Plautia-Papiria*, the very object of which was to benefit individual members of federate states refusing to avail themselves of the *lex Iulia*.

Apparently the accuser had tried to justify his untenable position by citing certain *foedera* (all made with tribes and not with urban communities) in which it was stipulated, *ne quis eorum civis Romanus recipiatur*, and by arguing that the same held good for all *foedera*. This, however, is confuted by the fact that no such *exceptio* occurred in the *foedus* with Gades, while, as the Gaditani strongly supported Balbus in the present trial, they would presumably, if anything in the *foedus* had required it, have made themselves *fundi* to the *lex Gellia-Cornelia*.

Cicero then proceeds to lay it down, as the principle on which federate states (*Latini et socii*) were allowed to become *fundi* to Roman laws, that, if such a state adopted a law passed by the Roman people, it would be bound by that law, the object being not to impair the validity of Roman rights or Roman law ('non ut de nostro iure aliquid deminueretur') but 'ut illi populi eo iure quod a nobis esset constitutum, aut ut commodo aliquo aut beneficio uterentur'. It seems safe to assert that, both historically and logically, this principle was primarily applicable to the first of these two objects, and that its application to the second, if indeed it was so applied, is known to us only from Cicero's line of argument in this speech. At any rate, Cicero's point is that it is only applicable, where the *beneficium* affects the whole federate state, and not merely some of its individual members.

In sect. 21 Cicero goes on without a pause to illustrate the first of the two objects he has laid down: 'Tulit apud maiores nostros legem C. Furius de testamentis, tulit Q. Voconius de mulierum hereditatibus; innumerabiles aliae leges de civili iure sunt latae; quas Latini voluerunt, adsciverunt.' We should have expected the second object to be illustrated in the same direct way, but the speaker's line of thought has somehow been diverted, and he proceeds: 'ipsa denique Iulia, qua lege civitas est sociis et Latinis data, qui fundi populi facti non essent, civitatem non haberent.' Of course the words are an illustration of the second object, since the *civitas* is a *beneficium* which the communities can only gain by becoming *fundi*; but why is the sentence introduced by *denique*? It implies, I cannot but think, a consciousness in Cicero's mind that the *lex Iulia* marked the end of the process indicated in the previous sentence, the process by which federate states had long since been assimilating Roman laws by consecutively becoming *fundi* to them. The sentence at best is awkward, abrupt, and the reverse of lucid, but, if *denique* and *ipsa* represent anything in Cicero's thought, I can only understand it thus: 'so far did this go, that even the *lex Iulia* itself, an enfranchising law for federate states, conferred its *beneficium* on those states only, which had become *fundi*, i.e. completely *fundi* to Roman law.' It was the objection to fulfil this condition which caused the hesitation at Heraclea and Naples, where many preferred the *libertatem foederis*, i.e. liberty to retain their own codes.

Prof. Reid limits the use of *fundi* here to the *lex Iulia*, and many scholars speak of states as making themselves *fundi* to this or that enfranchising law. But where, apart from the present passage, is the justification for using such a phrase? If a state, on accepting the citizenship, became *ipso facto* subject to Roman law, then of course it became *fundus* to the enfranchising law along with the rest. But, if the acceptance of the *civitas* made no difference to its municipal code, could it have been necessary, as a sign of acceptance, formally to adopt into its code a law, whose operation, as far as each accepting community was concerned, was terminated by the acceptance? We surely need more evidence for so clumsy a contrivance, which would have nothing in common but the name with the practice of adopting for actual use Roman laws *de civili iure*. Cicero sharply rejects the conception implied in the term *fundus* in connexion with any partially enfranchising law, and if he gives any countenance, which I doubt, to its application to general laws of the kind, he is, I imagine, merely adopting without prejudice the language of the accuser, no great authority on Roman law, who had obviously run the phrase to death (cf. in sect. 42, 'quoniam hoc magno opere delectaris verbo'). Perhaps it is in deference to this mode of speaking that in sect. 20 he draws a distinction between states which became *fundi*, in order to use some part of the *ius civile*, and states which became *fundi* to gain the *civitas*.[1] I suggest that the real difference which flashed on Cicero, when he introduced the word *denique*, was between becoming *fundi* for practical purposes of parts of the *ius civile*, and becoming *fundi* to the whole of it, as a condition of gaining the *civitas*.

If any other *commodum* or *beneficium* was conditional upon a state becoming *fundus* to the law conferring it, what instance can be adduced? Are we to believe that, unless the town of Termessus chose to become *fundus* to the *lex Antonia*, that piece of legislation was wasted and inoperative? Or, when the *lex Pompeia* of 89 B.C. gave to the *civitates foederatae* of Cisalpine Gaul the status and rights of Latin colonies, is it to be supposed that this settlement of the country was liable to be wrecked by the refusal of the states to become *fundi* to the law?

Cicero furnishes possible answers to these questions by laying down in sect. 22 a somewhat fluid principle, on which he declares the Roman government to have acted in deciding where free and federate states might voluntarily adopt (*fundi fieri*) a law,

[1] The *civitas* is not specified, but what else could fall under the vague *commodo aliquo aut beneficio*?

and where no choice was allowed. Where the matter was of such a kind that a state might reasonably be allowed to decide for itself *non de nostris sed de suis rebus, quo iure uti velint*, they had the choice of becoming *fundi* or not. But, where it was a question *de nostra republica, de nostro imperio, de nostris bellis*, &c., no such option was allowed (*fundos populos fieri noluerunt*). It is manifest that phrases so elastic as *de nostra republica* and *de nostro imperio* might easily be made to cover the two cases mentioned above, and possibly even that of the *lex Iulia*, but the circumstances under which the latter law was passed, when the crisis of the war was far from over, made it advisable to frame a permissive rather than a compulsory measure.

In my view the effect of the whole passage, considered in its logical connexion, is to explode rather than to support the theory that states could make themselves *fundi* to an enfranchising law, while retaining their own municipal codes of law. I call attention to the point that the argument from beginning to end is limited to the position of *civitates foederatae* and *liberae*, which alone are capable of becoming *fundi*. It is the Latini who *quas voluerunt adsciverunt*; it is for *populis sive foederatis sive liberis* that Cicero enunciates his principle in sect. 22. I submit that the legal conception involved in the term *fundus fieri* was applicable only to sovereign or semi-sovereign states, so that on the one hand subject communities are omitted, and on the other burgess communities, like Arpinum, which, as parts of the Roman body politic, were naturally subject to Roman law. Unless Prof. Reid is prepared to extend the doctrine of *fundus fieri* to burgess communities (and on what evidence can he do so?), he must either admit that they were already under Roman law, or affirm that they were permanently excluded from becoming so.[1]

[1] Prof. Reid has a great objection to the view that enfranchised towns were 'compelled' to adopt Roman law. He forgets that, if they became *fundi* to it, they were not compelled, since the essence of the process was its voluntary character.